Exit from Hegemony

Exit from Hegemony

The Unraveling of the American Global Order

ALEXANDER COOLEY AND DANIEL NEXON

OXFORD
UNIVERSITY PRESS

OXFORD
UNIVERSITY PRESS

Oxford University Press is a department of the University of Oxford. It furthers the University's objective of excellence in research, scholarship, and education by publishing worldwide. Oxford is a registered trade mark of Oxford University Press in the UK and certain other countries.

Published in the United States of America by Oxford University Press
198 Madison Avenue, New York, NY 10016, United States of America.

Library of Congress Cataloging-in-Publication Data
Names: Cooley, Alexander, 1972– author. | Nexon, Daniel H., 1973– author.
Title: Exit from hegemony : the unraveling of the American global order /
Alexander Cooley and Daniel Nexon.
Description: New York, NY : Oxford University Press, [2020] |
Includes index. |
Identifiers: LCCN 2019039322 (print) |
LCCN 2019039323 (ebook) | ISBN 9780190916473 (hardback) |
ISBN 9780190916480 (updf) | ISBN 9780190916497 (epub) |
ISBN 9780190054557 (Online)
Subjects: LCSH: Hegemony—United States. | World politics—21st century. |
International organization. | United States—Foreign relations—21st century.
Classification: LCC JZ1312 .C665 2020 (print) | LCC JZ1312 (ebook) |
DDC 327.1/140973—dc23
LC record available at https://lccn.loc.gov/2019039322
LC ebook record available at https://lccn.loc.gov/2019039323

9 8 7 6 5 4 3

Printed by Sheridan Books, Inc., United States of America

For Katherine Cooley and Leo Jouanny

and

Lyra Gemmill-Nexon

Contents

List of Tables and Figures

TABLES

FIGURES

Foreword

Though the presidency of Donald Trump provided an unavoidable focus for our discussions of international order and global US leadership, this book brings together a number of collaborative projects that we have been working on for well over a decade. We both have previously researched the evolution of state sovereignty, international hierarchy and empire, and the organizational dynamics of the contemporary system. In his previous work, Alex explored the rise of multipolar dynamics in the interactions of China, Russia, and the United States in Central Asia (*Great Games, Local Rules* 2012), while Dan outlined the transformation of dynastic empire in early modern Europe (*The Struggle for Power in Early Modern Europe* 2009). Together, we have collaborated on several projects involving such topics as the politics of US overseas military bases and US relations with Georgia.

Indeed, the origins of this book are something like fifteen years in the past. The project on transformations in the international order has ebbed and flowed through multiple American administrations, international crises, and research agendas. We are enormously grateful to Dave McBride from Oxford University Press for his multi-year faith in our project, his expert guidance, and his considerable patience. Dave also provided important guidance when it came to matters of accessibility and academic depth. If readers are interested in further exploring some conceptual and theoretical issues raised in the text, we recommend taking a look at the endnotes, many of which contain extended discussions of these matters.

Funding for substantial portions of this work was provided by the Norwegian Research Council under the project "Undermining Hegemony" (project no. 240647). From 2015 to 2018, the ideas and arguments found in this book received crucial feedback at various workshops and meetings with the research group in Norway and across Europe. We thank our colleagues at the Norwegian Institute of International Affairs (NUPI), especially Morten Skumsrud Andersen, Benjamin de Carvalho, Halvard Leira, Iver Neumann, Elana Wilson Rowe, and Ole Jacob Sending. The production of this book was supported by a faculty publication grant from the Harriman Institute at Columbia University and by research funds provided by Georgetown University. Alex would like to thank his colleagues at Barnard and Columbia for their collegiality and support. Dan would also like to thank his colleagues, from whom he learned a lot, during his 2009-2010 Council of Foreign Relations International Affairs Fellowship, which he served in the Russia, Ukraine, Eurasia unit of the Office of the Secretary of Defense (Policy).

We have richly benefited from the feedback we have received presenting earlier drafts of the project at the Ford Seminar at the University of Michigan, the Fung Global Fellows Program at Princeton University, Harvard University's Davis Center and Working Group on the Future of US-Russia Relations, the annual Central Asia Security Workshops at George Washington University, the National Endowment for Democracy, the Carnegie Endowment for International Peace, Air Force War College, the Analytical Outreach Program of the United States Department of State, the University Consortium, Chatham House, KIMEP University, the Institute for World Economy and International Relations of the Russian Academy of Sciences (IMEMO), the Department of Political Science at the University of Toronto, the Sié Chéou-Kang Center for International Security and Diplomacy at the University of Denver, various panels and roundtables at the International Studies Association, and almost certainly other venues that have slipped our minds. For their comments and insights, we are also grateful to Sam Charap, Maia Gemmill, Lyra Gemmill-Nexon, Stacie Goddard, Elise Guiliano, John Heathershaw, Nicole Jacoby, Nargis Kassenova, Robert Legvold, David Lewis, Kathleen MacNamara, Julie Newton, Abraham Newman, Jason Sharman, Jack Snyder, Hendrik Spruyt,

Josh Tucker, Leslie Vinjamuri, Alexandra Vacroux, Chris Walker, Stephen Ward, and Victoria Zhuravleva.

A number of individuals have provided invaluable research assistance and other support including Justin Casey, Alexander Sullivan, Zachary Karabatak, Gulya Tlegenova, Will Persing, and Aleksandra Turek. Alex Montgomery designed the network analysis of Chinese- and Russian-led IGOs in Chapter 4. Ahmer Arif, Leo Stewart, and Kate Starbird generously permitted us to republish their visualization of IRA social media activity as Figure 6.3. Seth Farkas, once again, was the creative force for the book's international order graphics. Dave Prout meticulously compiled the index.

Finally, we once again appreciate our families and friends who, over many years, have supported our research travel, deadline stress, and never-ending political banter. The book is dedicated to Alex's sister and nephew and Dan's daughter.

List of Abbreviations and Acronyms

ADB	Asian Development Bank
AFRICOM	United States Africa Command
AIIB	Asian Infrastructure Investment Bank
ALBA	Bolivarian Alliance for the Peoples of Our America
ASEAN	Association of Southeast Asian Nations
AU	African Union
BRI	Belt and Road Initiative
BRICS	Brazil, Russia, India, China, and South Africa
CA-CELAC	China-CELAC Forum
CASCF	China-Arab States Cooperation Forum
CDB	Chinese Development Bank
CEE	Central Eastern Europe
CELAC	Community of Latin American and Caribbean States
CFR	Council on Foreign Relations
China-CEE	China-Central Eastern Europe (17+1)
CICA	Conference on Interaction and Confidence Building Measures in Asia
CIS	Commonwealth of Independent States
CNPC	China National Petroleum Corporation
COMECON	Council for Mutual Economic Assistance
CPAC	Conservative Political Action Conference

CSTO	Collective Security Treaty Organization
CTBTO	Comprehensive Test Ban Treaty Organization
DNC	Democratic National Committee
EAEU	Eurasian Economic Union
ECOWAS	Economic Community of West African States
EIC	British East India Company
EODE	Eurasian Observatory for Democracy and Elections
EPA	EU Eastern Partnership Agreement
EU	European Union
FOCAC	Forum on China–Africa Cooperation
FVEY	Five Eyes
G20	Group of Twenty
G7	Group of Seven
GATT	General Agreement on Tariffs and Trade
GCC	Gulf Cooperation Council
GDP	Gross Domestic Product
GONGO	government-organized nongovernmental organizations
GOP	Grand Old Party, Republican Party
GWOT	Global War on Terror
IAEA	International Atomic Energy Agency
IBRD	International Bank for Reconstruction and Development
ICANN	Internet Corporation for Assigned Names and Numbers
ICC	International Criminal Court
IFI	international financial institution
IGO	intergovernmental organization
IMF	International Monetary Fund
IRA	Internet Research Agency (Russia)
IRI	International Republican Institute
JCPOA	Joint Comprehensive Plan of Action / the Iran nuclear deal / the nonproliferation deal concluded with Iran in 2015
LGBTQ	lesbian, gay, bisexual, transgender, and queer
LMC	Lancang-Mekon Cooperation Forum
LTTE	Liberation Tigers of Tamil Eelam
MFA	Ministry of Foreign Affairs
MoU	memorandum of understanding
NATO	North Atlantic Treaty Organization
NDB	New Development Bank
NDI	National Democratic Institute

NGO	nongovernmental organization
non-DAC	non-Development Assistance Committee member lenders
NRA	National Rifle Association
NRC	Norwegian Research Council
NUPI	Norwegian Institute of International Affairs
ODA	official development assistance
ODIHR	Office for Democratic Institutions and Human Rights
OECD	Organization for Economic Cooperation and Development
OPEC	Organization of the Petroleum Exporting Countries
OSCE	Organization for Security and Co-operation in Europe
QCCM	Quadrilateral Cooperation and Coordination Mechanism
RCEP	Regional Comprehensive Trade Partnership
SCO	Shanghai Cooperation Organization
START	Strategic Arms Reduction Treaty
SWIFT	Society of Worldwide Interbank Financial Telecommunications
TAN	transnational activist network
TPP	Trans-Pacific Partnership
UN	United Nations
UNESCO	United Nations Educational, Scientific, and Cultural Organization
UNGAR	United Nations Global Assessment Report
UNHRC	United Nations Human Rights Council
UNSC	United Nations Security Council
USAID	United States Agency for International Development
USSR	Union of Soviet Socialist Republics
WCF	World Congress of Families
WTO	World Trade Organization

1

Introduction

This Time Is Different

On July 11, 2018, at the North Atlantic Treaty Organization (NATO) summit in Brussels, American president Donald Trump berated Germany for its dependence on Russian energy; he demanded that NATO allies double their defense spending commitments to 4 percent of gross domestic product (GDP). Trump next traveled to the United Kingdom, where he chastised Prime Minister Theresa May for trying to negotiate the country's exit from the European Union (EU) rather than push for a "hard" Brexit; Trump threatened to withhold a favorable trade deal with the United States.[1] Then, Trump made a final stop in Helsinki for a bilateral summit with Russian president Vladimir Putin. At the summit, the world witnessed the extraordinary spectacle of an American president openly siding with the leader of an adversarial regime against his own intelligence services when Trump declined to acknowledge Russian hacking and interference in the 2016 presidential election. Trump's seeming obsequiousness toward the Russian president was made even more remarkable by the fact that, on the previous day, he had identified the EU as the United States' "greatest foe."[2]

Trump's European trip sent shockwaves through world capitals. It spurred a wave of popular commentaries about the impending collapse of the so-called liberal international order: a common, although problematic, way of describing the American-led system of alliances, institutions, and global governance that first developed after the Second World War.[3] And not without good reason. During his successful campaign for the presidency, Trump routinely disparaged NATO and other lynchpin American security relationships, rejected any serious role for democracy promotion and respect for human rights in American foreign policy, and scorned the value of multilateral diplomacy and institutions. His behavior and rhetoric in Europe suggested that despite inconsistency when it came to concrete policy, Trump remained ideologically and temperamentally committed to unraveling American-led international order.

Trump's dispositions also appeared to portend changing domestic US attitudes about America's global leadership role. In a public opinion poll following the summit, 48 percent of those surveyed expressed a belief that "the United States should not have to uphold its treaty commitments if allies do not spend more on defense," with two-thirds of registered Republicans agreeing that the United States should not honor its treaty commitments.[4] In tandem with President Trump's aggressive protectionist trade agenda—and the levying of tariffs on the EU and Canada—the anti-internationalist agenda of "America First" seemed to be shifting the attitudes of at least some Americans. Particularly troubling for the durability of the American international system, Trumpism may transform foreign-policy principles once underpinned by bipartisan consensus—including strong support for NATO—into subjects of partisan conflict.[5]

While debates over Trumpism currently consume foreign-policy watchers, scholars of world politics generally focus on longer-term developments. After the collapse of the Soviet Union in 1991, the United States faced no great-power peer competitors. It enjoyed uncontested status as the world's wealthiest country. The next seven largest economies all belonged to advanced industrialized democracies allied with the United States.[6] American officials believed that the Russian Federation would become an important strategic partner. The American foreign-policy establishment convinced itself that integrating China into the global economy would nudge Beijing toward political liberalization while creating a basis for ongoing cooperation. Many foresaw a durable world order based on international liberalism and market democracy, with the United States maintaining a position of global leadership—what international-relations scholars call "hegemony."[7]

By the mid-2010s, though, this future looked increasingly unlikely. The United States had spent over four trillion dollars fighting wars, with mixed results, in Iraq and Afghanistan. These conflicts, and especially the Iraq War, damaged American prestige and exploded the image of invincible American power. In 2014, in response to what it perceived to be a US-backed coup d'état in neighboring Ukraine that ousted President Viktor Yanukovych, Moscow annexed Crimea, supported insurgents in eastern Ukraine, and ramped up its efforts to destabilize Western democracies. In 2015, Russia intervened in the Syrian civil war. Far from a partner and ally, Moscow increasingly committed Russian resources to undermining the American international system.

As of 2019, the Chinese economy is, in nominal terms, on track to surpass that of the United States. In purchasing-power parity terms, it already did so in 2014.[8] After assuming power in 2013, Premiere Xi Jinping guided China toward a more assertive posture in international affairs. Beijing is using its economic clout to build a range of development initiatives alternative to those offered by the United States, Japan, and Europe; is flexing its muscle in the South China Sea; and has begun to construct a modest network of overseas military bases.

Scholars see these developments as signs of a general power transition away from the United States. During such transitions, the leading power—or "hegemon"—faces increasing difficulties in maintaining its preferred international order; its relative decline encourages other states unhappy with that order to seek to renegotiate terms, build alternative arrangements of one kind or another, probe for weaknesses, and even directly challenge the dominant power or its allies. In the worst-case scenario, peaceful adjustment to the changing distribution of military and economic capabilities proves impossible; as it did in World War I and World War II, the system collapses into a devastating great-power war.[9]

This possibility, which political scientist Graham Allison calls the "Thucydides Trap," is currently something of a minor obsession in foreign-policy circles. However, American hegemony can unravel without anyone ever firing a shot. In this book, we contend that the international system has already gone quite far down several pathways out of hegemony. These include great power challenges, changing behavior of small or weaker states, and new forms of transnationalism that destabilize previous norms and agreed-upon foreign policy frameworks. President Trump may be speeding up the journey, but major drivers of hegemonic unraveling predate him and will continue after his presidency. Indeed, Trump himself is as much a symptom of these developments as a cause, which has implications for those hoping to reverse his impact on international order.

DÉJÀ VU ALL OVER AGAIN?

This is not the first time that scholars and commentators have written an obituary for the American-led international order. The second half of the twentieth century saw a number of post-mortems for American hegemony, all of which proved premature. At the time, the moments that generated them all appeared to be key inflection points, ones often spurred by inward facing economic nationalism and rising geopolitical competitors.

In 1973, following the collapse of the Bretton Woods system, America's draining war in Vietnam, and the Organization of the Petroleum Exporting Countries (OPEC) oil shock, international-relations scholars widely viewed American hegemony—even within its Cold War sphere of influence—as collapsing under the weight of its fiscal strains and systemic commitments.[10] Scholars doubted whether, in the absence of overwhelming US power, the world economic system could remain open and its rules enforced.[11] And yet, as international-relations theorist Robert Keohane argued, the international system of rules and institutions governing economic relations proved remarkably resilient even in the face of eroding American power. Meanwhile, challenges from the so-called Third World to American global institutions seemed to lose steam as the decade progressed.[12]

Similarly, in the late 1980s, newfound concerns about the unsustainability of American overseas military commitments and mounting fiscal deficits prompted another wave of studies of American decline. Among these, Yale historian Paul Kennedy's highly influential 1987 book *The Rise and Fall of the Great Powers* argued that the United States, like a series of global hegemons before it, had succumbed to an enduring cycle of military overexpansion that was eroding its own internal capacity.[13] At the same time, public commentators argued that US standing in the world would be exploited by emerging challengers, especially Japan. Many believed that Tokyo, by spending less on defense and devoting more resources to national industrial policy, had discovered the recipe for a superior model of nationally directed capitalism.[14] One prominent book, published in 1991, even warned that Japan's rise would lead to open conflict and, quite possibly, war with the United States.[15] That very same year Japan entered a prolonged period of economic stagnation (its "Lost Decade"). Tokyo failed to secure a seat on the United Nations Security Council (UNSC), let alone a fundamental shift in global power.

Within just a few years of Kennedy's book, world politics itself shifted in a momentous and redefining fashion. Throughout Eastern Europe, Communist regimes, previously seen as enduringly stable, toppled in the face of street protests and demands for political and economic reforms. The Berlin Wall fell in November 1989, prompting immediate negotiations over the reunification of Germany. In the following year, the United States orchestrated a military buildup and accompanying diplomatic effort in support of a crushing defeat of Iraq—a former Soviet client state—that underscored its dominant status in the Middle East. Meanwhile, the Soviet Union unraveled under pressure from nationalist mobilizations and the collapse of planning structures previously relaxed as part of an effort to reform its economy.[16]

In August 1991, an old-guard of hardliners tried, and failed, to seize power. But the Soviet Union was already effectively hollowed out; its breakup assured by a series of independence referenda in its republics. On Christmas Day 1991, the USSR formally disbanded. Fifteen new sovereign states, including the new Russian Federation, replaced it. Almost overnight, the United States found itself alone at the top, a sole superpower with unmatched military might. It would soon experience a period of impressive economic growth, fueled by a technology boom centered around personal computers and internet communications. Rather than sliding into decline, the United States lacked viable competitors; instead of seeing its hegemony erode, Washington now could contemplate extending its preferred international order well beyond its Cold War sphere of influence.[17]

THE POST-COLD WAR ORDER RAPIDLY TAKES SHAPE: CHALLENGERS, EXIT OPTIONS, AND TRANSNATIONAL NETWORKS

The Soviet collapse transformed the global balance of power.[18] The jump to the "unipolar moment" led to the consolidation and expansion of the values, institutions, and networks underpinning the American international system and its elements of liberal international order. The collapse of Communist systems produced bold claims about the "end of history" in the form of the triumph of liberal democracy and capitalism.[19] Indeed, the first issue of the *Journal of Democracy*, published in the winter of 1990, featured articles about the ongoing crumbling of the Soviet system and the political reforms sweeping Eastern Europe. It also included critical pieces on the Chinese government's crackdown on what seemed like a growing tide of political dissent.[20] As the push to reform the bloc gathered momentum, Western policymakers adopted exaggerated ideas about the quality of democracy and market reforms, manifesting in new international rankings of state performance, benchmarks, and standards for membership in new regional organizations like the Organization for Security and Co-operation in Europe (OSCE).[21]

The Order of the "New World Order": Expand and Integrate into the West

The end of the Soviet Union led to the disintegration of the international institutions and governance arrangements that stitched together the Communist sphere. The Warsaw Pact, NATO's rival for over 40 years, dissolved with little fanfare in 1991. COMECON, the system that governed trade and economic relations between the Soviet Union and its Communist partners, also disintegrated in 1991; the now liberalizing post-Communist states began dealing with each other in the international market and transacting in convertible hard currency.[22] The Komsomol, the Soviet-led transnational movement of youth groups, disbanded. Moscow did manage to maintain a patchwork of international-ordering arrangements within the post-Soviet space,[23] yet these were ad hoc in nature. They would not be consolidated into regional institutions with functioning bureaucracies and permanent staffs until the 2000s.

This disintegration opened the door to the expansion of Western international institutions and arrangements into the former Communist sphere. There was nothing inevitable about this. The major players considered other possibilities during the critical window of 1989–1990; as historian Mary Sarotte argues, 1989 provided an opportunity for Western policymakers to consider many alternative ways of organizing Eurasian—and even global—international relations, including building new security architectures.

In the end, expanding (and modifying) Western organizations, principles, and norms won the day.[24] The Federal Republic of Germany absorbed East Germany. NATO soon issued membership invitations to Poland,

Hungary, and the Czech Republic. In fact, the broad expansion of the European Union[25] and NATO would become a crucial part of both organizations' agendas from the mid-1990s onward.[26] The United States' sweeping victory in the 1991 Gulf War underscored Washington's global leadership. It demonstrated a massive qualitative gap between its military capabilities and those of second-tier powers.[27] Washington enjoyed a network of multilateral allies and supporters, both providing input into American diplomacy and conferring legitimacy upon it. American-led military intervention in the Balkan Wars reinforced America's position at the top of the European security hierarchy. In 1998, Madeleine Albright, US secretary of state, declared the United States "the indispensable nation" and confidentially proclaimed, "We stand tall and we see further than other countries into the future, and we see the danger here to all of us."[28]

No Exit Options: Washington Consensus and Monopoly

The extinction of Soviet-ordering mechanisms underscored that American-led "liberal" international order would serve as the main source of global governance, international rules and standards. Any talk about Japan or Germany potentially providing alternative options to the US-led system soon evaporated. Germany became consumed with managing unification. Japan, after a decade of advocating a more state-friendly view of development in institutions like the World Bank,[29] dropped its own international aspirations as it turned inward to cope with chronic deflation and its own financial crisis.

Thus, the European Union, the United States, and other advanced industrialized democracies were, generally speaking, on the same page when it came to development assistance, human rights, international security, anti-corruption measures, trade, and other aspects of international order. While they might disagree over specifics, or sometimes let commercial or power-political interests take precedence, they tended on balance to push liberal notions of global governance. This meant that other countries lacked exit options when it came to matters of security or economic development; they had little choice but to play by the rules set by wealthy liberal democracies.

Further, the absence of exit options further empowered international organizations to embed liberal norms and values within their governance and membership criteria. For example, studies suggest that the economic conditionality associated with the International Monetary Fund (IMF) became more stringent for borrowing countries in the 1990s, precisely because they no longer had credible alternative patrons and thus little leverage. In consequence, states participating in the institutions of global governance faced the imposition of liberal political and economic conditions.

The Growth of Liberal Transnational Networks

The proliferation of a number of transnational networks reinforced the architecture of the post–Cold War order, often enhancing American and European power, by spreading broadly liberal values, standards, and worldviews.[30] In the economic sphere, the collapse and discrediting of centrally planned economies in the post-Communist world ushered in a wave of Western consultants and contractors. They designed new economic institutions and implemented transitions to the market—although, to put it mildly, not always with laudable result.[31] Networks of international financial institutions, government regulators, and economists worked to produce and reinforce an elite consensus in favor of free trade and the movement of capital across borders—a version of liberal order more market-oriented than earlier ones. Such tight networks spread norms about the importance of independent and non-interventionist central banks.[32]

On the political front, teams of consultants and technical assistance providers advised governments on how to design new constitutions, reform legal systems, and design political party systems. National elections themselves came under new scrutiny by international election observer missions, most of them Western in origin. More broadly, the period saw enormous growth in the scope and intensity of transnational civil society. Nongovernmental organizations (NGOs) advocating the expansion of human rights, gender equality, and environmental protection forged alliances with sympathetic states, media outlets, and international organizations. They scored victories in matters such as the campaign against landmines, which resulted in a treaty that secured a large number of signatories—but not the United States, Russia, and China.

Though not all such campaigns proved successful, the visibility and explosion of NGOs and transnational advocacy networks led some international-relations theorists to declare them a newly powerful type of actor in world affairs, one that even defied state sovereignty in the service of forwarding liberal norms and principles.[33] It seemed to many that activists fighting for their universal causes could now act nimbly and transcend borders. Nation-states, in contrast, often appeared clumsy, unable to cope with changes in communications and information technologies that non-state actors apparently exploited with great adroitness.

***

In sum, the Soviet collapse and the rise of (according to some) a "Pax Americana" occurred rapidly. It enshrined a whole set of institutions, networks, and norms that crystallized and gave shape to American power. American-led military action in Iraq and the Balkans cemented perceptions that the United States stood unrivaled as the leader of a unipolar system, but a wide variety of accompanying institutions—many initially developed during the Cold War—constituted the connective tissue, or critical infrastructure, of international order.

THIS TIME IT'S DIFFERENT: 2019 VERSUS 1989

Thirty years later, the United States maintains its primacy in terms of military spending. In 2017, US defense spending totaled $610 billion, reversing a decline since 2010, which was three times the level of the second biggest spender (China) and exceeded the $578 billion spent by the next seven largest spenders.[34] However, the state of play is very different from the time the Berlin Wall collapsed. In all three areas that once supported the American international system—the disposition and trajectory of potentially revisionist great powers, the availability of exit options from American-led order, and nature of new and growing transnational networks—we see opposite trends.

Great-Power Challengers

The United States faces at least two great powers, Russia and China, that seek to revise, in one way or another, the current international order. Though publicly unified as partners against American hegemony, they do not use all of the same tools, and they do not share all of the same strategic goals. Moscow, especially since its annexation of Crimea from Ukraine in 2014, wants significant changes in the rules, norms, and arrangements of world politics—the architecture of international order. Russian officials call for the replacement of the American international system with a more pragmatic "polycentric system," where great powers control spheres of influence and engage in a mix of situational cooperation and conflict. In his Crimean annexation speech, Russian president Vladimir Putin accused the West of failing to adhere to its own principles, ignoring international law and degrading its own institutions, thereby compressing Russia "like a spring" that forced it to "snap back."[35]

China also seeks to transform world order, but its approach does not, as of now, involve smashing existing institutions or norms, not least because its own rise and economic performance has depended on an open trading system and other economic arrangements associated with liberal international order. Rather, Beijing seeks to both amplify its voice within current international institutions and, critically, establish new regional and international bodies that can serve as vehicles to promote its interests and vision of a global community. By creating and underwriting new organizations like the Shanghai Cooperation Organization (SCO), the BRICS (Brazil, Russia, India, China, and South Africa), and the Asian Infrastructure Investment Bank (AIIB), Beijing has introduced new organizations that it dominates and substitutes for functions provided by American- and European-dominated arrangements.

China also launched the Belt and Road Initiative (BRI), which it announced to great fanfare (of its own making) in 2013. The BRI is a $1 trillion global vision to invest in neighboring and developing countries, especially in areas of infrastructure. It aims to embed recipients in an emerging, China-friendly political community. The BRI has important implications for international order, as it threatens to bind countries to Beijing's economic orbit, technologies and standards; China is also launching an international BRI court to adjudicate commercial and legal disputes that arise out of BRI programs. Accordingly, China's championing of these new vehicles and institutions may transform the ecology of international order itself, steadily increasing the power and activity of non-US sources of order.

Goods Substitution and Exit Options

If the emergence of Russia and China as revisionist competitors constitute a "top-down" challenge to the American international system, a less obvious, but no less significant, challenge comes from below. Even small and weak states now enjoy more readily available alternative patrons to allow them to exit the order on any given governance issue. This exit from hegemony via "death by a thousand paper cuts" operates precisely because regimes may simply seek domestic political advantage when they choose, or leverage, alternative suppliers of development assistance, military security, or other goods. That is, they may not intend to alter prevailing international order even as their actions have precisely that effect.

As we discussed earlier, in the early 1990s the lack of any alternative providers of such goods made a Western-dominated international order—one with significant liberal components—effectively the only game in town. Obvious and sustained deviation from its principles and institutions of global governance usually marked a regime as an international outlier or "rogue state." Such deviation made it more difficult for such a regime to secure international goods and provided important ammunition to political opponents. This "patronage monopoly" also imposed costs for state governments and regimes around the world, usually in the form of political commitments or economic conditions. Thus, international financial institutions (IFIs), such as the International Monetary Fund and the World Bank, imposed more stringent conditions on borrowers, while autocrats faced greater international scrutiny for holding problematic elections or otherwise violating democratic norms.[36] Thus, many of the popular and scholarly criticisms of globalization that emerged in the late 1990s emphasized the lack of alternative models or patrons for developed countries that did not want to implement the prescriptions and policies of the "Anglo-American" (or "neoliberal") model of open globalization.[37]

But, as time went on, a category of "competitive authoritarian regimes" overcame these external democratizing pressures and consolidated their regimes. Some did so with the help of revenues from the sale of important commodities, especially oil. Others positioned themselves as strategically important partners for the "War on Terror" prosecuted by the United States after the terrorist attacks of September 11, 2001.[38]

By the mid-2000s, the rise of alternative patrons in various areas of international governance started to mitigate the demands of Western patrons. The arrival of other providers of similar goods further diminished their vulnerability to the demands made by the United States and Europe—demands that often threatened recipient governments with political or economic disruption. For example, China's development bank provided increasing development and investment funds to impoverished states in Africa, Latin

America, and Central Asia, but without the conditions traditionally made by its liberal counterparts such as the World Bank.

Similarly, emerging patrons like Saudi Arabia and Qatar in the Middle East extended support to critical regional powers—for example, supporting the embattled Egyptian government following the 2011 Arab Spring—thereby also undercutting the West's ability to leverage its control over the major suppliers of global governance into political influence. Other emerging regional powers such as Turkey, India, and Iran (and, for a time, Venezuela) all adopted new strategies of influence that relied on their newfound ability to provide public, club, and private goods to neighboring countries of interest—but, again, without the demands made by advanced industrialized democracies.[39]

In the realm of political, military, and symbolic goods as well, these new patrons also began to supply alternatives. International election observation became a crowded and increasingly confusing field that featured dozens of new organizations. Many of these existed simply to rubber-stamp elections in hybrid and autocratic regimes.[40] In the post-Soviet sphere, monitors from regional organizations like the Russian-led Commonwealth of Independent States (CIS) and the SCO, beginning in the early 2000s, sent to member countries election monitors who provided favorable assessments of obviously flawed elections. In doing so, they muddied and undercut the much more negative signals sent by their Western counterparts, such as the Washington, DC–based Nixon Center or the Organization for Security and Co-operation in Europe's (OSCE) Office for Democratic Institutions and Human Rights (ODIHR).[41] Indeed, by the mid-2010s, regimes around the world, from Ecuador to Tajikistan to Sri Lanka, seemed to prefer procuring goods from alternative patrons precisely to avoid the political externalities and conditions demanded by Western and Western-backed external actors.

Contested Transnationalism

By 2019, the momentum once enjoyed by robust, generally liberal transnational networks had slowed, if not reversed. Right-wing illiberal counterparts now challenge them on matters ranging from lesbian, gay, bisexual, transgender, and queer (LGBTQ) rights to ethnic diversity to liberal-democratic governance. Meanwhile, illiberal regimes have found ways to limit—or even eliminate—the influence of liberal transnational advocacy networks and reformist NGOs.[42]

Waves of popular uprisings and regime changes—the so-called Color Revolutions of the mid 2000s in the post-Soviet Space and the 2011–12 Arab Spring in the Middle East—played a key role in this process. Western governments and media framed these political changes as democratically inspired. But they sent alarm bells ringing throughout authoritarian and illiberal regimes, who took note of the geopolitical threat posed by the democracy and human rights promotion agenda.

In response, concerned regimes soon adopted a sophisticated playbook to curtail the influence and operating space of NGOs with foreign and transnational ties. States imposed new restrictions on receiving foreign funds, they limited the scope of political activities, and they stigmatized such political activities by branding the actors as "foreign agents." In other words, the norms of democracy and their civil-society champions shifted from an often-desirable ticket into Western order to a security threat. By 2015, over 50 states had passed legislation banning or restricting NGOs, with 45 passing restrictions on their accepting foreign funds (38 of these since 2003).[43] At the same time, governments also diluted the influence of liberal transnational actors by sponsoring counterparts of their own—also known as Government Organized Nongovernmental Organizations (GONGOs). These conduct advocacy in the media spotlight but remain strongly supportive of government policies and positions.[44]

Important changes also happened within the core advanced industrialized democracies. By the mid-2010s, the proliferation of illiberal networks challenged the mainstream political consensus within the West. These sometimes took the form of left-wing radical parties but more often of right-wing parties and movements. They openly questioned the values of international liberalism. They attacked the authority and questioned the benefits of continued membership in major institutions such as the EU and NATO.

While such movements and ideologies dated back decades, two developments helped tip the balance more toward a generalized "illiberal turn" in the West: the Great Recession of 2008 and the refugee crisis in Europe. The latter, exacerbated by the civil war in Syria, pushed refugee and immigration issues to the top of the populist agenda, shattering the EU consensus on migration and transforming the domestic politics of Eastern and Central Europe.[45] As we will explore in greater detail in Chapter 6, illiberal parties also have developed transnational ties to one another; they receive both financial and moral support from, among others, Moscow—which views them as an instrument for wedging apart democratic governments and cultivating friendly regimes.[46]

For example, the 2010 electoral triumph and re-election of Viktor Orbán in Hungary allowed his government to launch assaults on key liberal institutions, such as judicial independence and civil society. The June 2016 Brexit vote in the UK, backed by a campaign with ties to Russian business interests, produced domestic turmoil in a European power known for its relatively hard line against Russia and driving a wedge through the EU. Not long after, investigative reporting into the Trump campaign found numerous ties to donors and organizations with an interest in weakening Western political institutions. Indeed, the Trump administration itself appointed several ambassadors to traditional NATO allies, including the Netherlands and Germany, who openly criticized EU values and the political norms of their host countries.

American Power without Order? The Trump Experiment Defined

Contrary to much public commentary, the Trump presidency is not a primary cause of the dynamics weakening the American international system. It is both a symptom and an accelerant of processes of hegemonic unraveling. Trump's presidency has certainly raised significant doubts about the durability of America's commitment to the system it helped construct. But, as we argue in this book, these pathways out of hegemony were already operating before 2017. Unfortunately, until very recently they have too often ignored or dismissed, whether by "the blob" (the mainstream consensus on foreign affairs associated with major liberal- and conservative-leaning think tanks and policy officials) or American international-relations scholars.

Indeed, past debates about the future of American primacy often revolved around comparing the power capabilities of a competitor—usually China—or highlighting the gap between revisionist ambitions and relative capabilities, especially in the case of Russia. Arguments about "unipolar stability" masked a steady, but unmistakable, transformation of the ecology of international order.[47] While commentators and observers did call attention to other processes of hegemonic unraveling and shifts in international order over the last fifteen years, some—such as the role of transnational anti-order movements in Europe and North America—received comparatively little attention before the success of the Brexit referendum and

Trump's campaign for the presidency. Moreover, it is becoming increasingly clear that these processes are interdependent and even "bootstrapping" on one another—that is, each is generating positive feedback for the others.

The central analytical question posed by the Trump administration is whether it is possible to decouple the maintenance of American power from key, and particularly liberal, elements of the American hegemonic system. The usual purpose of hegemonic orders is to lock in a system of benefits that accrue to the leading power. Thus, hegemons generally turn revisionist against the order that they've helped construct at their own peril. Yet this is where Trump's dispositions lie. Trump and some of his advisors openly regard supporting the infrastructure that helps maintain this system—multilateral alliances, international organizations, and at least some commitment to liberal values—as a threat to American power.

Moreover, Trump's public admiration for "strongman" regimes in Russia, China, and Saudi Arabia contrasts strikingly with his obvious disdain for traditional democratic allies and transatlantic partnerships. This suggests that he would prefer to replace America's current global role and international commitments with a series of bilateral (and more ephemeral) bargains. In other words, the wager is that stripping the global system of its ordering arrangements will yield a "dog eat dog" world where the sheer superior power of the United States will ensure that it most often comes out on top; the Trump administration believes that making aggressive increases in military spending, planning for nuclear modernization, and scrapping agreements that constrain American security policy will ensure that the United States retains the necessary military superiority to triumph in the geopolitical scrap heap.

In this respect, Trump's attempt at international disruptions exhibits key similarities and differences with that of Mikhail Gorbachev, who also attempted to reshape the foreign policy of a superpower in the service of a refocused domestic agenda. Gorbachev recognized that the Soviet Union's high levels of defense spending simply made it unable to meet the domestic demands and adjustments required in a globalizing world. Thus, he sought the Soviet Union's integration into the Western international system—and soon, quite unintentionally, oversaw the disintegration of the Soviet order. Whatever dividends these policies yielded were lost in the chaos of the final months of Soviet collapse and the immediate stress placed on Russia by its sudden independence.

Three years into his presidency, it is clear that Trump can rattle the infrastructure of the system constructed by the United States and its allies, but it remains uncertain how much of it he can, or is willing to, pull apart. But because Trump is both a symptom and an accelerant of general trends, his presidency calls attention to the broader pathways out of hegemony that the world is increasingly walking.

THE PLAN OF THIS BOOK

In Chapter 2, we explore the theory and practice of the American hegemonic system. We argue that there are three distinct principles of liberal international order: democratic political systems that broadly respect political and human rights, free economic exchange within and among states, and the management of international affairs via multilateral institutions and other forms of intergovernmental cooperation.[48] There is no reason that all three must coexist, but it became conventional wisdom in the 1990s that these three "pillars" of liberal order mutually reinforced one another. From the Clinton to the Obama administrations, American grand strategy sought accordingly to enlarge liberal order via the expansion of American leadership from its Cold War boundaries to the entire globe. Thomas Wright, a scholar at the Brookings Institution, refers to this as the "convergence" wager. It held that the major powers would come together around all three pillars of liberal order, and "stop treating each other as rivals and begin to work together to tackle common challenges." By the late twenty-teens, this wager appears to have failed.[49]

To better understand why and how the convergence wager failed—as well as the current trajectory of international politics—we take a close look at the concepts of hegemony and international order. We argue that international orders have *architectures*, made up of prevailing rules, norms, and values. International orders also have *infrastructures*, composed of the relationships, practices, flows, and interactions that underpin them. Overall, we suggest conceptualizing international orders as *ecosystems* or as having specific ecologies, within which a variety of different state and non-state actors operate. In Chapter 3, we use these concepts to make sense of the different pathways through which hegemonic orders—and, for that matter, international orders more broadly—unravel.

Chapters 4, 5, and 6 each explore and illustrate a different pathway that is undermining the US-led order. Chapter 4 focuses on the rise of Russia and China as revisionist powers, exploring their common grievances with the US-led international order but also the different strategies that they have adopted as challengers. Chapter 5 looks to uncover less obvious "bottom-up" dynamics by exploring how states in various regions, even smaller and weaker ones, are increasingly undermining the order by exiting from its institutions and rules and soliciting assets and governance from alternative providers. Our key analytical point in this chapter is to show how regime security, once thought by rulers to be guaranteed by the security as well as the governance and social status conferred by their association with the liberal international order, is now threatened by its intrusions into domestic sovereign affairs. New findings about the domestic political effects of Chinese aid in Africa as well as case studies of Hungary, Turkey, and the Philippines all demonstrate how regimes are shifting to new and alternative providers of public and club goods in a bid to consolidate their domestic power and authority. Chapter 6 explores how the transnational networks of the 1990s that enhanced the liberal order have been curtailed by states and tracks how new networks that promote illiberal forms of order—national culture, sovereignty, transitional values, and closed borders—are now interacting and openly disrupting what had appeared to be a domestic political consensus in the West.

Chapter 7 then turns to the foreign policy practices and agenda of the Trump administration. It examines the deeper domestic origins of Trumpism and highlights how Trump intersects with all three of the pathways that are eroding liberal internationalism.

Chapter 8 reprises the book's main findings and arguments and offers some possible scenarios for what a post-liberal international order might look like. We assess the likelihood of an emerging US-China Cold War, explore the dynamics of an international order without liberal values, and call attention to the rise of transnational oligarchy as a distinct political force that is supported by the institutions and legacies of the liberal order. Although we anticipate that a future new Democratic administration will attempt to revive American global leadership, to strengthen commitments to allies, and to uphold again liberal values and norms, we conclude that the international system is too far down multiple pathways to allow for a return of America's former hegemonic role. Exit is upon us.

2

The American Hegemonic System in Theoretical and Historical Perspective

Some theories of world politics remain locked away in the ivory tower, isolated from policymaking and the larger public. This is emphatically *not* the case when it comes to theories of hegemony and hegemonic orders. They permeate American policy and public debates about international affairs, even though many editorials and essays invoke them indirectly, preferring to use less technical and more anodyne terms such as "leadership." The same is true outside the United States, where theories of hegemony, especially when combined with ideas about liberal order, provide reference points for both critics and supporters of American power.

The idea that the United States is a hegemonic power that has been constructing and defending liberal international order since the end of the Second World War also routinely appears in official speeches and policy documents. Consider the *National Security Strategy of the United States of America*, which is supposedly the most important statement of official American strategic thought, one that signals to the world what values and policies America stands for. Nearly every recent *National Security Strategy* embraces the idea that America emerged from the Cold War as a global hegemon and that it has a duty to promote freedom, democracy, and open markets.

For example, President Bill Clinton's final *National Security Strategy*, written in 1999, emphasized that "the United States remains the world's most powerful force for peace, prosperity and the universal values of democracy and freedom" and that America's "central challenge—and our responsibility—is to sustain that role by seizing the opportunities of this new global era for the benefit of our own people and people around the world."[1] Even the 2017 *National Security Strategy*, crafted to make sense of Trump foreign policy, paints the post-1945 period as one in which the United States used its superior economic and military powers to construct a liberal international order; but it describes that order as outdated. It argues that other states have exploited liberal order to weaken American power and that the United States must change the way it relates to the world.[2]

This outlook explains why many critics of Trump foreign policy argue that his actions and rhetoric are undermining liberal order and, with it, American power (see Chapter 7). For instance, in January 2019, Stewart M. Patrick of the Council on Foreign Relations wrote, "Two years into his administration, Donald Trump's war on the liberal international order is still gathering steam, and the costs are mounting. The United States is increasingly going it alone—when it is not going home. As America abdicates global leadership, traditional allies and partners are reeling, authoritarians are rejoicing, geopolitical rivals are emboldened, and the world drifts without clear direction."[3] Such criticisms echo long-standing concerns that without American leadership, liberal order cannot survive.

Proponents of liberal order identify a number of its features that they think make it an especially successful way of organizing international affairs. These include voice opportunities, largely in multilateral institutions like the United Nations (UN) and the North Atlantic Treaty Organization (NATO) that give weaker states an unusual amount of input into the governance of a hegemonic order. They also contend that the United States, through a web of multilateral and bilateral agreements, engaged in an unusual degree of "self-binding": of voluntarily restricting its freedom of action internationally. Both of these characteristics are lacking in more exclusively coercive hegemonic systems; their presence, the argument goes, generates support among weaker powers for liberal hegemonic orders.[4]

Moreover, supporters note that in promoting and upholding this liberal order, Washington committed itself to open economic arrangements and financial policies that—even when those practices disproportionately served the interests of the leading states—at least spread the wealth around. They point to the success of Western Europe after the Second World War, and later East Asian allies such as South Korea and Japan, and still later countries such as China as evidence for the positive economic consequences of liberal order. Finally, while democratic waves have ebbed and flowed, the norms and values of liberal order emphasize human rights, equality, and self-determination—all of which make it relatively appealing to ordinary people.[5]

Is this argument right? Is there an American-led international order that, as a result of its liberal qualities, is particularly durable? Yes and no. It depends on the time and the place. Advocates of liberal international order often overstate their case—and then walk it back as they deal with anomalies. Critics correctly point out the tensions, contradictions, and inaccuracies in official rhetoric surrounding liberal order. But some dismiss the concept too easily, let alone how aspects of liberal ordering can prove very attractive to second-tier great powers and to weaker states. More important, we cannot understand key features of contemporary international order, as well as why some states and movements object to it, without reference to its liberal characteristics.

Discussions of international liberal order need to avoid conflating three different things: specific examples of US foreign policy; the regions and issue areas where the United States operates as a hegemonic power; and the broader international order within which US foreign policy and American hegemonic ordering takes place.[6] There are plenty of examples of illiberal American foreign policy; the United States has supported dictators, overthrown democratic regimes, violated international law, used force unilaterally, meddled in foreign elections, and directly abused human rights.[7] Many of these profoundly illiberal policies had long-term consequences in specific countries, regional politics, and even the overall international order (see Chapter 7).[8] But international order encompasses more than the specific foreign-policy actions taken by the United States. As international-relations scholar Rohan Mukherjee notes, this is "evidenced by the fact that many aspects of the order have challenged U.S. interests or constrained its freedom of action."[9]

In this chapter, we take a deeper dive into the concepts at play in so many official and media debates about American grand strategy. We begin with liberal international order. We then explore the concept of hegemony and the idea of hegemonic cycles. We next turn to elaborating the general notion of international order, which we argue is made up of architectures, infrastructures, and ecologies. We then elaborate on the distinction between broader international order and the more specific American hegemonic system, and we discuss how they mutually influence one another. Finally, we use the analytical tools and ideas developed in this chapter to revisit the broader question of liberal international order and the convergence wager that drove US foreign policy for most of the post–Cold War period.

INTERNATIONAL LIBERAL ORDER

There is no such thing as "the liberal international order." As we demonstrate later in this chapter, it never really makes sense to think about international orders as singular things. Nonetheless, it is true that liberal rules, norms, and arrangements suffuse (to varying degrees) contemporary regional and global orders. We ignore the liberal characteristics of both the American system and the broader international order at our peril. They help shape specific centripetal and centrifugal pressures in contemporary world politics, the ideologies of those who want to alter international order, and the terms by which states and political movements contest order.

But what, exactly, are these elements? We find it useful to think about three major dimensions of liberal international ordering. These can, and have, been combined in very different ways across history and in different regions and issue areas.[10]

Political Liberal Governance

Political liberal governance (or, simply, *political liberalism*) concerns one dimension of the content (or what we call "the architecture") of international order. The architecture of international orders is politically liberal to the extent that it establishes the responsibility for governments to protect some minimal set of individual rights for their citizens, with more liberal orders favoring developed liberal-democratic governance among their members.

The current international order is dense with treaties, agreements, covenants, and infrastructure that bakes in politically liberal principles. The United Nations Charter (1945) itself, the Universal Declaration of Human Rights (1948), the International Covenant on Economic, Social and Cultural Rights, and International Covenant on Civil and Political Rights (both

1966) constitute just some of the numerous arrangements that enshrine human rights, basic human equality, political rights, and other broadly liberal political principles as part of international order.[11] As such, they represent a potential threat to autocratic states and illiberal regimes. While the specific content, let alone the effectiveness, of this architecture has varied over time, it is simply impossible to ignore the fact that liberal rights are threaded throughout contemporary international order.

Economic Liberalism

Economic liberalism refers to the belief in, and commitment to, encouraging open economic exchange and flows among states. Different strains of economic liberalism have been more or less prevalent over the course of American hegemony. The immediate post–World War II economic order was characterized by "embedded liberalism." States committed to liberalizing trade by defending a system of capital controls designed to shield individual economies from destabilizing financial flows and shocks.[12] Many view the Nixon administration's abandonment of the gold standard in 1973 as an important marker in the transition from embedded liberalism to neoliberalism, understood in terms of the increasing deregulation that gathered steam in the 1980s and 1990s.[13]

In the wake of the Soviet collapse, neoliberalism became institutionalized in the so-called Washington Consensus of championing free trade—including establishing the World Trade Organization (WTO) in 2000—and financial liberalization. Both of these were rooted in the principles of major economic organizations, including the International Monetary Fund (IMF), Organization for Economic Cooperation and Development (OECD), and even the European Union (EU).[14] Indeed, the unwavering commitment to rules-based economic globalization in the 1990s and 2000s created a "democratic trilemma" for states, as governments are increasingly constrained in their domestic monetary and fiscal policies by adherence to international economic commitments, the threat of capital flight, and potentially punishing financial crises.[15]

Liberal Intergovernmentalism

Liberal intergovernmentalism concerns the *means*, or *form*, of international order. As a principle, liberal intergovernmentalism favors specific kinds of infrastructures: multilateral treaties and agreements, international organizations, and institutions that make rules and norms, monitor compliance with those rules and norms, resolve disputes, and provide for public, private, and club goods. Liberal intergovernmentalism also manifests in bilateral agreements and institutions that reflect principles of juridical sovereign equality even when concluded by states that are significantly unequal in their power relations.

However, relations among states can take on the trappings of liberal intergovernmentalism without embodying its spirit. States can, for instance, create multilateral arrangements that hide, or just barely conceal, highly coercive and unequal relationships. But the very fact that great powers feel the need to obscure, say, de facto imperial relationships suggests that liberal principles of ordering have concrete effects on state behavior.

International Liberal Order Is a Matter of Degree and of Kind

Contemporary critics and proponents of the idea of liberal order sometimes treat all three elements—political, economic, and intergovernmental liberalism—as a package deal. For critics, doing so makes it easier to point to inconsistencies and hypocrisies. Liberal internationalists like the notion that these three dimensions, at least eventually, go together. But political, economic, and intergovernmentalism need not mutually reinforce one another, let alone appear together.

For example, although certain strands of liberalism have always rejected the legitimacy of empire, liberal principles can also serve as a justification for imperial control; a number of British officials and intellectuals of the later nineteenth century saw themselves as promoting liberal order through empire.[16] Some supporters of the American-led occupations of Afghanistan and Iraq argued explicitly that the United States needed to embrace its status as a liberal empire and behave accordingly.[17] Indeed, liberalism need not reject imperial projects in favor of multilateral cooperation among sovereign states. The fact that we tend to see empire as incompatible with liberal order reflects, in part, the ascendency of liberal intergovernmentalist principles at the expense of the legitimacy of formal imperialism.[18]

For its part, post-war American-led order has always been unevenly, or inconsistently, liberal with respect to all three of these dimensions.[19] It took time for NATO to evolve into the more equitable alliance that exists today.[20] The first wave of American basing and access agreements included terms reminiscent of those we would expect to see between an imperial metropole and its provinces.[21] Washington extracted nearly unrestricted basing rights in the Philippines and Cuba as a direct condition of granting them independence. It did the same after 1945 to its vanquished foes Germany, Japan, and Italy. The former Axis powers, excluding the eastern part of Germany, became hosts to some of the largest US military facilities in the world after the formal end of their American-led occupations.

In East Asia, the United States eschewed multilateralism and opted for bilateral alliances specifically to prevent its allies, most notably South Korea and Taiwan, from colluding to influence the security order.[22] During the Cold War, Washington made frequent use of such wedge strategies in Latin America—as a way of maintaining American hegemony.[23] G. John Ikenberry, the most prominent theorist of American liberal order, notes that such aspects of the American alliance system have more than a passing resemblance to informal empire.[24] And it's difficult to describe a lot of this behavior as "liberal empire." Washington has supported dictators, subverted left-wing democratic governments, perpetuated and enabled human-rights abuses, and even run interference for mass violence.[25]

We discuss more illiberal facets of the American hegemonic system later in the book. But defenders of the idea of liberal order correctly note that it is simply unrealistic to suppose that any great power, no matter what its ideological disposition, will abandon its more parochial economic and security concerns. It makes no sense to think that hegemonic systems, or international orders more generally, will ever be free from violence and coercion: the "creation and maintenance of order involves violence and the suppression of certain interests in favor of others—on this count the post-1945 world order was no different from past versions."[26]

Post–Cold War Liberal Ordering

Despite what some debates over American foreign policy imply, liberal elements of the American system overall became more pronounced since the end of the Cold War. It is easy to focus on major counterexamples, such as the so-called War on Terror, to note Washington's continued support for dictatorial and illiberal regimes, or to point to the imperial character of the American occupation of Iraq. But the United States operated much more frequently as an informal empire during the Cold War. Washington was far more systematic in its support of authoritarian regimes, pursuit of covert regime change, and efforts at election meddling when its leadership was driven by anti-Communism and the US-Soviet rivalry.[27]

As we discussed in the introduction, Washington's post–Cold War approach to hegemonic ordering placed its bets on the wager that all three of these elements of liberal order would be mutually reinforcing. Over a decade and a half, the United States supervised the construction of new institutions. These included new international organizations where the United States, either by formal rules or tacit expectations, remained the dominant player. It consolidated its own security infrastructure by encouraging NATO enlargement and shoring up alliances and agreements for military bases. It promoted, but did not always practice, liberal principles such as democracy promotion, human rights, and the responsibility to protect.

The specific logic held that taking steps to integrate the states of the former Soviet bloc, as well as China, into liberal trading arrangements and liberal institutions would forward democratization and commitment to liberal norms.[28] Of course, US policymakers regularly sought exceptions from being bound by these ordering architectures. They negotiated country-by-country exceptions against the provisions of the International Criminal Court (ICC) for American service personnel stationed abroad. Washington ran up domestic debts and deficits at the same time that US-controlled international bodies like the International Monetary Fund (IMF) were demanding strict economic conditionality by countries hit hard by financial shocks, such as the East Asian crisis of 1997. However, the international ecology of the 1990s, where the United States was not only dominant but had virtually no competitors, made such exceptionalism easy and did not appear to interfere overmuch with broader liberal ordering efforts.

Now things look a good deal different. Under President Xi Jinping, China has reversed its tentative steps toward a more open political environment and doubled-down on surveillance and political repression. Russia explicitly advocates for the end of the American-led liberal international order and a turn to a polycentric world of spheres of influence and more pragmatic governing arrangements. The great financial crisis of 2008 shook the global consensus about the benefits of unfettered liberalism and gave rise to new demands for trade protection and more interventionist domestic policies. As we noted in the introduction, a number of central and eastern European states have swung, to various degrees, toward electoral authoritarianism. With a few exceptions, the democratic wave of the 1990s seems to have faltered and reversed.[29]

HEGEMONY AND HEGEMONIC CYCLES: A PRIMER

What happened? The most prominent explanation for the loss of the "unipolar moment" is simply that American power, like that of all great powers before it, has declined. End of story.

Indeed, a number of scholars see the history of world politics as driven by the rise and decline of leading powers. For them, the American "unipolar moment" of the 1990s and early 2000s provides only the most recent example of a larger pattern of recurrent bids for international dominance. Some of these bids succeed, leading to periods of international hegemony in which the leading power orders the international system according to its interests and values. Others fail, usually resulting in "multipolar" international systems where three or more great powers establish rough balances of power among them.

According to these theories, the most common and most stable international systems have a clear hierarchy of power characterized by a single dominant political community. In contrast, systems maintained by balances of power—in which states form alliances to block the emergence of a hegemon—are unstable arrangements. The hegemonic orders that dominant powers establish generally involve creating rules of the game; supplying international goods, such as security guarantees, suppression of piracy, and economic assistance; and allocating status and prestige. Such hegemonic ordering, in turn, sets the stage for the next dance between the incumbent power and rising challengers. Most of the great wars of history—such as the Thirty Years' War (1618–1648), the First World War (1914–1918), and the Second World War (1939–1945)—resulted when the declining hegemon and rising powers failed to reach peaceful accommodation over adjustments to international order. These wars sometimes swept away the old order, allowing the new hegemon to establish its own order—or giving the old one free rein to engage in a new round of hegemonic ordering.[30]

What Is Hegemony?

In his history of the concept, Perry Anderson notes that "the origins of the term hegemony are Greek" and, as "an abstract noun, *hēgemonia* first appears in Herodotus, to designate leadership of an alliance of city-states for a common military end, a position of honour accorded to Sparta in resistance to the Persian invasion of Greece."[31] A broadly similar idea appears in ancient China to describe military leadership of city-state leagues: the "ruler of the dominant state was given the title of 'senior' or 'hegemon' (*ba*) by the Zhou king, who charged him to defend what was left of the Zhou realm. Formally these leagues were hierarchical groupings of independent states, bound together through treaties."[32]

Most contemporary uses retain some of the spirit of *hēgemonia* and *ba*, but they expand the concept of hegemony well beyond the context of formal military alliances. Hegemons are usually states or other kinds of political communities—such as empires, confederations, and city-states—that use their superior economic and military capabilities to exercise leadership over weaker ones. In exercising that leadership, hegemons order relations among their subordinates. They establish rules and norms concerning warfare, economic exchange, and the allocation of status and prestige. This ordering may or may not result from conscious design—that is, it may not take the form of a deliberate "hegemonic project." Even when it does, the resulting order usually winds up deviating from whatever plan politicians and rulers might have had in mind.

Scholars have long argued over the relationship between hegemony and empire. In traditional understandings, hegemony involves the control over the foreign policies of subordinates, while imperial rule extends to control over their domestic policies as well. This distinction often breaks down in the real world. Domination of foreign security and economic relations usually entails at least some degree of control over domestic policies. Thus, some argue for "informal empire" as an intermediate relationship, one in which the practice of hegemony blurs into that of empire.[33]

But even this formulation produces protracted and, quite frankly, inconclusive arguments about the point where hegemonic relations cross over into imperial ones. These debates do not even matter very much for theories of hegemonic cycles. The cases that scholars draw on have always included well-known empires, such as the Roman and the Spanish. Thus, we think it easier to treat empire—along with confederations, federations, and other logics of political organization—as one of a number of different ways that dominant actors may order relations among subordinates. In practice, hegemonic systems often include a mix of imperial relationships and non-imperial ones.[34]

Hegemonic-order theory claims to distill international history to its essential characteristics, namely, a cycle of hegemonic powers. But what does that actually look like? Here we present a stylized "history according to hegemonic-order theory" that starts with the end of the Spanish Habsburg bid for European hegemony in the middle of the seventeenth century and concludes where Chapter 1 began: the period leading up to the end of the Cold War.

A Stylized History of Five Centuries of Hegemonic Cycles

In November 1659, Bourbon France and Habsburg Spain concluded the Treaty of the Pyrenees, which ended the last of the great-power conflicts that made up the Thirty Years' War (1618–1648). France, allied with Stuart England since 1657, saw its victory confirmed by territorial concessions, chiefly at the expense of Catalonia and Flanders—both part of the Spanish composite monarchy. The peace marked the total collapse of the Spanish Habsburg bid for dominance in Europe, a struggle that began in the early sixteenth century when Charles V cobbled together a patchwork, composite empire that included Castile, Aragon-Catalonia, most of what is now the Netherlands and Belgium, Naples and Sicily, and traditional Habsburg lands in Central Europe.[35]

Soon France, under the "Sun King" Louis XIV, made its own bid for European dominance. Great Britain emerged as France's principal antagonist, first in conflicts with Bourbon monarchs and then, after the French Revolution, Napoleon Bonaparte. During the nineteenth century, fueled by the industrial revolution and wealth extracted principally from India, the United Kingdom emerged as a global hegemon. The British system became the largest sphere of hegemony in human history. At its peak, it included not only formal colonies and possessions stretching from North America to Southeast Asia but also a network of protectorates and dependent states. Britain promoted interstate trade and pegged the UK pound to a fixed amount of gold, thereby generating a global monetary order; London used a variety of carrots and sticks to open markets.[36] In some reckonings, such international economic policies—combined with its elected parliament and the expansion of its domestic franchise—made Britain the first "liberal hegemon."[37]

As the nineteenth century came to a close, however, Britain faced multiple challenges. At the most basic level, the industrial revolution spread to other states and therefore undermined Britain's economic edge. Of particular importance was the rise of the United States in North America, and Germany (united by Prussia in 1871) in Europe. London ultimately opted for a peaceful accommodation to American power, trusting that good relations would keep Canada safe and the Atlantic free from American challenge. This process was so successful that London stopped considering American naval power a potential threat to its maritime security.[38] But Berlin and London failed to work out such an adjustment; after Wilhelm II replaced his father as kaiser, his *Weltpolitik* ("world politics") foreign policy frequently collided with British imperial interests. The Anglo-German naval arms race exacerbated tensions between the two powers. When Germany invaded Belgium in 1914 as part of its war plan against France, Britain declared war.

Britain was one of the victors in World War I. But the conflict left it exhausted and facing nationalist pressures throughout its empire.[39] London attempted to continue its role as manager of the global economy but lacked the resources to do so effectively. Washington, which might have been able to take up that role, failed to do so. The 1919 Treaty of Versailles established the League of Nations to prevent another great war, but the United States never joined.[40]

Perhaps because of America's absence, or perhaps because of fundamental flaws, the Treaty of Versailles proved not the start of durable peace but an interregnum before Nazi Germany made its bid for European dominance while its ally, Japan, fought for supremacy in Asia. The leadership of both countries saw themselves as squeezed between the ongoing rise of the United States and the newer threat represented by the Soviet Union and transnational Communism. As historian Adam Tooze writes, "Hitler warned in 1928" that "the 'threatened global hegemony of the North American continent' would reduce" all of Europe "to the status of Switzerland or Holland."[41] Germany and Japan signed the Anti-Comintern Pact in 1936—and thus established the Axis powers—as a bulwark against international communism.

In 1939, Germany invaded Poland; Britain and France declared war on Germany. The series of conflicts that became collectively known as the Second World War had begun. The war proved the bloodiest conflict in human history, leaving well over 50 million people dead and almost all of the major military and economic powers of the time devastated. The United States was the only great power to emerge with its industrial base intact—in 1945 it accounted for at least a third of global economic output.[42] American military forces were deployed in Europe and Asia, and wartime mobilization left it with significant ability to project power across the globe.

The Post-War Order

This privileged position allowed Washington to take the lead in shaping the post-war order. American proponents of taking on that role outmaneuvered their opponents—whom they branded "isolationists"—by pointing to the interwar period and the experience of World War II. Historian Stephen Wertheim argues that at the outbreak of the war, American planners believed that the best way to secure American security was global primacy via joint US-UK hegemony. But they eventually decided that ordinary Americans would be unlikely to support such an arrangement. Instead, the most effective way to sell global engagement to the public was by reviving ideas associated with the League of Nations.[43] This took hold and became integrated into American ordering efforts.

Washington's primary aim, aside from building a foundation for American global leadership, was to create arrangements that would prevent another round of fascism and world war. Leading thinkers identified the root causes of these threats in the Great Depression, the spread of protectionism, and the failure of the League of Nations. Thus, the United Nations (UN) was not an entirely novel creation. It evolved from "existing ideas and institutions" and its designers paid careful attention to the "successes and failures" of those ideas in the interwar period, especially when it came to the League of Nations.[44] The Bretton Woods Agreement of 1944 pegged currencies to the price of gold and made the dollar a de facto global reserve currency. It established the International Monetary Fund (IMF) and the International Bank for Reconstruction and Development (IBRD)—the first of the development banks that would together become known as the World Bank. A few years later, the General Agreement on Tariffs and Trade (GATT) rounded out the "Bretton Woods system" which aimed to facilitate open trade, economic development, and stability.[45]

That system came under strain in the 1960s. In 1971, President Richard Nixon suspended the gold standard. In 1973, the Bretton Woods System ended as such, but the IMF, World Bank, and GATT remained. It is no accident that the 1970s provoked a major wave of discussion of US decline. The collapse of the Bretton Woods System, the OPEC cartel's oil shock and general shifts in the global economy, and the inglorious end to the Vietnam War all raised serious doubts about the longevity of American economic and military leadership over its hegemonic sphere. But the end of the Bretton Woods System mutated, rather than ended, American economic leadership. As international-relations scholar Carla Norrlof argues,

"Far from being 'dethroned,' the dollar's resilience and unique position in the world economy would persist long after" the formal end of the Bretton Woods System.[46]

This takes us roughly to where we started Chapter 1. During the 1980s, many analysts looked at the Soviet Union and Japan and saw America as a declining hegemon. But the serious of events that ran from 1989 until 1991 propelled the United States into the position of dominant *global* economic and military power.

This history also highlights the fact that scholars built hegemonic-order theory largely from the experience of Europe and its immediate neighborhood, including the Greek city-state system and the rise and decline of the Roman Empire. Nonetheless, others adapt and apply the framework to many centuries of East Asian history, usually in the context of the rise and decline of different Chinese dynasties.[47] We also find similar dynamics in South Asia, such as during the transition between the Moghul Empire and the British East India (EIC) company in the 1700s, as the EIC took advantage of Moghul decline and fragmentation to establish dominance on the subcontinent.[48]

Moreover, all of this underscores a basic theme of this chapter: hegemonic orders take many forms. Specific ones change over time and look different as we travel across them; whatever their shared superficial commonalities, the Roman Empire, British Empire, American System, and Ming China are characterized by vast differences in, on the one hand, their rules and norms and, on the other hand, the political and economic infrastructure that held them together.[49] Accordingly, this brief overview of hegemonic-order theories leaves two crucial questions on the table: what is international order, and how does hegemonic ordering actually work? In the next two sections we address each in turn.

INTERNATIONAL ORDER

At heart, "international order" refers to relatively stable patterns of relations and practices in world politics.[50] These patterns emerge from the behavior of states, international institutions, transnational movements, and other important actors in international politics. They also constrain, enable, and channel how those actors behave. States created the Bretton Woods System and the international political economy that emerged in its wake, but once established, those systems profoundly shaped the states' behavior.[51] Because international orders are both cause and effect of the actions of many individuals and corporate actors, they can shift suddenly; the Persian Empire collapsed when Alexander the Great and his relatively small army conquered its center, and its ruler, Darius III, was killed by his own cousin. But they can also shift gradually through incremental alterations in economic, political, or military relations.[52]

In fact, it would probably be better to put an end to phrases like "the international order" and "international order" altogether. We use them because they serve as convenient shorthand, and because they play a big role in contemporary international affairs debates. But we do not use them without significant caveats.

Such phrases suffers from two major problems. First, they imply that international order is a stable "thing." Because the phrase is more of a shorthand for relative stabilities in relations and practices among international actors, it would probably be better to think in terms of a verb rather than a noun: international *ordering* rather than international *order*.

Second, there is no single international order. International ordering varies across issue areas and specific relationships. Until the nineteenth century, it is difficult to even contemplate a global international order. Regions interacted. Trade often flowed over long distances. But in terms of ordering, the world was polycentric. During the Cold War, parts of the world divided between two great ordering projects, that of the United States and that of the Soviet Union, each composed of different regional orders. At the same time, elements of international order—arms control, nuclear nonproliferation, order associated with the United Nations—crossed Cold War divides. In short, to the extent that there is an overarching international order, it takes the form of an assemblage of many different orders at different scales.[53]

All of this helps explain why not everyone thinks that "international order" matters very much, especially when it comes to power politics—and why some don't consider it a useful concept at all. We have to admit that "international order" does seem rather vague, and discussions often boil down to "I know it when I see it."[54] But at the very least, international orders shape how political communities pursue power and influence. The ideological content found within international orders also matters for challengers—whether great powers or political movements—because they tend to organize around alternative beliefs and values.[55]

A few examples, focused mostly on features associated with liberal order, illustrate how changes in international ordering materially affect world politics. We now take for granted the existence of large numbers of intergovernmental organizations—complete with their own bureaucracies—that provide focal points for diplomacy, provide goods and services to member states, and play a key role in international legal regimes. But they did not really exist as part of international order until the later nineteenth century.[56] The current international system includes over 200 of them, including the UN, the IMF, the EU, the African Union (AU), the Association of Southeast Asian Nations (ASEAN), and the International Atomic Energy Agency (IAEA). International organizations increasingly set the agenda for international politics, and they form policy networks with one another and with international nongovernmental organizations and other non-state actors.[57]

Similarly, we do not find much in the way of major multilateral diplomacy in Europe before the negotiations at Münster and Osnabrük that created the 1648 Peace of Westphalia. But in the current international order, multilateralism provides a fundamental tool for cooperation and a key site of contention. Still, the form and settings of multilateral diplomacy have shifted along with the international orders that it helps constitute. Calling a great-power "congress to address territorial conflict" was "a routine tool of statecraft in nineteenth-century politics." There have been no such meetings, with the possible exception of allied conferences during World War II, in over a century.[58]

Even in the domains of international security and how states project power, the texture of international order can change significantly. Until the end of World War II, it was pretty unusual for militaries to maintain a peacetime presence on foreign territory.[59] After World War II the pillars of the American security order involved highly institutionalized arrangements, such as NATO or the bilateral alliances and basing treaties with Japan and South Korea. These days, American power projection capability depends on a network of basing and access agreements that span the globe.[60]

In addition to new types of actors and practices, consequential changes in international order extend to the density of interactions among international actors. An important aspect of "globalization" involves extensive growth in economic and political interdependence across the globe. These interdependences almost certainly alter the calculations of governments as they consider, for example, whether to go to war or to borrow money. Significant economic activity in the industrialized world now depends on globally distributed supply chains, such that multiple countries contribute to any particular finished product. This makes major wars even more disruptive to economies than under conditions of simple trade interdependence in goods produced entirely, or largely, within one country.[61]

The Components of International Order

Because "international order" covers so much ground (both literally and metaphorically), many scholars break it down into more manageable components. We find it useful to divide it into two different dimensions, which we call "architecture" and "infrastructure," and to conceptualize international orders overall as ecosystems or in terms of ecologies (see Figure 2.1). We briefly discussed these at the start of the chapter, but here we develop them further. In particular, we identify two important sources of variation in the ecology of international orders: the *density of their infrastructures* and

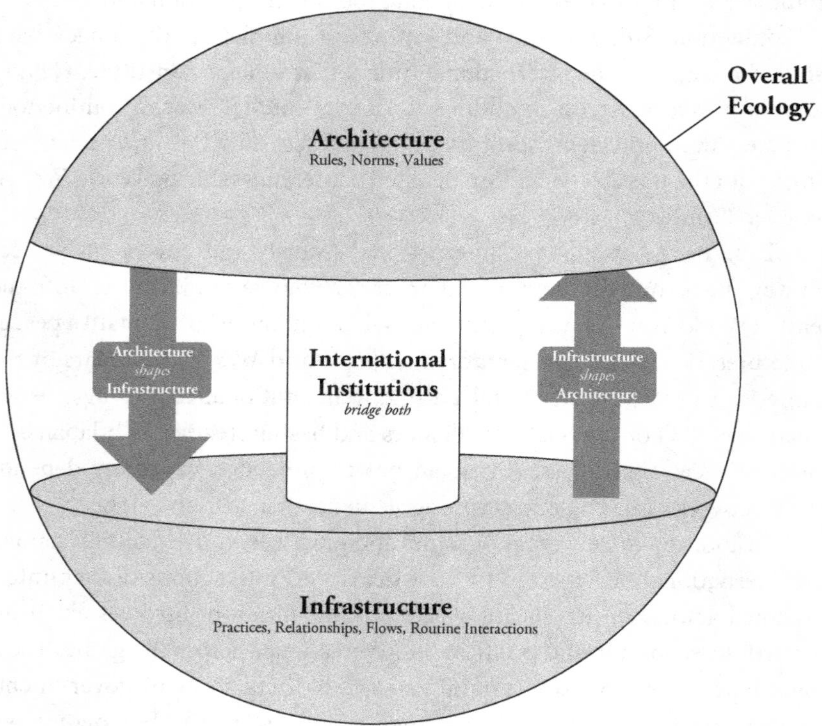

FIGURE 2.1 International Order: Architectures, Infrastructure, and Ecology

the degree to which their *architectures are harmonized or conflictual.* As we show in subsequent chapters, this variation matters for understanding how hegemonic orders unravel.

Architecture

Most discussions of international orders center on their architectures: their guiding principles, norms, rules, and values.[62] G. John Ikenberry, one of the preeminent theorists of liberal order, notes that "international order is manifest in the settled rules and arrangements between states that define and guide their interaction."[63] Such rules and arrangements include basic procedures for resolving disputes—such as those found in the long-standing system of arbitration found among the ancient Greek city-states or in the multilateral, rule of law–oriented institutions that proliferated after the Second World War.[64] They also include specific norms and rules concerning, for example, the legitimate use of force,[65] the conduct of trade and finance, and how governments should treat their citizens.[66]

Even in hegemonic orders, these rules, norms, and procedures are never entirely the result of a single architect, nor do they necessarily wind up precisely as anyone envisioned. Adding a norm here or a principle there can produce a composite order whose architecture, in practice, looks different from what its designers intended or expected. In this respect, international orders are a kind of bricolage, constructed over time through the addition of layers and pieces.[67]

As this suggests, the architecture of international orders is often more bumpy than smooth, patchwork rather than uniform.[68] This creates room for states to violate some norms and rules while claiming to uphold others. For example, even though the United Nations Security Council (UNSC) refused to authorize the 2003 American-led invasion of Iraq, officials in the Bush administration maintained that existing UN resolutions provided sufficient legality for the operation. Administration officials also argued that the Iraqi regime's systematic abuses of its citizens justified overriding norms of state sovereignty; that they made a war of American aggression, in effect, legitimate on humanitarian grounds.[69] But such ambiguities and tensions in prevailing rules, norms, and principles do not render the architecture of international orders irrelevant—merely the ongoing product of many designers, builders, and suppliers.

Infrastructure

International organizations, such as the UN and the IMF, embody rules and norms concerning diplomacy, the resolution of disputes, and the conduct of states. But they are also sites of contestation and negotiation over those rules. And they serve as providers of goods and services—such as peacekeeping operations and development assistance—that undergird international order. In other words, they are simultaneously part of the architecture of international order and its *infrastructure*: the ongoing, often everyday relations, flows, arrangements, and practices that serve as the sinews of international orders. Critically, they might even be arenas of competition among great powers about which rules and norms should prevail or orient the body. Hence, in Figure 2.1, we illustrate how they bridge the different dimensions.

The broader relationship between the architecture and infrastructure of international orders also runs in both directions. For example, the architecture of contemporary order, in effect, transfers some of the functions once carried out by coercive empires—such as the suppression of piracy and the containment of conflict—to alternative infrastructures, namely, multilateral and cooperative institutions. Those infrastructures reflect the illegitimacy of the formal empires of the past. They also shape the rules and norms that, in turn, make up the architecture of contemporary international order.

Of course, the infrastructures of imperial systems are also not terribly uniform. They vary a great deal, even within specific empires. The Spanish monarchy, for instance, was a hodgepodge of governance mechanisms, practices, and security arrangements spread across different kingdoms, counties, duchies, allies, followers, and subordinates.[70] As we noted earlier, there was no such thing as "the British Empire." There was a British system, constituted by a wide variety of different movements of people, trade flows, and military forces. Over time and in different places, governance practices and relationships within the British system might more resemble those of a colonial empire, a protectorate, a patron-client relationship, or a federation.[71]

The infrastructure of contemporary world politics is also composed of complex networks. These include, to list only a few elements, military alliances, partnerships, and basing and access agreements; embassies and consulates; trade and financial flows; and patterns of economic and development assistance. If we take a more granular look at the security infrastructure of the American hegemonic system, we will find recurring joint exercises among militaries, long-standing officer exchange programs, routine bilateral meetings among defense officials, and everyday interactions at standing multilateral security institutions, such as NATO.[72]

In crucial ways, this security infrastructure is likewise an adaptation to liberal aspects of international architecture. As we alluded to earlier, states interested in projecting power well beyond their borders must now generally rely on military basing and access agreements, which imply consent by a host or transit country, rather than simply seizing territory and establishing an imperial garrison.[73] Instead of mobilizing colonial armies,[74] great powers acquire "auxiliaries" by forming close defense partnerships (based on different combinations of carrots and sticks) with other states.

The Ecologies of International Orders

The architecture and infrastructure combine to constitute an ecology of international order. Overall, international order resembles an ecosystem.[75] Like ecosystems, international orders involve the distribution of resources—including not just security and economic goods but also, for example, cultural and environmental ones. Instead of different species, they include various kinds of actors, such as states, international organizations, transnational activist networks, and multinational corporations. Such actors, including different states, occupy various niches related to the tasks they perform. As we noted above, one interesting difference between contemporary and older international orders is that intergovernmental organizations and multilateral groupings of states have taken over some of the tasks once performed by empires.[76]

The ecology metaphor also calls attention to how the uneven character of international orders affects behavior. States and other actors are positioned in the ecosystem by geography, by the arrangement of international infrastructures,[77] and by their compliance or rejection of prevailing aspects of international architecture.[78] For example, international orders often entail standards of civilization, usually initially set by the powerful, that arrange political communities as more civilized or more barbaric. Political communities that can meet those standards often enjoy specific benefits, which can include better treatment in treaties or being spared from imperial conquest.[79]

Similarly, variation in the contemporary infrastructure of telecommunications and finance empowers some while disempowering others. As Henry Farrell and Abraham Newman argue, "New flows of money, information and manufacturing components required the construction of a correspondingly vast infrastructure. Global finance relied on a complex system of institutions to clear transactions and facilitate messaging and communications between different financial institutions." The "Internet was built on routing systems, physical 'pipelines' and redundant information storage facilities to move and house data. Complex supply chains needed equally complex networks that drew together a myriad of assemblers, suppliers and sub-suppliers."

In practice, these developments "tended to channel global flows through a small number of central data cables and switch points." This "did not just transform economies; it transformed international security. A global economy meant that states' economies were interdependent with each other." The ability of the United States to use the Swift (Society for Worldwide Interbank Financial Telecommunication) system—designed to facilitate international financial flows—to target terrorist financing and also to enforce sanctions on countries like Iran and Russia stemmed from its central position in global financial networks.[80]

Thus, the ecology of international orders can vary by issue area or region. The overall global international order is an ecosystem of ecosystems.[81] East Asia during the Cold War had a significantly different ecology from what it had during the American unipolar moment in the 1990s. Then again, in the mid-2000s, when China's rise added new infrastructure to the international ecology, the US-Japan relationship took on different ordering effects. For example, when in 2015 China led the establishment of the Asian Infrastructure Investment Bank (AIIB), the United States and Japan remain the only two major states that refused to join. During the 1990s this solidarity might have constituted an exercise of hegemonic maintenance, but in the year 2015 it actually underscored not just American and Japanese miscalculation but also their relative decline as exclusive providers of development assistance, including in the form of physical infrastructure such as roads, ports, and mass transit.

Regardless of the level of analysis or the issue area, we can conceptualize variation across international orders along at least two dimensions: the relative density of ordering infrastructure and the degree that related architecture is conflictual or congruent (see Figure 2.2). Note that even though we describe the extremes for illustrative purposes, real ecologies will always occupy more complex, intermediate points in the conceptual space.[82]

- *Conflictual–Congruent*. At one extreme, existing ordering infrastructure may be highly integrated and harmonized. At the other extreme, we find rival infrastructures that directly clash over rules and norms. In between, we find *coordinated* infrastructures, which lack integration but generally work toward the same ordering ends, and *uncoordinated* ones, which can work at cross-purposes but in the absence of zero-sum conflict.[83]
- *Dense–Sparse*. We can think of density in terms of the ratio of existing to potential infrastructure.[84]

In highly dense international ecologies, there are very few empty "niches" for new international infrastructure to fill, and we may find redundant or overlapping infrastructures—international organizations, bilateral treaties and partnerships, diplomatic flows, and the like—engaging in the same tasks.[85] In highly sparse ecologies, we find lots of open space for new ordering infrastructure. In Chapters 4 and 5, we will see how Russia and China find their own order-building activities channeled toward states

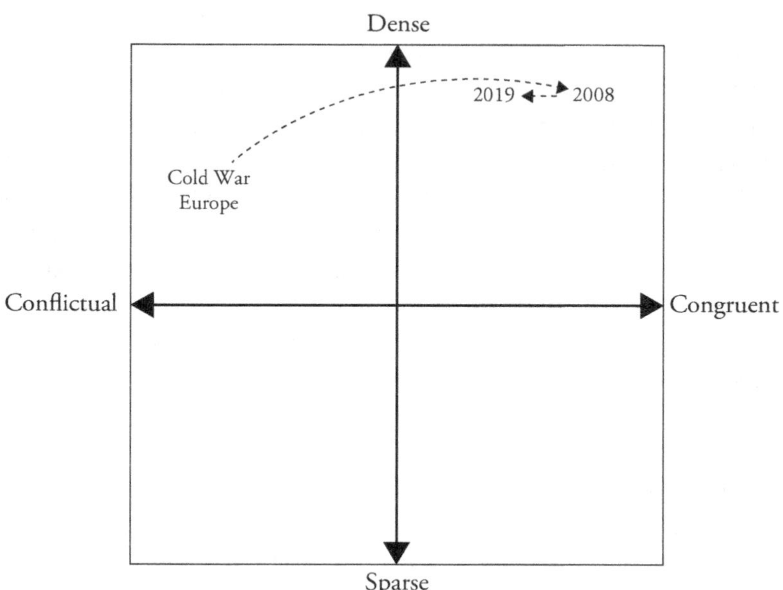

FIGURE 2.2 Variation in International Ecosystems

and regions, such as Central Asia, Africa, and Southeast Asia, characterized by sparser American hegemonic infrastructure. This provides more open niches for Beijing and Moscow to fill when it comes to extending their influence.

Sparse ecologies where the ordering architectures are more conflictual (work at cross-purposes) may be ripe for geopolitical competition; such geopolitical competition may, in turn, drive the emergence of denser ecologies. At the extreme, it can bifurcate a region into two distinct, but dense and complementary, ecologies. In the 1970s and 1980s, during the era of Soviet domination and the Warsaw Pact and COMECON, the ecology of the Eastern European order was relatively homogenous and dense. But Europe *overall* was heterogeneous, with NATO and the European Economic Community forming part of a rival order that interacted with, but only barely overlapped with, its Eastern counterpart.

After the Communist collapse, which took its infrastructure with it, the American system—along with broader agents and infrastructure of liberal international order, including the EU—expanded across Eastern Europe. This process remained incomplete in most of the former Soviet Union, giving rise to a sparser and less complementary regional ecology, complete with both legacy infrastructure, and new Russia- and China-centric infrastructure. It is from this "periphery" that counter-order contention pushed back toward the European core in the 2010s.[86]

Ecologies with dense and complementary infrastructures, on the other hand, can be tough nuts to crack for rising powers positioned on the outside. This is the case for much of Europe, where NATO, the EU, and other arrangements saturate much of the security and economic ecology. Actors that want to directly contest such an order generally need to adopt "wedge" or "divide-and-conquer" strategies to break apart the cohesiveness of ordering infrastructure. We explore in Chapter 6 how Moscow has been trying to do just that by cultivating, and supporting, political movements on the basis of shared dislike for prevailing international rules and norms. It hopes that introducing such conflict will undermine major aspects of European ordering infrastructure.[87]

This provides just one way to analyze features of the ecologies of international orders. For example, international-relations scholar Stacie Goddard focuses solely on how rising powers are positioned within institutional ordering infrastructure. She argues that states that are embedded in core great-power institutional arrangements but lack outside options—potential partners not closely tied to other great powers—are least likely to try to significantly alter the existing order. These states gain from their access to its infrastructure but they cannot leverage external partners and institutions against it. Great-power challengers that enjoy high "access" but also have outside options that they can leverage for influence behave differently. They engage in "rule-based revolution." Thus, in the 1860s and early 1870s, Prussia seized territory from Austria-Hungary, Denmark, and France on its way to forming a united Germany. In doing so, it significantly shifted the existing balance of power in Europe. Yet it did not fundamentally challenge the architecture of the system.[88]

Regardless of how we parse it, variation in the ecology of international orders shapes power politics in profound ways. As we argue in the next section, this is as true for hegemons as it is for rising powers and weaker states.

HEGEMONIC ORDERING AND AMERICAN HEGEMONY

Some influential theories see the existence of a hegemon as a necessary condition for stable international ordering. They contend that only a state or empire with overwhelming military and economic power can make and enforce rules in international politics, let alone provide public goods, such as open trade and a relatively peaceful system. It should be clear by now that we disagree. Great-power cartels can, and have, created and upheld international orders. The most famous example comes from after the Napoleonic Wars, when a combination of great power congresses and multilateral alliances helped manage the European order between 1815 and 1854.[89] International orders may also emerge from processes independent of great-power orchestration: through the convergence of a broad group of states on general practices, norms, and rules. In other words, international orders develop and evolve through a variety of different pathways, and often many different processes contribute to their architecture and infrastructure.

We should therefore view hegemonic orders as a subcategory of international orders—ones profoundly shaped by the presence of a hegemonic power. Hegemonic ordering typically works through the use of carrots and sticks. The possession of preponderant wealth and military capabilities gives a hegemonic power outsized "market share" when it comes to offering security guarantees, economic assistance, status and prestige, market access, and the like. Hegemons can also issue potent threats when it comes to the use of force, withdrawing of existing benefits, or excluding a state from those benefits in the first place. Leading powers deploy these tools to persuade and coerce others to support their preferred international architectures—whether in the context of specific hegemonic ordering projects or simply as they advance more pedestrian policy goals.

For example, British efforts to suppress the slave trade in the nineteenth century centered around signing treaties with a diverse group of actors, including sovereign states in Europe and Latin America, Hanseatic towns, African chiefs, and Muslim sultans. While some willingly signed the treaties, many had to be cajoled through threats and bribes.[90] The United States, in effect, provided Japanese companies access to its markets in exchange for Tokyo to subordinate its security decision making to Washington.[91] Washington has long used carrots and sticks to uphold the nonproliferation regime, such as when it compelled South Korea (in the 1970s) and Taiwan (in the 1980s) to abandon their nuclear programs.[92]

The Importance of Goods Provision to Hegemonic Ordering

As all of this suggests, one of the most important ways that hegemons order international politics is through the provision of some combination of economic, security, and cultural goods. These might include public goods, such as combating piracy or, in the classic formulation of Charles Kindleberger, maintaining an open market that can absorb the exports of countries experiencing crises.[93] But hegemons much more frequently provide club goods, such as the collective security provided by NATO, to its member-states, and private goods, such as aid and trade arrangements specific to individual countries or bilateral alliances like the US-Japan defense agreement.[94]

But the provision of goods is more than a mechanism for making and enforcing order. The forms through which such goods are channeled could be strictly bilateral in character, but they might also involve broader international agreements, international organizations, and even designated or contracted third parties. Much of the infrastructure of international orders is formed via goods provision, and the manner and substance of those goods themselves shape and are shaped by international architecture. The mix of public-like, club, and private goods shapes the ecology of international order.[95] Much of the infrastructure of contemporary international order consists of institutions and practices associated with goods provision. For example, the infrastructure of the nonproliferation regime includes institutions such as the IAEA and the Comprehensive Test Ban Treaty Organization (CTBTO), and a host of relationships and practices involving bilateral and multilateral assistance for nuclear safeguards and nuclear security, as well as technical assistance for peaceful uses of nuclear energy and nuclear technology,

Hegemonic ordering also influences what particular goods matter for international status and prestige, from membership in international organizations, such as the Group of Seven (G7); to the performance of specific norms and values, such as having democratic institutions; to the possession of specific weapons systems, such as aircraft carriers. Not all of these are the result of deliberate policy. No one in the United States held "a meeting" and decided that possession of an aircraft carrier is a sign of great-power status. Rather, what mattered was "the long-standing role of aircraft carriers in" America's "practices of power projection and its global presence."[96]

Hegemons can also shape international order through persuasion and socialization, the halo effect created by their superior capabilities, and other mechanisms sometimes associated with "soft power."[97] We discuss the significance of these processes in greater detail in subsequent chapters, but here we stress two things. First, a good deal of what makes dominant powers attractive is their success—the fact that they are wealthy and powerful. Rome impressed outsiders in no small part because of its material prowess, and other hegemons are no different.[98] Second, soft power is not something that descended from the sky upon the United States or is coded into its DNA. It took significant investments to build American soft power. Much of American hegemonic "socialization" occurs via its diplomatic, security, and economic infrastructure.

Hegemons Shape Order, but Order also Shapes Hegemons

Traditional hegemonic-order approaches tend to treat the great-power wars that give birth to new leading states as a kind of "big bang" that creates a "blank slate" on which hegemons write a new order. But slates in international politics are never truly blank, even after major wars; "hegemons emerge in preexisting" international orders; "they rarely, if ever, enjoy" enough military and economic might to entirely overwrite existing aspects of international order. We lose important perspective on challenges to contemporary order and understanding how order might evolve if we neglect the effects of preexisting architecture and infrastructure shape.

For example, recall that the United States drew upon interwar rules and norms—concerning international law, multilateralism, and the use of force—as well as infrastructure (such as the League of Nations and the Permanent Court of International Justice) in constructing the post-war order. Spain and France both bid for hegemony in a Europe where most states were ruled by dynastic lines and where patterns of marriage and inheritance shaped territorial claims and thus avenues for expansion within Europe. The War of Spanish Succession (1701–1714) centered on Louis XIV's efforts to secure his grandson's rule over Spain, to which the Austrian branch of the Habsburg dynasty also had a plausible claim.[99] Neither Spain nor France at the peak of their power could alter the architecture of the international order to dispense with dynastic norms and rules—in no small measure because the legitimacy of their own rulers depended upon them.[100]

The combined effects of existing international order with interstate contestation over the nature and terms of international order can profoundly affect the trajectory of hegemonic ordering. As we have noted before, when the United States emerged from World War II in a position of hegemony it confronted a world structured not only by that war but also by rising anti-colonial sentiment. It is possible that the United States could have—in collaboration with France and the United Kingdom—sunk significant military and economic resources into resisting the demands of imperial subjects for independence and national self-determination. But Washington feared the consequences of Moscow becoming the sole champion of national liberation. It saw its bid for global leadership as best served by playing up America's history as the product of a successful rebellion against a colonial empire. Thus, the United States generally supported decolonization and helped, both passively and actively, to dismember the empires of its own military allies.[101]

These developments also meant that neither the United States nor the Soviet Union would seek to control its allies and clients as formal imperial provinces.[102] Of course, Washington clearly set the parameters of security policy for countries like Italy, the Netherlands, Norway, and West Germany.[103] In Latin America, Washington often exercised stronger influence, including dictating aspects of domestic policy to local officials. Most scholars accurately characterize the Warsaw Pact as an unofficial Soviet imperial system. The Soviet Union led invasions of two of the pact's member-states, Hungary (1956) and Czechoslovakia (1968), in order to enforce Communist rule and prevent exit from the alliance system.[104]

But in all of these cases, subordinates remained—in legal terms, sovereign states with their own independent governments and presence in international organizations.[105] In general, even when the relationship was one of informal empire, client states enjoyed greater autonomy than, say, Gaul in the Roman Empire, India in the British Empire, or, for that matter, New York and Texas in the federal republic that is the United States.[106]

Thus, critically, hegemons don't just "make" international orders. They must also "take" international order. Leading powers are affected by both the international orders that they inherit and those that they help create.[107] Their alliances structure future commitments, interests, and even how they conceptualize their own identities—such as how NATO has reinforced the notion of the West as a broader political community that includes the United States.[108] Over time, their clients and partners learn how to manipulate and influence them.[109] Moreover, this interactive relationship between international order and hegemony extends into domestic politics. For instance, the United States promoted successive waves of globalization, but, in turn, unleashed economic forces that also reshaped the American political economy, shrinking and weakening trade unions and manufacturing sectors while empowering industries and businesses that benefited from cheap imports, globalized supply chains, and capital mobility.[110]

The United States, like other hegemonic powers, is part of the ecology of international order and does not stand outside of it. We see it in the opportunities and constraints faced by the United States as a rising power. We see it in the ways in which its international ordering has reshaped its domestic economy and politics. And we also see it in terms of how much its position in the international hierarchy of power has come to depend on its relationships with a broad range of powers and allies.

The American Hegemonic System in Practice

The United States has been engaged in international ordering pretty much since its beginnings. The example set by the American Revolution encouraged others; Americans spent much of the nineteenth century engaged in hegemonic projects in the Western Hemisphere, chiefly through imperial expansion westward and warfare, most of which took place against Native American political communities. In the latter part of the nineteenth century the United States turned to overseas imperial expansion. It acquired a number of colonies from the Spanish after the Spanish-American War (1898), including the Philippines and Puerto Rico. It was also on its way to establishing hegemony over the Americas, a process helped along by London's decision not to contest rising American power in the region.[111]

Many associate the period between World War I and World War II with the American rejection of Woodrow Wilson's international ordering project. Some refer to the 1920s and 1930s as a period of isolationism, but what that really meant was absence from the League of Nations and the lack of military commitments to Europe.[112] Still, after 1945 the United States has clearly, often with assistance from other countries, engaged in broader hegemonic projects—and either directly or indirectly helped played a key role in ordering world politics writ large. But global international order is not synonymous with American hegemony. This was true during the supposed peaks of American relative power: immediately after World War II and in the wake of the Cold War. It is certainly true today.

Instead, within broader international order we find an *American hegemonic system* (or simply *American system*), within which the United States most directly orders and takes leadership of economic, security, and political relations. Of course, like the British system before it, the American system is really a number of overlapping orders. It contains a variety of different bilateral and multilateral arrangements, formal alliances and informal partnerships, and a host of different trade and economic relationships.

The core of the American system is the United States itself—which international-relations scholars sometimes forget is not a standard nation-state but a federal republic complete with a number of remnant imperial territories, such as Guam and Puerto Rico. In terms of security, the greater core extends to its immediate neighbors, especially Mexico and Canada. Some overseas countries, such as Japan and most NATO member states, form semi-cores—not quite peripheries but not really part of the core either. The exact forms of this infrastructure, as we have seen, vary across regions and issue areas. But in nearly every region of the world the United States maintains a handful of close security relationships that serve as local hubs or anchors for the American security system.[113]

This ordering infrastructure is absolutely crucial to American global influence. As we have already noted, it plays a key role in the ability of the United States to project military power abroad. The existence of a wide number of security partners magnifies American relative military capabilities, as well as providing the everyday basis "for negotiation and coordination of security affairs" while creating settings for "socialization and influence among militaries and military personnel."[114] Beyond the sheer breadth and depth of this network, it includes a number of the wealthiest, most technological advanced countries in the world—including Japan, South Korea, Germany, and Italy.

As long as the infrastructure remains intact, the United States retains a significant geopolitical advantage. Great-power challengers, such as Russia and China, face an ecosystem already dense with American-centered alliance networks and political associations. It makes sense, then, that Russia doubled down on keeping its allies in power during the Syrian civil war—Syria is home to the only overseas Russian military base not on former Soviet territory, and Moscow is now constructing additional facilities there. But to truly compete, Russia will need to break down or fragment existing American security relationships. As discussed earlier, this should be easier in the context of states and regions with more conflictual architectures. China also faces limits on where it can secure client states or pursue basing agreements—although its wealth gives it far more options than Russia—and these limits create constraints, but also opportunities, for China's growing efforts to build power-projection capability.

American security commitments almost certainly depress military spending by its major allies.[115] This is a perennial source of friction—one that Trump routinely complains about, for example. But it also means most of the major players in the First and Second World Wars, including Germany, France, the United Kingdom, and Japan, are not engaged in great-power rivalries with one another, or with the United States. Instead, they are all part of an American-centric security system that has removed many of their incentives, as well as their ability, to become military challengers to the United States.[116]

Historian Hal Brands nicely summarizes the advantages that derive from American security infrastructure:

> The protection that Washington has afforded its allies has equally afforded the United States great sway over those allies' policies.

> During the Cold War and after, for instance, the United States has used the influence provided by its security posture to veto allies' pursuit of nuclear weapons, to obtain more advantageous terms in financial and trade agreements, and even to affect the composition of allied nations' governments. More broadly, it has used its alliances as vehicles for shaping political, security, and economic agendas in key regions and bilateral relationships, thus giving the United States an outsized voice on a range of important issues. To be clear, this influence has never been as pervasive as U.S. officials might like, or as some observers might imagine. But by any reasonable standard of comparison, it has nonetheless been remarkable.[117]

Moreover, even hegemonic ordering *within* the American system creates spillover effects—that is, shapes broader international order. NATO's existence shapes the global security ecology in general, and that of its neighbors, such as Russia, in particular. States and non-state actors, whether they like it or not, adjust their own security policies in light of American alliance commitments, counterterrorism and counter-proliferation efforts, direct military training and aid, and overseas basing agreements.[118] Nonetheless, this system does not exhaust the overall security ecosystem: many states stand more or less outside of direct American security governance, and there are security orders where the United States is a peripheral or external player.[119]

Despite the gravitational pull it exercises on the policies of other states, the American security system is easier to isolate from broader international order than the economic dimensions of American hegemonic ordering. This is, in no small measure, because the United States pushed along economic globalization. But it is also because some of the major institutions of the international economy, such as the IMF and the WTO, are broadly inclusive of other states. Still, as we revisit in Chapter 7, this could change if regional trading blocs, such as the Trans-Pacific Partnership (TPP), continue to proceed without US involvement, or if other markets "route around" the United States, as in the case of the free-trade agreement between the EU and Japan.

A number of scholars have chronicled the infrastructural advantages that the United States, both deliberately and inadvertently, engineered over the last eight decades in the international economy. We emphasized some of those in the stylized history presented earlier: embedding the dollar as the unit of exchange in global trading regimes, such as the oil market, to ensure its status as a reserve currency; weighting the system of decision making in major international financial institutions to represent US interests; protecting US intellectual property within the pillars of the global trading regimes; and so on.[120] In fact, between 2000 and 2010, the network structure of the global banking system became significantly more interdependent; "the increase in cross-national bank holdings has been highly skewed towards the US and the UK," making both, but particularly the US, "more central to the system."[121] This augmented Washington's ability to leverage financial instruments—often in the form of sanctions—as tools of statecraft.

Underlying American domestic wealth and national military power is necessary, but not sufficient, for maintaining this hegemonic infrastructure. It depends on ongoing interactions, often boring diplomatic activities, and the management of a large number of very different relationships with states, international organizations, and other international actors. We have stressed how it does crucial work in underpinning American hegemony and leadership. Indeed, the American "unipolar moment" was only possible because second-tier powers such as Germany, France, and Japan did not behave like traditional great powers and build militaries geared for competition with one another and the United States. In this sense, military unipolarity does not explain hegemony; hegemony explains military unipolarity.[122]

REVISITING THE CONVERGENCE WAGER AND THE TRANSFORMATION OF THE POST–COLD WAR ECOLOGY OF INTERNATIONAL ORDER

This American international leadership, understood as the degree of overlap between the American hegemonic system and international order writ large, and broader liberal international ordering, appears to have reached its zenith around 2004. In that year, NATO and the EU both admitted ten new members each, mostly post-Communist states. It was also the year in which the US military was conducting two major overseas military campaigns in Iraq and Afghanistan that required extensive cooperation from allies and security partners, including NATO member states. And the year 2005 was also the last year before the world began backsliding into authoritarianism. According to the democracy watchdog Freedom House, 2006 marked the first time during the post–Cold War era that the number of states with declining democracy scores outnumbered the number of improved country scores by 33 to 18.[123]

If we look solely at American military capabilities, wealth cannot account for 2004 as an inflection point. Between 2001 and 2010, for example, US military spending continued to steadily increase (as a result of the Afghanistan and Iraq campaigns), and from 2005 to 2010 so did US military spending as a percentage of the world total. Moreover, even the decline in military spending after 2010 was actually reversed in the 2018 and 2019 budgets of the Trump administration.

The Great Recession of 2008 certainly has contributed to current contention within the advanced industrialized democracies. It eroded American financial power and shifted geo-economic power toward China and emerging countries. But although it triggered a debt crisis in the Eurozone—and the real possibility of Greece's exit from the single European currency—the United States had recovered by June 2009. It has to date enjoyed 10 years of uninterrupted growth. Indeed, the United States held all the advantages of a hegemon using a monetary and fiscal toolkit to weather the shock; as Dan Drezner shows, the American-led economic "system worked" by facilitating the necessary international cooperation and coordination to prevent the financial crisis from producing a worldwide depression comparable to the one before World War II.[124]

As we discuss more in Chapter 7, the combination of the debacle of the Iraq War and the effects of the 2008 Great Recession have clearly undermined support for liberal international architecture and eroded some of the infrastructure of the American system. But what's remarkable, in retrospect, is confidence in the convergence wager both *before* and *after* these challenges—whether in Washington or in allied capitals. After 2004, Washington continued to push for the expansion of its hegemonic infrastructure and to support the growth of broader liberal infrastructure, including NATO and the EU expanding into Eastern European and the Balkans, increasing WTO membership, greater IMF and World Bank jurisdiction, and supporting US-based democracy monitors and human rights watchdogs. Even the George W. Bush administration, much derided for its unilateralism and antipathy toward international institutions, worked through international organizations in a variety of different policy arenas. It staunchly supported NATO expansion into new countries bordering Russia, including Georgia and Ukraine. Agreements such as the Obama administration's proposed Trans-Pacific Partnership and "pivot to Asia" sought to lock in even greater levels of economic and security cooperation across Asia and the Pacific.

So What's the Problem?

First, there are deep and real tensions between political, economic, and intergovernmental liberalism. We can see these tensions clearly in terms of liberal intergovernmentalism. Intergovernmentalism *can* promote liberal domestic governance under some conditions, but it also often creates barriers to the spread of political and economic liberalism. To the extent that it privileges sovereign equality, it makes it difficult to pressure illiberal states to reform. Moreover, it restricts the ability of states to impose liberal governance unilaterally, including through force.

These tensions have long been the subject of debate in American foreign policy circles. During the 2000s, neoconservatives routinely expressed frustration with the ways in which the UN and other international institutions can empower autocratic states and provide them with a mechanism to constrain Washington's ability to promote liberal democratic principles.[125] As we see in Chapter 7, some liberal and most progressive internationalists see this as a virtue. They consider aggressive democracy promotion, whether militarized or not, as dangerous and self-defeating. More hawkish liberal internationalists split the difference, generally affirming the intrinsic importance of liberal intergovernmentalism but also—like the neoconservatives—being more willing to bypass it, or attempt to harness it for aggressive liberal enlargement.[126]

Moreover, liberalism is also compatible with different positions on political identity. Some associate the architecture of contemporary international order with transnational dimensions of identity, which a number of people on the right derisively label "globalism."[127] But national self-determination—the claim that every nation deserves a state and every state should be a nation—was a major liberal principle of the nineteenth and twentieth centuries. Many liberals in that period were nationalists. They supported movements for national self-determination of various kinds. The architecture of contemporary liberal order includes both nationalist and transnationalist principles.[128] This tension *within* liberalism has also emerged as sites of contestation in the current moment.

Second, convergence presented a threat to a number of illiberal regimes. For them, pressure to respect political and civil rights opens them to domestic political challenges. Leaders in countries like Russia and China noted American and European material and symbolic support for "Color Revolutions" and other mobilizations of civil society against illiberal regimes in Ukraine, Georgia, and Kyrgyzstan. Moscow increasingly viewed the EU as a threat to its sphere of influence and, to the extent that it succeeded in post-Communist states, the legitimacy of its regime. The 2010 Arab Spring—which saw American and European support for some uprisings—and the 2014 collapse of the Yanukovych regime in Ukraine—during which the United States and the European Union strongly backed anti-regime forces—further exacerbated such fears.[129]

The combination of these two problems matters a great deal. Convergence meant that the United States, as well as the EU, expanded liberal ordering infrastructure with the assumption that congruence around liberal norms, values, and principles would follow. In some cases, policymakers believed that newly incorporated states and regions would be "locked into" liberal architecture by acceding to the requirements of joining international institutions or through subsequent socialization pressures. But this hasn't always turned out to be the case. Backsliding within the European Union by countries like Hungary and Poland has allowed increasingly illiberal governments to coopt EU funds to entrench their regimes and to form blocks to insulate themselves from EU pressure.

The uneven expansion of both infrastructure and architecture shaped international ecology in other ways. It generated a series of reactions, countervailing strategies, and, eventually alternative-order building efforts using liberal intergovernmental modes of cooperation but without commitments to political liberalism. In organizations such as the Chinese-led Shanghai Cooperation Organization (SCO) or the Russian-led Collective Security Treaty Organization (CSTO), intergovernmentalism is used explicitly to support norms deemed in opposition or at least in tension with liberalism, including sovereignty and non-interference, regime security, civilizational diversity, and "traditional values." Moreover, regimes such as Moscow and Beijing figured out ways to target weak spots and challenge the ecology of the order in regions like Africa, the Middle East, the post-Communist space, Southeast Asia, and even within the West itself.

* * *

At the risk of repetition, the convergence wager produced practices of liberal ordering. These practices, in turn, have structured contemporary international ecology in ways that empowered its very antagonists, including illiberal states and political movements. It did so while also providing them with reasons to oppose various aspects of liberal ordering. It turns out that some of the liberal aspects of international economic ordering can also be "weaponized" against American leadership or turned against other aspects of liberalism, such as when states use intergovernmentalist principles to strip mechanisms supporting political liberalism from international institutions.

Our conclusion—that a good deal of contemporary international architecture and infrastructure reflects liberal beliefs—does not necessarily imply that, for example, the American system and broader international order are either good or benign. Liberal ideology has played a role in many American interventions—whether in terms of protecting the putative property rights of American multinationals, combating communism, or notionally spreading democracy.[130] What it does mean is that we cannot ignore that liberalism if we want to understand the subject of the next chapter: the unraveling of hegemonic orders in general, and American hegemony in particular.

3

How Hegemonic Orders Unravel

In his classic articulation of the theory of hegemonic war, Robert Gilpin writes that "the dynamic of international relations is provided by the differential growth of power among states." He credits the famous Greek historian Thucydides for the "essential idea" that "a stable system is one in which changes can take place if they do not threaten the vital interests of the dominant states and thereby cause a war among them." In contrast, "an unstable system is one in which the economic, technological, and other changes are eroding the international hierarchy" and thus "the position of the hegemonic state."[1]

For scholars of hegemony, the inevitability of uneven economic growth matters, in no small measure, because wealth and industry undergird military capabilities. So as economic vitality shifts, so too does the international balance of military power. However, as Gilpin notes, it is also possible for new military technologies—such as aircraft carriers or nuclear weapons—to suddenly alter the balance of capabilities in world politics.[2] Strategic overextension provides another potential source of hegemonic decline. Leading powers, the argument goes, often overinvest in protecting or expanding their orders. They do so at the expense of their underlying economic vitality, thus undermining their long-term international position.[3]

Once the hegemon enters relative decline, its fate—and that of its order—depends on the attitudes of other powers, especially rising ones. Those that are satisfied with the general parameters of the order adopt, in the language of international-relations scholars, *status quo* orientations. They uphold important aspects of international order either through passive acquiescence or active support. Their efforts might entail adopting policies, such as shouldering some of the hegemon's economic and military burden, that bolster the hegemonic power. They might even become part of a great-power cartel in which they join the declining hegemon as roughly equal partners in upholding order. Those that are dissatisfied—that want more territory, greater status, or different rules of the game—push *revisionist* agendas. If the hegemon fails to accommodate them, they will increasingly mount challenges against the hegemon and its order.[4]

System-wide conflicts, in turn, result from power transitions involving revisionist challengers. The dominant power might launch a preventive war to stop a rising power from overtaking it; the challenger, finally seeing a window of opportunity, might turn toward military aggression; or some local conflict might draw in the declining power and its challenger—and then escalate into a large-scale military confrontation. These power-transition wars often, the argument goes, drive major alterations in international order—especially if a challenger emerges victorious and in a position of system-wide dominance. The stylized narrative we presented in Chapter 2 described European history as a series of hegemonic cycles and conflicts triggered by power transitions, with Spain, France, the United Kingdom, and the United States taking up the role of hegemon or challenger during different periods. As we have noted many times, a great deal of attention is currently focused on whether the United States and China are headed toward a power-transition war.[5]

There are a number of issues with this account. It's not entirely clear that power transitions are closely associated with major-power wars, especially in periods when rulers constantly warred with one another and peace provided no more than a temporary break between conflicts.[6] But more important, for our purposes, is that states, international organizations, and non-state actors challenge hegemonic orders in a variety of ways that do not involve military conflict, let alone warfare among the great powers. These challenges sometimes do culminate in system-wide war. But they can unravel hegemonic orders whether or not they ultimately lead to a clash of great-power militaries. By the time the power-transition war does or does not happen, the old order may already be gone.

Consider the end of the Cold War. Scholars of hegemony, much like many American political commentators, see the United States after the end of the Cold War and the collapse of the Soviet Union as a victorious hegemonic power.[7] The struggle between the United States and the Soviet Union produced significant bloodshed, but these encounters took the form of indirect conflicts. The United States fought Soviet allies in North Korea and Vietnam. Washington supported the Mujahedeen against the Soviets in Afghanistan. More often, the Cold War was marked by civil wars fought by proxies of the two superpowers or by interstate wars fought between their clients.[8] The Cold War ended without a direct great-power war—and with Moscow, not Washington, making significant adjustments and concessions.

In some reckonings, the basic weaknesses of the Soviet command economy forced it to decide between accommodation with the United States or collapse.[9] Soviet Premier Mikhail Gorbachev ultimately chose accommodation—including abandoning the Soviet Union's Eastern European satellites—and saw his country collapse anyway.[10] The order that existed within the Soviet sphere mostly unraveled through revolutions and secessions.[11]

Standard theories of hegemony do not have a lot to say about counter-order mobilization by non-state actors. But as political scientist Mark Beissinger shows: "The tides of nationalism that emerged in the USSR . . . transcended Soviet boundaries, moving into East Central Europe and the Balkans in 1989–90, reflecting back into the USSR, and outward once again in connection with the Soviet break-up."[12] In this chapter, we suggest that the end of the Cold War was less anomalous than it might seem; transnational and subnational movements often play an important part in the fate of international orders in general, and hegemonic orders in particular.

More broadly, the end of the Cold War demonstrates that international orders can undergo major shifts without a cataclysmic war. It also illustrates the interdependent character of great powers and their transnational infrastructure. Moscow's hegemonic infrastructure was a major source of its international power; the loss of that infrastructure not only ended its status as a superpower but also undermined the Soviet Union itself. The significance of these dynamics risks getting lost in the power-transition story and the general narrative of an American "victory" followed by expansion of the American international system. Both of these downplay the fact that the Soviet Union's sphere of hegemonic order unraveled, and unraveled quickly.

THREE PATHWAYS OF CHANGE

In this chapter, we look more closely into three proximate causes of the unraveling of hegemonic and international orders:[13]

- *Great-power challenges* in the form of contesting international orders from within or constructing new, alternative infrastructures. Some of these involve great powers offering to substitute for the economic, military, and cultural goods provided by the hegemon.
- *Challenges from below*, with a focus on how small and weak states shape demand-side pressure for order contestation and alternative order building. Paying attention to smaller powers provides an important corrective to the tendency to focus almost exclusively on the preferences and choices of great powers.[14]
- *Transnational contention*, which we use as a covering term for all non-state counter-order movements. These movements usually object to aspects of international architecture on ideological grounds. Those objections can also lead them to challenge existing infrastructure. Counter-order movements pose the most serious challenge when they coordinate with or otherwise support fellow travelers across borders, and when they can secure state sponsorship.

All three of these pathways revolve around some mix of two broad approaches to challenging international order. Great powers, weaker states, and non-state actors can try to contest aspects of international architecture from within existing infrastructure (*order contestation*) or they can try to construct alternative infrastructures that embed their preferred rules, norms, and values (*alternative-order building*). Not only can challengers engage in mixed strategies, but they can try to combine them by, for example, using the threat of exit via alternative infrastructure to exert leverage in favor of order contestation.[15]

One reason for such contestation is that prevailing rules and norms of international order can threaten some states while empowering others. For example, Russia and China have been reluctant to allow the United National Security Council (UNSC) to authorize uses of force to protect human rights. Given their own human-rights records, it makes sense that they would resist normalizing militarized violations of sovereignty to prevent atrocities. In the one major recent instance where Moscow and Beijing allowed the UNSC to support a militarized responsibility-to-protect norm, Libya in 2012, they quickly came to regret it as the resulting NATO campaign produced regime change.

When these struggles happen within, say, the UNSC or the UN, they reflect order contestation. Indeed, we should expect that, given the stakes, norms concerning military intervention will often prove highly contested.[16] But plenty of other kinds of rules, norms, and values are subjects of conflict, such as those involving human and political rights, trade and markets, and the possession or use of specific military technologies—such as chemical and biological weapons.[17]

Challengers can also contest order by appropriating and deploying norms that they would probably prefer to consign to the dustbin of history. Moscow has used responsibility-to-protect rhetoric to justify its own interventions in its self-styled "Near Abroad," including its 2014 invasion of Ukraine and annexation of Crimea. Moscow's increasing efforts to disrupt liberal ordering principles stems from long-gestating concerns about "perceptions of human rights trumping national sovereignty . . . starting with NATO's intervention in the Balkans to protect Kosovars from Serbs."[18] Only a few states have backed any of these interventions, which gives Moscow's action more the flavor of alternative-order building. But there are plenty of examples of more full-fledged alternative-order building efforts in the current international system, which we examine more closely in Chapters 4 and 5.

Note that academics and American policymakers often associate revisionism toward the architecture of international order with rising challengers. They presume that dominant states always uphold the status quo. The example of responsibility-to-protect doctrine suggests otherwise. It amounted to a *change* in prevailing norms, one backed by the United States and some of its allies. In this case, opposition comes from states that we normally associate with revisionist aspirations, such as Russia and China. Indeed, some argue that American revisionism—concerning the spread of democracy, norms concerning the use of force, and the expansion of NATO—during the "unipolar moment" drove them to want to end American hegemony.[19] As we see in Chapter 4, it goes too far to pin all the responsibility on the United States; Russian and Chinese commitments to a multipolar order go back to the early 1990s. But the key point is that we need to be extremely careful that we don't conflate "revisionism" with opposition to the United States. The desire to undermine hegemony and replace it with a multipolar system entails revisionism with respect to the *distribution of power*, but it may or may not be revisionist with respect to various elements of international architecture or infrastructure.[20]

Thus, while we sometimes speak of "revisionism" or its cognate terms, we prefer to focus on the more neutral notion of contestation, to talk about counter-order movements that reject liberal ordering, or to specify what, precisely, states and movements want to revise.

Wedging and Brokering

In addition to the general mode of contestation, challengers usually deploy some mix of two distinct logics, both of which we've already mentioned in passing: *wedging* and *brokering* (or *brokerage*). In brief, wedging involves trying to *break apart* existing relationships, while brokering involves trying to *create* new relationships by linking together different individuals, groups, and organizations. States and other actors can also attempt to position themselves as brokers (or, put differently, place themselves in a brokerage position)—that is, to insert themselves as the key site linking together other individuals, groups, and organizations.[21]

Wedging

Timothy Crawford defines wedge strategies in the context of alliance politics, "as a state's attempt to prevent, break up, or weaken a threatening or blocking alliance at an acceptable cost. When the strategy is successful, the state (i.e., the divider) gains advantage by reducing the number and strength of enemies organized against it."[22] But wedge strategies operate in many different contexts. Empires use wedge strategies ("divide and rule") to heighten tensions between their subjects in order to prevent successful rebellions.[23] States have long sought to weaken their opponents by exacerbating *domestic* political conflict, thus hindering, for example, their ability to mobilize wealth and manpower.[24]

The mirror opposite of wedging is *binding*, a strategy aimed at preventing another actor from exiting a relationship. For example, states attempt to bind other states by making them economically or militarily dependent, creating formal alliances with the expectation that these will be more difficult to break, and a variety of other means. Binding efforts matter in the context of struggles over order. Much of hegemonic infrastructure is oriented toward "locking in" or binding other states. But binding is best understood as a way of countering wedging; when it comes to challenging international order, brokerage is more important as a discreet logic.

Brokerage

In the study of contentious politics, brokerage refers to "the linking up of two or more currently unconnected social sites by" an individual or organization "that mediates" the relations among those newly connected sites. Successful brokerage appears frequently in the evolution of social and political movements. Because it builds coalitions and common purposes among previously distinct networks, it allows for larger-scale, better coordinated, and thus frequently more effective mobilization.[25]

However, very few states lack some kind of connection with one another; at the least, all recognized states interact to some degree through their representatives at the UN. Thus, we often use "brokerage" to refer to an entity's efforts to create *new connections* among actors around some *common purpose*, often with the explicit aim of making itself the key mediator between them. As such, brokerage is a widespread practice in world politics. Diplomats, on behalf of their governments, can attempt to broker voting coalitions at the United Nations or the IMF.[26] The United States engaged in brokerage when it constructed multilateral military coalitions for the Korean War, the 1991 Gulf War, and the 2003 Iraq War.[27]

Figure 3.1 provides some examples of the ways that approaches to challenging order—order contention and alternative-order building—mix with wedging and brokering. These examples focus more on relations among states (rather than, say, wedging and brokerage involving nongovernmental organizations, political movements, or domestic societies). But they should give a flavor of how the two dimensions combine to map a variety of different kinds of challenges. They also suggest how they often complement one another. States that engage in alternative-order building can offer the possibility of exit to those in hegemonic infrastructure; when it comes to order contestation, breaking apart a rival coalition can facilitate building one's own. Indeed, wedging often complements brokerage precisely because

	Order Contestation	**Alternative-Order Building**
Wedging	Disrupting Coalitions that Support Existing Rules, Norms, and Practices within International Organizations	Sabotaging the Ability of a Hegemon-Backed Multilateral Development Bank to Function Convincing a State to Exit from a Bilateral Alliance with the Hegemon
Brokering	Building Coalitions for Changing Rules, Norms, and Practices within International Organizations	Building a New Rival Multilateral Development Bank Forming a Rival Bilateral Alliance Infrastructure

FIGURE 3.1 Combining Logics of and Approaches to International Order

it breaks down old relationships and partnerships, thus making one of the isolated parties ripe for new ones.

POWER TRANSITIONS AND STRUGGLES OVER ORDER

Great-power challengers, challenges from below, and transnational contention can appear at any point during the life cycle of an international order or hegemonic order. So can order contestation and alternative-order building. Wedging and brokerage are extremely general logics of power politics. But they all become particularly potent threats to existing order during power transitions.

Power Transitions and the Loss of Monopoly Patronage

In hegemonic systems, the dominant power enjoys a near monopoly on the provision of international goods—what we have termed a "patronage monopoly." No other state can, for example, provide credible security commitments. We illustrate this condition in Figure 3.3 (legend in Figure 3.2), which depicts an idealized American hegemonic international infrastructure comparable to the 1990s. Even though other actors may contest order, they must contend with significant ordering pressure, whether directly though the hegemon's interstate relations or indirectly via international institutions.

But the ecology of international orders comes under strain during power transitions because the hegemon loses its patronage monopoly; more states can compete when it comes to providing economic, security, diplomatic, and other goods.[28] Dominant powers may be less able, or less willing, to provide those goods themselves. But even if the hegemon and its allies remain committed to supplying public, private, and club goods,

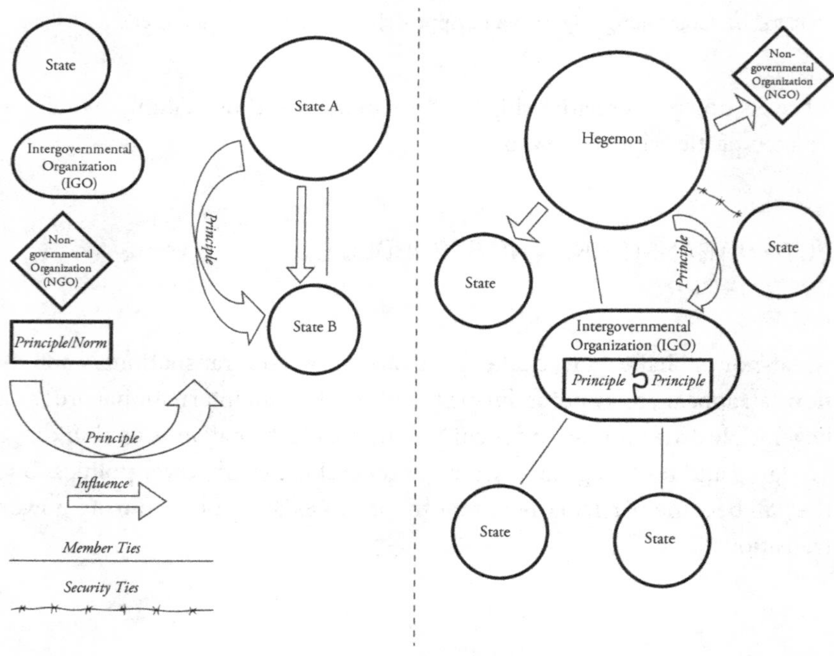

FIGURE 3.2 Visual Legend of International Order

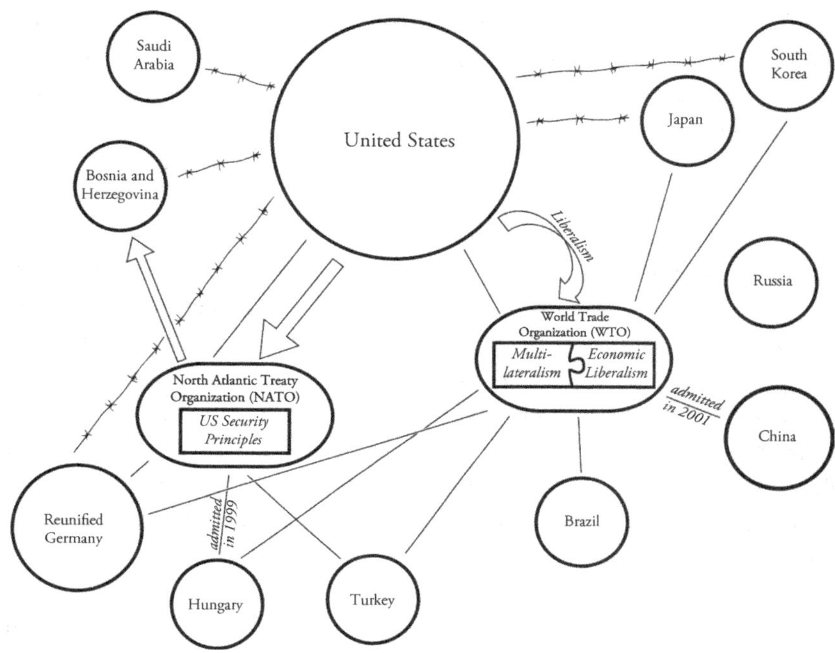

FIGURE 3.3 Idealized American Hegemonic Infrastructure

the greater availability of alternative suppliers—of exit options—affects the calculations of other states.[29] If the hegemon threatens to withdraw development aid, for example, then the recipient has alternatives.[30]

Rising powers may also find themselves with bigger sticks that they can use to enforce their own preferences. For example, throughout the 1990s, the United States and the European Union controlled far and away the largest consumer markets on the planet. They offered, or threatened to withhold, access to their markets as a way of influencing other states. The size of their markets also meant that they enjoyed unrivaled ability to set regulatory standards for products and how those products are produced. Now China's market is as large as, if not larger than, that of the United States.[31] Beijing has traditionally used its market power to require "foreign companies in strategic sectors to form joint ventures with Chinese state-owned partners—and share their technology as a condition to gain access to the Chinese market."[32] It has also already "used economic coercion in support of its political objectives, such as curtailing economic ties with South Korea over its deployment of a U.S. missile defense system."[33]

Thus, power transitions make it possible for a wider variety of states to engage in consequential challenges to international order using wedging and brokerage logics, as well as to use them to pursue order contestation and alternative-order building.

Power Transitions Increase the Likelihood of Contention

Power transitions don't simply provide means. They also provide motives. They encourage revisionist sentiments among rising powers, who often find fault with aspects of the prevailing architecture. Those norms, rules, and values, after all, reflect the ideology and interests of the great powers that created it. Rising powers may also lack what they believe is an appropriate level of influence in existing international infrastructure—or even find themselves excluded from it entirely. As they grow economically and militarily, they may demand influence commensurate with their sense of their own place in the pecking order.[34]

Power transitions may also encourage revisionist sentiments among declining powers. Their leadership may blame their circumstances on aspects of the existing order and thus seek to reform or alter some combination of its architecture and infrastructure. These actions can, in turn, alarm otherwise status-quo powers, whose leadership may conclude that they need to develop their own capabilities to hedge against, or directly contest, a revisionist hegemon. In doing so, they accelerate the relative decline of the leading power. As we discuss in Chapter 7, some observers argue that Trump foreign policy risks producing such an outcome.[35]

These same pressures operate not just on great powers. Importantly, they also influence weaker states as well as political parties, social movements, and other non-state actors. Power transitions produce winners and losers, creating resentment against the current order. Those who never felt well served by the order may harbor preexisting revisionist sentiment. Because rising powers are doing relatively well in economic and military terms, those with different political or economic systems often look like attractive models to those with grievances against the current order. At the same time, the existence of alternative patrons makes it easier for movements and regimes to contemplate pushing back against the incumbent leading powers—they no longer have as much to fear from reprisals.

Right now, many parties and regimes point to China as demonstrating that robust economic growth is compatible with a rejection of liberal democracy. As we discuss in Chapter 6, despite its serious economic problems Russia has positioned itself as a model for cultural conservatives, one that looks more attractive as liberal democracies appear to flounder. Both have emerged as alternative sources of support for regimes unhappy with American international ordering, such as Nicaragua under Daniel Ortega and Venezuela under Nicolás Maduro.[36]

It may be tempting to dismiss counter-order movements, but a number of textbook revisionist states, such as Fascist Italy and Nazi Germany, were cases of counter-order movements successfully taking control of governments.

GREAT-POWER CHALLENGERS

Everyone agrees that great powers can present major challenges to the hegemon and its ordering efforts. What we worry about is the lack of sufficient attention to the *independent* importance of great-power order contestation and alternative-order building when it comes to unraveling hegemonic orders. Such challenges are more than an indicator of revisionist intentions. They aren't only important as a prelude to hegemonic wars. They have major power-political implications in their own right.

Contemporary efforts at alternative order reflect those of prior international systems. Rising powers often build new infrastructures. Recall our discussion, in Chapter 2, of Stacie Goddard's findings concerning great powers who are integrated into the institutions of international order but vary in terms of their outside options: their network of potential allies, partners, and clients beyond the core of the order. Those that lack opportunities for alternative order-building tend to focus on order contestation and exercise caution about undermining the very infrastructure that contributes to their own international influence.

However, imperial Japan during the 1920s and 1930s provides an example of a state that found itself marginalized within the core institutional infrastructure of the order and also lacked existing outside options. This drove it from order contestation and, when that failed, to militarized alternative-order building. As Goddard notes, after World War I, Japan integrated into the infrastructure of the developing international order, including the League of Nations, where it was a permanent member of the League Council—the executive body of the League. But Tokyo's efforts to achieve a favorable international architecture foundered on the major European powers, especially Britain and France, which consistently treated Japan as a second-class citizen, largely on racist grounds. In the face of such exclusion, Japan's attitude toward international order became increasingly revolutionary during the 1930s.[37] "Japan's territorial claims grew ever more expansive, as it moved to conquer China, subdue southeast Asia, and drive the United States out of the Pacific." Moreover, "Japan's challenges to the order were not simply territorial. As early as 1933, Japanese officials were proclaiming a new institutional order. . . . By the end of the decade, Japan" would attack the United States as part of its project for building an alternative order in East Asia, its "Co-Prosperity Sphere."[38]

Imperial Japan's trajectory ended in war. On the surface, it fits nicely with standard stories of transformations in international order in general, and hegemonic unraveling in particular. But Japan's pathway also helps illustrate broader patterns in great-power challengers to international order. Japan had already reordered the Pacific before World War II and before it attacked Pearl Harbor on December 7, 1941. Although Japanese alternative-order efforts were channeled into warfare, this is not the only possible trajectory for great powers. Such efforts can focus on the use of non-military means, such as economic leverage, diplomatic capital, and cultural and ideational sources of power.

Indeed, Japan's challenge reflected its position with the broader ecology of international order. Although formally within the existing infrastructure, it pulled out of the League in 1933 and, in the years before and after, shifted from order contestation to full-scale alternative-order building. Because it faced an ecosystem already saturated with rival, exclusionary political systems—most notably the British Empire and the United States—Japan believed it had little choice but to build an alternative order through aggressive, bellicose means.

Of course, not every government that sees prevailing norms and rules as undermining its legitimacy will embark on such an aggressive course, let alone turn toward extensive construction of alternative international infrastructure. Contesting ordering principles—and trying to block their implementation—from within existing international infrastructure provides another option. However, as we noted earlier, the creation or availability of exit options (in the form of alternative infrastructure) can strengthen the hand of regimes that otherwise wish to remain within older infrastructure.

The development of institutionally denser ecosystems with greater levels of architectural heterogeneity can also facilitate "forum shopping": allowing states to choose international organizations and institutions that are more congenial to their values and preferences. For example, in the realm of election observation, after the post-Soviet Central Asian states endured nearly a decade of critical and even negative assessments of the quality of their national elections by the OSCE's ODIHR election-observations teams, the Central Asian governments welcomed the introduction of additional teams of election monitors from the Russian-led Commonwealth of Independent States and the Chinese-led Shanghai Cooperation Organization observation missions, both of which now issue far more favorable assessments and erode the criticism of the ODIHR assessment. Thus, alternative-order building does not have to produce actual exit to shift international order and weaken hegemonic ordering.[39]

These kinds of dynamics are not specific to modern, more liberal international orders. We can find them in any international order—or hegemonic system—that promotes principles that some political communities find threatening. In the sixteenth and seventeenth centuries, Protestants worried about the prospect of Catholic hegemony in Europe under the Spanish and Austrian Habsburgs. When efforts to contest order within the Catholic Church and the Holy Roman Empire failed in the first half of the sixteenth century, they sought to construct various leagues and alliances outside of existing infrastructure.[40] In the late eighteenth century, fears that Bourbon hegemony would ultimately lead to a Catholic restoration in England pushed Parliament to join the Dutch in their war with France.[41]

We also find plenty of examples of the creation of rival infrastructure in the context of economic competition. Before the Second World War, Nazi Germany pursued trade with Latin America. It even met with some success in displacing the United States and the United Kingdom. In the end, however, this effort came to little because "Nazi policies aimed at achieving economic hegemony had been applied in an extremely haphazard fashion in Latin America." Still, these efforts alarmed Washington, which saw "the activities of German officials . . . as an extremely serious example of the threat the Nazi regime posed to vital US interests and . . . to Roosevelt's vision of an open and undivided world market."[42]

Imperial Japan also engaged in efforts to expand its market presence. In the early 1930s, British policymakers believed that Japan was "dumping textiles into the British Empire" but found it impossible to negotiate an agreement that would resolve competition through "a global demarcation of markets."[43] Japan's "exceptionally intense competitive onslaught" triggered complaints that Japanese companies were receiving subsidies from their government—a concern about unfair trade practices that should seem familiar.[44]

But Japanese competition was particularly pronounced in China, where its success in expanding its "economic presence during the first three decades of the twentieth century was nothing short of extraordinary." If "the values of foreign assets in all of China are compared, those of Japan exceeded all the other foreign powers' combined. The Japanese predominance owed much to their control of the South Manchuria Railway Company, which in 1931 controlled assets worth over 570 million dollars."[45]

We also find examples from before World War I, most of which also involved Germany or German firms, whether successfully or not, attempting to wrest market share away from the British or, in some cases, to build railroads in areas that the British considered within their sphere of influence.[46] Here, German banking, especially in Latin America, seems particularly interesting. As George F. W. Young writes, for example, on the eve of the First World War German overseas banks "had securely established themselves in Latin America as second in importance only to the British banks," thereby allowing German companies to bypass British banks. "These banks . . . surely did further German trade and investment in the region. In contemporary parlance, they strengthened the 'German influence' there, which translates of course into 'German imperialism' in much of present day historiography."[47] Indeed, "German banks were also set up with a view to taking business away from the previously established British banks. . . . [M]uch of the whole German economic effort after 1870 was colored with this nationalist tint: . . . German banks should have the profit from the international transactions engendered by German trade" and "should actively promote German trade at the expense of British trade."[48] Such activities are reminiscent of Chinese attempts to move away from conducting trade in US dollars.[49]

Of course, prevailing rules and norms may enhance, rather than undermine, governments. For example, regimes that build their domestic legitimacy around specific international ordering principles may uphold, say, those of a hegemonic system even when the leading power is too weak to enforce order. International-relations scholar Ji-Young Lee documents this pattern in Korean relations with Ming and Qing China: "Korea's surprisingly consistent acceptance of Chinese hegemony was due to the fact that Korean leaders were made vulnerable to attacks from their subordinates in the absence of external recognition from the Chinese emperor."[50]

But contesting order is not just for states we would normally classify as revisionist challengers. Great powers—whether those within a single region or those that can project power into multiple regions—routinely jostle over the rules and norms of international politics.[51] States and other international actors *always* have incentives to maintain or alter at least some of the elements of existing international order—and thus to engage in order contestation or alternative-order building. Even in a relatively stable system, we will find various kinds of revisionism among a large number of international actors.

Indeed, there are circumstances where status-quo dispositions among great powers can contribute to hegemonic unraveling via the construction of infrastructures that route around the hegemon. Here, the attempt by Europe, Russia, and China to keep the JCPOA (the nonproliferation deal concluded with Iran in 2015) going after the Trump administration withdrew from the agreement is particularly instructive. It provides an example of great powers seeking to uphold an existing arrangement in the absence of hegemonic participation—one potentially driving an alteration in infrastructure (via the proposed Special Purchase Vehicle as an alternative to SWIFT) that could further undermine American influence. A similar point, potentially on both counts, could be made about how the Trans-Pacific Partnership (TPP) went ahead without American involvement, as well as other examples of trade liberalization (such as the EU-Japan Economic Partnership Agreement) that have continued even as the Trump administration has pushed back against open trade.

Such examples show that international orders can shift and hegemonic order unravel even in a world where second-tier great powers are generally supportive of the status quo. By trying to uphold the order in ways that route around the incumbent hegemon, or that substitute for hegemonic goods provision, they can undermine the incumbent hegemon's influence and infrastructural power. If it subsequently turns out that the broader architecture and infrastructure cannot be sustained without the efforts of the hegemon, then the larger order may come crashing down.[52]

Keep in mind that the leading power may trigger these processes if it sends credible signals that it has reformist ambitions, especially in terms of renegotiating basic aspects of the prevailing international order—or significantly altering the character of its hegemonic system—in ways that core allies and partners find worrisome.[53] This is a major concern of those who see Trump as a threat to liberal order: not *simply* that Trump wants to make the order less liberal and holds the reins of the incumbent hegemonic power, but by merely exacerbating fears about Washington's reliability he encourages other traditional American partners and allies to seek alternative arrangements that enhance their own capabilities—while eroding those of the United States.

CHALLENGES FROM BELOW

Weaker states and movements are generally less effective at directly contesting order or alternative-order building than great powers. Nonetheless, regional powers sometimes find themselves in a position to attempt either. Saudi Arabia has used its petroleum wealth to influence the regional order of the Middle East and to shape the Islamic world—including underwriting hardline Sunni movements. Under Hugo Chávez, Venezuela briefly engaged in alternative-order building in Latin America, mostly by supplying economic assistance to regimes receptive to creating a "Bolivarist" bloc.

But the more important role played by less powerful states is not on the supply side of alternative-order building, but on the demand side. Weaker states have a number of different reasons to seek new providers of economic, security, and cultural goods.

- They may simply want more, say, development aid or military hardware. That is, they have no intention of abandoning their existing relationship with the hegemon and the current international order.
- They may want a better deal than they currently receive and believe either that they can get that from a new supplier or that they can leverage the threat of exit to negotiate a better bargain with the hegemon.
- They may worry about whether the hegemon will continue to supply, and thus see new suppliers as a hedge against future change.[54]

One of the reasons that governments may find fault with their current portfolio of goods resides in the implicit or explicit conditions attached to them. Prevailing norms, rules, and values might threaten weaker states for the same basic reasons that they threaten great powers: abiding by them undermines the legitimacy or power of their governments. Corrupt regimes do not particularly want to put their practices under the spotlight, let alone have to change them, in exchange for economic aid, foreign direct investment, or security guarantees. Authoritarian ones do not want to have to admit Western NGOs or comply with human-rights requirements. Governments may not want to liberalize their economies in ways that threaten key supporters.

Now, it is true that sometimes governments welcome conditionality as a way to make preferred policy changes while blaming donors.[55] It is also true that Western governments are rather inconsistent when it comes to applying pressure on illiberal regimes, often giving a free pass when it serves their security or economic interests.[56] But there is a whole range of practices, standards, conditions, and pressures that governments potentially open themselves up to. When push comes to shove, even many liberal democracies would rather maximize their domestic policy autonomy.

Such demand-side pressures create opportunities for wedging and brokering strategies by great-power challengers. Before World War I and World War II, Germany did not simply impose itself on markets in Latin America and the Middle East. When it succeeded in displacing the Americans or the British, it did so because it offered attractive goods to individual consumers or governments seeking a broader range of options. The desire to defend their religious principles led Protestant German princes to ally with Catholic France against Habsburg hegemonic ordering.

Even if great powers do not have a grand plan to undermine existing international architecture, such dissatisfaction provides them with arbitrage opportunities in the form of omitting such conditions and other sources of pressure. French Catholic kings and strategists hoped for a future Europe free of Protestantism; uprising by their Huguenot subjects continued after the French Wars of Religion. But that did not stop them from repeatedly seizing the opportunity offered by German Protestants to weaken Habsburg power.[57]

Only in the last few years have these dynamics started to receive sustained attention in the scholarly literature on power transitions. Ironically, this is because scholars of hegemony generally take them for granted and thus fail to emphasize them as much as they should. It should be clear by now that the bottom-up politics of international goods substitution, and their consequences for international ordering and hegemonic systems, are not a unique feature of the last two decades.

As we discussed in the introduction, they were features of (and the subject of extensive study in) the Cold War.[58] Small states around the globe regularly leveraged their alignment with the US-led or Soviet camps to demand increased economic aid, security assistance, and technical transfer in exchange for offering military basing rights and/or political support at the United Nations. One of the more interesting, but lesser-known examples, involved the active switching of geopolitical patrons by Albania in the 1960s during the Sino-Soviet split. The Albanian government leveraged the rupture of the socialist giants' split to substitute Soviet aid, skilled technical personnel, and security assistance with yet unproven equivalents from China and North Korea. According to historian Elidor Mëhilli, the principal driver of Tirana's decision to switch patrons was not the quality of the goods themselves—Soviet assets and aid were generally regarded as superior and were also tied into a broader and more influential transnational patronage network—but rather the Albanian government's determination to purge the party of possible rivals and reformists under the guise of opposing the de-Stalinization that Khruschev had introduced into the Soviet system, and which Albanian authorities found ideologically threatening.[59]

More broadly, the availability of exit options, among other things, explains why the United States and the Soviet Union faced difficulty in using aid as a lever of influence.[60] Of course, regimes that considered either the United States or the Soviet Union a key threat had less ability, or desire, to credibly threaten exit from their respective systems. Both powers sometimes turned to informal imperial control of their subordinates to make it impossible for them to exit, as Moscow did in forming the Warsaw Pact.[61]

During the 1990s, the United States was the primary and, in most regions, the only goods supplier, enjoying a patronage monopoly. The role of China grew in the 2000s, which saw that state expand as a major aid provider throughout Africa and as a significant investor and development assistance provider to energy-producers in Eurasia and Latin America. Many of these targeted states—such as Cambodia, Turkmenistan, and Venezuela—had been relatively neglected by the liberal order. It is also no accident that many of the states that are seeing sustained attention from China are authoritarian or skeptical of the United States, in need of as much aid as they can get, of limited geopolitical significance to American policymakers, of the view that the liberal order has failed them, or some combination of these.

No one state that switches from the United States to China (or another emerging donor) as its patron will by itself fundamentally alter the ecology of international order. However, over time, the accumulation of small states either defecting, or even threatening to exit in order to secure more favorable political and economic conditions, can hollow out international order, effectively inflicting "death by a thousand papercuts" in a fashion that doesn't appear so significant until after the unraveling is well under way.

Goods substitution can alter the ecology of the order not only by bringing in more infrastructures of influence, such as via the Chinese aid system, but also by shaping the form and influence of the liberal order itself. It can make aid conditionality less stringent, encourage more authoritarian and kleptocratic practices due to the availability of external funds, and make Western revocation of aid—especially in conflict settings—less consequential because regimes that have been abandoned, say for violating human rights, can readily substitute Chinese aid or that of other alternative patrons. We look more closely at contemporary dynamics in Chapter 5.

TRANSNATIONAL CONTESTATION

Scholarship on hegemonic orders, with a few notable exceptions, focuses almost exclusively on relations among states.[62] This is a mistake. The collapse of the Soviet system and the post–Cold War expansion of liberal ordering are far from the only cases where transnational and subnational mobilization played significant roles in the rise or decline of international orders—hegemonic or otherwise. The significance of counter-order movements as a cause of hegemonic unraveling varies across different cases. For any number of reasons, some international orders prove more vulnerable than others, and some movements prove more capable than others. But where we see orders unravel, we often see important transnational and subnational movements contesting international order.

The fate of Habsburg Spain, which is something of the poster child for stories of the rise and decline of great powers, highlights the importance of transnational and subnational anti-order movements. Standard accounts of the collapse of the Spanish Habsburg bid for European hegemony stress strategic overextension and the repeated (among other conflicts) wars with, and intervention in, France during the sixteenth century; the Dutch Revolt, which became Spain's decades-long war (1568–1648) against the Dutch

Republic; the catastrophic failure of the Spanish Armada sent to prosecute Philip II's claim to the English throne; and, finally, the Thirty Years' War and Spain's eventual defeat by an Anglo-French alliance. As historian Paul Kennedy writes, "At the center of Spanish decline . . . was the failure to recognize the importance of preserving the economic underpinnings of a powerful military machine."[63]

Such accounts often note that new religious movements, primarily Lutheran and Calvinist, played a role in this process. But then they move on. Habsburg Spain, as we noted in Chapter 2, was actually a composite monarchy that included, among other territories, Castile, Aragon-Catalonia, Naples and Sicily, modern-day Belgium and the Netherlands, Portugal (from 1580), and the Spanish New World. But it was only part of a larger composite empire that Charles V (1500–1588) inherited or acquired between 1516 and 1540—one he divided between his son Philip II of Spain and brother Ferdinand I, Holy Roman Emperor and ruler of the Austrian Habsburg domains. Charles was embroiled in multiple wars and faced multiple rebellions. But his ultimate defeat, as we alluded to in the prior section, came in Germany at the hands of Protestant forces supported by the French, in the Second Schmalkaldic War (1552–1555). By then, German Protestant princes and cities had become a revisionist force, opposed to a Catholic order upheld by Charles.

While the uprisings against Charles's son, Philip II, in the Netherlands originally crossed religious lines, they eventually became a much more sectarian affair, with Calvinists forming the major part of the Dutch Revolt. The rebels received assistance from and allied with a transnational network of Calvinists anchored in Geneva and extending through France and Germany. Elizabeth II of England also provided important aid; indeed, one motivation for the Spanish Armada and its attempted conquest of England was to cut off support for the Dutch Rebels.

What would have become of Charles's ambitions absent the German Reformation is very difficult to tease out. More broadly, religious counter-order movements had complicated effects on the European balance of power. From 1562 to 1598 they plunged France into a series of civil wars. In doing so, they temporarily sidelined Spain's most important European rival. But no uprising in the Netherlands would have succeeded without the transnational support afforded by co-religionists, nor without the barriers that religious disagreements created against compromise. The Dutch Revolt drained Spanish wealth and manpower. It eventually produced a potent naval rival that created significant problems for the Spanish and Portuguese overseas empires. For both reasons, the Revolt significantly undermined the infrastructure of the Spanish system, and likely greatly shortened the lifetime of Spanish hegemony.[64]

In fact, we find transnational contention associated with many cases of hegemonic collapse or the unraveling of international orders. Without the emergence of anti-colonial movements, driven by ideals of national self-determination and equality, the European colonial empires—in one form or another—would still exist.[65] Uprisings by liberal political movements helped polarize the European great powers of the nineteenth century and thus undermined their ability to manage the system.[66]

Fascism and Marxist-Leninism began as political movements that became interconnected transnationally. When in control of governments, they adopted revisionist postures and pursued them aggressively. As movements, they engaged in social disruption, subversion, and political mobilization against the existing political order.[67]

Consider international fascism. Historian Joseph Fronczak recounts the story of an American financial broker, Gerald MacGuire who, in 1934, sought to "raise a private army to march on Washington, as Italian *squadristi* had marched on Rome, and establish a fascist dictatorship in America."[68] The *Baltimore Sun* described MacGuire as an "amiable, ruddy-faced person of middle age with the shoulders of a football player and the waistline of an alderman."[69] MacGuire had become devoted to brokering "transatlantic fascism" after he returned from "a wide-ranging European tour taken on behalf of a committee of Wall Street bankers, evidently to study veterans' movements associated with fascism" intent on "broker[ing] transatlantic fascism."[70]

As Fronczak stresses, while MacGuire's foiled plot makes his experience unusual, nothing about fascist tourism was out of the ordinary. The diffusion of fascist practices, "performances," and ideas to "local actors around the depression-era world made a global Right."[71]

While fascist movements grew in the 1920s and democratic governments struggled, "democratic institutions were not completely discredited and even in countries where democracy had in reality broken down" the result was generally "multiparty elections and only moderate repression of civil liberties." It was really in the 1930s, when "the domestic and diplomatic successes of Nazi Germany" tipped the scales away from democracies, that a wave of governments fell to right-wing seizures of power.[72] Fascism was by then a truly global phenomenon, with prominent supporters throughout Europe, North America, Latin America, India, and even China.[73]

Fascism is a slippery concept, but what united these movements was antipathy toward, first, the existing order and its liberal characteristics and, second, left-wing movements, especially revolutionary socialists. Fear of the radical left drove many moderate conservatives, owners of business, and industrialists to see fascism as a useful ally and bulwark. While a number of right-wing authoritarian governments, particularly Catholic ones, disliked the Nazis, they still adopted fascist trappings. Mussolini himself began to emulate aspects of Nazi Germany, and adopted its racist orientation.[74]

These dynamics of emulation and diffusion—involving both governments and political movements—are not the only similarity between fascism and other examples of transnational anti-order contention. By the 1930s, both Italy and Nazi Germany were providing material support to fascists in other countries. Mussolini's *Comitati d'Azione per l'Universalità di Roma* hosted the only two Fascist International Conferences in 1934 and 1935. According to press coverage, the 1935 conference featured "aspirant dictators of Ireland, Norway, Belgium, and Czechoslovakia" and saw the creation of "the Fascist Foreign Legion of Volunteers" comprising primarily "one thousand Irish Blue Shirts, all spoiling for a fight" alongside Mussolini.[75] Efforts to construct a united movement ultimately foundered on an inability to come to agreement "on issues such as racism, anti-Semitism, corporatism, and state structure."[76] But that did not deter German or Italian support for fascist, far-right, and other ideologically convivial movements throughout Eurasia and North Africa.[77]

Jørgen Møller and his collaborators provide an important description of the processes that underpinned the fascist and far-right anti-order wave of the 1920s and 1930s: "As democratic great powers are challenged internationally and become less inclined to protect and promote democracy abroad, anti-democratic demonstration effects are likely to become stronger and to spur democratic regression by increasing political polarization."[78]

Such developments involve distinct but mutually reinforcing processes. They help explain the processes through which transnational anti-order movements threaten prevailing international orders, hegemonic or otherwise.

- Revisionist positions tend to be incubated in political movements *before* those movements have secured election or seized power. Many, but certainly not all, of the states that have sought to overturn international orders did so because hardline leaders and movements came to power, or put pressure on incumbent leaders to adopt more aggressive international policies.[79] Once they do start taking control of states, they can trigger feedback processes that increase radicalization and bring more anti-order movements to power.

- Even when counter-order movements fail to seize power, they can still weaken and fragment political communities that might otherwise be able to invest more resources into conserving existing international orders or hegemonic systems. Think of how the Brexit referendum effectively sidelined the United Kingdom, paralyzing its political system and creating deep fissures in its two major parties, after 2016.[80]
- Transnational linkages, when they develop, provide opportunities for coordination, strategic learning, and financial support among anti-order movements and parties. They also create opportunities for specific revisionist states to position themselves at the center of these networks and act as brokers across them. The Soviet Union played this role in the Comintern, through which it exerted significant influence on other Communist movements in other countries.[81]

BOOTSTRAPPING AND POSITIVE FEEDBACK

We expect that many readers will have noticed how different aspects of the same periods, such as that of the Habsburgs or of the 1920s and 1930s, appear across all three of the pathways we identify: great-power challengers, bottom-up pressures, and transnational contention. This is no accident. It reflects a crucial way that power transitions exacerbate all three pathways—by making it more likely that they will start bootstrapping on, or mutually reinforcing, one another.

Figure 3.4 illustrates the dynamics that obtain when all three pathways converge in patterns of positive feedback. For example, because rising powers often provide alternative models of successful political orders, they encourage the emergence of counter-order movements. Rising powers also, especially if they wish to challenge the order, have incentives to develop ideological connections with and provide support to counter-order movements—especially within incumbent powers and their allies. By

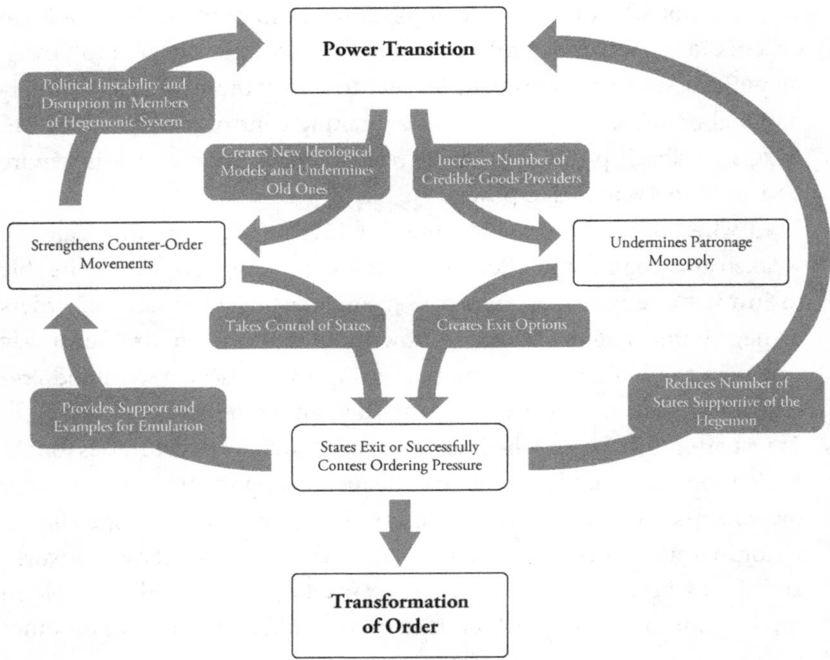

FIGURE 3.4 Power Transitions and Positive Feedback Loops for Hegemonic Unraveling

inserting themselves as brokers among different local and regional counter-order movements, challengers give themselves some ability to direct those movements in ways that serve their interests, including wedging apart hegemonic infrastructure and destabilizing status-quo powers.

This is the story of Russia's support for the far right (and sometimes far left), which we look closely at in Chapter 6. Moscow is too militarily and economically weak to truly threaten the bulk of the American hegemonic system directly, but it can assist anti-order movements *within the core* to secure power, and rely on those movements wedging apart liberal order and its institutional manifestations, such as the EU and NATO. France was more evenly matched with Spain than Russia with the United States, but it supported Protestant rebels and princes for similar reasons. Even Spain provided assistance to Protestant Huguenot rebels in France in the seventeenth century, but its leadership dithered over the matter until it was too late to stop France from putting down the uprising.[82]

To the extent that these efforts work, the success of counter-order movements further weakens existing hegemonic infrastructure, which gives an additional boost to rising powers while also accelerating the spread and mobilization of counter-order movements elsewhere. Meanwhile, the growing number of alternative patrons makes it easier for these movements to seize and retain power, thereby increasing the scope of alternative ordering arrangements and order contestation. All of this accelerates the underlying power transition, as more states break off from the hegemon, negotiate more favorable bargains, or resist its ordering efforts.

The degree that these positive feedback loops kick in matters a lot for whether or not the system can come in for a relatively "soft landing"—that is, one in which the hegemon conserves some of its system and the overall order alters without collapsing. Figure 3.4 only shows positive feedback loops, but there are also sources of negative feedback, including failed or discredited counter-order movements, an increasing sense of threat from rising powers that inclines weaker powers to support the hegemon, and successful mutual adjustment between leading and rising powers. Sometimes the power transition itself fizzles out.

However, just as the period from 1989 to 1992 was marked by the sudden Soviet unraveling and the rapid onset of a credible American bid for global hegemony, we see signs of accelerating bootstrapping of challenges to the American order in the current moment. We chronicle those over the next three chapters, starting with the rise of China and Russia as producers of alternative-ordering infrastructure and architecture.

4

Exit from Above

Russia and China Seek to Transform the International Order

In April 1997, Russian President Boris Yeltsin and Chinese General Secretary Jiang Zemin signed a declaration in Moscow that pledged "to promote the multipolarization of the world and the establishment of a new international order."[1] At the time, the declaration attracted little attention from American policymakers who, during the previous year, had aggressively supported Yeltsin in his 1996 reelection bid and were busy laying the groundwork to admit China into the World Trade Organization (WTO) as a full member. In a now forgotten op-ed, former US secretary of state and *realpolitik* advisor Henry Kissinger warned that Clinton administration officials lacked an appreciation of the structural balance of power. In their post–Cold War euphoria, Kissinger charged, Washington had allowed Russia and China to separate themselves from the US orbit.[2]

Twenty years later, Kissinger's observations appear prescient, but with a twist: Russia and China managed their rise as strategic competitors to the United States primarily by targeting international infrastructure that benefits American power while constructing their own alternatives. These efforts accelerated considerably following the Ukraine crisis in 2014, when Moscow theatrically pivoted toward the East; but the building blocks of this cooperation were well in place even before the presidency of Vladimir Putin.

Both Russia and China now refer to the "multipolar world" in two ways: as the state of the current international order and as one of their key foreign-policy priorities. Both call for the "democratization of international relations," oppose unilateral US action, seek an elevated international status, and denounce Western hypocrisy—especially the American self-image as a promoter of political "values" such as democracy and human rights. For Russian policymakers, the quest for a multipolar (or polycentric) world is intimately tied to its broader desire for status as a great power, one with a regional sphere of influence in the post-Soviet space and position as a global player.[3] China's rhetoric has, to date, become more assertive since the rise to power of President Xi Jinping. Some believe that Beijing has abandoned the principle of "peaceful rise," in favor of flexing its geopolitical muscles while asserting its preferences in the system of global governance.[4]

Russia and China both worry that the American hegemonic system, particularly if unchecked, poses a threat to their geostrategic interests. Russia faces NATO to its west, China a system of American-centered alliances and partnerships to its east and south. Both Moscow and Beijing view a number of the liberal norms and standards baked into current global governance arrangements—particularly involving human and political rights, democracy, and transparency—as threats to their regimes. They both would like to see the architecture of the post-US international order oriented toward stronger norms of sovereignty and non-interference, at least as it concerns the rights of citizens.[5]

Thus, while Russia and China do not yet form a classic alliance, their cooperation has so far proven durable and adaptive. It has increased in scope across different governance arenas (security, economic, cultural, and informational) and regions (Eurasia, Africa, and the Middle East). Yet the notion of Russia and China forming a counter-hegemonic and order-revising entente continues to meet with some skepticism, especially within Western academic and policy communities. This skepticism focuses on three main objections.

First, skeptics argue that regardless of whether Moscow or Beijing intends to disrupt the American hegemonic system, both would still like to preserve key aspects of existing international order. They contend that while China, in particular, seeks greater accommodation, voice, and influence when it comes to international ordering, it does not want to upset the main institutions of the international order; it seeks to "play by the rules of the game."[6]

Second, some focus on the relative capabilities of Russia and China, respectively, arguing that they lack the military and economic power to actually dislodge the United States from its dominant position in world politics, let alone undermine the American system or fundamentally alter the architecture of international order. In many Washington think tanks and policy circles, analysts dismiss Russia as a "declining power" with only regional reach. A number of recent studies seek to dispel the notion that China's rising trajectory will ensure its superiority in military, technological, or other domains.[7]

Third, another group of scholars and analysts argues that the China-Russia relationship is itself fraught, merely an "axis of convenience."[8] The superficial entente masks a number of ways in which Moscow and Beijing compete with one another, Russian insecurities about becoming a junior partner to China, and historical legacies of distrust that, over the long run, cannot be overcome by common concerns about American power. At some point, the argument goes, Sino-Russian rivalry will likely reassert itself.

In this chapter, we argue that Russia and China, both as individual and cooperating challengers, have already undermined liberal international ordering in several critical ways. The question of whether "China or Russia will play by the rules" is already overtaken by events. In the UN's General Assembly, China and Russia voted the same way 77.4 percent of the time (China voted only 24.5 percent of the time with the United States) between 1991 and 2005; between 2006 and 2018, that number rose to 85.4 percent of the time (versus China's voting 22.2 percent with the United States).[9]

The question also misses the point. Beijing and Moscow are *already* altering the ecology of the international order. They have introduced a number of new international and regional organizations, forwarded counter-norms within global governance institutions, and undertaken unilateral military and economic actions aimed at redefining international understandings of what constitutes "shared rules."

Measures of Chinese and Russian military capabilities and spending matter, but raw military power is only one element of the broader toolkits by which Moscow and Beijing influence their immediate regional environments and project power and influence farther afield. Along the way, they have learned from both successes and failures. Moreover, even if ongoing and future Russian and Chinese efforts to promote their own respective global projects end in failure or stagnation,[10] they will still have contributed significantly to alterations in international ecology. They will also continue to do so, even if the United States remains, in terms of gross capabilities, a major power without serious peer competitors.

Finally, we agree that growing asymmetry characterizes the China-Russia relationship. Moscow does fear that it has become Beijing's "junior partner" and that its relative position will continue to erode.[11] But that very growing power imbalance is, for now, less a source of tension than a catalyst for their joint efforts to target international order. In essence, and over a growing number of issue areas, Moscow has increasingly accommodated itself to China's strategic ambitions and initiatives and redefined its own foreign policy interests in the process. These efforts reflect a deliberate effort to mitigate potential areas of tension and rivalry.

ALTERING THE GLOBAL GOVERNANCE ECOLOGY: THE RISE OF POST-WESTERN REGIONAL ORGANIZATIONS

Dreaming of the BRICS

In June 2001, Jim O'Neill, chief economist of the prominent investment bank Goldman Sachs, released a highly influential report in which he argued that the international institutions of governing the global economy no longer represented the changing distribution of world economic power.[12] O'Neill specifically singled out the rapid growth and economic rise of four emerging economies: Brazil, Russia, India, and China. The "BRIC" group (as he termed them) should be represented in an upgraded G7 "in order to allow more effective policymaking."[13] The grouping was first realized in 2006 when, at the initiative of Russian President Vladimir Putin, the foreign ministers of these same countries founded an informal group that met on the sides of the UN General Assembly.[14]

In 2009, in the midst of the disruptive global financial crisis and in the high-profile G-20 meeting that year, the BRIC group held its first formal diplomatic gathering in Yekaterinburg, Russia. Though, the group's initial communiqué does not explicitly make reference to the United States or "the West," the document does use the Sino-Russian formulation: the signatories pledged to support a more democratic and just multipolar world order, one based on the rule of international law, equality, mutual respect, cooperation, coordinated action, and collective decision making of all states.[15] Two years later, the group admitted South Africa. The BRICS became, at least for a time, an actual thing.

Since 2009, the BRICS have held annual summits, rotating through the member countries. They have announced several high-profile global governance initiatives. Although it initially focused on fostering dialogue and coordination to weather the global financial crisis, the group came to promote "non-Western" global governance in an eclectic fashion. It continues to serve as an informal forum for consultations within the meetings of established international organizations such the WTO, IMF, and World Bank. At the same time, the group has also opposed US primacy in some global governance areas—most notably internet governance by the American private agency the Internet Corporation for Assigned Names and Numbers (ICANN).[16]

In 2014 the group made headlines by founding the New Development Bank (NDB), an international financial organization paid for by the BRICS (but mainly by China). The NDB explicitly adopted as its institutional mission the funding of infrastructure in developing countries but without Western-style conditions.[17] The group has also launched an extensive dialogue about monetary issues, including developing its own payment system to reduce dependence on the US-led SWIFT system.[18]

The future of the BRICS remains uncertain. Brazil backed it strongly while under left-wing leadership that vigorously embraced alternative-ordering building. In 2018, Brazil elected a right-wing president, Jair Bolsonaro. Despite his own rejection of aspects of liberal ordering—early indications suggest Brazil is at high risk of serious democratic backsliding—Bolsonaro holds strong anti-China dispositions. Whether those translate into a demobilization of BRICS alternative-order building remains to be seen. Brazil's foreign minister emphasized continuity after the BRICS summit in July of 2019.[19] But the BRICS provide merely a single example of current trends; Beijing's efforts to push the group in its preferred direction reflect a broader pattern. The BRICS represents one of a plethora of new regional and international fora, founded, and promoted by regional- and great-power challengers angling to expand their global influence and erode the power of Western institutions in global governance.

New Organizations under Chinese and Russian Leadership: Developing Counter-Order Infrastructure

Russia began to craft its own regional institutions as a means of re-establishing its primacy and leadership over post-Soviet space in the late 1990s and early 2000s. The most important of these regional institutions are the Collective Security Treaty Organization (CSTO) in the security and defense field and the Eurasian Economic Union (EAEU) in the economic realm. For Moscow, leadership in these organizations provides infrastructure for asserting hegemony in its immediate neighborhood: its sphere of influence (or "privileged relations"), a pillar of Russian foreign policy publicly announced by Russian President Dmitri Medvedev shortly after the Russian military's triumph in the August 2008 war with Georgia. In turn, establishing such a sphere of influence justifies Russia's self-image as a great power in an increasingly multipolar, or polycentric, world.[20]

For China, the 2001 establishment of the Shanghai Cooperation Organization (SCO) in 2001 provides a template for a non-Western organization dedicated to multilateral governance (liberal intergovernmentalism) but that places norms of noninterference over political liberalism in both the economic and security spheres. China also subsequently helped found the Conference on Interaction and Confidence Building Measures in Asia (CICA) and established the Asian Infrastructure Investment Bank (AIIB). The AIIB launched with 56 state members in 2016, with the mission of promoting lending for the purposes of investment in physical infrastructure.[21]

In addition, China has created a slew of new fora and dialogue groups to structure its engagement with overseas regions, including the Forum on China-Africa Cooperation (FOCAC), founded in 2006, the Forum for Ministerial of China-Community of Latin American and Caribbean States (CELAC), which hosted its first ministerial forum in 2015, and the China-Central Eastern European States Cooperation forum, which launched the 16 + 1 group in 2012 that features 16 countries from Eastern Europe and the Balkans, including 11 EU members.[22] Again, such efforts mimic the multilateral form, but not necessarily the political content, associated with liberal ordering.

We provide visual renderings of the network properties of these new Russian and Chinese-led IGO (intergovernmental organization) infrastructures in Figures 4.1 and 4.2 (with a detailed list of these

FIGURE 4.1 Percentage Increase in Intergovernmental Organization (IGO) Co-membership with Russia from 1999 to 2018 (through organizations in Chapter 4, Appendix 1)

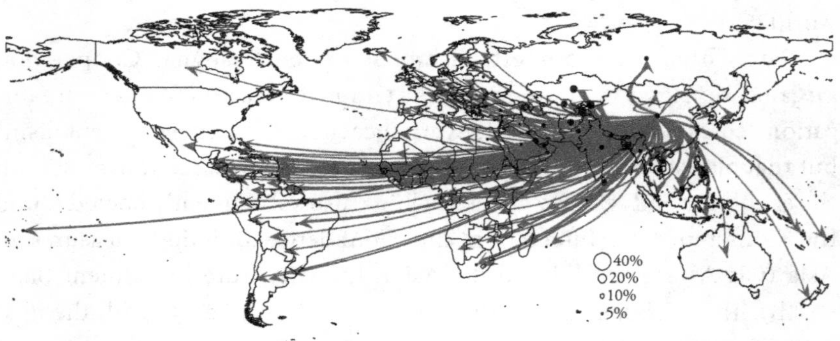

FIGURE 4.2 Percentage Increase in Intergovernmental Organization (IGO) Co-membership with China from 1999 to 2018 (through organizations in Chapter 4, Appendix 1)

organizations and their membership in Appendix 1 at the end of the chapter).

Taken together, these renderings suggest an increasingly dense networking of non-Western IGOs, especially in regions such as Central, South, and Southeast Asia, underscoring that the that the international ecology of these areas is becoming both more dense (with a growing number of IGOs) and contested (with more Russian- and Chinese-led groups whose norms and values are, in some domains, incongruent with those generally pushed by liberal-democratic states)

Observers vociferously debate the implications of all these new regional organizations. For now, American and Western European leaders refuse to recognize or engage with the Russian-led CSTO and EAEU. In both cases, they point specifically to Russia's coercive role in these organizations. Then–Secretary of State Hillary Clinton even dismissed the economic bloc as an attempt to reconstitute the Soviet Union.[23] Similarly, analysis of much of Chinese-backed alternative infrastructure remains more speculative than grounded in strong evidence. The jury is still out on the SCO. It remains unclear whether new international lenders like the AIIB and the New Development Bank (NDB) will challenge or complement their Western counterparts, such as the World Bank and IMF.

Russian and Chinese scholars tend to represent these "post-Western" regional organizations and their significance in very different ways.[24] Russian scholars like to portray groups like the BRICS and EAEU as challengers to Bretton Woods institutions, even while noting how they often attempt to mimic their Western counterparts.[25] Chinese scholars usually adopt a more measured tone, presenting new organizations like the AIIB and NDB as complementary to existing international institutions and the roles that they play in global governance.[26] Some evidence suggests that Chinese-led development banks are adopting similar practices to, and cooperating with, the World Bank. This suggests that we should see the AIIB and the NDB as more of a response to Beijing's lack of clout in older international development institutions than a desire to "'change the rules.' China "has an effective veto in" the AIIB, and the NDB gives the BRICS a voice that they lack in the Bretton Woods institutions.[27] But, as we argue below, even if such alternative-order building does not directly contest existing ordering principles, it still has implications for the American hegemonic system and the broader ecology of international order.

HOW NEW ORGANIZATIONS TRANSFORM THE ECOLOGY OF GLOBAL GOVERNANCE

How are such Russian- and Chinese-led institutions transforming the liberal international order? We see two major ways: first, by networking among themselves and, second, by disrupting the functional activities and jurisdictional reach of Western-controlled IGOs.

Defining the Contours of the World without the West

First, as new regional organizations proliferate, they establish mutual contacts and confer recognition upon one another. Their contacts, dialogues, and cooperative initiatives with other non-Western organizations contribute to a networked infrastructure that bypasses, or at least parallels, the existing "Western" infrastructure. Barma, Weber, and Ratner refer to this process as the creation of a "world without the West," and note that these networks take on particular significance as they come to comprise a greater share of overall global governance and economic exchange.[28] In our terms, they add up to a major shift in the ecology of international order.

Russian- and Chinese-led international organizations treat mutual recognition as a high institutional priority, and thus emphasize various forms of coordination among elements of new infrastructure, including holding plenty of joint summits and meetings. For example, the 2015 BRICS summit (in Ufa, Russia) took the form of a joint summit with the SCO and the EAEU, while the SCO takes care to list its memoranda of understanding (MOUs) with various UN bodies, the CSTO, ASEAN, CICA, and even the Red Cross.[29] Moreover, all of these groups appear committed to expanding their membership and external partnerships.

After the EAEU launched, it sparked an argument over whether the United States and the European Union (EU) should confer legitimacy on the group by engaging with it, despite its own self-image as a regional counterweight to the EU within the post-Soviet space.[30] Western reluctance to engage helped push Moscow to seek partnerships more globally. The EAEU concluded a free trade agreement with Vietnam (in 2016) and has reached accords to negotiate similar agreements with Iran, Egypt, and Serbia. At the same time, Moscow has undermined its own rhetoric about the EAEU by, for instance, bypassing consultations with other members when it imposed countersanctions on EU agricultural products in 2014.[31] The United States aggressively but unsuccessfully opposed the AIIB at the behest of its Treasury Department but, as noted above, the AIIB, now boasts a framework for co-financing projects with the World Bank and cooperative memoranda of understanding with both established and new international financial institutions including the African Development Bank, Asian Development Bank, Eurasian Development Bank, and New Development Bank.[32]

Russian- and Chinese-led institutions also alter international order by producing new intergovernmental groupings and new forms of interactions among states that were previously unaccustomed to dealing with one another. Such state groupings amount to important geopolitical constructions. In hegemonic systems their formation and boundaries owe much to the ordering efforts of the leading power. As international-relations scholar Peter Katzenstein shows, and we discussed in Chapter 2, American hegemony rests on regional groupings of alliances and proxy powers: a multilateral system with Germany in Europe and a hubs-and-spokes systems with Japan as its center in Asia.[33] But as Figure 4.3 reveals, from 1999 to 2018 the growth of state ties with Russian- and Chinese-led IGOs as a percentage of their overall IGO affiliations is particularly acute in Central and South Asia. Interestingly, about half of these countries exhibit new network ties with predominantly Chinese IGOs, about half with Russian and Chinese-led IGOs, but very few with the Russian-only group. In other words, the network map suggests that while we are seeing a considerable increase in non-Western ordering infrastructure, very little of it exists within a clear, exclusive Russian sphere of influence.

Because the BRICS is perhaps the most prominent of these new "post-Western" groupings, it has spawned some imitators—such as the next tier of emerging economies, also identified by O'Neill as the "MIST" (Mexico, Indonesia, South Korea, Turkey).[34] The Trump administration's abandonment of the TPP accelerated negotiation of the Regional Comprehensive Trade Partnership (RCEP), a mega-trade agreement of 16 states comprising 50 percent of global GDP that would link China with Japan and

FIGURE 4.3 Combined Increase in Intergovernmental Organization (IGO) Comembership with Russia and China from 1999 to 2018 (through organizations in Chapter 4, Appendix 1)

include India, South Korea, Australia, New Zealand, and ten Association of Southeast Asian Nations (ASEAN) members.[35]

On the security front, beginning in 2016 China has convened annual meetings of the Quadrilateral Cooperation and Coordination Mechanism (QCCM), a counterterrorism group dedicated to training and information sharing. Its membership includes China, Pakistan, Afghanistan, and Tajikistan. This grouping is interesting for two reasons. First, the countries are either confirmed or rumored hosts for Chinese military or counterterrorism facilities. Second, it cuts across traditional groupings of South Asia, post-Soviet Central Asia, and East Asia. Thus, it provides further indications of potential reconfigurations of the boundaries of regions. Similarly, the 2017 official expansion of the SCO to include Pakistan and India signaled a shift from the organization acting as a forum for cooperation in the post-Soviet Central Asian region to a much broader engagement with Eurasia and South Asia.[36] In this light, Chinese efforts to resurrect and promote Conference on Interaction and Confidence-Building Measures (CICA) appears aimed at establishing an Asian-wide security dialogue that also adopts the language of "confronting unilateralism" and promoting "fairer multilateralism."[37]

Disrupting Jurisdictions and Functions of Existing IGOs

By entering the ecology of international order, these new organizations also may disrupt the traditional activities of Western actors and undermine their ability to use membership in international organizations as carrots and sticks. Russia aimed to use the EAEU and CSTO as institutional mechanisms for checking the influence and activities of Western organizations in its perceived sphere of influence. Accordingly, in 2013 Russia openly pressured Armenia and Ukraine not to join the EU's Eastern Partnership agreement and, instead, negotiate for membership in the EAEU. Similarly, European Commission officials in Brussels have treated the 16 + 1 initiatives with suspicion. They have expressed particular concern that China might leverage the forum—and promises of investment in European physical infrastructure—to water down EU common positions on China-related policy, such as human rights declarations.[38] In the field of international election observation, across Eurasia, both the SCO and the Russian-led Commonwealth of Independent States (CIS) have, since 2003, sent election observation missions to member countries. These observers consistently pronounce obviously flawed elections acceptably free and fair, or at least provide much more positive assessments than those traditionally offered by the OSCE's Office of Democratic Initiatives and Human Rights.[39]

The proliferation of these organizations also affords opportunities for states to demand more concessions or better terms of engagement from Western organizations, thereby potentially altering the routines, standards, and conditions usually imposed by them as organizational practices. We will explore this dynamic of "international goods substitution" in greater detail in Chapter 5, but here we note that even relatively weak states—ones that traditionally lack leverage with Western organizations—can increasingly use the availability and partnership of a new institution to demand better terms. For example, the historian Peter Frankopan observes that Balkan states have invoked Chinese interest and engagement to try to push the EU to take greater interest in the region.[40]

In sum, public pronouncements about the intention of these new regional organizations suggest little to challenge most elements of contemporary international order. But in practice their networking efforts, combined with how they disrupt the functional and regional monopolies once enjoyed by their Western counterparts, means that, over time, those pronouncements may not matter. Even those designed for congruence with contemporary international architecture and infrastructure may begin to alter the ecology of international order in profound ways.

DISCREDITING LIBERAL NORMS AND SPREADING COUNTER-NORMS

Of course, Moscow and Beijing have not been passive reproducers of prevailing liberal norms. Instead, they have sought to discredit aspects of contemporary international architecture—particularly those related to human and political rights. One way that they pursue this goal is through the creation and diffusion of counter-norms within their IGOs and other ordering infrastructures.

As we discussed in Chapter 2, observers have long (and with good reason) criticized the United States for its inconsistency in promoting liberal democracy across its network of allies and partners. During the Cold War, US officials publicly championed liberal democracy as ideologically superior to Communism, but they regularly supported anti-Communist authoritarians and readily intervened in the domestic affairs of political clients.[41]

In the post–Cold War era, the collapse of the Communist bloc gave new impetus to liberalism. It created the impression that democracy had triumphed. Certainly, many American actions (military intervention in the Balkans) and inactions (the Clinton administration's passive role during the Rwandan genocide) drew strong criticism about Washington's actual commitment to upholding liberal principles and human rights. But the default position of the United States was to openly advocate greater democratization and political reform. It fostered a large and international democracy promotion apparatus, with the two major party affiliates—National Democratic Institute (NDI) and the International Republican Institute (IRI)—both playing visible international roles as advocates and government contractors.[42] Certainly, Moscow and Beijing, even in the mid-1990s, remained cynical about Washington's professed normative commitments. Recall that they openly called for the democratization of international relations, but they lacked the capacity to build significant global or regional networks of opposition to liberal-democratic values. But since the 2000s, important trends have undercut Washington's ability to promote liberal democracy.

Democracy Becomes Conflated with Regime Change

The Bush administration routinely invoked the spread of democracy—what later became its "freedom agenda"—as a justification for its disastrous 2003 Iraq War. In doing so, it confirmed a willingness to unilaterally topple governments and reorder entire regions in the name of democratization. For Russia and China, the notion that the United States sought to directly undermine authoritarian regimes received further substantiation by Washington's support for "Color Revolutions" in Eastern Europe and Central Asia (see below).

During the Obama administration, Washington attempted to reassure Moscow (and other autocratic governments) that it had no interest in actively pursuing regime change. Moscow and Beijing remained wary, and their skepticism seems justified by American behavior during the Arab Spring (2010–2012). The Obama administration abandoned, for example, long-time allies like Egyptian president Hosni Mubarak in the face of widespread street protests, and while it remained relatively mute in some cases, such as severe repression in Bahrain, it generally seemed supportive of the aims of activists.

For several Russian commentators, Libya marked a watershed moment in post–Cold War foreign policy.[43] As noted in prior chapters, Washington persuaded Russian president Medvedev to abstain on, rather than veto, a UN resolution that authorized Western bombing strikes in the country. Although the resolution was open-ended, Washington emphasized it was for the limited responsibility-to-protect purpose of preventing Libyan forces from massacring the population of Benghazi. Instead, the United States joined French and British forces in dismantling the Libyan military; President Muammar Qaddafi was tortured and killed by a rebel mob as he tried to flee a battle scene. Libya underscored that the American penchant for militarized regime change was inexorable—as Clinton, Bush, and Obama had all used force to overthrow autocratic governments.

Grounding the Activists: Cracking down on NGOs

In the mid-2000s a wave of largely peaceful uprisings swept post-Soviet space. Demonstators protested the results of fraudulent elections and managed to topple entrenched leaders—most of whom were more supportive of Moscow than their successors. American and European backing played a significant role in the fall of Serbian president Slobodan Milošević in 2000, and then in the so-called Color Revolutions that produced regime change in countries like Ukraine and Georgia.

These developments not only alarmed Moscow but also Beijing. Both regimes took note of how fast and easily post-Soviet governments crumbled. For China, the March 2005 collapse of the regime in its small Central Asian neighbor, Kyrgyzstan, proved particularly worrisome. In consequence, Western civil-society building efforts and liberal NGOs went from being mere annoyances to security threats. Russia imposed a series of restrictive registration laws that many of the post-Soviet states—including the Central Asian states, Belarus, and Armenia—subsequently emulated.

Soon after the Color Revolutions, Russia and China embarked on what became a global effort to stigmatize, restrict, and even ban the activities of NGOs. The Kremlin's concerns mounted following the Bolotnaya protests in Moscow in 2011, which broke out in reaction to the announcement that then-prime minister Putin would run again for president. In 2012, Russia passed a law mandating that all NGOs receiving foreign funding would have to self-declare as "foreign agents." In 2015 Moscow went one step further and passed the "Undesirable Organizations" law that effectively criminalized the activities of a number of groups, including the George Soros–funded Open Society Foundations, National Endowment of Democracy, National Democratic Institute, and International Republican Institute.[44]

Beijing, which enacted its first major restriction in 2009, passed a more restrictive law in 2016. It mandated that all foreign groups working in China—even in philanthropic and cultural spheres—had to find a sponsoring Chinese organization and register with the police.[45] We further explore this blockage of liberal transnational advocacy networks in Chapter 6. Here, we note that Russia and China have led a seemingly successful global effort to delegitimize and curtail the activities of liberal NGOs engaged in political issues, especially democracy, anti-corruption, and human rights.

Supporting Counter-Norms in the International Arena

Russia and China not only learned how to better insulate themselves from political liberalism ordering, but they also developed ways to go on the offensive. Moscow and Beijing now openly highlight the weaknesses of Western democratic political systems and offer alternative ordering principles.[46] Across much of the globe, liberal democracy appears in retreat. But in the post-Communist space, according to Freedom House, since 2007 more countries have declined in terms of democracy scores than improved; countries once viewed as consolidated democracies, such as Hungary and Poland, saw substantial backsliding in 2017 and 2018.[47]

Analyst Christopher Walker argues that Russia and China are increasingly practicing "sharp power": informational practices that "limit expression" and weaken "the health and credibility of democratic regimes."[48] These include targeting formal democratic processes (such as Russia did when it interfered in the 2016 US presidential election) and the broader "spheres of culture, academia, media, and publishing—sectors that are crucial in determining how citizens of democracies understand the world around them." Walker thus sees clear patterns in, for example, Beijing's successful efforts to pressure private actors, including Hollywood, to censor how they talk about or represent China; the aggressive targeting of journalists and Western publishers; the flooding of social media and online stories about Russia and China through the use of paid trolls and bots designed to control the information space; and the penetration of US academic and cultural space by networks of Chinese Confucius centers.[49] In one of the first systematic analyses of the global impact of Confucian centers on the "grassroots" image of China, Samuel Brazys and Alexander Dukalskis found that the proximity of an active Confucius Institute improves the tone of local media reporting on events involving China.[50]

Critics worry that the "sharp power" argument overemphasizes the novelty of the basic logics at stake, the effectiveness of these efforts, and the degree that they actually come together into a pattern of behavior. For our purposes, what matters is the degree that they represent a reversal of the dominance of liberal ordering in the 1990s and 2000s—and sometimes by appropriating techniques that the United States and Europe used to spread liberal norms and values.

Finally, Moscow and Beijing have also introduced alternative principles of international order to those associated with political liberalism, both as ways of contesting aspects of international architecture and as a roadmap for shifts in global governance.[51] Beijing has been a vocal advocate of the principle of "civilizational diversity." The argument is that since countries all enjoy distinct and important cultures, they do not have the right to make value judgments about one another's domestic conduct. These same principles form the basis of the so-called Shanghai Spirit, the founding principle of the SCO that seeks to promote cooperation through "mutual respect and mutual trust between the states belonging to different civilizations and having different cultural traditions."[52]

Political scientist David Lewis observes that in Central Asia these SCO principles have steadily displaced the liberal values espoused by the OSCE. East European leaders, including Hungarian illiberal champion Viktor Orbán, have also invoked these principles. Moscow has promoted a so-called traditional values agenda, which it pushed at the regional and international level; this includes emphasizing the importance of organized religion in public life; the centrality of the family unit; and opposition to Western attempts to promote lesbian, gay, bisexual, transgender, and queer (LGBTQ) rights. Moscow itself worked with political allies to pass a declaration supporting traditional values in the United Nations Human Rights Council (UNHRC). Finally, both Russia and China forward strong notions of national sovereignty, especially with respect to foreign interference in domestic affairs, broadly understood to include pressure and criticism on human, political, and civil rights issues.

DEVELOPING COMPETING INFRASTRUCTURES: TWO INTERVENTIONS AND A GLOBAL PLAN

Beijing and Moscow have established new international organizations. They have directly challenged liberal democratic norms. But since 2014 they also have pursued individual unilateral foreign policy initiatives that promote their preferred visions of international order. For Moscow, unilateral military actions in Ukraine and Syria affirm Russia's status as a great power, one capable of making its own rules concerning the use of force and territorial annexation. The Belt and Road Initiative (BRI) has provided President Xi Jinping with a way to build physical and ordering infrastructure that connects multiple countries and regions to China. Xi has used it to stake a claim to global leadership and proactive international ordering.

Russia's Interventions in Ukraine and Syria as "Rule-Changing" Acts

The 2014 Ukraine crisis marked a turning point in Russia's relations with the West.[53] The immediate cause of the conflict was the collapse of the regime of Ukrainian president Victor Yanukovych. Yanukovych was Moscow's preferred candidate in the disputed 2004 election that led to the "Orange Revolution." Yanukovych went on to legitimately win the 2010 election. He relied on a network of Western advisors, including Paul Manafort, to present a more Western-friendly image while consolidating power. But in 2013 Yanukovych found himself caught between the EU and Russia. Ukraine had been negotiating an EU Eastern Partnership Agreement (EPA), which would include a trade arrangement and facilitate visa-free travel for Ukrainians to EU member states. But as the November 2013 Vilnius summit approached, at which Yanukovych was supposed to sign the EPA, Russia intensified pressure on Yanukovych to abandon the agreement and endorse future Ukrainian membership in the Russian-led Eurasian Economic Union. Moscow used a combination of carrots and sticks. It first closed down trade and then offered an economic assistance package that included Russian purchases of Ukrainian bonds and additional discounts on energy purchases.

When Yanukovych announced his withdrawal from the EPA, his decision triggered a wave of demonstrations in Kyiv's Maidan Square. After Yanukovych's interior forces shot protestors, EU negotiators brokered an agreement calling for early elections and the restoration of the constitution, but soon afterward Yanukovych fled the country as his authority over the Interior Ministry and troops collapsed.

Moscow responded on two fronts. First, it launched an operation to take control of the heavily Russian-speaking province of Crimea. In March, the Russian-backed government of the Autonomous Republic of Crimea held a referendum, observed by friendly election monitors and regarded with skepticism in Europe and the United States, that approved membership in the Russian Federation. Second, Moscow funneled support to separatists mobilizing in the Eastern Ukrainian provinces of Donetsk and Lugansk. In the summer of 2014, as the Ukrainian army threatened to overrun the rebels, Russia increased its support, effectively freezing the conflict as separatist forces consolidated control over eastern areas. The United States and the EU imposed rounds of economic sanctions on Russia, triggering Russian countersanctions.

Western and Russian interpretations of the longer-term origins could not be more different. EU officials claim to have been completely surprised by the unfolding of the crisis. Indeed, Russia failed to communicate its opposition to the EPA in regular meetings between the EU and Russia.[54] For the United States and the EU, the conflict represented a blatant case of Russian aggression as Moscow violated the sovereignty and security of a neighbor in contravention of the norms and rules of the post–Cold War European security architecture. Russia committed to uphold Ukraine's sovereignty and territorial integrity when it signed the Budapest memorandum (1994) and the Black Sea Fleet accords, which apportioned the Soviet-era Black Sea fleet and leased naval facilities in Sevastopol to Russia for a period of 20 years (1997).

But for Moscow, events in Ukraine represented nothing less than a crisis of the US-led international order itself. President Putin's own speech following the annexation of Crimea featured a laundry list of Russian grievances about the American-led international order and post–Cold War developments, including a denouncement of US exceptionalism, NATO expansion, Western recognition of Kosovo's unilateral intervention, and Western military interventions.[55] Tellingly, Putin described Russia as a coil, ready to snap back.

Despite coming under a robust package of economic sanctions, Russia found narrower international opposition to its annexation in Crimea and its support for breakaway republics in Ukraine than for its similar support of independence for the breakaway Georgian territories of Abkhazia and South Ossetia following the 2008 Russia-Georgia War. Then, despite an extensive global diplomatic lobbying campaign by the Russian Ministry of Foreign Affairs, Moscow proved able to secure recognition only from Venezuela, Nicaragua, and a handful of small Pacific states.[56] However, when the United Nations considered a non-binding resolution affirming "Ukraine's territorial integrity" following the March referendum and annexation (UNGAR 68/262), 100 states voted in support and 11 countries in opposition.[57] Strikingly, 68 countries abstained from the vote (and 24 missed the vote), including all of the other BRICS members—a fact that Putin himself acknowledged in his Crimea speech and pointed to as demonstrations of support for the Russian position from India and China. Though Russia by no means secured widespread support for its action, it found itself significantly less marginalized than it had been in the aftermath of the Georgia conflict.

Syria: Protecting Traditional Clients, Projecting Global Power

In 2015, Russia intervened militarily in the Syrian civil war to support the government of Syrian president Bashir Al-Assad. Syria had been a longtime client of the Soviet Union, and, after a period of engagement with the West in the 1990s, was once again a major purchaser of Russian military equipment. But for Moscow, the Syria conflict represented its most important concerns about international order and provided a prime opportunity for challenging American primacy in international "rule-making."

Russian operations in Syria amounted to its first significant attempt at power projection outside of its neighborhood since the collapse of the USSR. They required extensive political and military coordination with the other powers involved, including the United States (with which Russia established de-conflicting procedures), Turkey, Iran, and Israel. Moscow also actively pushed for the Astana peace process, which has excluded the United States as a negotiating party. And Russia actively shrugged off criticism from liberal-democratic governments and international NGOs concerning the devastating humanitarian consequences of its air campaign, particularly the mounting civilian casualties from Russian aircraft bombings in an effort to retake provinces from rebel hands.[58]

Despite warnings that Russia would become bogged down in Syria, its intervention appears to have been decisive in turning the tide of the conflict and allowing Assad to re-establish control over broad areas of the country. In October 2019, President Trump impulsively decided to withdraw US troops embedded with the largely Kurdish Syrian Democratic Forces. He thus allowed Turkey to establish a buffer zone in northeast Syria, ensuing events—including active cooperation between Syrian and Turkish forces to secure the region—seemed to underscore the success of Putin's decision to commit to backing Assad, solidify his working ties with Turkey and Prime Minister Erdogan, and demonstrate to the world that Russia remained an influential power with extra-regional ambitions and military capabilities.

Russia's actions in Ukraine and Syria involved the use of military force and information warfare to challenge the liberal international order and re-establish its position as a great power with the authority to participate in global affairs. The conflicts have also contributed to greater uncertainty in Russian relations with Western powers. As scholars Andrej Krijovic and Yuval Weber argue, the two sides are now at an impasse because Russia cannot commit to limiting its revisionism and willingness to use force, but the United States, NATO, and the European Union cannot reassure Russia that it will avoid exploiting Russia's continuing structural weaknesses, such as its natural resource–dependent economy and insecure regime.[59]

China's Turn to the Belt and Road

Just as the Ukraine crisis was escalating in September 2013, Chinese Premier Xi Jinping delivered a landmark address at Nazarbayev University in Kazakhstan. There he invoked the ancient Silk Roads of the past to announce that China would launch a "Silk Road Economic Belt" across Eurasia intended to promote mutual trust, connectivity, and the exchange of people, development, and cooperation.[60] Over the next year, Chinese experts and officials unfurled more details of a highly ambitious plan to fund a number of large-scale infrastructure projects, energy investments, and transportation upgrades to connect China with Europe, the Middle East, and South Asia. Together with a "Maritime Silk Road" that will upgrade and expand a number of overseas strategic ports, the two projects were referred to as "One Belt, One Road"; by 2015, Chinese agencies usually referred to the overall projects as the Belt and Road Initiative (BRI).

A 2015 government report further developed Beijing's vision for the BRI. It called for the promotion of "the connectivity of Asian, European and African continents and their adjacent seas," and proposed to establish regional partnerships, to set up "all-dimensional, multi-tiered and composite connectivity networks, and realize diversified, independent, balanced and sustainable development in these countries."[61] As part of "embracing the trend to a multipolar world," the paper refers to strengthening partnerships with new institutions like the AIIB, the NDB, the SCO, and the China-ASEAN Interbank association, as well as promoting "collaborative governance" with a range of other regional organizations and international financial institutions (IFIs). According to the *South Morning China Post*, the initiative would partner with 65 countries and would constitute "the most significant and far-reaching the nation has ever put forward."[62]

Both strategic and domestic considerations drive the BRI. China seeks to more actively shape, on a bilateral basis, the political attitudes of its neighbors with the aim of making them friendlier and more responsive to Chinese foreign policy and strategic priorities. Beijing also wants to accelerate the internationalization of the renminbi and establish additional coordination mechanisms to elevate the role of its new institutions like the AIIB and NDB. Along with BRI investment, documents also discuss the harmonization and convergence of Chinese standards with its partners, including in areas such as public administration, technology transfers, and professional training. The BRI also targets new markets for Chinese industries already operating at overcapacity, especially steel and cement manufacturing. Chinese financing arms, such as the China Development Bank or the Export-Import Bank, can set terms that award project contracts to specific Chinese companies and mandate the use of Chinese labor. Finally, the BRI umbrella also offers opportunities to regional and local governments to expand their regional and foreign activities as they vie to become transit hubs.[63]

Western reactions to the BRI have been divided. Some emphasize the global economic opportunities afforded by the BRI—not only when it comes to improving global infrastructure but also to allowing Western companies and banks to play an active role in various projects. More geopolitically minded observers caution that the BRI represents a significant departure from the "peaceful rise" paradigm and, if left unchecked, will become a vehicle to rival Western-controlled Bretton Woods institutions as an alternative source of a Chinese-led economic order.

How the BRI Transforms the Ordering Ecology

Western alarmists greatly exaggerate the coherence and unitary purpose of all the Chinese companies, political agencies, and parochial interests that have attached themselves to the BRI as China's flagship national cause. But the BRI is likely to exert five significant impacts on the ecology of international order across its partner states.

First, the management and legal governance of this panoply of investments, loans, and contracts will require new legal forums and dispute-resolution mechanisms. Between January 2015 and August 2017, Chinese companies, as part of the BRI initiative, reportedly signed over 15,300 projects worth $303 billion.[64] Rather than rely on traditional investment dispute mechanisms like international arbitration, in 2018 China announced that it will establish an "international commercial court" (CICC) with three tribunals—in Shenzen, Beijing, and Xian.[65] These courts will be staffed exclusively by eight Chinese judges and will also be advised by a committee of experts. The CICC promises more efficient dispute resolution than the current system of international arbitration venues, which many Chinese companies use. Although international companies might find dispute resolution in China difficult to stomach, cash-strapped states might well accept these terms as part of an overall aid and investment package.[66] When the government of Montenegro in 2017 halted an $800 million Chinese-funded road project due to excessive debts and cuts in government spending, it faced the prospect of a Chinese court enforcing the contract.[67]

Second, major BRI partners will likely prove increasingly reluctant to buck China and its foreign-policy priorities in the UN and in other international settings. In a possible prelude to future developments, in June 2017 Greece, a major BRI partner because of a Chinese firm's investment in the upgrade of the Piraeus port, blocked a customary EU annual statement at the UN Human Rights Council in Geneva criticizing China for its human rights practices.[68] Indeed, Beijing's growing normative influence via its economic power was on display in June 2019 when, in response to a UNHCR letter condemning China for its mass detentions of Muslims in Xinjiang that received 22 signatories (mainly advanced industrial democracies), Beijing countered by mobilizing 50 countries, spread over Africa, the Americas, and Asia, in a direct reply lauding "China's contribution to the international human rights cause."[69] Figure 4.4 depicts the geographical

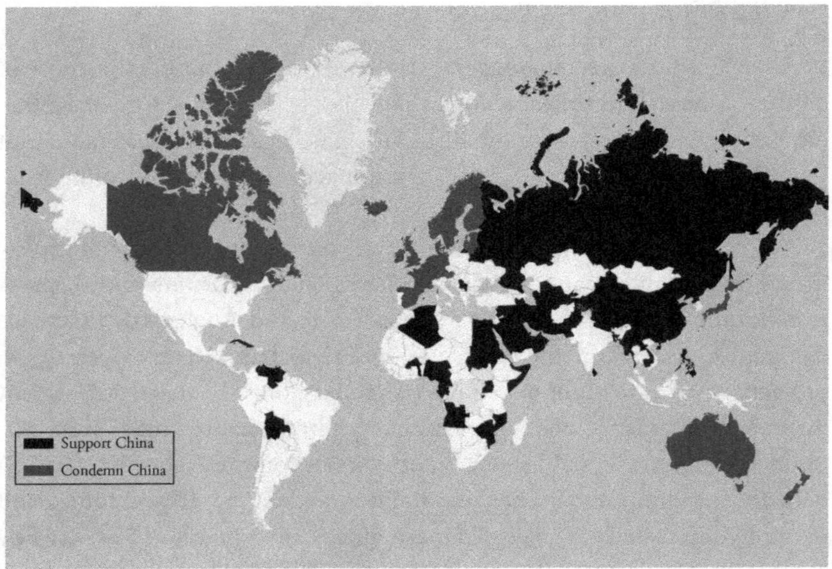

FIGURE 4.4 United Nations Human Rights Council (UNHRC) Members Who Condemned or Supported China on the Xinjiang Re-education Camps (as of July 30, 2019)

origins of the signers of the condemnatory and supportive letters (Qatar withdrew its signature in August 2019).

Third, large injections of Chinese lending into already indebted economies threaten to explode recipient states' external debt. A report by the Center for Global Development found that of the 68 BRI partners, 23 are significantly or highly vulnerable to debt distress and that eight of those—Djibouti, Kyrgyzstan, Laos, Maldives, Mongolia, Montenegro, Pakistan, and Tajikistan—were placed in "particular risk of distress" because of a BRI-associated pipeline project.[70] In turn, mounting debt obligations raise questions about whether China would coordinate with IFIs over terms of debt relief and what Beijing might demand to repay or restructure these debt burdens. For example, the decision of the Sri Lankan government in 2018 to restructure its debt incurred for upgrading the Hanbantota port into extending a 99-year lease sparked anti-government and anti-China demonstrations in the country. A subsequent investigative story revealed that large payments from the Chinese construction fund had been funneled into the 2015 campaign of the Sri Lankan president who negotiated the deal, while the Sri Lankan authorities were pressed by the Chinese side to grant more equity in the port in exchange for $1 billion in debt relief.[71] One report suggests that China has learned from the backlash and generally imposed much less harsh terms or even forgiven debt, but how this ultimately will play out remains unclear.[72]

Fourth, it seems increasingly likely that certain BRI partners are now also becoming major security partners and even basing hosts for Beijing. For example, in 2017 China established its first formal overseas military base in Djibouti (also host to a major US strategic facility), while in 2018 China formally unveiled a naval facility in Gwadar, the southern port city of Pakistan that has been one of the largest recipients of Chinese funds for the construction of highways and power plants. Indeed, one of the concerns in Sri Lanka over China gaining more control over Hambantota was the potential of using it for military and strategic activities not readily agreed to by Colombo. The co-mingling of BRI funds as unofficial quid pro quo for security and access agreements with China remains an additional potential lever for Beijing.

Finally, the global reach of the BRI has already prompted responses from other major powers who either find themselves threatened by the BRI or want to support China's geo-economic foray. After the Obama administration maintained a relatively sanguine view of China's efforts to promote "connectivity" in third regions, the Trump administration announced in December 2018 that it would actively seek to counter "predatory" Chinese and Russian practices in Africa that are "deliberately and aggressively targeting their investments in the region to gain a competitive advantage."[73] Similarly, Japan and India have also advanced their own development and transit corridors intended to mitigate the geopolitical impact of the BRI. In short, the BRI is now being widely understood as China's attempt to profoundly shape international order.

Tellingly, the one major power that seems to have adjusted its own regional ambitions to align with the BRI is Russia. Over the last 10 years, Russian planners have consistently recalibrated their own regional plans to accommodate Chinese initiatives. In 2016, Russian and Chinese officials announced a coordinating mechanism between the EAEU and the BRI designed to harmonize tricky questions like tariff levels, standards, and regulations. But perhaps the most important evidence to date of Moscow's increasing acquiescence to China's geo-economic ambitions came in 2017, when Putin called for a "Greater Eurasia," a concept that leading analysts now use to describe Russia as occupying a central role in the integrating super-continent.[74] This move to "scale up" from Russia's immediate post-Soviet neighborhood to the Eurasian landmass appears to concede that Chinese-led economic initiatives on the continent are unstoppable. Rather than openly oppose China or even formally negotiate and delineate spheres of economic interest, it now seems that the Kremlin is satisfied with, or at least resigned to, claiming that even Chinese-led Eurasian integration is in Russian interests. Russia's embrace of the Greater Eurasia concept also suggests that whatever concerns Russian officials might have over growing asymmetries of power with China, they prefer a strategy of accommodation and a focus on collaborative efforts to create new institutions of international order, to confrontation or even hard bargaining with Beijing.

Indeed, on July 23, 2019 Russia and China engaged in a joint operation to violate airspace claimed by South Korea and Japan in the Sea of Japan.[75] Some more hawkish analysts see this as evidence that Sino-Russian cooperation has passed a major inflection point. As one put it, "The latest incident should not be dismissed as an isolated event. It is further confirmation that a military quasi-alliance between China and Russia is emerging where both countries assist each other in undermining the U.S. and its allies despite the absence of formal commitments to defend each other against attack."[76]

CONCLUSIONS: EXIT FROM ABOVE

It is almost a cliché of international-relations theory to view international orders in terms of a series of great power transitions, where declining hegemons give way to revisionist challengers, often as a result of major power conflict or even hegemonic war. This brief survey of Russian and Chinese post–Cold War activities suggest that these states have targeted key features of the American hegemonic system and the broader international order without directly confronting the United States militarily. By establishing new regional and international infrastructure, challenging liberal democratic architecture, and entering into unilateral assertive foreign policy initiatives, Moscow and Beijing have taken important steps to shape the ecology of international order in line with their own preferences. The ecology of the 1990s—when the US ordering infrastructure was nearly congruent with the overall ecology (recall Figure 2.4)—has given way to a far more crowded and contested ecology of international order (see Figure 4.5).

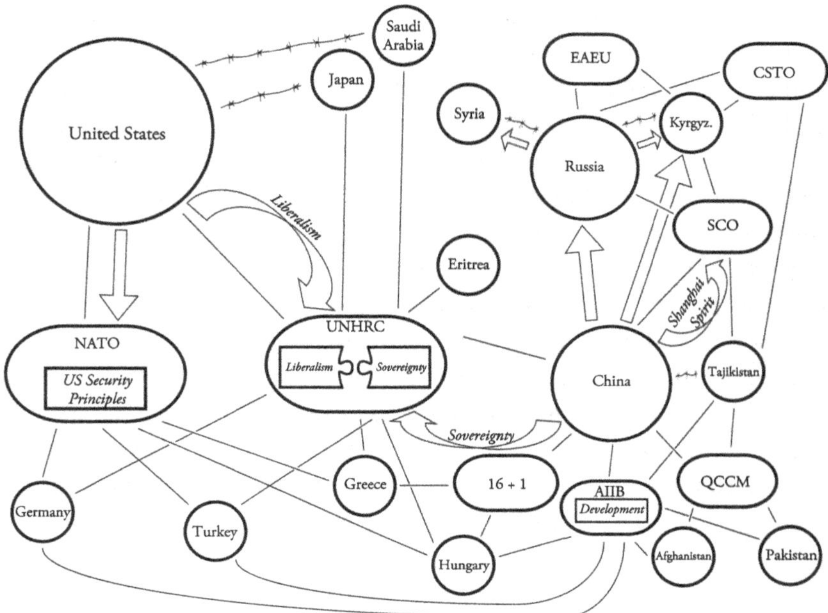

FIGURE 4.5 Ecology with Chinese and Russian Counter-ordering Infrastructure, c. 2019

To be sure, neither Russia nor China has replaced the United States as a new global hegemon. Opinion surveys suggest global skepticism about their revisionist intentions and relatively low public favorability ratings.[77] Nevertheless, the key wager that China and Russia—through their socialization into the rules, institutions, and standards of the international system—would become "responsible stakeholders" that largely accept the ordering principles established by the United States and its allies now appears to have been wrong. American advocates for China's WTO membership in 2000 and the architects of the US-Russia reset policy of 2009 both maintained that through interaction with established international institutions, China and Russia would develop a shared interest in upholding existing pillars of international order. These assumptions appeared to be founded on a 1990s view of the liberal order, where international integration seemed nearly congruent with the expansion of the American hegemonic system.

But, contra such expectations, integration has produced experimentation and adaptation in ways to block and reverse elements of liberal ordering. At times, Russia and China have openly challenged prevailing aspects of international order. But, perhaps much more consequentially, they are also more subtly repurposing its institutions, replacing its norms, and creating parallel institutions that fundamentally alter the interactions and network connections of global governance actors.

This push "from above" by great-power challengers seems to have accelerated since 2014. But it has also been affected by policies and actions of the Trump administration. Washington's *National Security Strategy* of 2017 argued that great-power competition with Russia and China now presented the most pressing threat to US security. The Trump administration's "trade war" with China has underscored, for Moscow and Beijing, the importance of coordinating their responses to the United States.[78]

Yet, these developments are just one of several pathways that have facilitated exit from American hegemony. As we explore in Chapter 5, those smaller countries being courted by emerging global and regional powers play an equally consequential, though perhaps less visible, role.

APPENDIX 1

Post–Cold War China- and Russia-Led International Organizations, End of 2018

Name	Year Founded	Membership (later Members)	Issue Area
Commonwealth of Independent States (CIS)	1991	Russia, Armenia, Azerbaijan, Belarus, Georgia (1994–2009), Kazakhstan, Kyrgyzstan, Moldova, Tajikistan, Uzbekistan	Security
Conference on Interaction and Confidence-Building Measures in Asia (CICA)	1999	Afghanistan, Azerbaijan, Bahrain (2011), Bangladesh (2014), Cambodia (2011), China, Egypt, India, Iraq (2010), Iran, Israel, Jordan (2008), Kazakhstan, Kyrgyz Republic, Pakistan, Palestine, Qatar (2014), Republic of Korea (2006), Russia, Sri Lanka (2018), Tajikistan, Thailand (2006), Turkey, UAE (2008), Uzbekistan, Vietnam (2010)	Security

Name	Year Founded	Membership (later Members)	Issue Area
Forum on China-Africa Cooperation (FOCAC)	2000	China, Algeria, Angola, Benin, Botswana, Burkina Faso, Burundi, Cabo Verde, Cameroon, Central Africa, Chad, Comoros, Congo, Cote d'Ivoire, Djibouti, Egypt, Equatorial Guinea, Eritrea, Ethiopia, Gabon, Gambia, Ghana, Guinea, Guinea-Bissau, Kenya, Lesotho, Liberia, Libya, Madagascar, Malawi, Mali, Mauritania, Mauritius, Morocco, Mozambique, Namibia, Niger, Nigeria, Rwanda, Sao Tome and Principe, Senegal, Seychelles, Sierra Leone, Somalia, South Africa, South Sudan, Sudan, Tanzania, Togo, Tunisia, Uganda, Zambia, Zimbabwe, Commission of the African Union	Various
Shanghai Cooperation Organization (SCO)	2001	China, Russia, Kazakhstan, Kyrgyzstan Tajikistan, Uzbekistan, India (2017), Pakistan (2017)	Security
Asian Cooperation Dialogue (ACD)	2002	Afghanistan (2012), Bahrain, Bangladesh, Brunei Darussalam, Bhutan (2004), Cambodia, China, India, Indonesia, Iran (2004), Japan, Kazakhstan (2003), Republic of Korea, Kuwait (2003), Kyrgyz Republic (2007), Lao PDR, Malaysia, Mongolia (2004), Myanmar, Nepal (2016), Pakistan, Philippines, Oman (2003), Qatar, Russia (2005), Saudi Arabia (2005), Singapore, Sri Lanka (2003), Tajikistan (2006), Thailand, UAE (2004), Uzbekistan (2006), Vietnam, and Turkey (2013)	

Name	Year Founded	Membership (later Members)	Issue Area
Collective Security Treaty Organization (CSTO)	2002	Russia, Armenia, Belarus, Kazakhstan, Kyrgyzstan, Tajikistan, Uzbekistan (2006–2012)	Security
China-Arab States Cooperation Forum (CASCF)	2004	Algeria, Bahrain, Comoros, Djibouti, Egypt, Iraq, Jordan, Kuwait, Lebanon, Libya, Mauritania, Morocco, Oman, Palestine, Qatar, Saudi Arabia, Somalia, Sudan, Syria, Tunisia, UAE, Yemen	Security
Eurasian Development Bank (EDB)	2006	Russia, Armenia, Belarus, Kazakhstan, Kyrgyzstan, and Tajikistan	Development Finance
BRICS	2008	Brazil, Russia, India, China, South Africa (2010)	Various
China-Central Eastern Europe (17 + 1) (China-CEE)	2012	China, Albania, Bosnia and Herzegovina, Bulgaria, Croatia, Czech Republic, Estonia, Hungary, Latvia, Lithuania, Macedonia, Montenegro, Poland, Romania, Serbia, Slovakia, Slovenia	Trade and Investment
China-CELAC Forum (CA-CELAC)	2014	China, Antigua and Barbuda, Argentina, Bahamas, Barbados, Belize, Bolivia, Brazil, Chile, Colombia, Costa Rica, Cuba, Dominica, Ecuador, El Salvador, Guatemala, Grenada, Guyana, Haiti, Honduras, Jamaica, Mexico, Nicaragua, Paraguay, Peru, Panama, Dominican Republic, Saint Kitts and Nevis, Saint Vincent and The Grenadines, St. Lucia, Suriname, Trinidad and Tobago, Venezuela, Uruguay	Trade and Investment
Eurasian Economic Union (EAEU)	2014	Russia, Belarus, Kazakhstan, Armenia, Kyrgyzstan (2015)	Economic Integration

Name	Year Founded	Membership (later Members)	Issue Area
Asian Infrastructure Investment Bank (AIIB)	2015	Afghanistan (2017), Australia, Azerbaijan, Bahrain (2018), Bangladesh, Brazil, Brunei, Cambodia, Canada (2018), China, Cyprus (2018), Denmark, Egypt, Fiji (2017), Finland, France, Georgia, Germany, Hong Kong (China), Hungary (2017), Iceland, Ireland (2017), India, Indonesia, Iran, Israel, Italy, Jordan, Kazakhstan, Kuwait, Kyrgyzstan, Laos, Luxembourg, Madagascar (2018), Malaysia, Maldives, Malta, Mongolia, Myanmar, Nepal, Netherlands, New Zealand, Norway, Oman, Pakistan, Philippines, Poland, Portugal, Qatar, Romania (2018), Republic of Korea (South Korea), Russia, Samoa (2018), Saudi Arabia, Singapore, South Africa, Spain, Sri Lanka, Sudan (2018), Sweden, Switzerland, Tajikistan, Thailand, Timor-Leste (2017), Turkey, UAE, United Kingdom, Uzbekistan, Vanuatu (2018), and Vietnam.	Development Finance
New Development Bank(NDB), formerly BRICS Development Bank	2015	Brazil, Russia, India, China, and South Africa	Development Finance
Lancang-Mekong Cooperation forum (LMC)	2016	China, Cambodia, Laos, Myanmar, Thailand, Vietnam	Water management, Investment
Quadrilateral Cooperation and Coordination Mechanism (QCCM)	2016	China, Afghanistan, Pakistan, Tajikistan	Security

5

Exit from Below

Regime Security, Exit Options, and the Rise of New External Patrons

In the immediate post–Cold War era, the advanced industrialized democracies emerged as the main source of international goods. The United States, Europe, and Japan—either directly or through multilateral institutions such as the IMF and the World Bank—were the main "game in town" for development assistance, access to private capital and wealthy consumer markets, and the provision of other public, club, and private goods. With a few exceptions, such as France in West Africa, the United States appeared to be the only state capable of providing truly credible security guarantees and effectively projecting military power.

As we have already seen, the "unipolar moment," during which the United States could make a credible claim to global hegemony, resulted from three developments. First, Japan, the world's second largest economy, became mired in a "lost decade" of recession and slow economic growth. Second, Germany, the world's third largest economy, had to divert significant political and economic resources to the task of integrating the former German Democratic Republic. Third, the collapse of the Soviet Union, along with the crippling economic and political problems that followed for the Russian Federation, left Washington without a major geopolitical rival.

This last development assured at least a decade of unrivaled American global power. It also robbed the larger community of liberal democracies of a major competitor. The United States and its allies emerged as the only significant source of interstate patronage and global governance.[1] In practice, the resulting American-led "patronage monopoly" on the supply of public, club, and private goods meant that if governments around the world wanted access to emergency finance, development loans, or broader political legitimacy, they would have to subject themselves to liberal ordering. That is, they would need to signal adherence to Western economic and political norms, such as by agreeing to potentially intrusive verification monitors and mechanisms.[2]

It should not be surprising, then, that during the 1990s the conditions imposed by agents of liberal governance become more pronounced. With Communism discredited as a viable alternative, "neoliberal" principles of international economic architecture could proceed unconstrained. The so-called Washington Consensus enshrined free-market orthodoxy and led to significant pressure for trade liberalization, reduced controls on finance, and shrinking government welfare programs.[3] Governments seeking loans from the IMF had little choice but to accede to its strict conditions, as the absence of intense geopolitical competition reduced their leverage over Washington. We see similar dynamics when it comes to pressure on recipients to make progress on corruption, human rights, and democracy.[4] Indeed, scholars find more stringent international financial institution (IFI) conditionality in Africa in the 1990s than during the Cold War, when concerns about US-Soviet geopolitical competition previously shaped decisions on when and how to grant loans to countries in distress.[5]

With the United States and advanced industrialized democracies functioning as a cartel in many arenas of global governance, otherwise reluctant regimes signed and ratified international treaties promoting human, political, and physical-integrity rights. They accepted the presence of international monitors to adjudicate the quality of their elections.[6] The rise of state-based rankings and ratings further entrenched Western norms and standards of governance. These indexes publicly judge states on how they meet liberal criteria in areas like democracy, media freedom, control of corruption, and economic freedom.[7]

Not all countries adhered equally to liberal economic and political principles. Rather, the lack of alternative patrons and norms meant that the United States and other liberal great powers generally enjoyed significant latitude when it came to deciding *when* to make exceptions. Notably,

Washington gave Yeltsin's government in Russia a pass when it came to many dimensions of liberal ordering.[8] But the dynamics of such exceptions and non-enforcement took on different implications during the 1990s from what they had had during the Cold War. Overall, regimes saw few options other than to join the institutions, rules, and arrangements of the expanding "liberal order." At the very least, governments generally had to pay lip service to liberal principles. In doing so, they reinforced the perception of those principles as both natural and universal.

International-relations scholar Steven Krasner reminds us that leaders, elected or otherwise, have long ceded aspects of their sovereignty to external actors when it helps them to make their regimes more secure against foreign threats or domestic challengers.[9] Governments that want to pursue unpopular policies may even find it useful to shift the blame to requirements imposed by international institutions or foreign patrons.[10] In general, however, leaders would prefer to receive unconditional economic, security, trade, or other benefits. External conditions, as well as the intrusive monitoring that often accompanies them, curtail their authority and constrain decision making. Implementing foreign-imposed conditions may signal weakness to domestic public and political opponents. As a result, all else being equal, regimes would rather accept goods that come with minimal strings attached; they would prefer to limit negative externalities and policy concessions associated with receiving international goods.[11]

During the 2000s, governments started to find it easier to reduce their exposure to the American hegemonic system. The rise of alternative patrons—not only China and Russia, but also Saudi Arabia and a number of regional powers—offered new sources of economic patronage, trade relationships, and international development assistance. Often, these were accompanied with reduced pressure for liberal ordering, especially when it came to democratization and neoliberal economic policies. Here, the global financial crisis of 2008 proved especially pivotal. It thrust emerging donors, such as China, into the role of providing emergency credit and development lending. For some recipients, the crisis underscored the perils of accepting the kind of unregulated financial liberalization pushed by Western lenders.[12]

At the same time, shifts in US policy undermined American liberal ordering. That is, the American hegemonic system reduced, sometimes significantly, its commitment to the protection of human rights. After Al-Qaeda's attacks on the United States on September 11, 2001, Washington embarked on a so-called Global War on Terror. American policymakers focused on combating and destroying transnational terrorist networks. To that end, Washington adopted a number of directly illiberal policies, such as the use of "enhanced interrogation techniques" (specific forms of torture) against suspected radicals and "extraordinary renditions" that transferred suspected radicals to authoritarian regimes willing to engage in far more abusive tactics in questioning these individuals. Such policies provided "other governments with a convenient way to justify their own bad behavior" and "with a specific set of practices to emulate." They also undermined the legitimacy of US pressure on other countries to respect human rights.[13]

Moreover, the United States disbursed massive amounts of security assistance, in the name of counterterrorism, that aimed to strengthen the security services of partner countries and to secure cooperation against revolutionary Islamist movements. Soon, non-Western security organizations, such as the Shanghai Cooperation Organization (SCO) or Gulf Cooperation Council (GCC), converged on tackling these same concerns. But they did so in the deliberate absence of any pressures to respect human rights and democratic norms, and even sometimes with the aim of displacing Western powers from their regions. Meanwhile, the 2003 intervention in Iraq without UN authorization, and its disastrous aftermath, underscored that forcible regime change was an extension of US unilateralism and democracy promotion. This, along with the Color Revolutions and, much later, the Arab Spring, convinced many authoritarian powers that the United States was itself a revisionist power when it came to sovereignty norms. Overall, in the 15 years following the September 11 attacks, Washington's policies increased incentives for autocratic powers to seek ways around the American hegemonic system, while (perhaps paradoxically) frequently subordinating human rights and democratization to counterterrorism policy.[14]

In this chapter, we examine how "exit from below" has taken shape after the 1990s. The rise of states interesting in altering international order—ones with little interest in promoting domestic liberal institutions—broke the post–Cold War near-oligopoly over international patronage enjoyed by the advanced industrialized democracies. The existence of new patrons allows recipients of international aid to push back against, and attempt to loosen, many of the kinds of conditions and principles demanded by incumbent donors. And, as we explore at the end of this chapter, these same dynamics play a role in the rise of illiberal, populist leaders within the "core" of the American system.

"Exit from below" dynamics thus pose a challenge to both the American system and liberal ordering, but sometimes in different ways. On face, these dynamics more directly threaten liberal ordering than the American hegemonic system, inasmuch as the American system has never depended on anything resembling a uniform commitment to democratic enlargement and consolidation. To date, core alliances and partnerships in Europe and Asia have remained intact, yet there are warning signs. As we discussed in the previous chapter, Russian influence, driven primarily by connections with illiberal and right-wing parties, is currently on the upswing within some NATO member states. China is nosing around the "soft underbelly" of the American system—states, such as Greece and Italy,[15] that desperately need foreign investment that the United States and the rest of Europe are unwilling or unable to supply. Exit-from-below dynamics play a critical role in the end of the "unipolar moment" as they have enabled China to find partners in its efforts to build an alternative global security infrastructure.

These dynamics clearly attenuate the American hegemonic system at its periphery, and potentially within its core alliances. But their effects on liberal ordering writ large are more complex. We still find broad commitment to multilateral principles of international governance among those taking advantage of shifting bargaining leverage and greater exit options, including those with counter-hegemonic and anti-democratic agendas. This suggests that liberal intergovernmentalism is in better shape than liberal principles concerning democratic institutions.

In 2019, many of the big regional powers, such as Brazil, are governed by politicians who contest aspects of liberal ordering. However, many of these regional powers are not, or not yet, authoritarian states. Thus, while exit-from-below processes already undermine some instruments of liberal ordering, it does not follow that non-Western powers always have or always will eschew democratization and human rights. What we may see, instead, is the emergence of new flavors and configurations of democracy.[16]

REGIONAL ORGANIZATIONS AND REGIME SUPPORT

Throughout the 1990s, Western scholars and policymakers took an optimistic view of the power of regional organizations. They saw them as sources of liberal ordering that promoted democratization and economic integration. Much of that analysis implicitly generalized from the experiences of the European Union and NATO as expanding organizations. Both developed extensive membership conditions that promoted deep and comprehensive institutional reforms. These seemed to socialize aspirant countries into accepting liberal democratic governing principles on issues such as guaranteeing minority rights.[17] Scholars also noted that the EU indirectly prompted liberal ordering in peripheral states. In countries with aspirations to join the EU, its standards provided important focal points for opposition activists and political parties to use in pressuring regimes for being insufficiently democratic, transparent, or European.[18] Thus, many believed that regional organizations served to lock down reforms, socialize elite groups into democratic values, and confer legitimacy on young democratizing regimes.[19]

Over the last 15 years, however, a different pattern has developed. Many governments wield their membership in regional organizations as shields against international criticism. As we saw in the last chapter, regional organizations are now an important part of the toolkit of great-power alternative-order building. The trend toward constructing alternative infrastructure includes both the repurposing of existing organizations and the creation of new ones. For great powers, the development of infrastructure decoupled from the American system offers an important counter-hegemonic power resource. It also provides a way to influence the architecture of regional and international politics in ways that better reflect their interests—especially those with authoritarian regimes.[20] The same is true of those weaker states whose leadership would prefer access to private and club goods without accompanying pressure to crack down on corruption or engage in domestic liberalization.

Protecting Regimes from the Liberal Order in a New Regional Context

Across Latin America, Africa, Eurasia, and the Middle East, the 2000s saw regional organizations play an increasingly prominent role in regional affairs. But their activities often focused on promoting the status and sovereignty of their member states—especially authoritarian ones. Such regional organizations promoted the intergovernmental multilateralism associated with liberal order, but not the domestic political liberalism otherwise baked into the architecture of international politics.

As we noted at the outset, the War on Terror ushered in a much broader global turn to prioritizing security as part of the overall approach to confronting transnational extremist threats. Whereas the 1990s saw a wave of democratization and the diffusion of constitutionalism, the sociologist Kim Lane Scheppele refers to the 2000s as the decade of the global "state of emergency." Regimes across the world exploited counterterrorism to consolidate executive power, expand surveillance capabilities, reduce civil liberties, create new extra-legal processes, and increase informal cooperation among state security services.[21] Regional organizations emerged as crucial players in these trends.

For example, both the 2009 Anti-Terrorism Treaty of the SCO and the Joint Security agreement of the GCC institutionalized previously informal illiberal security practices. These included the adoption of common and overly expansive blacklists of transnational threats, allowing the rapid extradition of suspected terrorists and extremists to other signatories without adequate due-process safeguards, and facilitating cooperation among regional internal security services in the absence of safeguards against abuse.[22] In both cases, the agreements also allow for the criminalization of criticisms of one member-state regime by people located in a different member state.[23] In this sense, regional organizations play a sometimes underappreciated role in extra-territorial authoritarianism: the trend of authoritarian governments deploying repressive practices against people living abroad, whether their own citizens or citizens of another country.[24]

Moreover, regional great powers sometimes prove reluctant to use their newfound positions of leadership to criticize the domestic practices of other countries in their region. On the contrary, countries like South Africa, Saudi Arabia, and Russia often close ranks with human-rights abusers or authoritarian regimes in their regions. In doing so, they reaffirm principles of sovereignty and domestic non-interference. For example, in May 2005 the EU imposed targeted sanctions on the government of Uzbekistan for the brutal crackdown by its security services on protestors in the city of Andijon. Moscow vigorously supported the actions of the Karimov regime. Tashkent expelled the US military, which had established an airbase in support of its operations in Afghanistan, as well as a number of Western NGOs. Uzbekistan then openly re-aligned with Russia by joining the CSTO.[25] This, in turn, gave Tashkent significant leverage over the United States when, in 2008, it agreed to become part of a new a supply route for Afghanistan, the

Northern Distribution Network. The United States sent substantial transit fees to the Uzbek government and refrained from pressuring Tashkent when it came to matters of domestic governance.

To take another example, in the wake of the Arab Spring in 2010, Saudi Arabia led an intervention in Bahrain. It invoked GCC security agreements as its military rolled in to support the beleaguered ruling regime in Manama against democratic and sectarian political protests.[26] In these and other cases, regional organizations help shield and support autocratic regimes against external, and especially Western, criticisms and sanctions.

Political developments after 2004 show the limits of even the EU's capability to consolidate liberal governance within its member states; the Eurozone crisis, triggered by the 2008 financial crisis, revealed significant structural problems in the EU. As the EU prepared for the 2004 expansion, which admitted 10 new states (with Romania and Bulgaria following in 2008), it configured much of its bureaucracy in Brussels around the process of accession negotiations and overseeing the implementation of *acquis communautaire*—the 20,000 pages of social, economic, and political conditions required of EU member states—by aspirant countries.

However, the power of EU conditionality severely attenuated once countries joined the organization. The rise to power of right-wing nationalists in Poland, Hungary, and the Czech Republic—and their subsequent targeting of the media, judiciary, and civil society—exposed deep problems with the tools available to the EU to enforce its standards on existing members. To date it has been unable to sanction Hungary in the face of Poland's ability to veto those sanctions.

The Eurozone crisis of 2010, which saw Greece nearly expelled from the Eurozone, unleashed anti-EU populist movements in southern member states. These groups promised a more confrontational stance against Brussels and its strict budgetary rules. The results of the Brexit referendum in June 2016—in which a narrow majority of UK citizens vote to leave the EU—demonstrated that the domestic political power of nationalist appeals based on anti-immigration platforms can score majorities or pluralities even in the most consolidated European democracies. Though the EU is by no means in danger of falling apart, populist movements commonly take anti-EU stances. Bashing the EU, often while benefiting from its policies and subsidies, has proven a successful political strategy for many political parties.

The Rise of Regime-Protecting Shadow Regional Election Observers

The area of election observation provides a striking illustration of how regional organizations have weakened liberal ordering by shielding regimes from international assessment and opprobrium. A few specialized groups, such as the Carter Center, traditionally provided election observers. They did their best to make sure that observers were well trained in evaluating both short-term concerns—such as polling day access, abuse of administrative resources, and tabulation integrity—and longer-term ones, such as whether governments created a highly unequal media environment.

In the 1990s, the monitoring of elections by outside observers rapidly became an international norm. Even insincere authoritarians accepted incursions on their sovereignty to host external observers.[27] In the post-Communist sphere, the newly constituted Office for Democratic and Human Rights initiatives (ODHIR), an autonomous division within the Organization for Security and Cooperation in Europe (OSCE), sent election observers to every national election among countries in the OSCE. It provided summary reports and assessment about whether the elections had been "free and fair."

But the onset of the Color Revolutions in the mid-2000s led authoritarian and autocratically inclined leaders to see the ODHIR, and other comparable observers, as threats to their power. In all three successful Color Revolutions (Georgia in 2003, Ukraine in 2004–2005, and Kyrgyzstan in 2005), ODIHR observation missions declared that the elections had not been "free and fair" and, in doing so, sent clear signals that helped the opposition mobilize against and topple incumbent regimes.[28]

In response, beginning in the mid-2000s, member states began curtailing the size and scope of ODHIR missions. Some refused to admit the group's observers altogether. Within the OSCE, Russia and a number of supportive countries tried to implement organizational changes designed to reduce the threat posed by election monitors to their regimes. These included transferring the right to appoint the head of the mission from the Warsaw ODIHR office to the OSCE assembly and requiring ODHIR missions to make their recommendations about elections in consultation with the host government. These efforts went beyond contesting liberal ordering from within existing liberal infrastructure. Governments also increased the number of international observers and invited observer missions from other regional organizations. In Eurasia, both the CIS and the SCO began to send election observation teams in 2003.[29] These regional mission assessments, of course, proved far more favorable to host regimes than those of the ODIHR; from 2003 through 2018, ODHIR and CIS/SCO observers only agreed that one national election, the 2010 election of Viktor Yanukovych in Ukraine, was fair. With all others, they reached divergent conclusions.

Increasing regional monitors diluted the assessments and dulled the criticisms of more seasoned monitors like those authorized by ODIHR. In a classic instance of the "multiple principals problem," with more sources of external monitoring issuing verdicts, a regime can pick and choose the supportive and positive comments among these different observers.[30] The trend of regional organizations signing off on obviously flawed elections in member countries has gone global. Regional organizations such as the CIS and SCO (Eurasia), the Community of Latin American and Caribbean States (CELAC), the Bolivarian Alliance for the Peoples of Our America (Latin America), and the AU and Economic Community of West African States (Africa) have all given the seal of approval to elections that their liberal counterparts argued were fundamentally flawed.

Not content with how the entrance of election teams from more regional organizations make it difficult for other observers to send clear signals about electoral impropriety, some regimes now encourage (and likely fund) new "zombie monitors" or "shadow observers."[31] According to political scientist Lee Morgenbesser, these shadow groups come from nongovernmental or intergovernmental bodies mostly comprising authoritarian states, do not subscribe to the UN Declaration of Principles on International Observation, and tend to issue favorable comments on elections in the international media.[32] From Uganda to Cambodia to Kazakhstan, autocratic regimes increasingly deploy shadow monitors strategically to confer international legitimacy on even the most blatantly flawed elections.[33] For example, the 2013 presidential elections in Azerbaijan were monitored by over 40 international election monitors, with only the ODIHR issuing a critical statement of obviously unfree and unfair elections.[34] Moreover, some governments are also drawing on observers from authoritative-sounding regional groups to validate otherwise internationally controversial referenda. For example, in March of 2014 the Kremlin used a hastily convened referendum to justify its annexation of the Crimea. It invited in, and received a favorable evaluation from, a group of pro-Russian parliamentarians from EU countries as well as observers from the Eurasian Observatory for Democracy and Elections—a group that denounces the "monitoring missions of Western international organizations" and is committed to a "multipolar world."[35]

In sum, in the 1990s, international election observation became a robust global norm. Specialized, expert, and usually impartial monitors worked to ensure that elections were free and fair. By the mid-2010s, autocratic regimes had found ways to hollow out the norm by rigging not just elections but also the pool of monitors evaluating them. Many of these monitors came from regional organizations, which thus helped to shield their member states against liberal ordering.

NEW PATRONS AND PUBLIC GOODS SUBSTITUTION

A second significant process in the unraveling of American global hegemony and contestation of liberal ordering involves the rise of alternative patrons capable of supplying economic and security assistance. Charles Kindleberger, one of the founders of modern hegemonic-stability theory, argued that leading powers help stabilize the global economy by discharging "public goods" and other governance functions. These include providing emergency financing and countercyclical lending.[36] While the 1990s saw a near monopoly over global development finance by US-backed IFIs, in the 2000s the situation changed as new emerging donors, such as China, Saudi Arabia, and Turkey, entered the international development arena.

The rise of the so-called non-Development Assistance Committee members (non-DAC) lenders ignited controversy among policy analysts. The foreign policy commentator Moises Naim coined the term "rogue aid" to refer to the emergence of these alternative donors. He argued that their politically motivated lending, which lacked conditions associated with liberal ordering, was working to support authoritarianism and state-led cronyism in developing countries.[37] Defenders of the new emerging donors took issue with Naim's stylized depiction of Western lenders as principled and credible.[38] They pointed out that long-standing IFIs, like the World Bank and Asian Development Bank, no longer could cover the infrastructure needs of the developing world.[39]

Soon, the theme of illiberal lending and its possible promotion of authoritarianism began to animate academic debates and policy discussions, especially in the context of China's role as a major lender in Africa. Books explored the differences between Chinese and Western aid negotiations on the continent. Some compared the West's tendency to impose its assumptions and conditions on recipients to Beijing's more iterative and demand-based approach with respect to tailoring aid packages to specific government wishes—what Halpern coined as the contrasting "Beijing Consensus."[40]

From a bottom-up perspective, it is of little surprise that regimes all around the world have increasingly embraced non-Western donors. Critics have long targeted IFIs such as the IMF, World Bank, and the Asian Development Bank for their insistence on politically damaging economic conditions that starve the public sector for funds, even as the need to build public infrastructure becomes increasingly pressing.[41] Regardless of China's intentions to compete as a donor, and well before the announcement of the BRI in 2013, Beijing's overseas lending and investment started to provide financing to cash-strapped regimes that were unable or unwilling to turn to the West.

Chinese Aid and Regime Substitution Effects

More recently, researchers have explored some of the political consequences of Chinese and non-traditional lenders in the developing world. The task has been difficult, both because China does not release detailed data of its foreign aid disbursements and because distinguishing between Chinese Official development assistance (ODA)-type aid and investments can be difficult. Nevertheless, the availability of more comprehensive data—most notably the crowd-sourced AidData initiative at William & Mary[42]—has generated a number of important new studies that explore more systematically some of the previously reported domestic political effects of Chinese lending. The results are both striking and broadly consistent with our observation that regimes and leaders are increasingly pursuing external substitution strategies for political and personal advantage. The availability of Chinese credit provides otherwise weak and politically vulnerable regimes with a new external source of support and even diluting the conditionality of Western aid itself in competitive settings.

First, recent Chinese aid is more likely than Western lending to be used by rulers for patronage purposes. A common observation among both critics and defenders of Chinese aid is that borrowing governments have a greater say in both the types of funds received and the allocation of those funds. In practice, greater agency over aid allocation means that leaders will use funds to shore up their bases of political support and award projects to supportive regions, co-ethnics, and political clients. In an innovative study of the geographical allocation of Chinese assistance to 117 African leaders of 47 countries over the period of 2000–2012, researchers found that the Chinese lending principles that privilege sovereignty and non-interference permit African rulers to allocate Chinese funding to their birth regions—the volume of such funding triples after they assume power.[43] By contrast, the authors found no comparable local allocation effects in the case of World Bank projects within the same countries, leading the authors to conclude that "when provided with the discretion to do so, African leaders seem to play favorites by allocating substantial additional resources to their home constituents to the detriment of citizens who face greater economic need."[44]

Second, the availability of Chinese aid is more likely to stabilize incumbent regimes and even help them remain in power in the face of domestic conflict. A dramatic illustration of this dynamic occurred in 2009 when the government of Sri Lanka effectively concluded a 25-year civil war by emphatically defeating the Tamil group LTTE; at the time, China had assumed the position of Colombo's main external donor—just a few years after it had been cut off by Western donors over concerns of human rights violations by the government in its counterinsurgency campaign.[45]

The Chinese aid-substitution effect especially matters in light of evidence that the sudden withdrawal of Western aid in conflict settings tends to generate political shocks and increase conflict.[46] In a cleverly designed paper, a team of political scientists replicated this study, but added Chinese aid that had not been included in the original dataset.[47] They found that Chinese lending actually mitigated the political shocks associated with Western aid withdrawal; the availability of Chinese substitute aid "reduces the ability of Western donors to intentionally weaken governments that have chosen to pursue policies which do not fall in line with Western policy preferences."[48]

More broadly, cross-regional studies of "illiberal peace building" have explored how, in areas such as Central Asia and Africa, emerging donors like Russia and China have promoted alternative norms and arrangements to the Western-led consensus on liberal peace in post-conflict settings. These have helped governments to consolidate their control over the political system, monopolize economic resources and revenue streams, promote the rule of the dominant ethnic minority, and secure control over the domestic flow of information.[49]

Third, Chinese aid projects appear to fuel local corruption, especially in comparison to Western IFIs, though they often also simultaneously promote economic development. In Central Asia, Chinese highway projects have been the source of high-profile corruption scandals in Tajikistan, where in 2010 a mysterious British Virgin Islands–registered company with ties to the president's family began collecting tolls from a Chinese-built national highway just after its completion,[50] and in Kyrgyzstan, where in 2016 Prime Minister Temir Sariyev resigned after a parliamentary commission found that his government had rigged a $100 million road tender in favor of the Chinese recipient.[51]

More broadly, economists Ann-Sofie Isaksson and Andreas Kotsadam have explored the issue of corruption by matching geolocated Chinese aid projects in 29 African countries from 2000 to 2012 with over 98,000 respondents to the Afrobarometer surveys on corruption perceptions.[52] Strikingly, they found more widespread corruption within 50 kilometers of active Chinese project sites (measured by increased likelihood to pay a bribe to a policeman or to secure a license or document) as opposed to not yet active sites, as well as more accepting local attitudes toward corruption; they found no such effects for areas surrounding geocoded World Bank sites, even in areas with increased economic activity, leading them to argue that the presence of Chinese projects may legitimize increased local corruption, possibly as a result of the transmission of China's non-interference norm (as opposed to simply the economic benefits created by the projects).[53]

Along these lines, a team of researchers conducted an in-depth study of local perceptions of corruption in Chinese and World Bank projects in Tanzania that found spillover effects from Chinese projects. Although Chinese development projects are associated with higher local levels of corruption that World Bank projects, the co-location of Chinese and World Bank projects within 40 kilometers of each other increases perceptions of corruption in both, leading to a possible "fog of aid" effects in which the clustering of multiple projects weakens anti-corruption norms in general.[54]

Finally, we now have strong evidence, both case-based and quantitative, that the presence of Chinese lending impacts the degree of Western IFI conditionality, leading to a "race to the bottom" in competitive country settings. Sometimes analysts call this dynamic the "Angola effect," after the 2006 case in which the Angolan government broke off negotiations with the IMF at the last minute and, instead, chose to accept a loan from China, backed by Angolan oil sales, with less stringent conditions.[55] A study by economist Diego Hernandez examined the effects of new donor (mainly China) lending to countries with World Bank projects in 54 African countries over the period of 1980–2013.[56] Strikingly, he found that the World Bank provided loans with significantly fewer conditions in countries that were also the recipients of Chinese aid. By contrast, World Bank conditionality was rarely affected by the entrance of other Western or Developmental Assistance Committee donors, though he found that after the year 2000 borrowers that were allies of or of strategic interest to the United States received fewer conditions. But conditions attached to aid became stricter when new UK and French donors entered a country, most likely as a result of improved Western aid coordination.[57] Moreover, despite countries' potential bargaining disadvantages and problems in repayment, Hernandez found that the lowest-income countries that received Chinese aid were most strongly associated with the World Bank's making its project conditions less stringent.

Though most of this new research has studied Chinese aid and projects, similar effects with respect to substitution and regime support may also apply to other non-DAC or emerging donors. For example, following the Arab Spring and the ouster of long-time president and US ally Hosni Mubarak in Egypt, the government of Mohamed Morsi forestalled negotiating a financing package with the IMF that would have imposed domestically unpopular cuts in public expenditures by courting, soliciting, and receiving over $10 billion in emergency financing from Gulf lenders Qatar and the UAE. We show the international ordering effects of goods substitution—in the realms of election observation and development and financial assistance—in Figures 5.1 and 5.2.

The Financial Crisis and the Emergence of Loans-for-Energy Deals

Of all its activities in the developing world, China's pursuit of energy and natural resources generates perhaps the most controversy. In a bid to secure reliable supplies of oil and gas, China has extended concessional loans, secured by energy suppliers, to many countries. These lending practices effectively fuse the roles of investor and development assistance provider; but Chinese energy loans, in practice, also have allowed recipient governments

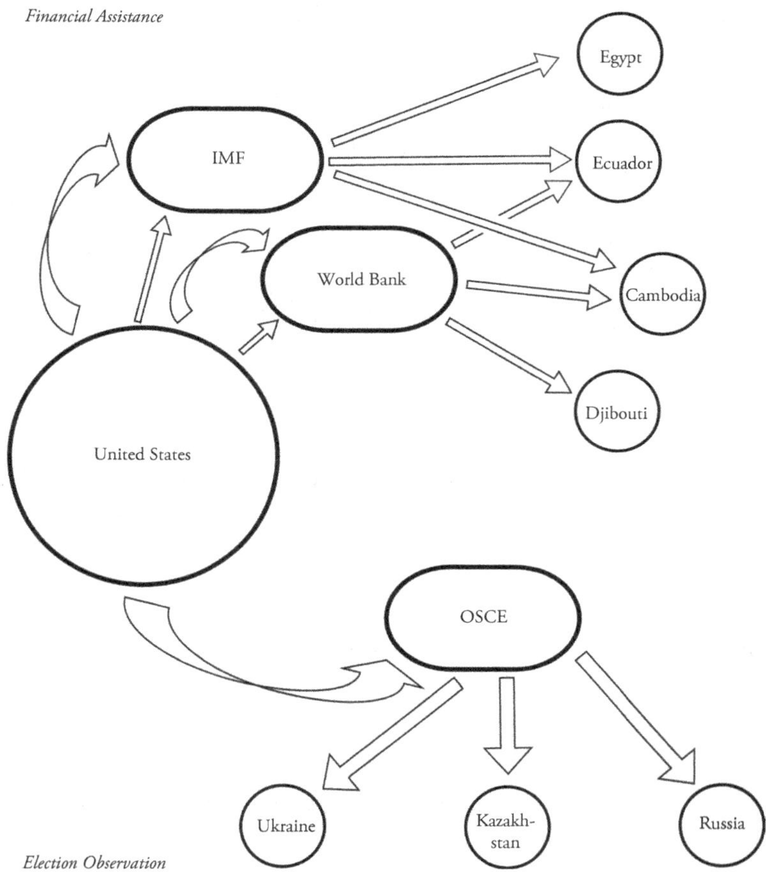

FIGURE 5.1 US Monopoly Patronage of the 1990s

to turn away from Western-backed sources of credit. The global financial crisis of 2008 proved pivotal for China as a "global governance" actor as it thrust China into the role of a "countercyclical lender," providing substantial financing packages to struggling energy-rich countries during this sharp economic downturn.

Consider the case of China's loans-for-energy deals that it concluded in 2008–2009 with six different countries at the peak of the global financial crisis, three in Latin America (Brazil, Ecuador, and Venezuela) and three in Eurasia (Kazakhstan, Russia, and Turkmenistan). The estimated total of these deals (see Table 5.1) was about $85 billion (rising to $107 billion with an additional $22 billion extended to Venezuela from 2011 to 2015),

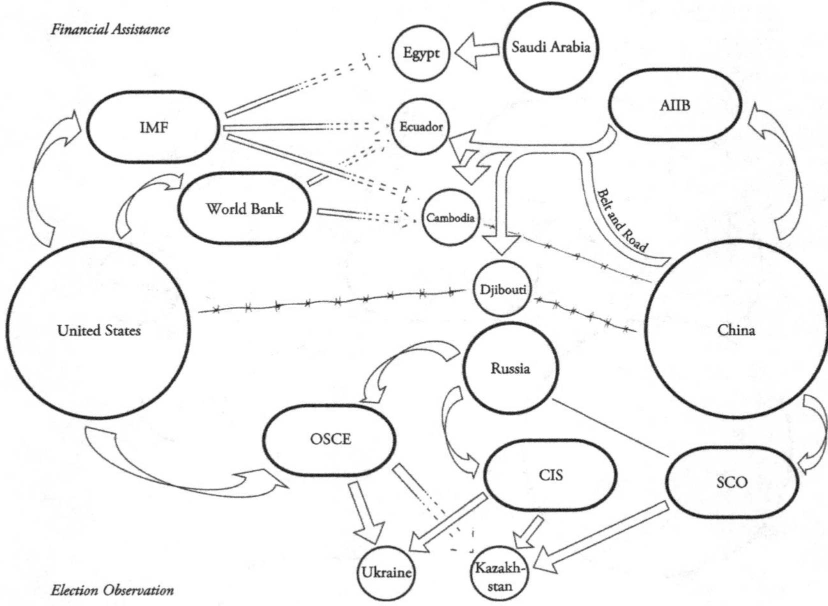

FIGURE 5.2 Alternative Patrons and Asset Substitution, c. 2019

financed mostly by the China Development Bank on behalf of Chinese state energy companies. All six of the repayment arrangements reportedly included guarantees that recipients would export a certain volume of energy or transfer energy assets to China.[58]

Unlike pure "investments," these Chinese loans also functioned as a practical alternative source of global governance, shielding these borrowers from the shocks of the financial crisis and the pressures of having to turn to Western sources of lending. Russia now stands as the largest recipient of Chinese aid and concessionary financing, having received over $36 billion since 2000. Of that, $25 billion took the form of a loan in 2009 from the China Development Bank to Transneft, the Russian state-owned oil pipeline operator, while a 2010 loans-for-coal project provided an additional $6 billion;[59] the rest was injected into various Russian banks to support them during the financial downturn, removing the need for them to turn to Western financing.[60]

In December 2008, President Rafael Correa of Ecuador, prior to his courting of Chinese loans, actually defaulted on payments of his country's international bonds worth $3.9 billion.[61] Soon after the default, China

TABLE 5.1 China's Energy-Related Loan Agreements in Eurasia and Latin America, 2008–2010

Country Recipient	Borrower	Chinese Issuer	Amount ($ Billions)	Repayment Structure
Eurasia				
Kazakhstan	KazMunaiGaz, Kazakh Development Bank	CNPC, Exim Bank	10 (5 + 5)	Not energy supply backed; CNPC $5 billion for joint acquisition w/ KazMunaiGaz of MangistauMunaiGas
Russia	Rosneft, Transneft	Chinese Development Bank (CDB)	25	Oil sales of 180,000 barrels per day (bpd) and 120,000 bpd, December 2011–December 2030
Turkmenistan	Turkmengaz	CDB	8	Unknown
Latin America				
Brazil	Petrobras	CDB	10	150,000 bpd year 1, 200,000 bpd years 2–10
Ecuador	Ministry of Finance	Petrochina	1	36,000 bpd for 4 years
Venezuela	Bandes	CDB	30.5	Various supply contracts

Sources: Erica Downs, *Inside China, Inc: China's Development Bank's Cross-border Energy Deals* (Washington, DC: Brookings, 2011), 38–57; https://www.wsj.com/articles/venezuela-oil-loans-go-awry-for-china-1434656360; https://www.wsj.com/articles/SB123996097676128865.

provided an emergency $1 billion and subsidized the Ecuadorian budget through additional loans. By the end of 2018, the small Latin American country had racked up over $6.5 billion in debt for which it had promised 90 percent of its oil production in repayment.[62]

Similarly, the isolated and autocratic state of Turkmenistan concluded two successive loans-for-energy deals with China in 2009 and 2010. These promised a share of its natural gas output in exchange for $8 billion in stabilization funds. The Central Asian state, ineligible for IMF borrowing, had been in discussion with German banks for private financing prior to the deal. Very shortly after, Turkmenistan became a key energy supplier for Beijing, as China National Petroleum Corporation concluded a production-sharing agreement for developing the second largest natural gas field in the world, which would augment the Turkmen supply exported through the Central Asia-China pipeline, inaugurated in 2009.[63] Almost immediately, Turkmenistan became one of the most dependent countries in the world on Chinese trade, effectively replacing its previous reliance on the old Soviet-era pipeline operated by the Russian gas giant Gazprom with its new Chinese partnership.[64] In all of these energy-for-loans cases, regardless of Chinese intentions, the recipient regimes used the availability of Chinese funds to either shun or substitute for Western sources of financing.

These energy deals also reveal the selective but significant geography of China's foray into providing international aid and credit. In Africa, China remains engaged across the whole continent; since 2012, it has become the single most important outside creditor. In Latin America, Beijing has selectively targeted certain regimes—mostly energy or natural resource producers—for partnership.[65] Not coincidentally, Venezuela, Ecuador, and Bolivia also were governed by left-leaning populists who openly criticized the West and sought to demonstrate to their publics that they could secure new international partnerships. By 2013 and the announcement of the Belt and Road Initiative, China had secured partnership with its immediate neighbors by becoming the most important creditor to Russia, Pakistan, Myanmar, Laos, and the bordering Central Asian states of Tajikistan, Kyrgyzstan, and Kazakhstan.

China wasn't the only emerging powers that tried to use the economic downturn of the financial crisis to their political advantage by offering development funds and other goods to regional neighbors they hoped to influence. Although it was itself badly hit by the financial crisis, Russia attempted to assert its geopolitical influence in the post-Soviet space by offering emergency lending packages to Belarus and Kyrgyzstan, the former in an effort to convince Minsk to recognize the Georgian breakaway republics of Abkhazia and South Ossetia and the latter in a bid to shut down the US military base at Manas airport; both efforts proved ultimately unsuccessful.[66]

In Latin America, the government of Hugo Chávez initiated a number of international foreign aid and barter arrangements with countries including providing oil-based assistance to Bolivia, Dominica, Cuba, Honduras, and Nicaragua. Cuba, which at its peak received $1 billion in

Venezuelan oil a year, in return provided medical, educational, and military assistance to Venuzuela.[67] In 2004, a group of left populist governments in Latin America, led by Chávez, founded the explicit anti-American bloc ALBA—including Venezuela, Cuba, and Bolivia—with the purpose of promoting selective integration and economic cooperation as an alternative to a US-dominated Latin American free trade area. The Venezuelan president courted and forged closer relations with Cuba, China, and Russia, visibly embracing the onset of a multipolar world.[68] And in the Middle East, the onset of the Arab Spring so alarmed the monarchic states of the Gulf, that they initiated their own economic assistance programs in a bid to halt the spread of popular protests and stabilize threatened regimes.

Goods Substitution and the Rise of New Global Security Arrangements

The rise of alternative patrons also constitutes a distinct pathway for understanding how China and other emerging powers are likely to challenge the military and security dominance and global reach of the US military. In Chapter 4, we noted that Russia and China have sought to blunt a number of long-standing American alliances and transatlantic institutions by creating their own regional organizations. However, US global military primacy is predicated on a much wider network. It includes a number of basing and access arrangements with countries that are not traditional allies or members of the Western security system. In these cases, US planners often have to provide rent, club goods, or other forms of informal quid pro quos (logistical arrangements that benefit host regimes) in order to secure continued access. For example, during the Cold War the United States regularly pressured international financial institutions like the IMF and World Bank to extend loans and credits to the Philippines which, under Ferdinand Marcos, was a crucial host of US military facilities.[69]

This type of competitive bidding for security allegiances occurred frequently during the Cold War, when the United States and the Soviet Union regularly provided side payments of economic aid, security assistance, and political support to clients in the Third World in exchange for loyalty and military access. Historian Radoslav Yordanov shows how Moscow's policy toward the Horn of Africa not only offered Soviet economic and security assistance in its efforts to woo local regimes but also connected these African regimes with the educational, informational, economic, and cultural outreach efforts of its Eastern Bloc allies.[70]

In the immediate post–Cold War era, the United States closed a number of overseas facilities and reduced its base-related expenditures. However, after September 11, 2001, US planners concluded a number of new security and access arrangements to support the Global War on Terror (GWOT). These included agreements with the Central Asian states of Uzbekistan and Kyrgyzstan, and the establishment of a large facility for its new United States Afrian Command (AFRICOM) center in Djibouti. These facilities were smaller in size than the main overseas bases in Germany and Japan, but also less institutionalized and more vulnerable to the whims of their hosts and broader political crosscurrents.

In fact, the United States faced access denials and evictions from several hosts in the 2000s. Some US observers described these examples of "soft-balancing."[71] But a closer look reveals that in almost all cases an alternative patron either threatened to withdraw ongoing assistance or offered the host government a new package that met or exceeded American support.[72] In Kyrgyzstan, President Kurmanbek Bakiyev initiated a base-bidding war in 2009 between the United States and Russia, during which he secured the promise of a $2.1 billion economic package from Moscow in exchange for closing Manas. But after he received a transfer of $300 million from Moscow, he concluded a new deal with the United States that raised the base's annual rent from $17 to $63 million a year.

Uzbekistan evicted the United States in July 2005 following a government crackdown on protestors in the eastern city of Andijon. In the aftermath of the protest, US officials criticized the actions of the Uzbek government, while Russia and China publicly voiced strong support. In 2007, Ecuadoran President Correa refused to renew the 10-year lease of the US military at Manta after his government secured an offer from a Hong Kong–based firm to renovate the nearby port and its surrounding facilities.

From this more "bottom-up" perspective, we see instructive similarities in China's recent acquisition of formal overseas basing and access relationships. These appear connected to offers of broader packages of club and private goods to base hosts. China inaugurated its first formal overseas military base in August 2017 in the small Horn of Africa state of Djibouti, also the site of Camp Lemonnier, the main US military hub in Africa. Though Washington objected to the Djiboutian government prior to this agreement, China's economic largess seems to have been the determining factor in securing basing rights, with the Export-Import Bank of China offering over $1 billion in loans to Djibouti and 40 percent of new major infrastructure project financing.[73]

The Chinese presence appears to mix support of security and commercial interests, but the acquisition in early 2019 of the Port of Doraleh by China Merchants Port Holdings raised additional concern that China could effectively block the transit of supplies bound for the US base.[74] Similarly, in Pakistan, China has augmented its $62 billion investment in the high-profile China-Pakistan Economic Corridor and reportedly secured port access for the Chinese navy to Gwadar in a secretive basing deal.[75] Port access has also been accompanied by the Pakistani government's agreement to build a network of Chinese satellite stations within the country to support the Beidou Navigation System, a Chinese-built alternative to the US Global Positioning System network.[76]

In early 2019, an investigative story revealed that China has maintained a security presence in Tajikistan since 2016;[77] not coincidentally, during this time period, Chinese aid and assistance to Tajikistan increased dramatically. A subsequent report revealed that Tajik authorities had also ceded to Chinese troops the right to patrol different swaths of territory on the Tajik-Afghan border.[78]

But perhaps Cambodia provides the most revealing illustration of how Chinese basing rights might be entangled with development assistance and goods provision. In July 2019, several international news outlets published investigative stories of a secret agreement between the Cambodian and Chinese governments to allow the Chinese navy exclusive access for 30 years to a refurbished naval base at Ream, on the Gulf of Thailand.[79]

The port would increase Chinese capacity to enforce its territorial claims in the South China Sea. The agreement also includes granting access to the Chinese military to use a new large airport at Dara Sakor, 40 kilometers away from Ream, whose construction was also completed by a Chinese company. One report includes comments from US defense officials that pressing Cambodia for human rights improvement made American security partnership less attractive for Cambodia's authoritarian government than alignment with China.[80]

Still, Cambodia's marked move away from relying on Western-backed and multilateral creditors also appears to be an important enabling condition for the new Chinese security accord: whereas in 2007 Cambodia's debt to multilateral creditors constituted 63 percent of its total external debt, by

2017, as Chinese lending and investment became dominant, that percentage had plummeted to just 16 percent. Similarly, in the other three identified Chinese base hosts—Pakistan, Djibouti, and Tajikistan—overall multilateral debt had peaked in the mid-2000s and by 2017 had dropped to just 19 percent in Tajikistan, 29 percent in Djibouti, and 32 percent in Pakistan, from highs, respectively, of 56 percent, 62 percent, and 48 percent.[81]

These facilities provide China with a formal security presence. At the same time, Beijing seems to be globalizing its security footprint by gaining access and transit rights to facilities that it denies serve a strategic purpose. Chinese state-owned companies have begun upgrading or constructing new facilities in a series of strategic ports across the Indian Ocean, including in Sri Lanka, Malaysia, and Bangladesh. In all of these cases the Chinese government denied that it intended to use these facilities for military purposes. In the disputed South China Sea, Beijing has recently announced a number of completed Chinese construction projects. For example, the Chinese Ministry of Transport has referred to a newly constructed runway and facility in Fiery Cross reef, part of the disputed Spratly Islands in the South China Sea, as a "Maritime Rescue Facility."[82]

In sum, viewing security partnership from the perspective of goods substitution and regime survival suggests that Moscow and Beijing already have developed more global infrastructures than what an exclusive focus on military cooperation agreements or alliances might imply. In fact, Beijing's recent moves to bundle economic sources of cooperation with its strategic presence agreements is consistent with how the United States has sought to obtain and maintain military access outside of its enduring military allies.

THE RISE OF MULTIPOLAR POPULISM

Regimes are now more willing to defect from association with aspects of liberal international order and embrace patrons that can provide new sources for substitute goods. At the same time, we see the rise of regimes that combine both fiery strongman populism domestically with open skepticism of liberal international order—what we refer to as "multipolar populism."

According to political scientist Jan Werner Müller, contemporary populists combine identity-based claims to political authority with anti-elite with anti-pluralist appeals. They attempt to hijack the state apparatus and use it for the purposes of clientelism—as opposed to impartial representation.[83]

We agree, but note that such accounts miss the foreign-policy dimensions of contemporary populism. In particular, populist leaders identify prevailing international liberal rules, norms, and values as a domestic threat. They point to alternative international goods providers as better partners who will help preserve the strength and cultural integrity of the nation. Indeed, populists actually signal international strength by explicitly rejecting international liberal order and playing up their relationships with illiberal providers of international patronage.

Consider the foreign policy trajectories of three such multipolar populist regimes—Prime Minister Viktor Orbán of Hungary (since 2004), President Recep Tayyip Erdoğan of Turkey (since 2002), and President Rodrigo Duterte of the Philippines (since 2016). All three of these rulers are overt about their illiberalism. They also have, at one point or another, used public statements about potential, or actual, foreign-policy realignment to signal their political strength and their stewardship of national sovereignty.

These countries are otherwise strikingly different from one another. Hungary is a post-Communist country that was absorbed into the first wave of transatlantic expansions of liberal ordering (joined NATO in 1998 and the EU in 2004). Turkey has been a member of NATO since 1952 and emphasized its Western orientation for most of its Cold War and some of its post–Cold War history. The Philippines is a former Pacific colony of the United States. Since attaining independence in 1946 it retained close security and economic ties with Washington. Yet, by the later 2010s, all three of these states are actively hedging their association with the West in similar ways.

All three leaders have targeted prominent domestic political opponents, dismantled or sought to undermine the judiciary and other institutions of accountability, and tried to intimidate or neutralize independent mass media that could otherwise scrutinize their practices. Orbán made significant waves with a 2014 speech in which he announced that his government was actively building an "illiberal state" within the EU.[84] After five years of steady democratic backsliding, in 2019 Freedom House downgraded the political status of Hungary from "Free" to "Partly Free."[85]

In Turkey, Erdoğan's steady consolidation of power accelerated following a failed coup attempt in summer 2016, which he attributed to military members loyal to the exiled cleric Fethullah Gülen. A narrow victory in an April 2017 constitutional referendum followed. It gave the presidency almost complete control over the parliament.[86]

Duterte, the long-serving mayor of the island of Mindanao, won the 2016 presidential election on the explicit promise to act as a strongman; he pledged to eradicate corruption and the drug trade. His tenure as mayor, as well as president, has been associated with the creation of death squads and rampant extra-judicial killings.[87] In addition, like his illiberal counterparts in Turkey and Hungary, Duterte has targeted civil society groups and imprisoned journalists that publish pieces critical of his presidency.[88]

Asserting Multipolarism as Defending Sovereignty

Multipolar populists publicly reject liberal elements of international order for the same reasons that they appeal to illiberal principles domestically—they argue that the rules, norms, and institutions of liberal order impose unnecessary constraints on their regimes and place conditions on their sovereignty that reflect alien interests and influences. In turn, all these leaders have turned toward authoritarian power as either possible or actual alternative patrons, while invoking them as models for their regimes. They therefore publicly portray breaking free from the constraints of liberalism as a means of upholding national self-determination; they dismiss external criticism of their democratic backsliding as attacks on national sovereignty.

Orbán's own embrace of illiberalism includes the claim that democratic societies can no longer compete economically. He has argued that Hungary should look outside of the EU—including to China, Russia, Turkey, and Singapore—for potential role models that are neither liberal nor democratic.[89] Similarly, at a German investment forum, Orbán pointed to Beijing as an alternative patron to Brussels, commenting that "if the European Union cannot provide financial support, we will turn to China."[90]

President Erdoğan has overseen a similar transformation, steering Turkey away from Western ordering infrastructure and toward cooperating with other emerging powers. Moscow and Ankara have increasingly coordinated efforts in Syria, both anticipating a division of regional influence after Trump suddenly announced the withdrawal of US forces in October 2019. The Turkish president also infuriated US officials and lawmakers by defiantly purchasing the advanced S-400 air defense system from Russia, leading the United States to expel Turkey from the F-35 military aircraft program.[91] Geopolitically, Erdoğan also regularly invokes the SCO—which Turkey joined as a dialogue partner in 2013—as a dynamic new partner for Turkey and a hedge against faltering negotiations with the European

Union.[92] Though Erdoğan himself has not publicly questioned Turkey's position in NATO, US-Turkey security relations remain frayed, potentially also jeopardizing US access to its airbase at Incirlik.

Upon his election, Duterte announced what he referred to as an "independent foreign policy" that rejected using the US strategic presence in the Philippines to balance against China in favor of openly courting both China and Russia in an effort to extract increased economic aid and investment. This apparent shift proved all the more dramatic given that, in 2014, Washington and Manila had signed the Enhanced Defense Cooperation Agreement (EVA), which formalized renewed basing rights of US forces in the country on a rotational basis.

Following the Philippines victory over China in the Permanent Court of Arbitration's decision on the South China Sea in 2016, Duterte embarked on a visible campaign to mend relations with Beijing and publicly distance himself from Washington, declaring a halt to joint patrols in the South China Sea and mandating the withdrawal of US Special Forces from its counterterrorism operations on the island of Mindanao.[93] On September 27, 2016, amid steep currency and stock market declines, the Philippines president declared that he would seek closer trade and economic ties with China and Russia.[94] The next month, China pledged $24 billion to Manila in new investments ($15 billion) and soft credits ($9 billion), including support for 10 major infrastructural projects, among them a high-profile new Mindanao Railway under the BRI.[95]

Who Defends the Order?

In Hungary, despite calls by EU member state officials and the EU parliament to rebuke Orbán, Brussels has taken no punitive actions. Orbán's Fidesz Party has long been a member of the European People's Party (EPP) caucus. Despite a vote of denunciation by the European Parliament (448–197, with 48 abstentions),[96] EPP leaders have not acted to *expel* Orbán's party—though in March 2019 they did vote to *suspend* the party. Another red line appeared to have been crossed when, in late 2018, pressure from Orbán's government forced the Central European University—a university founded by the liberal philanthropist George Soros after the Soviet collapse—to announce that it would depart Budapest and relocate to Vienna.[97] The year before, the Hungarian government forced the closure of Soros's Open Societies Foundation as part of its effort to criminalize advocacy efforts on behalf of immigrants. But despite broad US and EU condemnation of the move, US Secretary of State Mike Pompeo made no mention of CEU or Hungary's democratic backsliding during a visit to Budapest in 2019.

In both Turkey and the Philippines, the Trump administration appeared ready to put its military cooperation and basing access on a purely transactional footing and de-emphasize concerns about democratic backsliding and human rights violations. Not only did the Trump administration refrain from criticizing Duterte's drug policy, but the US president approvingly cited the Philippine leader's crackdown as a model that the US should emulate—contradicting his own State Department's Human Rights report that expressed concern about the Philippine president's violations of human rights and due process.[98] In fact, as Chapter 6 will explore, President Trump's own foreign policy statements and actions indicate that he has more affinity for the multipolar populists than for the liberal international order that they actively question.

CONCLUSIONS: EXIT FROM BELOW

The field of international relations tends to privilege the study of great powers at the expense of small states. But, as we have seen, even some of the smallest and weakest of states provide important indicators about the evolution of international order. The governments of countries such as Ecuador, Tajikistan, Sri Lanka, and Djibouti are successfully leveraging the emergence of China and other alternative patrons to increase their share of economic, security, and cultural goods. They are also using the emergence of new potential patrons to push back against the conditions sought by Western donors. In consequence, the changing ecology of the international order is providing new opportunities for authoritarian regimes to protect themselves from external criticism and political pressures. These dynamics lack the drama of Russia's actions in Ukraine or China's announcement of the Belt and Road Initiative, but cumulatively, they are hollowing out aspects of liberal architecture that underpinned the patronage monopoly of the West.

6

Exit from Within

Right-Wing Transnationalism as Counter-Order Movements

On March 15, 2019 an Australian right-wing terrorist attacked the Al Noor Mosque and Linwood Islamic Center in Christchurch, New Zealand, killing 50 people.[1] As one commentator put it, the shooter was apparently "inspired by a thriving online ideological structure that recruits and radicalizes mostly men to save 'Western civilization' from a foreign 'invasion.'"[2] In a manifesto uploaded to the internet, he invoked the Norwegian far-right terrorist Anders Behring Breivik who, in July of 2011, murdered 77 people at a Norwegian Labor Party youth camp and exploded a bomb in downtown Oslo. Breivik "killed his victims because they embraced multiculturalism." He has inspired a number of other terrorist attacks and plots in many democracies, including in the United States and Germany.[3]

After September 11, 2001, most discussion of transnational counter-order movements centered on radical violent jihadism. Washington declared and waged a Global War on Terror; President George W. Bush aggressively militarized the fight against jihadi groups, expanded counterterrorism support to embattled regimes and their security services, and advocated democratization and intervention in parts of the Middle East. Some argued that organizations like Al-Qaeda ultimately wanted to overturn fundamental norms of contemporary international order, including state sovereignty.[4] Scholars noted that the rising global movement of money, people, and ideas enabled such groups to adopt more adaptable networks and cell structures.[5] These kinds of movements still mount challenges to various aspects of international order and violently oppose US policies and military interventions, particularly in the Islamic World. But radical jihadists are clearly not the only significant counter-order movement of the twenty-first century.

This is not unusual. Anti-order contention by subnational, national, and transnational movements often involves multiple, conflicting groups. Sometimes these movements reinforce one another through mutual antagonism and conflict, producing cycles of radicalization and polarization. We see this pattern between fascists and far-left movements, particularly Communists and revolutionary socialists, during the interwar period. Other times the primary axis of contention is between counter-order movements and ideologies already represented by established governments and powers, as in the case of the liberal uprisings that rocked Europe in 1848. Movements seeking to alter the prevailing order may intermingle with one another, such as in anti-colonial campaigns led by socialists and Communists.[6]

As we saw in Chapter 3, counter-order contention that originates primarily with non-state actors, including political factions and religious movements, plays a generally underappreciated role in the unraveling and transformation of international orders, including hegemonic ones.[7] Whether or not counter-order movements take control of governments and adopt revisionist strategies—such as alternative-order building, contesting norms and principles from within existing infrastructure, and cooperating with other anti-order movements and states—they can still disrupt the ability of incumbent powers to engage in international ordering. At the extreme, they can produce widespread political violence and civil conflicts that alter the distribution of capabilities among states and drive great powers into strategic overextension.

The heart of the American hegemonic system rests on dense strategic cooperation that creates military, political, and economic interdependencies. This may make it a favorable ecology for both the development and diffusion of transnational anti-order movements. The combination of interdependence and liberal democratic institutions—with their relatively open political systems—likely makes the core of the system asymmetrically vulnerable to illiberal movements and their sponsors.[8]

Right-wing, illiberal transnational movements are not the only ones capable of transforming international order and the American system. But we focus on them for a number of reasons. First, they are currently on the upswing. We see this in Trump's capture of the Republican Party and subsequent election as president of the United States; the number of illiberal, right-wing parties that hold or share power in Europe; and the largely right-wing coalition that successfully pushed for the United Kingdom to trigger withdrawal from the European Union—and thus sent one of the most stalwart, stable great-power supporters of liberal order and the American system into political chaos.

Second, the transnational right, however fragmented and diverse, explicitly opposes important aspects of international liberal ordering. It takes aim at, variously, economic openness and free trade, migration and immigration, liberal global governance, and the universal legal and normative claims of the international human rights regime.[9] We should stress that only a tiny percentage of this movement engages in political violence, let alone terrorism.[10] But many of the ideas expressed by the New Zealand murderer—the threat to Western civilization posed by Muslims as well as liberal and left-wing multiculturalists—echo those not only associated with other right-wing militants,[11] but also in broad circulation among the more mainstream far-right parties and movements in Europe and the United States.[12]

Third, the Kremlin has inserted itself into a number of transnational right-wing networks, and marketed itself as an international conservative cultural beacon for illiberal parties and movements. The same techniques that Moscow uses abroad—such as disinformation and sponsorship of civil society actors that share its political agenda—it initially pioneered to disrupt and demobilize its liberal domestic opposition.[13] This process—of first halting non-state liberal movements and networks, then shifting to roll back liberal ordering itself—reflects broader geopolitical trends that threaten the current unraveling of the American-led order.

As we explore in this chapter, Moscow has made multiple efforts to position itself as a broker among existing transnational illiberal movements, coalitions, and formal political parties that span across the West and Eurasia. The Kremlin has also attempted to exacerbate existing domestic social and political cleavages within Western democratic polities and societies. Its wedge strategies seek to magnify discord on hot-button social issues like immigration, religion, public health policy, and race relations—especially through online disinformation and active interventions in social-media communities.

Brokering and wedging, as we saw in Chapter 3, are ubiquitous in power politics. Hegemonic and imperial powers make use of them to manage their subordinates and undermine challengers. Beijing uses them as well; its attempts to influence Taiwanese politics resemble Moscow's efforts to affect Western democracies.[14] But Moscow's efforts, especially over the last fifteen years, showcase how a relatively economically weak power has, with some real success, targeted the dense architectures and infrastructures *within* the liberal order's Euro-Atlantic core.

THE GREAT REVERSAL: TRANSNATIONAL ORDERING AND COUNTER-ORDERING

In the 1990s, some scholars began to see transnational networks and nongovernmental organizations (NGOs) as an essential component of international order. They considered them, in effect, elements of international infrastructure as well as critical agents in shaping international architecture. Political scientists Margaret Keck and Katherine Sikkink produced the single most influential, even genre-defining account of transnational activist networks (which international-relations scholars often refer to as TANs).[15] They argued that such networks represented a third kind of actor in global governance, one motivated neither by power-political ends (like states) nor by profit (like private sector actors). Instead, principles drove transnational activism.

Keck and Sikkink focused exclusively on transnational networks that promoted broadly liberal values, including political rights, human rights, gender equality, environmentalism protections, and physical advocacy. The networks themselves linked together a variety of actors holding similar principles, including NGOs and civil society activists, media personalities, university researchers and students, international organizations, and even specific governments and governmental agencies that shared the relevant values.

Keck and Sikkink developed the idea of the "boomerang effect" to explain how transnational activists can successfully pressure even closed sovereign states to change their policies. They described a process in which governments reject appeals for policy concessions by domestic civil society; those groups then turn to like-minded allies within the international system—such as international NGOs or foreign governments. Once a coalition comes together, these international actors pressure the government to concede.

For scholars working in this tradition, successful advocacy campaigns—including those that reduced the use of child soldiers worldwide and banned the use of landmines by most countries—demonstrate that transnational advocacy networks could even affect matters of military security.[16] Committed activists could, through a skillful and nimble use of the architecture of the liberal international order, successfully challenge state sovereignty and authoritarian governments.

In retrospect, the "boomerang" model overestimated the extent to which shared principles could overcome organizational barriers to mobilization. As it turned out, NGOs balance their values with their need to fundraise; many transnational NGOs suffer from bureaucratic conflicts between headquarters and field chapters; and international gatekeepers block some causes from ever getting on the agenda.[17] Such problems generally diluted, but did not eliminate, the influence of advocacy networks as agents of liberal ordering.

The Backlash against NGOs

In the 2000s, states began to actively undermine NGOs and their non-state allies, especially on matters of democratization and human rights—that is, the political dimensions of liberal ordering. What happened? First, regimes that found such NGOs troublesome started to place significant legal obstacles in their path. Governments severely restricted the activities of NGOs, impeded their ability to obtain foreign funds or, in certain cases, banned their political and social advocacy altogether.[18] One study by Dupuy, Ron, and Prakesh found that between 1993 and 2012, 39 countries adopted laws restricting foreign funding for NGOs. The data shows evidence of diffusion, learning, and emulation: 33 of these countries passed their restrictive laws or significantly expanded existing ones after 2002.[19]

These restrictions proved remarkably effective. For example, in 2008 the Ethiopian government enacted a new law restricting foreign funding of NGO political advocacy. The result: 90 percent of the groups previously involved in political and social work either entirely dissolved or shifted from political activism to providing social services.[20] Moreover, new informational technologies—which policymakers and scholars once assumed would facilitate the mobilization of civil society against the state—provided effective ways for autocratic regimes to monitor and block the activities, especially the transnational ones, of those seeking liberalization.[21]

Second, it turned out that illiberal and anti-democratic movements could *also* organize transnationally. We should note that, from the very start, scholars knew that they might be inappropriately focusing on what they considered to be "good" groups (that is, ones that generally liberal and left-wing academics approved of). After September 11, 2001, for instance, researchers noted that radical, violence-wielding jihadist groups were a form of transnational advocacy network—and that the almost total lack of interest in these groups among scholars of transnational movements might suggest a problem. But only a few researchers working on transnational advocacy networks looked closely at illiberal, let alone simply conservative, movements.[22]

In the 1990s this oversight seemed defensible. After all, the focus on liberal, democratizing, environmentalist, and social justice movements fit with the spirit of the times. The infrastructure of international order was increasingly encroaching on state sovereignty in the name of liberal principles. For example, the Rome Statute established the International Criminal Court (ICC), following the creation of UN-mandated war crimes tribunals in the former Yugoslavia and in Rwanda.[23] The UN adopted Responsibility to Protect (R2P) principles that created room for legitimate military interventions in states unable or unwilling to protect vulnerable populations.[24]

But the very same infrastructure and strategies—building coalitions of NGOs, international organizations, media, and supportive states—could also mobilize in support of conservative, and sometimes outright counter-ordering causes. In 2012, international relations scholar Clifford Bob pointed out that precisely this pattern was well under way. The Vatican led a global anti-abortion movement. The National Rifle Association worked transnationally to oppose the UN small arms ban treaty, as well as anti-gun referenda and legislation in countries like Brazil. Religious conservative groups, often based in the United States, developed transnational networks to oppose rights for sexual minorities.[25]

Taking both of these developments together makes clear that the tide of transnational mobilization in favor of liberal ordering was not only slowing but facing at least partial reversals. Moreover, in the 2000s, illiberal and authoritarian regimes not only took concrete steps to block the activities of liberal advocacy networks, but they also started to seed and support illiberal groups and networks that could push back against liberal and pro-democracy movements.

GROUNDING THE ACTIVISTS

Soon after the Color Revolutions of the mid-2000s, the Kremlin began to pioneer new kinds of efforts and "political technologies." Western democracy promotion, often through NGOs and transnational networks, looked like an increasing threat—not only to Russia's self-styled sphere of privileged interests but to the regime itself.[26] The Kremlin imposed new and burdensome registration requirements on NGOs. In 2012, it enacted a law that restricted access to foreign funding and made recipients self-identify as foreign agents. The "undesirable organizations" law of 2015 subsequently banned liberal advocacy groups deemed a "threat to the constitutional order of the Russian Federation" or "state security" altogether.[27]

At the same time, Russian authorities began to develop a range of domestic and international political infrastructure that took liberal forms, but absent the liberal political principles that they found threatening. Soon after the Orange Revolution in Ukraine, the Kremlin founded and supported the youth movement Nashi, which encouraged patriotic volunteer work for the Russian state, in an effort to contest the influence of Western-sponsored youth organizations and exchanges.[28] Russia and other authoritarian governments promoted government-backed nongovernmental organizations (GONGOs) to act as agenda-setters in international fora and otherwise act as instruments of authoritarian power.

Even in the UN, bodies such as the UNHCR became contested sites in which clusters of countries pushed back against aspects of liberal ordering. Tellingly, from 2009 to 2014, Russia led, in two distinct illiberal campaigns, a coalition of Middle Eastern and Eurasian states at the UNHCR against the United States and Western Europe. The first advocated "traditional values" and the second the "protection of the family." Both of these sought to counter pro-LGBTQ advocacy; they appealed to cultural, moral, historical, and religious traditions, broadly defined across faiths. Indeed, scholars Kristina Stoeckl and Yuliya Medvedeva show the key role played in these efforts by the strategic use of NGOs and GONGOs, which engaged in orchestrated actions designed to support the campaign, such as submitting briefs and memos in support of illiberal resolutions.[29] Tellingly, Stoeckl and Medvedeva find that 65 percent of submissions by outside actors between 2009 and 2016 came from ones that favored the pro-traditionalist platforms.[30]

DIFFUSION, EMULATION, AND BROKERAGE

In addition to blocking liberal NGOs and promoting illiberal ones in the domain of global governance, Russian officials and funders have engaged in efforts to cobble together new transnational coalitions—or at least lay the groundwork for their cooperation—among various movements, organizations, and politicians across the world. What these groups have in common is a shared a dislike of political liberalism and the trajectory of post–Cold War international order.

In Chapter 3 we saw how the spread of Protestantism in early modern Europe linked rulers, nobles, and ordinary people in ways that we would now consider "transnational." This process gave impetus to perennial sources of contention—such as opposition to taxation and the defense of local rights against centralizing rulers—and layered on new ones, in the form of religious disagreement. This overlay made it easier for contentious movements to spread beyond localities and regions. It gave some of them greater access to financial and military support.[31] We also saw similar dynamics in the rise of fascism during the twentieth-century interwar period. Fascists shared ideas and practices. They learned from examples of unsuccessful and successful counter-order mobilization. Fascists supported fellow travelers across borders. All of this helped produce a devastating crisis for the fragile post–World War I international order.[32] And during the Cold War, both the Soviet Union and the United States routinely interfered in third country elections—about one out of every nine between 1946 and 2000. Washington and Moscow provided open and covert support to those political parties and regimes that they viewed favorably.[33]

We find extensive patterns of diffusion, emulation, and brokerage among present-day right-wing movements and parties. This makes a lot of sense in contemporary Europe. For one thing, the EU parliament is organized into pan-European ideological coalitions, a structure that builds on an older history of transnational cooperation among like-minded European parties. For another, even nationalist movements operate in a context of a broader, everyday European identity that facilitates cross-national connections.[34] But ideological transmission, influence, and debate has pretty much always had a transnational dimension in the region, as our illustrations of past transnational contention over international order should make clear.

The same is true of the major ideological configuration linking right-wing populist parties: opposition to "multiculturalism, existing immigration policies, and immigrants."[35] Hostility toward Muslim immigrants, represented as impervious to true assimilation and an inevitable threat of "Islamic fundamentalism," became part of the rhetorical matrix of right-wing populist and post-fascist parties even before the Syrian refugee crisis.[36] In Europe, these convergences developed through a combination of emulations, diffusion, and concrete networking. In 2008, one of the leading members of Vlaams Belang, a right-wing populist party in Belgium, "invited the leaders of several right-wing parties—among them Heinz-Christian Strache of the [Austrian] Freiheitliche Partei Österreichs (FPÖ)—to Antwerp to launch a transnational project to resist the 'Islamization' of Europe's cities."[37]

But it would be a mistake to overlook the transatlantic character of the populist right. Some right-wing European figures, including Nigel Farage—one of the inescapable faces of the Brexit movement—have cultivated connections with Trump and Republicans; we also see evidence of emulation and learning between North American and Europe.[38] When Marion Maréchal-Le Pen of the right-wing *Front National* (now renamed *Rassemblement National*) spoke at the annual Conservative Political Action Conference (CPAC) in 2018, her presence proved divisive among American conservative commentators, but the fact that some prominent voices defended her highlights broader convergence among the populist right.[39]

Mounting evidence suggests that American financing plays an important role in promoting European right-wing movements. As journalists Mary Fitzgerald and Claire Provost report: "America's Christian right spent at least $50 million of 'dark money' to fund campaigns and advocacy in Europe over the past decade," which is a "formidable" amount of money by "European standards" of "political financing." Moreover, they contend, these "numbers are also likely the tip of the iceberg: our analysis looked at only 12 US Christian right groups, and there were many obstacles to disclosure that limited the information we could extract. Institutions registered as churches, for example, are not required to publish their overseas funding."[40]

We highlight these ties not only to drive home that the populist and culturally conservative right is already transnational and transatlantic, but also to emphasize that Moscow is not a grand puppet-master without which there would be no global right-wing movement challenging political liberalism. Nonetheless, Russia's relationship with European far-right parties and movements, which began to develop in the 1990s, matters a great deal, precisely because it appears to be part of a larger strategy that seeks to weaken the liberal order by supporting anti-liberal parties, regardless of their exact ideological affinity with Moscow.

According to scholar Anton Shekovtsov, the 2008 Georgia War marked an important inflection point in this post–Cold War counter-networking. Russia engaged in numerous attempts at brokerage with the aim of positioning itself as the hub of anti-liberal movements in Europe. In 2005, Moscow had already rebranded *Russia Today* as *RT*, which it now uses not only for propaganda purposes but to give exposure to far-left and far-right political movements and personalities.[41]

In more recent years, Russia has developed—through a combination of its own efforts, its branding, and outreach from European politicians—a range of supportive parties. These range from openly fascist to populist.[42] In addition to the former *Front National*, which received Kremlin-orchestrated bank loans to keep it afloat,[43] these include "Jobbik, UKIP, Golden Dawn, the Freedom Party of Austria (Freiheitliche Partei Österreichs, FPÖ), Attack (Ataka) from Bulgaria and the North League [now just the League, or Lega] from Italy."[44] In May 2019 the Austrian government dramatically collapsed when a video recording that captured Heinz-Christian Strache, then vice chancellor of Austria and leader of the Freedom Party, offering a variety of lucrative government contracts in exchange for campaign support to an actress that he thought was the daughter of a Kremlin-friendly oligarch.[45]

The Russian-Italian nexus showcases both the supply and demand for transnational brokerage. In 2016, Russia's ruling party, United Russia, signed a cooperation agreement with the Freedom Party. In 2017, it signed an agreement with the Lega.[46] The Lega is currently the junior partner in the Italian coalition government. As of the summer of 2019, it is the most popular single party in Italy. It has run interference for Russia on a variety of international controversies. The FPÖ did the same before its coalition with the Austrian People's Party collapsed. Both parties have been enmeshed with Russian interests through business ventures, institutes, and likely political financing.[47]

In July 2019, a news outlet published an audio recording and related transcript of a Moscow meeting between three representatives of the Lega—including Italian deputy prime minister's Matteo Salvini's long-standing aide Gianluca Savoini—and three Russian officials. At the October 2018 meeting at the Metropole hotel in Moscow, Savoini listed a group of far-right European parties and remarked, "We really want to begin to have a great alliance with these parties that are pro-Russia," later remarking that "we count on sustaining a political campaign which is of benefit, I would say of mutual benefit, for the two countries."[48]

The two sides discussed a funding scheme that would evade Italian legal prohibitions on foreign political contributions by funnelling Russian oil sales into Lega campaign coffers. The Russian company would, over the course of a year, sell around $1.5 billion worth of oil to the Italian company Eni through a network of intermediary sellers. These sellers would, in turn, apply a discounted trade to these transactions; in total, the scheme would net about $65 million that would be shifted to the right-wing Italian party.[49] The discussions included technical details of prevailing oil prices, ports of delivery, volume, payment structures, and possible personal commissions. Just days after the news story broke, Italian prosecutors in Milan announced that they would open an investigation into the incident to investigate possible charges of international corruption involving Lega.[50]

Though the Lega report offers the first actual "smoking gun" for such meetings and clandestine support, it did not come as much of a surprise to many observers. Moreover, as we noted in previous chapters, we see similar patterns in Russia's relations with Hungary's illiberal government and with political power brokers in the Czech Republic. Such (often indirect) methods of brokerage—through businessmen and oligarchs, research institutes, organizations affiliated with right-wing parties, and travel invitations to cultivate relationships—are essentially the way that Moscow has attempted to cultivate relationships with not just American conservatives and the Republican party but also some of the progressive left.[51]

In sum, we see strong indications of the development of a diverse configuration of right-wing counter-order movements and parties, some allied and some not, in Europe and even the United States. They generally share some combination of skepticism if not hostility toward immigrants; an ethnic conception of Western civilization, often as a white racial-cultural community; the belief that Islam and Muslims are a threat to Western civilization; a view of multiculturalism as a mechanism for the destruction of traditional Western values and identities; and culturally conservative attitudes toward the status of women, the family, and sexual minorities.

At the same time, they disagree on a great deal. Some are committed to representative democracy while others are authoritarian in disposition. Some are fascist or even neo-Nazi. Some are overly anti-Semitic, while others are more favorably disposed toward Jews in general, and Israel in particular. Many online right-wing extremist movements are deeply misogynist; some researchers believe that hostility toward women may be a "gateway" into radicalization. But some parties and groups emphasize support for women's rights, especially in the context of their criticisms of Islam and Muslim immigrants. Indeed, the contemporary European and North American right differ on many other issues, such as matters of explicit racism, hostility toward the United States, and support for Trump.[52]

But, as we saw in Chapter 3, this kind of diversity, and even competition, is typical of counter-order movements in general, including those that have played a major role in the collapse of hegemonic systems and power transitions.

Brokering New Transnational Counter-Ordering Networks: The Case of the World Congress of Families

The Kremlin's brokerage efforts extend beyond formal political parties. They include other kinds of actors dedicated to challenging aspects of contemporary liberal architecture—ones that echo the kinds of strategies and tactics found in the liberalizing transnational actors of the 1990s.

The World Congress of Families (WCF) provides a revealing case study of how illiberal actors, social movements, and groups—across the United States and Eurasia—have been networked and scaled up to generate transnational counter-ordering networks with global reach. The WCF was founded in the 1990s by two American organizations associated with the Christian Right: the Howard Center for Family, Religion, and Society (which is also the WCF's permanent global headquarters) and the Family

Voice (later called the World Family Policy Center). The WCF held its first forums in Prague (1997) and Geneva (1999) as part of an effort to network the Christian Right with non-American, overwhelmingly Christian, partners.

The choice of Geneva was no accident. Geneva serves as a de facto UN hub. The UN's head of NGO relations even delivered the conference's opening address.[53] The conference focused on themes revolving around defining the "natural family," which provided the main focus of the Geneva conference's declaration. Discussions of homosexuality and gay rights movements remained limited to passages in a couple of speeches.[54]

The WCF went on to hold conferences in Mexico City (2004), Warsaw (2007), and Amsterdam (2009). Its engagement with Russian partners and patrons reportedly began in 2010 when director Larry Jacobs traveled to Moscow to speak at an event organized by the Russian pro-life group Sanctity of Motherhood.[55] In 2011, the WCF held a "demographic summit" in Moscow. Participants included Christian evangelical leaders, leaders from the Orthodox Church, and Russian patrons. Promotional material from the 2011 summit claims that the summit "helped pass the first Russian laws restricting abortion."[56]

Putin's return to the Russian presidency in 2012 led to a rightward shift on social issues, perhaps, in part, as an effort to delegitimize remaining pockets of liberal civil society in Russia. Putin developed a closer public relationship with Orthodox leadership. In 2013 a new same-sex "anti-propaganda law" prohibited the public promotion of LGBT relationships as equal to heterosexual relationships.[57] Further anti-LGBT legislation followed, banning adoptions by same-sex couples and Pride parades. In foreign affairs, the emphasis on "traditional values" became a geopolitical platform for opposing the liberal West, especially in opposition to the Obama administration's global push to promote LGBTQ rights.[58]

A series of subsequent forums in Eastern Europe demonstrated the WCF's increasing transnational ties as well as its specific targeting of liberal ordering via Western NGOs and American foreign policy. The 2014 WCF conference was initially scheduled for Moscow in September, but Russia's annexation of Crimea led to its cancellation—because the United States placed sanctions on its main sponsor, Vladimir Yakunin, the former chairman of Russian railways. But despite the official WCF cancelation,

American evangelical leaders attended a conference on the similar topic of "Large Families: The Future of Humanity" in Moscow in September, where they mingled with Russian legislators, religious leaders, and conservative activists.[59] Yakunin's own network sponsors a number of transnational conferences, organizations, and networks promoting "traditional values." These include the Association Dialogue Franco-Russe, Dialogue of Civilizations Research Institute in Vienna, the World Public Dialogue of Civilizations in Berlin and a charitable foundation—St. Andrew the First-Called Endowment Fund—that funds Russian-related causes and Orthodox values abroad.[60]

The 2016 WCF summit was held in Tbilisi, Georgia, and focused on the theme of "Civilization at the Crossroads: The Natural Family as the Bulwark of Freedom and Human Values." Its agenda involved combating the influence of "sexual radicals" as well as promoting the "natural family" as "the fundamental unit of society" and "the basis of healthy and progressive civilizations." The conference aimed to "help the international pro-family movement to establish a beachhead in [Eastern Europe]."[61] Like the planned Moscow meeting, a high-profile patron sponsored the Tbilisi session: the Georgian conservative activist and businessman Levan Vasadze. During his address, Vasadze asserted that the main US foreign policy priority was "supporting homosexuality all over the world." He demanded that the West stop interfering in "internal affairs" and "family traditions" through "hundreds of your NGOs."[62]

The following year the conference went to Hungary, again with a "pro-family" agenda. There, Hungarian prime minister Viktor Orbán delivered the opening speech, criticizing the EU for being guided by a "relativizing liberal ideology that's an insult to families."[63] The Hungarian government's apparent endorsement of the forum took place as Budapest continued its standoff against Brussels over its anti-migration platform and attacks on the Central European University and the Open Society Foundations, both closely associated with George Soros. After a 2018 meeting in Moldova, formally hosted by Moldovan president Igor Dodon, the 2019 WCF forum was held in Verona, Italy, a stronghold of the Lega.

Overall, the WCF may or may not amount to much, though the increasing eagerness for illiberal country leaders like Orbán and Dodon to host suggests that it has gained an important measure of acceptance and even prestige. Analytically, it exhibits many of the same networked

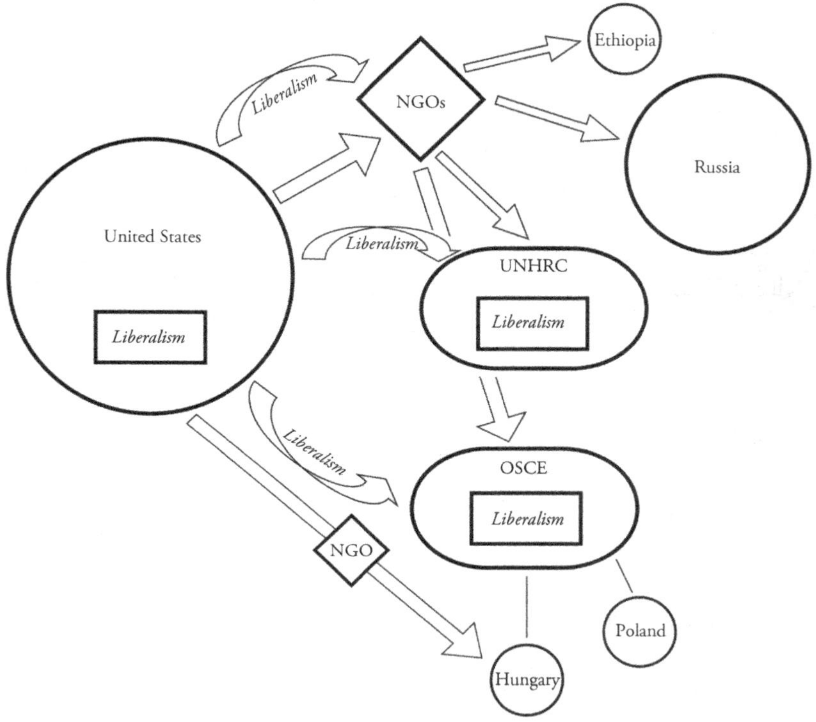

FIGURE 6.1 Transnational Networks of the 1990s

qualities as its liberal counterparts. Overall, as with other transnational illiberal networks, it has helped to transform the ecology of transnational networks that, in the 1990s, were strongly championed by the United States and seemingly dominated global governance (see Figure 6.1 and Figure 6.2). Started by a coalition of Christian Right organizations, it developed international partners and patrons. It adopted similar practices as those associated with liberal transnational actors. As Kristina Stoeckl observes, "The WCF acts as transnational norm entrepreneur, much of the same kind as norm protagonists . . . only . . . it is illiberal and conservative, not liberal and progressive. It contributes to the rise of illiberal civil society in Eastern Europe and the former Soviet Union. It also makes its influence felt in Western Europe, with actors from the Christian Right, who are a minority in their home countries, finding large audiences."[64]

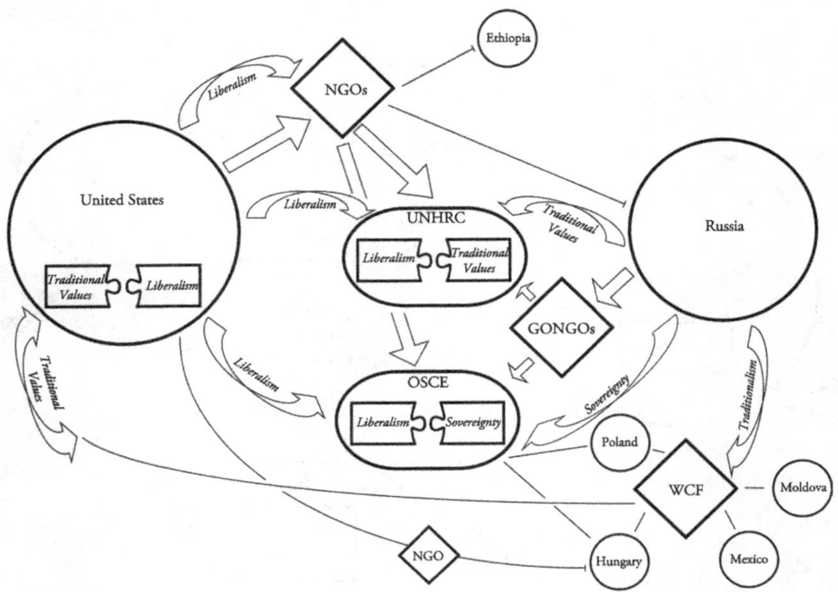

FIGURE 6.2 Contested Transnational Networks, c. 2019

WEDGE STRATEGIES: SOWING CHAOS AND DEEPENING DOMESTIC POLITICAL PARTISANSHIP

Brokerage is only one way that transnational counter-order movements, and the governments that would support them, can challenge the consensus about international order within the hegemon's core infrastructure. Another is through the use of "wedge strategies" aimed at undermining the cohesion of interstate alliances and states themselves. In prior chapters, we focused on the first variant: efforts by challengers to split the infrastructure that supports the American system and liberal ordering. But the second variant is also critically important. If successful, it significantly undermines the ability of great powers to uphold the order.[65]

In practice, serious threats to, say, hegemonic orders involve successful combinations of wedging and brokerage. The two strategies often complement one another, insofar as the counter-order state or movement seeks to *wedge apart* domestic societies and *form* coalitions with those disposed to undermine the hegemon and the prevailing order. We have already discussed Russia's attempts to form coalitions with far-right parties in Europe. But the biggest coup would be to wedge apart existing social fractures in the dominant power while forming ties with one of its major parties. In 2016, it became blindingly obvious that Moscow was trying to do both in the United States.

New Russian-American Social Networks?

Even before the 2016 campaign, the Russian government, often through oligarchs and other intermediaries, was courting influential American social, political, and religious actors. On July 15, 2018, just before the Trump-Putin summit in Helsinki, federal officials arrested Maria Butina, a student at American University. They charged her with acting as an unregistered agent of the Russian government. On December 12, 2008, Butina pleaded guilty to working as an agent of Moscow from 2015 to 2018 and of conspiring with a senior Russian official—Alexander Torshin—to infiltrate conservative groups in the United States in order to gain their support and influence the 2016 presidential election.[66]

Butina organized a Russian tour for several prominent members of the National Rifle Association (NRA), one of the most powerful conservative lobbies and contributors to efforts to elect Republicans. It took place in December 2015 and was pretty clearly an effort to form political ties between the NRA and Russian political players. In the area of political campaign finance, various media investigations suggest that Russian and Russian-American oligarchs may have increased their donations, in coordination with Moscow and often laundered through various intermediaries, to support Trump's candidacy and the campaigns of Republican senators. A *Dallas Morning News* story revealed a series of substantial political contributions in 2015 and 2016 by Russian-linked wealthy donors. For example, Len Blavatnik—US-UK citizen whose family had emigrated to the United States in the 1980s—proved to be one of the biggest Republican donors of the cycle, donating $6.35 million to GOP political action committees—despite the fact that until 2014 his political contributions had been relatively modest and evenly distributed among Democrats and Republicans.[67]

As we explore in the next chapter, it is not difficult to understand why Russia saw specific upsides to Trump's election. Even into the campaign, Trump was pursuing a deal for a Trump-branded property in Moscow. This may help explain his praise for Putin and general indications of sympathy toward Russia and Russian foreign policy. Trump's campaign made numerous overtures to Moscow suggesting that Trump's own diplomatic and foreign-policy goals aligned with Russian interests. Trump's own hostility to liberal ordering in general, and to critical infrastructure of the American system in particular, suggested that his election would be the equivalent of a successful "hail Mary" for Moscow: an opportunity to let Trump further polarize American society while undermining American standing and strategic partnerships abroad.[68]

The IRA, Information Warfare, and Wedge Politics

In the final report released by the Office of the Special Counsel, Robert Mueller and his team wrote that the "Russian government interfered in the 2016 Presidential election in a sweeping and systemic fashion."[69] The backbone of the investigation's findings focuses on indictments of two groups of Russian actors: one for hacking and releasing emails and memos from the Democratic National Committee (DNC) and coordinating the release via a third party (understood to be WikiLeaks); and the second, for crimes involving the Internet Research Agency (IRA), based in Saint Petersburg.[70]

In February 2018, the US Department of Justice indicted 13 nationals and three entities, including the IRA, for crimes related to interference in the 2016 US presidential election. The indictment charged Yevgeniy Prighozin, a close ally of President Putin and, since 2016, a target of State Department sanctions, with funding the IRA operation and its employees. The indictment noted that the IRA's strategic goal was to "sow discord in the U.S. political system" by posing as Americans and operating internet accounts that "addressed divisive U.S. political issues."[71] The troll factory operated with a $1.25 million monthly budget; it generated content on major social-media platforms including Twitter, Facebook, Instagram, and Google. Twitter's Elections Integrity Initiative revealed that about 3,600 IRA-linked accounts sent over nine million tweets in 2016. The indictment described the account as "primarily intended to communicate derogatory information about Hillary Clinton, to denigrate other candidates such as Ted Cruz and Marco Rubio, and to support Bernie Sanders and then-candidate Trump."[72]

The posts employed classical wedge tactics by magnifying social and political tensions on issues including migration, religion, and race. They targeted users in swing states such as Florida, Pennsylvania, and Michigan. Fictitious accounts like "Being Patriotic" championed Trump's support for Pennsylvania miners, while accounts such as "Army of Jesus" linked Hilary Clinton to Satan and "Heart of Texas" promoted secession in case of a Clinton victory.[73] In one prominent example, for 11 months the account "@Ten_GOP" impersonated a state-approved Republican account and produced inflammatory race-related content. It attracted 136,000 followers before the real Tennessee Republican Party shut it down.[74]

With access to a complete dataset of IRA-linked Twitter content, a number of political communications scholars extensively studied the IRA and discovered important dimensions of the strategy and reach of the troll-farm.

Almost all researchers noted that the IRA created both left-leaning and right-leaning accounts in an effort to promote political polarization. For example, Darren Linvill and Patrick Warren analyzed 3,865 IRA Twitter human-operated troll accounts and identified five basic categories of users: *right troll, left troll, news feed, hashtag gamer*, and *fearmonger*.[75] In terms of their content, they found that the "right troll" handled themes that "were distinct from mainstream Republicanism," predominantly broadcasting nativist and populist messages, President Trump's own campaign slogans, and sending divisive messages that targeted moderate Republicans.[76] Left-wing troll handles focused on socially liberal issues, especially issues of race and identity politics. They attacked both mainstream Republicans and Democrats, especially Hilary Clinton, and broadly supported Bernie Sanders prior to the election.[77] Overall, these handles sought to increase polarization and decrease trust in domestic institutions, including the electoral process, media, science, and academia.[78]

The researchers also found distinct ebbs and flows in the volumes of tweets in each category in response to changing campaign-related news—for example, troll activity spiked the day before and during the WikiLeaks release of hacked DNC emails on October 7. The researchers therefore concluded that the IRA was strategic as "effort was reallocated amongst account types in response to shocks, depending on the segment of the U.S. electorate the IRA wished to engage, changing IRA strategic goals, or both."[79]

Another feature of the IRA campaign was the sophisticated way in which it focused on race-related themes and contentious issues; trolls sought to embed themselves within grassroots communities to shape the framing of issues. Kate Starbird, of the University of Washington, and her colleagues zeroed in on the extreme polarization in the framing of issues surrounding race and especially involving #BlackLivesMatter online exchanges. They found two distinct, polarized, and "toxic" clusters. By overlaying confirmed IRA handles on their previous research on the known universe of Black Lives Matter exchanges, the researchers found that the IRA accounts forged both profiles of "the proud African-American" and of "the proud White Conservative," each with distinct geographical locators. They also created fictitious "grassroots" accounts and media groups for each of these sides.[80] Overall, they concluded that the IRA accounts "imitated ordinary users to systematically micro-target different audiences, foster antagonism and undermine trust in information intermediaries."[81] In Figure 6.3, we see striking visual confirmation of this "wedging" strategy, as Russian IRA retweets are embedded in the core of both sides of the polarizing social media map.

Moreover, a team of New York University researchers, led by Joshua Tucker, uncovered a sophisticated appeal to local news from the more informationally oriented IRA accounts. Overall, they found that IRA-operated accounts shared news and content from local media sources 15 times more often than did a comparison group, and five times more than junk news or "fake news" content, "possibly trying to take advantage of the trust local media outlets enjoy in the US."[82]

Finally, the scope of IRA networking and attempts to embed itself in community discussion were not just limited to the election campaign. IRA

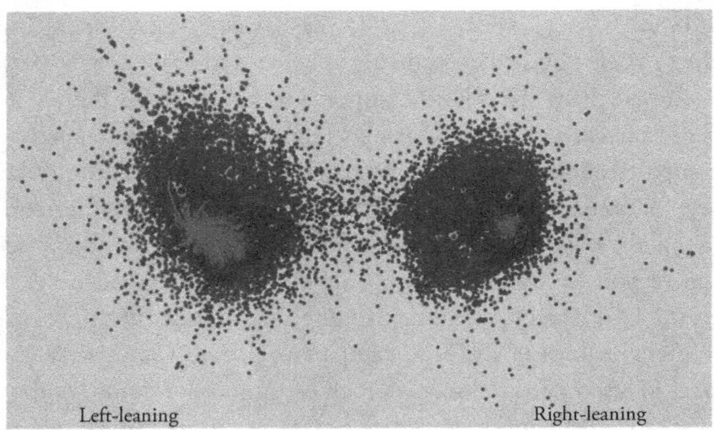

FIGURE 6.3 Retweets of Known Russia-Internet Research Agency Trolls in Polarized #BlackLivesMatter Retweet Map.

Republished from Figure 2 in Ahmer Arif, Leo Stewart, and Kate Starbird, "Acting the Part: Examining Information Operations within #BlackLivesMatter Discourse," *Proceedings of the ACM on Human-Computer Interaction*, Vol. 2, No. CSCW, Article 20, November 2018, 11.

operatives have also involved themselves inflaming online debates about social or public health issues. For example, a team of public health researchers found that a subset of IRA activities promoting health content sought to "weaponize" internal American debates by spreading disinformation and misinformation about vaccination.[83] The study found that IRA-generated Russian trolls sought to create discord by promoting both sides of the vaccine issue, while unidentifiable accounts acted as "content polluters"—they tweeted at higher rates and with more anti-vaccine messages with the aim of "eroding public consensus on vaccination." The study also found that the IRA messages that used the hashtag #VaccinateUS, tended to connect the anti-vaccine messages with overtly political, rather than family-oriented, themes like "freedom" and "Constitutional Rights." These messages promoted divisive topics that were otherwise not regularly discussed in other vaccine-related tweets.[84]

Commentators and policymakers continue to debate how consequential this Russian involvement was on the outcome of the election. In our view, this is a question that is nearly impossible to answer with certainty. Skeptics, both within the United States and Russia itself, correctly argue that Russia did not cause the extreme polarization and political fault lines that currently characterize US domestic politics. The question of how consequential individual components of the campaign were, such as the IRA's activities, raises even more difficult methodological challenges.

We are less interested in whether Moscow's efforts "made a difference" than in their logics and goals. When viewed through the prism of counter-order efforts, the IRA's role was to splinter and magnify social and political tensions, precisely with the aim of further destabilizing the willingness and the ability of the United States to promote liberal architecture and sustain its hegemonic infrastructure.

In that sense, it's important to keep in mind that social media are just new platforms for strategies that are likely as old as politics itself. Invaders, empires, political rivals, warring states, rising challengers, and incumbent hegemons have long attempted to weaken their opponents by manipulating (or creating) societal fault lines. Sometimes the means involve economic inducements, radio broadcasts, infiltrating agents who spread disinformation, or some other technique. But we see the same patterns again and again.[85]

Russian efforts are updated versions of Soviet information warfare, which often sought to divide the American system. The United States and many of its allies did the same, including encouraging uprisings in the

Warsaw Pact.[86] As Keir Giles has pointed out, Russian social media and cyber campaigns are a part of a more integrated and broader national strategy—one that aims to reassert state control over information spaces deemed vital to state sovereignty and security. In this sense, the logic directly challenges post–Cold War understandings of liberal ordering while the tactics "weaponize" liberal-democratic openness to information.[87]

Crucially, and in keeping with the focus of this chapter, subnational and transnational counter-order units are not merely instruments of great powers. They are often actors in their own right, and they deploy some of the same repertoires when it comes to weakening the existing international order. One of the possible ironies of focusing on Russian efforts to exacerbate partisan divides in Western countries is that they're often superfluous. There's nothing IRA employees can do that, say, partisan media in the United States isn't already doing—and usually with greater success.[88]

Put differently, if counter-order movements within the core play a major role in the collapse of hegemonic systems collapse or transformation of international orders, then even without Moscow's attempts at orchestration, other efforts at brokerage are already linking up illiberal, right-wing movements and helping them gain strength across the West. These movements also benefit from highly polarized societies; they piggyback on media ecosystems that cultivate that polarization. There are also some signs of growing mobilization by left-wing counter-order elements. We know these kinds of conditions are dangerous for international order and hegemonic systems, because we've seen the movie before.

7

Exit Made in America

The Trump Presidency

We discuss Donald Trump in the present tense. The reason is straightforward: as we write this book, we do not know whether he is headed for defeat in 2020, re-election to a second term, or even toward impeachment and removal from office. Trump's attitude toward the existing American hegemonic system and to many principles of liberal order means that the fate of his presidency matters for both. But, as we have seen in the preceding chapters, the forces eroding them extend far beyond the specifics of Trump foreign policy. Trump did not cause the emergence of great-power challengers. Russia's increasing assertiveness extends back to the George W. Bush presidency, and has its roots in the 1990s.[1] China's economic and military expansion started decades ago; anti-order movements from within the American system did not spontaneously generate on November 8, 2016.

Trump and Trumpism are accelerants and symptoms of broader processes.[2] It is not unheard of for the leadership of great powers, including hegemonic ones, to adopt policies of retrenchment;[3] (as we have seen) reformers, such as Gorbachev, sometimes—usually without intending to—pursue a course that collapses their systems.[4] However, few expected that American politics would produce a president with as thoroughly revisionist an outlook as Donald Trump.[5] But it did. Trumpism is the American wing of a counter-order movement—one challenging the American international system and liberal ordering from within the advanced industrial democracies. Thus, whatever Trump's own fate, we need to grapple with the ideas he represents and the policies he has pursued.

When it comes to international principles of human rights, democracy, and transparency, Trump's predecessors were inconsistent and hypocritical. Trump, in contrast, is generally indifferent if not outright hostile. By scaling back American influence in international organizations, seeking to reduce Washington's role in the field of foreign aid, and generally lifting America's thumb off the scales of human rights and democracy, Trump does his best to help strip contemporary international architecture of some of its liberal features.

Where Trump differs not just quantitatively, but qualitatively, is his disposition toward the infrastructure of the American system. For example, the Bush administration sidelined the State Department, but it did not do lasting damage to its core competencies. As the international-relations scholar Daniel Drezner notes, under Trump a "combination of budget cutting and politically motivated personnel moves winnowed the senior ranks of the diplomatic corps" and denudated "foreign policy bureaucracies of expertise and authority, letting those agencies drift and atrophy."[6] Trump has denigrated and dismissed lynchpin alliances and partnerships of the American system, most notably the NATO alliance. Even when he has failed to make good on his rhetoric, his behavior has spooked officials and publics throughout the American system.

All of this helps explain why Moscow attempted to help Trump win in 2016. Whether or not Trump could deliver on a "grand bargain" that suited Russian interests, he would certainly be (as 2016 rival Republican Jeb Bush put it) a "chaos president"[7] inclined to disrupt the architecture and infrastructure that sustains American leadership. Trump underscores the fact that the United States, like other hegemonic powers, does not stand outside of its own order: it is a site of contestation within that order.

Whatever his campaign promises or his occasional statements, where Trump has remained squarely within the Republican orthodoxy is his approach to domestic political economy. His administration has promoted economic deregulation, undermined environmental protections and efforts to curb climate change, pushed through large tax cuts that greatly benefit wealthy Americans, driven up deficits during a period of economic growth, and failed to produce new major investments in infrastructure, education, or research and development.

Thus, while the Trump administration national-security policy prepares for a future of great-power competition, especially with China, its policies toward both the international and domestic infrastructure of the American system undermine key sources of Washington's power and influence. As international-relations scholars Brian Blankenship and Benjamin Denison keenly observe, "With an American economy more focused on tax cuts than investment in physical and human infrastructure," "alienation of core American allies," and "distrust of U.S. leadership growing among America's strategic partners," current American policy looks exactly the opposite of what the United States should be pursuing if it wishes to prepare for great-power challengers.[8] Put differently, Trump is continuing policies that hasten hegemonic decline at home while adding ones that hasten it abroad.

It remains to be seen whether these policies and dispositions will outlive Trump's presidency. We also will not know for some time if Trump himself permanently undermined the American system, let alone some liberal dimensions of international order. But even if the Republican Party returns to its pre-Trump foreign-policy equilibrium, it will take major changes in the political landscape to reverse self-inflicted strategic overextension via tax cuts, upward redistribution of wealth, and neglect of the domestic infrastructure that sustains American global power and influence.

FEAR OF TRUMP

In the months before Donald Trump secured the Republican nomination, the American foreign-policy establishment began issuing warnings about the danger he posed to liberal order and the American international system. This was far more than a matter of Trump's statements about Russia and its president, Vladmir Putin. All during the campaign, Trump bashed American allies as deadbeats, happy to rely on American military protection while running up trade deficits with the United States. As Thomas Wright, a Senior Fellow at the Brookings Institution, wrote in January of 2016, Trump is "deeply unhappy with America's military alliances and feels the United States is overcommitted around the world. He feels that America is disadvantaged by the global economy. And is sympathetic to authoritarian strongmen. Trump seeks nothing less than ending the U.S.-led liberal order and freeing America from its international commitments."[9]

After Trump won election with a minority of the popular vote, that worry intensified. By December of 2017, Mark Landler of the *New York Times* could report that Trump "has left the rest of the world still puzzling over how to handle an American president unlike any other. Foreign leaders have tested a variety of techniques to deal with him, from shameless pandering to keeping a studied distance." As he quoted Richard Haas, president of the Council on Foreign Relations and former director of policy planning in George W. Bush's State Department, "We're beginning to see countries take matters into their own hands. They're hedging against America's unreliability."[10]

A little over six months later, experienced Republican foreign-policy hand Kori Schake wrote, "We may look back at the first weeks of June 2018 as a turning point in world history: the end of the liberal order." His "aggressive disregard for the interests of like-minded countries, indifference to democracy and human rights and cultivation of dictators" represents "the new world Mr. Trump is creating. He and his closest advisers would pull down the liberal order, with America at its helm, that remains the best guarantor of world peace humanity has ever known."[11] After the 2019 Munich Security Conference, Wright argued that efforts to pretend things are fine in US-European relations had proven futile: "The American position is collapsing under the weight of its own contradictions. The Europeans are defaulting to nostalgia for a multilateral order. Meanwhile, the true challenge of a rising authoritarian bloc goes largely ignored."[12]

These are not isolated opinions. Many scholars of American foreign policy believe that Trump's "transactional bilateralism" and zero-sum approach to foreign policy threatens to negatively transform the American system—and potentially cause its collapse.[13] Even those optimists who think that the "liberal order can survive Trump" still consider him "a meaningful threat to the health of both American democracy and the international system."[14]

Other scholars, even those hostile to Trump, find this analysis overwrought. A significant part of this pushback surrounds the concept of liberal order, which we discussed in Chapter 2. As we argued there, we need not succumb to ahistorical nostalgia or whitewash the very mixed record of US foreign policy to recognize that there are important liberal elements in international order. Nor should we assume that these elements are unequivocally good. Still, to the extent that Trump contests or actively seeks to reorder them, he does undermine lynchpin components of the current

American system. To the extent that he takes the United States out of the game of pushing for broader liberal ordering, Trump does increase the likelihood that international order will evolve in ways more convivial to authoritarian and kleptocratic regimes.

WHY TRUMP IS UNUSUAL

It has become fashionable to stress continuities between Trump and his predecessors, especially in light of Trump's failures to fully implement his foreign-policy dispositions. While such analysis does serve as a useful corrective, it risks understating Trump's distinctiveness. Recall the three major arenas of liberal ordering: political, economic, and intergovernmental. As the Cold War developed, a number of tensions emerged around liberalism in American foreign policy rhetoric and practice. Should the United States prioritize multilateral governance, even when doing so empowers illiberal forces, helps rival powers, or requires setting aside immediate strategic gains? Should the United States instead ignore multilateral governance when it, for example, protects illiberal domestic arrangements in other states—whether in the form of violations of human rights, undemocratic institutions, or closed economic policies? Even within these broad trade-offs, policymakers often faced more specific dilemmas, such as whether to privilege democracy or open markets. This led American policymakers, for example, to sometimes support autocratic regimes that pursued economic liberalization, while opposing democratic regimes that adopted socialist policies.[15]

Power-political expediencies often attenuated, or simply overwhelmed, these tensions between different dimensions of liberal ordering. The United States supported plenty of autocratic governments, human-rights abuses, and atrocities—whether out of broader geostrategic concerns or narrower economic interests. Some of the governments it formed close partnerships with, such as that of the Kingdom of Saudi Arabia, remain major human-rights abusers. Washington also overthrew or undermined democratically elected governments.

For example, in 1954 it ousted the president of Guatemala, Jacobo Árbenz. Both fears of Communism and Árbenz's conflicts with the American United Fruit Company played an important role in President Eisenhower's decision to orchestrate the coup[16] (the partnership between Saudi Arabia and the United States had as much to do with oil as shared anti-Communist principles).[17] The military governments that succeeded Árbenz committed, with American active and tacit support, a series of atrocities that culminated in genocidal military operations against rural Mayans.[18] In the 1970s and 1980s, the United States backed massive campaigns of torture and executions in Argentina and Chile.[19] Although Washington ultimately forced out autocratic regimes in South Korea and the Philippines during the 1980s, it did so only after decades of support.[20] Throughout the Cold War, ideological, economic, and geostrategic considerations often fused together to drive American support for authoritarian, anti-Communist governments and movements.

These tensions did not disappear after the Cold War. Rather, they mutated. The collapse of the Soviet Union and, with it, any sense of Communism as a geostrategic threat to the United States and liberal democracy, eventually enhanced the importance of tensions between liberal intergovernmentalism and enlargement. The central grand-strategy debate of the early 2000s, which played out during the George W. Bush administration, pivoted on the relative importance of the two.

After the September 11 attacks on the United States, the Bush administration firmly embraced neoconservative foreign-policy principles. It took up, at least rhetorically, the cause of democratic enlargement, while strongly affirming the right of the United States to use force unilaterally. The so-called Bush doctrine emphasized the central importance of American primacy in promoting democracy and international peace and reserved the right to wage preventive warfare (confusingly, or perhaps misleadingly, referred to as "preemption") against threats—particularly involving nuclear, biological, and chemical weapons—before they truly emerged.[21]

Some proponents of the Bush doctrine of preemptive war argued against multilateralism on grounds of necessity. For many neoconservatives, "the influence of illiberal regimes in institutions such as the UN hampered effective multilateral responses in institutions. Moreover, democratic allies—whether from corrupt economic entanglements, a lack of commitment to liberal principles, or willful ignorance—sometimes fail to recognize the threat posed by the enemies of liberal order."[22] That is, they privileged the spread of political and economic liberalism, what we might term "liberal enlargement," over liberal intergovernmentalism. As international-relations scholars Brian Schmidt and Michael C. Williams argue, by "embracing democracy as the universally best form of government, and by committing themselves to spreading democracy across the globe, neoconservatives are in important respects the heirs of Wilsonian liberalism."[23] Neoconservatives still hold that the best way to assure American leadership, security, and liberal order—which they often see as essentially synonymous—is to maintain American military supremacy and freedom of action. Trump's third National Security Advisor, John Bolton, rejected the neoconservative label, but his outlook converged with an extreme variant—one inherently hostile to agreements that restrict the "free hand" of the United States. As he told journalist Graeme Wood, "The greatest hope for freedom for mankind in history is the United States, and therefore protecting American national interest is the single best strategy for the world."[24]

In contrast, liberal internationalist critics of the Bush doctrine emphasized the importance of liberal intergovernmentalism for the stability of liberal order and American leadership. For them, liberal order fundamentally depends on institutionalized international cooperation and a commitment to general rules of state conduct—rules that apply to hegemonic powers as well as to weaker ones. Multilateral cooperation and rule-based order, according to liberal internationalists, play a key role in reducing pressures for military competition and the likelihood of great-power war. Multilateralism also facilitates open economic relations and international action on collective problems—such as environmental challenges, terrorism, and the spread of nuclear weapons. Liberal internationalists also argued, and still argue, that a commitment to multilateral consultation and restraint is central to making American hegemony acceptable to other states, especially second-tier great powers.[25]

Generally speaking, most of "the action" in establishment foreign-policy debates, prior to Trump, happened within these parameters. Most participants agreed on the broadest contours of the convergence wager but disagreed on how to handle the trade-offs between liberal intergovernmentalism and liberal enlargement. They differed in their assessment of the relative threats to American interests and liberal ordering posed by non-state forces, such as transnational terrorism and climate change, and states, such as China, Russia, and Iran. They argued over how much to compromise concerns for democracy and human rights in light of other geostrategic interests. But very few challenged the idea that the

United States benefited from *some kind* of liberal order or from preserving the pillars of the American international system, most notably the NATO alliance.[26]

This helps explain why some Trump critics downplay the backlash among many allies created by the Bush administration's doctrine of preemption and the American-led invasion of Iraq. Liberal internationalists have incentives to stress that, whatever else his problems, Bush at least shared some commitment to liberal order and the American system. This emphasis also arguably makes it easier to find common cause with establishment conservative and neoconservative critics of Trump foreign policy, many of whom supported the Iraq War. Those further on the left, as well as some on the right who opposed the Iraq War, find all of this preposterous. Iraq and the Bush doctrine produced a severe crisis in transatlantic relations;[27] the war itself killed an estimated 400,000 people.[28] For some of these critics, it suggests that there really is no daylight between liberal internationalists and neoconservatives.

There are important truths in both these perspectives; they highlight different, important things about Trump's place in the arc of recent American foreign policy.

First, the Bush doctrine and the Iraq War provide a crucial backdrop for the Trump administration. Among other things, Trump is more worrisome for many American partners and allies *precisely* because of the disruption of the first term of the Bush administration.[29]

Second, we do not need to downplay the ways in which the George W. Bush administration spooked many European allies—more generally, damaged American prestige abroad,[30] killed a lot of civilians, and initiated a war that drained American blood and treasure—to recognize that Trump really is an outlier among post–Cold War American presidents. Trump offered a way to resolve the standard trade-offs of American liberal ordering and to address perennial concerns about the hypocrisy created by Washington's championing of "liberal values" while supporting brutal dictators or invading other countries. That is, he put on the table the possibility of dispensing with liberal ordering altogether.[31] Bush sought to modify aspects of the architecture of international order and the American system. Trump not only rejects its architecture but portrays all of its infrastructure—from NATO, to trade agreements, to America's relatively small foreign-aid budget—as horrible deals struck by idiots.[32]

Every flavor of foreign-policy liberalism, and even some forms of realism, believe that international agreements can be positive-sum: that all participants can find themselves better off. Trump's rhetoric was, and continues to be, relentlessly zero-sum: the United States does better when other states are doing worse.[33] Trump trashes institutionalized multilateralism and prefers cutting bilateral deals. He's not wrong that multilateral negotiations can dilute American bargaining power by allowing other states to form united fronts against American demands.[34] But those agreements may also be less durable and thus riskier given the continued erosion of American relative economic leverage.[35] The advantages of isolating negotiating partners also erode if other states pursue cooperation, multilateral or otherwise, while the United States sits on the sidelines. This is precisely what we've seen: traditional American allies have moved forward with the Trans-Pacific Partnership (TPP); Japan and the EU have created a major free-trade agreement. Note that such alternative-order building reinforces liberal aspects of international order, but at the potential cost of the strength of the American system.[36]

Trump's distaste for multilateral settings and negotiations leads him to privilege selective engagement with those foreign leaders he feels personally comfortable with. These officials tend to hail from authoritarian states, have authoritarian dispositions, readily affirm Trump's worldview, or are intertwined with the business world from which Trump hails—one of shell corporations, money laundering, and wealthy investors willing to sink resources into money-losing ventures if it serves their political interests. In practice, this means that Trump appears most comfortable with the leaders of great-power challengers, such as Vladmir Putin of Russia and Xi Jinping of China, and those who form part of the recent wave of democratic backsliding, such as Viktor Orbán of Hungary and Recep Erdoğan of Turkey.

Scholars Rebecca Lissner and Mira Rapp-Hopper put it this way in early 2018: "Regardless of whether Trump supporters voted for or despite his foreign policy positions, the 'America First' vision, with its defiant nationalism and ruthless transactionalism, is a decidedly radical departure from the strategic mainstream. Indeed, it explicitly repudiates the core tenets of liberal internationalism and implicitly rejects the United States' position atop the liberal international order."[37]

HOW TRUMP FACILITATES ANTI-ORDER CONTENTION AND ALTERNATIVE-ORDER BUILDING

Proponents of liberal order advanced a number of fears about Trump foreign policy, especially given early positions taken by the Trump administration. Trump sought to scale back development assistance but now seems to have softened his position under pressure to respond to China's Belt and Road Initiative.[38] Overall, Trump has not completely abandoned some of the traditional ordering mechanisms used by the United States. But he has increased the profile of the United States in terms of *contesting* liberal elements of international order. Trump and his representatives articulate an alternative vision of international order to that previously found in major statements of American foreign policy. It combines a narrowly conceived self-interest with an emphasis on the inviolability of national sovereignty.[39] This vision accords, for better or worse, with that of many autocratic powers, such as Russia, which, as we saw in Chapter 4, prefer an order focused on "state sovereignty and bargaining between great powers in a multipolar system."[40]

The Trump administration has actively contested, or pushed back against, both dimensions of liberal ordering. For example, it has sought to cut aid to the United Nations, going so far as to try to find ways to circumvent congressional appropriations.[41] It withdrew from the UN Human Rights Council (UNHRC) and the UN Educational, Scientific, and Cultural Organization (UNESCO),[42] decisions likely to further enhance the influence of authoritarian states in those bodies.[43] In December 2017 it pulled out of negotiations for the Global Compact on Migration, citing sovereignty concerns.[44]

Few of the actions taken by Trump—from slapping tariffs on US allies to pulling out of treaties—are unprecedented in post–Cold War American foreign policy. The Bush administration, for instance, withdrew from the Anti-Ballistic Missile (ABM) Treaty in 2002 and from the Optional Protocol of Vienna Convention on Consultation Relations in 2005. Still, Trump is dumping international agreements at a much higher rate than any of his predecessors. By 2019, the Trump administration had withdrawn from (or signaled its intent to withdraw from) three treaties, one executive agreement, one political commitment, and two international organizations (see Table 7.1). Some of these, such as the Joint Comprehensive Plan

TABLE 7.1. US Withdrawals (or Declared Intent to Withdraw) from International Agreements, Organizations, and Treaties, 1991–2019

President	Year	Name	Type
Clinton	1995	Pan-American Railway Congress Association	International Organization
	1995	World Tourism Organization	International Organization
	1996	United Nations Industrial Development Organization	International Organization
Bush	2002	1972 Antiballistic Missile Treaty	Treaty
	2005	Optional Protocol of Vienna Convention on Consular Relations	Treaty
Trump	2017	Paris Agreement	Executive Agreement
	2018	Joint Comprehensive Plan of Action (JCPOA)	Political Commitment
	2018	United Nations Human Rights Council	International Organization
	2018	Universal Postal Union	International Organization
	2018	Treaty of Amity with Iran	Treaty
	2018	Optional Protocol of the Vienna Convention on Diplomatic Relations	Treaty
	2018	UNESCO	International Organization
	2019	1987 Intermediate Range Nuclear Forces (INF) Treaty	Treaty

of Action (JCPOA) (the "Iran Deal") and the Paris Agreement on climate change, were painstakingly negotiated multilateral arrangements.

The Trump administration's hostility toward liberal aspects of international order finds reflection in a broad range of settings. The United States has generally, albeit with some exceptions, supported European integration. Surveying world politics from the early twenty-first century, it is easy to forget that, since World War II, one of the central pillars of American grand strategic thought is that great-power warfare in Europe endangers

American security, as it creates the possibility of a hostile power achieving European hegemony and thus putting itself in the geostrategic position to threaten North America.[45]

European integration, perhaps paradoxically, provided a vehicle to achieve this objective. During the Cold War, it promised to enhance Western European solidarity and, through economic gains, capacity to stand against the Soviet threat. In the post–Cold War era, most American policymakers saw European integration as a way of suppressing potential interstate rivalries in the region and embedding European countries in a strong, constitutively liberal confederacy. Both would make the emergence of an expansionist, anti-American power less likely. Thus, while American strategic calculations varied over time, the project became increasingly central to Washington's visions of liberal ordering.[46] Indeed, some analysts see European integration as providing an important hedge against American decline. It offers the possibility of a strong partner helping to uphold, at least in broad terms, the American system and liberal facets of international order.

Trump, however, views the EU primarily as a geopolitical rival. He has, at least rhetorically, consistently aligned with right-wing, sometimes post-fascist, movements within Europe—all of which treat the EU as a key political foil. As Patrick Kingsley reported in 2018, "Some European diplomats and analysts" believe that "his administration is trying to divide the European Union, a bloc that he regards as a powerful trade competitor." Trump "has frequently criticized the union, even describing it as a trade 'foe,' while praising the Continent's insurgent, populist forces. His . . . new ambassador to Germany, Richard A. Grenell, has said he hopes to empower conservative forces across the Continent."[47] Trump's antipathy to the EU finds reflection in his repeated support for Brexit and the ties between his campaign and pro-Brexit politicians.[48] As columnist Natalie Nougayrède put it in December 2018, "Trump is interested in an isolated UK and a disemboweled EU which would no longer be able to set rules and standards in trade. Putin wants to secure geopolitical gains for Russia in Europe in a quest for a sphere of influence."[49]

The Trump administration has consistently de-emphasized the importance of human rights and democracy in its rhetoric and practices while adopting language and tropes similar to those of right-wing, illiberal movements. In his 2017 speech in Warsaw, Trump effectively endorsed European ethno-nationalist discourse, declaring at one point that "we must work together to confront forces, whether they come from inside or out, from the South or the East, that threaten over time to undermine these values and to erase the bonds of culture, faith and tradition that make us who we are."[50] As one of us wrote at the time, "For Trump to utter these lines in Poland, while unequivocally praising its government, amounts to full-throated support for Law and Justice's erosion of democratic safeguards. It's a gut punch to those fighting for civil liberties and the rule of law in the country. It explicitly endorses the arguments of the Polish nationalist right. More broadly, it transforms the entire meaning of Trump's speech into an articulation of an ethno-civilizationalist vision of the West."[51]

At home, the Trump administration adopted similar policies and strategies as those found in backsliding regimes. It created significant barriers to accepting refugees and took a hard line—including in ways that violate basic human rights—against asylum-seekers. Trump's efforts to delegitimize reporters and media outlets that he views as unfavorable reflect the strategy of the leaders of autocratic and backsliding regimes—some of those leaders have added Trump's signature cry of "fake news" to their rhetorical toolkit. While the current wave of gerrymandering—which is so intense in some states that Republicans cling to power even when they receive an outright minority of the vote—predates Trump, his judicial appointments and Department of Justice directives make such electoral manipulation (again, a feature of electoral authoritarian regimes) more difficult to dislodge.[52] Indeed, in June 2019 the Supreme Court of the United States, including two justices appointed by Trump, voted 5–4 that federal courts could not rule on the constitutionality of political gerrymandering.[53]

Of course, the United States has not been a consistent champion of liberal democracy and political rights at home either. Until the 1960s, many American states were racialized authoritarian enclaves under the rubric of "Jim Crow."[54] But these developments—both specific to Trump and more general—come at a time of an "authoritarian wave" that is, as political scientists Anna Lührmann and Staffan I. Lindberg find, "affecting an unprecedentedly high number [that is, twenty two] of democracies." The wave does not take the form of coups or revolutions, but slow erosion under the cloak of legality. That is, it involves "democratic backsliding" as officials manipulate electoral processes, undermine independent media, and pass laws designed to consolidate their hold on power.[55]

Recall from earlier chapters that this wave is almost certainly related to the rise of authoritarian capitalist and kleptocratic great powers, which stand as both alternative potential patrons and political models. It follows that the current moment seems an inauspicious time for the United States to abandon even everyday mechanisms, such as diplomatic pressure, for encouraging democratization and open societies while also taking active steps to closely align itself with backsliding and authoritarian states. Moreover, the fact of America's *own* backsliding in this environment (the United States has even been downgraded in global democracy indexes),[56] combined with domestic political dysfunction driven by high levels of partisan polarization,[57] affects the ability of the United States to serve as a successful democratic model. Indeed, only a handful of countries, most notably Russia and Israel, have seen improvements in public opinion toward the United States since the end of the Obama administration,[58] especially on matters of respect for freedom.[59]

Finally, the affinities among Trump and American right-wing counter-order movements, European right-wing counter-order movements, and Russia help explain Trump's reluctance to take steps against Moscow's information-warfare and brokerage efforts—and thus to limit their ability to disrupt the current order from within. Trump himself is a creature of the kleptocratic financial flows that have played a role in these efforts, as they not only provided material support for the American right but also kept the Trump organization afloat.[60] This nexus exploits vulnerabilities in both the domestic systems of many advanced industrialized democracies and also the way that liberal order has facilitated capital mobility—the flow of money and finance across borders.[61]

These challenges obviously predate Trump and will continue after he has gone. They create avenues not only for Russian influence, but also for that of other illiberal, cash-rich countries—including China and a number of Middle Eastern autocracies.[62] As Diana Pilipenko and Talia Dessel of the Center for American Progress warn, "Unless Congress . . . enacts significant legislative reforms to address faults in the U.S. financial system and campaign finance laws," American "elections—and, by extension, [the U.S.] Constitution—will remain vulnerable to the 'profligacy of corruption' and 'pestilence of foreign influence' that President Adams warned our nation of more than two centuries ago."[63] Given the desire of Republican officials, and judicial appointments, for deregulation of campaign finance, and the influence of the financial sector on both parties, it may prove extremely difficult to respond to these vectors for undermining contemporary international order.

Thus, Trump's contestation of liberal order, especially in terms of its democratization and liberal rights components, is both symptom and accelerant of broader trends at home and abroad. Shifts in global power reduce Washington's ability to engage in liberal ordering, especially in the face of opposition from other great powers. Trump is not responsible for longer-term trends of democratic erosion and partisan dysfunction in the United States. But he seems to be making them worse while encouraging broader pushback against liberal order overseas—especially from members of the American hegemonic system.

TRUMP AND THE AMERICAN SYSTEM

Trump's unprecedented number of withdrawals from international agreements, often with minimal consultation with those allies and partners likely to be most affected, and his demands to renegotiate others has made him deeply unpopular among core US allies.[64] This has contributed to an overall sense that Trump is damaging the lynchpin relationships and infrastructure of the American system.

Some view these characterizations as alarmist.[65] Secretary of Defense Donald Rumsfeld disparaged France and Germany as "old Europe" in 2003, and conservatives engaged in a systematic campaign against France for opposing the Iraq War,[66] yet the alliance persisted. They also point out that for all his denigration of NATO, Trump has continued to increase military support for the alliance via the European Deterrence (Reassurance) Initiative first developed under Obama in the wake of Russia's 2014 invasion of Ukraine.[67] Calls for burden sharing by American allies have been a feature of American politics for decades.[68] In classified remarks to the National Security Council in 1963, President John F. Kennedy stressed the need "to seek to prevent European states from taking actions which make our balance of payments problem worse" and noted that the United States "cannot continue to pay for the military protection of Europe while the NATO states are not paying their fair share. . . . We have been very generous to Europe and it is now time for us to look out for ourselves, knowing full well that the Europeans will not do anything for us simply because we have in the past helped them."[69] Indeed, both major Democratic contenders for the 2016 nomination, Hillary Clinton and Bernie Sanders, called for greater burden sharing. The agreement for NATO members to aim for military budgets of

2 percent of GDP, which Trump repeatedly invoked, was negotiated under the Obama administration.[70]

Some observers consider it ridiculous that more European officials than ever are talking about developing the capabilities to decouple from their alliance with the United States. They note that despite Trump's rhetoric, NATO's infrastructure remains robust. James Kirchick argues that "as long as Trump remains in the White House, expect most European thought leaders to continue using him as an excuse to avoid contending with the continent's serious, systemic and structural problems, or pretend that these challenges are somehow the fault of the ogre in the White House."[71] Here we see echoes of accusations of European political opportunism during the Bush years. In 2002, for example, German Chancellor Gerhardt Schroeder secured re-election by running against Bush foreign policy.[72]

However, Trump's intense pressures for burden sharing come in a radically different context from those of, say, the 1950s and 1960s. As historian Francis J. Gavin points out, "it is hard to underestimate the economic and domestic political pressure on American policy makers to pull U.S. troops out of Europe during" that period: "Eisenhower, Kennedy, and Johnson all expressed a strong desire to 'redeploy' out of Europe in order to strengthen the U.S. balance of payments." But they also fundamentally wanted to keep NATO intact in order to deter the Soviets and prevent the destabilizing consequences of Western European powers all going their own way on security policy.[73] Never before has an American president so routinely attacked NATO and questioned its strategic value to the United States.

The degree to which Trump overtly treats the American security system as an extortion racket may be even greater than his public rhetoric suggests. In March 2019, Nick Wadhams and Jennifer Jacobs reported that "under White House direction, the administration is drawing up demands that Germany, Japan and eventually any other country hosting U.S. troops pay the full price of American soldiers deployed on their soil—plus 50 percent or more for the privilege of hosting them, according to a dozen administration officials and people briefed on the matter." Indeed, they wrote, "Trump has championed the idea for months. His insistence on it almost derailed recent talks with South Korea over the status of 28,000 U.S. troops in the country when he overruled his negotiators with a note to National Security Adviser John Bolton saying, 'We want cost plus 50.'" Moreover, some countries would get a "good behavior discount" if "their policies align closely with the U.S."[74]

Such a policy might, like many of Trump's proposals, go nowhere. But even its serious consideration indicates a great deal about Trump's dispositions—as does the fact that numerous government officials leaked word of it, presumably in the hope that congressional and public pressure would derail it. The very fact that Trump produces a united front among many European governments merely underscores the depth of the problem. More broadly, Trump's election raises questions about the ability of the American electoral systems to produce candidates committed to key pillars of the American system and to some degree of liberal ordering. The recent memory of the Bush years certainly suggests that recurrent Washington-driven crises in transatlantic relations are the "new normal."[75]

HOLLOWING OUT AMERICAN INFRASTRUCTURE IN THE FACE OF GREAT-POWER CHALLENGERS

Trump's attacks on the architecture and infrastructure of the American system are clearly a gift to challengers. Repeatedly calling into question America's commitment to NATO forwards the Russian goal of undermining transatlantic cohesion. To the extent that Trump succeeds in convincing major European states that the United States cannot be trusted, and thus encourages them to decouple their military security from NATO, then Trump is both undermining, for good or for ill, the European pillar of the American security system. For China, the situation is more mixed. But any unforced disruptions to the American system open up the possibility of favorable changes in the international political ecosystem. For example, whatever one thinks of the TPP in terms of its distributional effects in the American economy, it was the main mechanism on the table for Washington to create trade arrangement that might mitigate, if not counterbalance, Chinese economic leverage in East Asia. Trump has not put forward anything resembling a credible "Plan B" after pulling out of the process.[76]

It is easy to focus on the anxiety and uncertainty produced by Trump among some American allies. Some suggest that this reflects an isolationist worldview or, more positively, greater realism when it comes to the sustainability of American global power. This kind of picture is complicated by the Trump administration's interest in expanding virtually every facet of American *military* power. Trump routinely signals that he wants to see defense cuts and campaigned on reducing the defense budget, but he also approved and boasts of larger defense budgets.[77] Independent of specific levels of military spending, Trump routinely calls for American military dominance in the air, land, sea, and space.[78] Whether he can achieve that, of course, is another matter entirely. But the Trump administration clearly aims to better challenge Beijing's own growing military capabilities. While the underlying policy of preparing for possible military confrontation with China—including countering Chinese "anti-access/area denial" capabilities designed specifically to inhibit Washington's ability to project military power into China's neighborhood—remains similar to that of prior administrations, the Trump administration is also intent in deploying new capabilities. Withdrawal from the Intermediate-Range Nuclear Forces (INF) Treaty, for example, will allow the United States to deploy its own conventional and nuclear intermediate-range missiles in the region, thus addressing China's current advantage.[79] A central motivation for the Trump administration's nuclear policy appears to be to counter Russian capabilities.[80]

However, this combination—of a major push to double down on American military supremacy while creating uncertainty about at least some of America's core alliances and partnership—may be particularly risky. Among other things, it suggests an approach to hegemony more dependent upon military instruments, and thus on the ability (and willingness) of the United States to continue extremely high defense spending. It depends on the wager that the United States both can and should substitute raw military power for its hegemonic infrastructure. It assumes that if America takes its toys and goes home from international institutions, their diminished relevance will outweigh the consequences of lost American influence. And these wagers come in the context of domestic policies that seem designed to erode, rather than enhance, America's ability to engage in long-term great-power competition.

We normally associate the push for burden sharing with policies of retrenchment. Such policies, which can range from incremental tweaks to systematic changes in grand strategy, aim to cope with the problem of strategic overextension. Retrenchment entails some combination of shedding international security commitments and shifting defense burdens onto allies and partners.[81] This allows the retrenching power, in principle, to redirect military spending toward domestic priorities, particularly those critical to long-term productivity and economic growth. In the current American context, this means making long-overdue investments in transportation infrastructure, increasing educational spending to develop human capital, and ramping up support for research and development. This rationale makes substantially less sense if retrenchment policies do not produce reductions in defense spending—which is why Trump's aggressive, public, and coercive push for burden sharing seems odd. Recall that Trump and his supporters want, and have already implemented, increases in the military budget. There is no indication that the Trump administration would change defense spending if, for example, Germany or South Korea increased their own military spending or more heavily subsidized American bases. Nor does it seem likely that those resources would even go toward deficit reduction.[82]

The other rationale for retrenchment is to better match capabilities to strategic priorities. This was the idea behind the Obama administration's 2011 "pivot" to Asia. It believed that its drawdown from the Middle East and the "Reset" of relations with Russia meant that it could, and should, prioritize Asian security. As Secretary of State Hillary Clinton explained, "We need to be smart and systematic about where we invest time and energy, so that we put ourselves in the best position to sustain our leadership, secure our interests, and advance our values." It followed, she argued, that "one of the most important tasks of American statecraft over the next decade will therefore be to lock in a substantially increased investment—diplomatic, economic, strategic, and otherwise—in the Asia-Pacific region."[83]

The legacy of the pivot remains contested.[84] Critics contend that it sent the wrong signals to Europe, Russia, and China. European leaders worried about abandonment, Moscow interpreted the announcement as giving it more room to push its agenda, and Beijing saw it as confirmation that the United States wanted to contain and encircle China. It is entirely possible that the Obama administration could have pursued the same expanded partnerships and diplomatic activity without calling it a "pivot," especially because it did not really change the trajectory of American allocation of military and economic resources.[85]

In the end, the pivot did not produce retrenchment. Russia's invasion of Ukraine in 2014 led to expanded commitments to Europe. In this context, some of the ideas circulating in the early Trump administration represent a more radical run at Obama administration policy—that is, the notion that the United States could make a sweeping accommodation with Moscow, which in turn would allow Washington to shift toward more aggressive containment of China—perhaps with Russia ultimately joining in the anti-China coalition.[86] In this scenario, the "savings" would be over the long haul: by significantly decoupling from European security, the United States would spend less than it would if deterring both Russia and China.

In March 2017, both authors participated in a forum on the failure of the Reset and the prospects for the Trump administration when it came to striking a grand bargain.[87] The general consensus was that the Reset collapsed for a variety of reasons, but the fundamental problem was that there was no way to translate cooperation on areas of mutual interest into a grand bargain without Washington making sweeping concessions on NATO policy and liberal ordering. Trump himself seemed perfectly comfortable with those concessions, as they matched his apparent outlook on foreign policy. But his ability to fully reorient American foreign policy would be limited by institutional constraints, Republicans in Congress, and the political pressure generated by the growing investigation into connections between the Trump campaign and Russian contacts.

Put differently, absent Moscow deciding that China posed a sufficient threat that Russia would accommodate the United States, there are only two possible outcomes. On the one hand, the United States could deliberately transform the American system and reorient its ordering activities in line with Russian interests. On the other hand, Washington could fail to strike a grand bargain. What Trump has done, instead, is a series of half measures that risk weakening the American system and facilitating illiberal order-contestation—but without any grand bargain that *might* produce strategic upsides.

Thus, the first few years of Trump policy reveal two fundamentally flawed assumptions about American global power. One concerns a lack of appreciation of the critical importance of the international infrastructure of the American system—and the broad range of power resources that it provides to Washington. The notion that the United States can retain hegemony largely on enormous military budgets dates back to the 1990s, when many future Bush administration officials wagered that shoveling money into the Defense Department would deter other states from even trying to compete.[88] This was clearly a bad bet, as evidenced by China's military expansion. Indeed, the idea that American security can rest largely on raw military capabilities should have been buried after the failure of the occupation of Iraq.

As we discussed in Chapter 2, the American system is sustained through an extensive web of alliances and partnerships, which itself rests on a variety of routine cooperative practices; transnational networks that include bureaucracies, diplomats, and military personnel; and other infrastructure that generates significant military and political interdependencies. This infrastructure is supported by a range of non-military (sometimes called "non-kinetic") instruments, including diplomatic capital and cultural capital. We earlier pointed out some of the damage that Trump policies have done to the State Department. We also noted that Trump's efforts to slash funding for diplomacy and foreign aid were rebuffed by Congress. But Trump remains intent on making the United States increasingly dependent on military instruments. Trump's most recent budget called for budget cuts of "around 25 percent" to the "State Department and US Agency for International Development."[89] And while many Republicans have recently opposed these efforts, they have a history of slashing funding for non-military capabilities.[90]

Even without such cuts, there are indications that the United States has been underinvesting in non-military sources of power. At the same time, many policymakers make an implicit assumption that "American values" and "American culture" are a kind of perpetual-motion machine for moral authority and cultural capital, what the eminent international-relations scholar and foreign-policy practitioner Joseph Nye calls "soft power." America, by virtue of being "America," can retain significant non-military instruments of power. As we touched on in prior chapters, American moral, cultural, and ideological capital is much more dependent than not on the existence of a strong economy, high standard of living, and functional political institutions. Moreover, these sources of power were cultivated, again largely during the Cold War, through significant investments by the State Department, the United States Information Agency, and the Central Intelligence Agency.[91]

Thus, while the infrastructure of the American system, from its diplomatic networks to its cultural capital to its web of alliances and partnerships, has helped maintain the American system in the face of Trump's inconsistent antipathy and disruptive dispositions, it cannot persist without ongoing efforts and commitments by their participants. As we discussed in Chapter 2, the web of institutionalized international cooperation depends on trust and consent from American allies. It operates as a force multiplier for the varied instruments of state power, including diplomacy and intelligence. American influence is, both literally and figuratively, subsidized by allies and partners. It also includes, or closely overlaps with, almost all of the great powers *other* than Russia and China. This means that the United States need not worry about great-power challenges from, for example, Germany, France, and Japan; instead, it can treat their capabilities as components of the American security system.

In short, the hegemonic system built by the United States now underpins America's position as a global superpower.[92] It will take significant resources and years of diplomatic labor for China to hope to create something equivalent; absent the kind of rivalry seen during the Cold War, it may simply be impossible for any great power to construct such a system. As long as Washington conserves the core of its system, Beijing will be hard-pressed to find an equivalent coalition of allies. As of now, it is very difficult to imagine how Russia can ever match it. Thus, as we have already seen, Moscow sees its best hope as breaking the system apart, whether by exacerbating existing cleavages or by supporting friendly political movements. Trump does not have to proactively aid in these efforts to accelerate them. Doing little, while eroding American diplomatic capital and encouraging allies to route around the United States, is problematic enough.

The other flawed assumption concerns not the international, but rather the *domestic*, infrastructure that undergirds American power. Here the problem lies not just with Trump but with orthodox Republican domestic policies. Trump's signature legislative achievement, a massive round of pro-cyclical tax cuts, did little to produce sustainable economic growth while helping to produce big increases in the federal budget deficit.[93] It was only the latest part of a downward drift in revenue driven by Republican policy preferences (see Figure 7.1),[94] combined with accumulating debt (see Figure 7.2) from the failure of federal revenue to keep up with government spending (see Figure 7.3).[95]

The hold of anti-tax ideology is now so strong in the Republican Party that, as former Ronald Reagan advisor Bruce Bartlett notes, "I'm not sure how many Republicans even know anymore that Reagan raised taxes several times after 1981," let alone pay attention to the overwhelming evidence that tax cuts have not really improved long-term economic growth.[96] The overall package—of keeping taxes well below levels compatible with robust growth, inadequate domestic investment, tolerating increased deficits for the purpose of eventually starving the welfare state, and general policies of redistributing wealth upward—is exactly the opposite of what

FIGURE 7.1 US Federal Tax Receipts as Percentage of Gross Domestic Product, 1940–2018

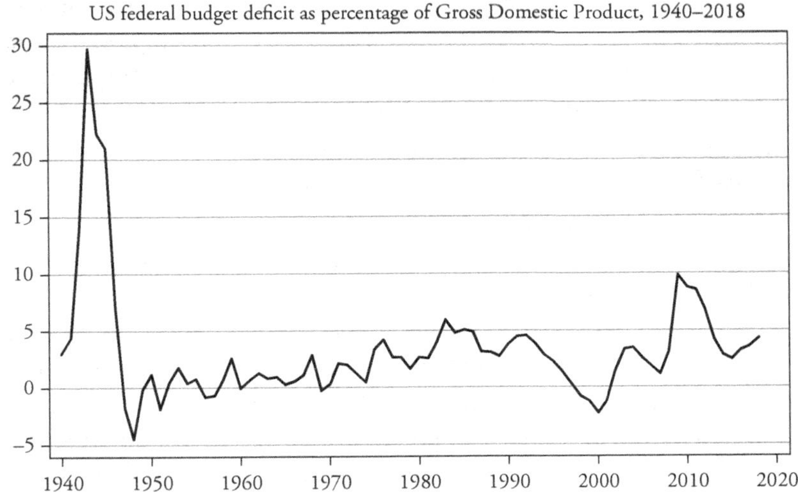

FIGURE 7.2 US Federal Budget Deficit as Percentage of Gross Domestic Product, 1940–2018

you would expect for a domestic program designed for a coming period of great-power competition.[97] Moreover, as international political economist Thomas Oatley argues, financing large wars and other large military outlays through debt may help drive American boom-and-bust cycles.[98]

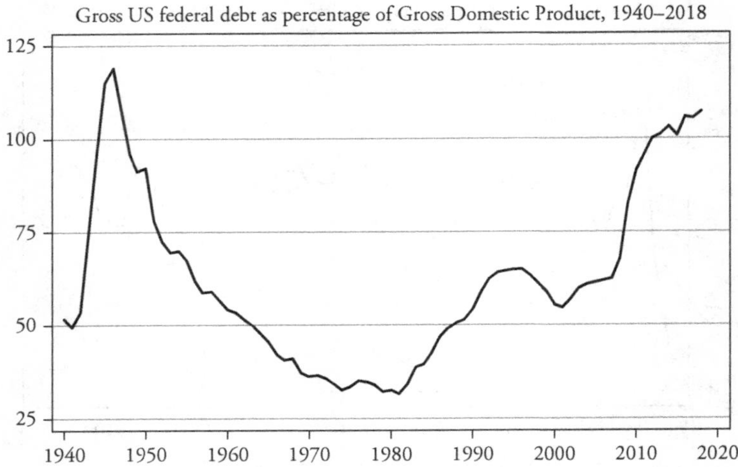

FIGURE 7.3 Gross US Federal Debt as Percentage of Gross Domestic Product, 1940–2018

In many respects, the United States is essentially coasting on major investments in transportation, technology, and human capital that date from the Cold War. These formed the basis of continued American scientific leadership and, with it, its advantages in military technology. But while Beijing has been massively investing in these areas—and perhaps overinvesting—the United States is not on track to maintain its historical edge. True, overall American spending on research and development as a percentage of GDP is near post-war highs, but most of that spending is from sources other than the federal government (see Figure 7.4), and thus does not necessarily reflect strategic priorities.[99] In the absence of a renewed commitment on these fronts—what political scientist Sean Kay calls "new Sputnik moments"—the United States will find it much more difficult to compete with other international powers, let alone maintain the underlying engines of US military and economic strength.[100]

At the same time, Trump's domestic priorities may further erode the social bargain that makes Americans willing to divert resources overseas. Trump campaigned on the idea that America was getting a bad deal from the international order, but tax cuts, underinvestment, and attempts to weaken America's already (when compared to other advanced industrial democracies) restrained social-insurance policies will only make matters worse.[101]

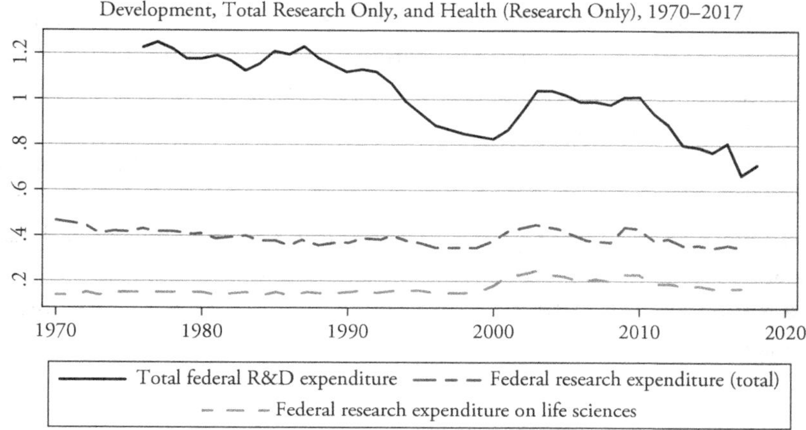

FIGURE 7.4 Federal Expenditure as a Percentage of Gross Domestic Product: Total Research and Development, Total Research Only, and Health (Research Only), 1970–2017

Few Americans want to hear that the United States should raise taxes not just on the wealthy but also on the middle class. No one really likes paying taxes. But these circumstances highlight a basic fact about American global power. The United States has, without question, wasted significant blood and treasure in peripheral wars. These conflicts harmed America's standing and its ability to wage conventional war with great-power challengers. On paper, they fit the pattern associated with hegemonic overextension. However, the United States is not overextended in the traditional sense. Strategically sensible reductions in defense spending, combined with higher taxes and productive domestic investments, would enable Washington to maintain much of the American security system and rebuild and expand its non-military instruments of power. This task will be made considerably easier if the United States stops entering wars of choice, particularly for the purposes of regime change. In sum, Washington can do a fair amount without suffering from the kind of domestic social and economic erosion that is associated with hegemonic cycles. But this will be much harder if American politics and policy choices produce, as they do now, the *effects* of strategic overextension.

Moreover, the United States has been able to run large fiscal deficits and accumulate substantial debt precisely because of its hegemonic ordering, especially in terms of the position of the dollar as a reserve currency. This reflects the economic infrastructure of the American system, much of which is baked, for now, into international order. This advantage will not last forever, and policies that accelerate hegemonic unraveling could undermine it sooner than later.

None of this means that the United States should, or even can, maintain all of its current international commitments. We personally favor retrenchment that focuses on core areas of the American system in Europe and East Asia. But what it does suggest is that policies that take the domestic and international infrastructure of American hegemony for granted will undermine, rather than enhance, American's global position.

CHOOSING ADAPTATION OVER EXIT

The United States is no longer a truly global hegemon. Even the apex of American hegemonic ordering was not really a solo effort; it depended on ongoing, negotiated bargains with second-tier great powers and the European Union. As of now, fundamental trends are producing a rebalancing of economic and military power, with China one of the main beneficiaries. It is *possible*, but unlikely, that we will look back at the 2010s and 2020s as just another period of alarmism about American relative decline.

Already realized changes in the international ecology mean that Washington has less ability to influence these processes than it did just 20 years ago. For example, China's consumer market has *already* surpassed that of the EU and is set to overtake that of the United States, Washington "still retains significant reservoirs of structural power. But in the arena of regulation, the United States is not even first among equals."[102] It will now need to coordinate with not only the EU, but also China, if it wants to create global regulatory standards.

The United States probably can't prevent the rise of the "rest," and trying to do so isn't a particularly good idea. It would condemn many people to poverty while greatly increasing the risk of destructive conflict. But these shifts do not mean that the United States will, absent some kind of catastrophe, cease to be a global great power. Nor does it have to mean the end of the American system or the end of liberal ordering when it comes to human and political rights. A shift in relative power need not mean a loss of absolute power, the end of international arrangements that have served

American interests extremely well, and the ability to positively reform international order, whether in terms of reducing globalized kleptocracy or combating climate change. It certainly does not require the erosion of American democratic institutions and the transformation of the current authoritarian wave into a tsunami.

The likelihood of these outcomes depends on policy choices, for which the next decade will prove crucial. But rather than making America great again, Trump and Trumpism represent impulses toward geopolitical suicide. While some, such as those on the extreme right or the "anti-imperialist left" (for whom "the enemy of my enemy is my friend, and my enemy is American influence") might welcome such an exit from within, we do not think any of the likely alternative orders it will produce are particularly convivial. We turn to those in the conclusion.

8

Heading for the Exit

This book is scheduled to come out during the 2020 presidential campaign. Democrats will almost certainly campaign on a platform to restore American leadership. They will promise to recommit to international agreements such as the Paris Accord on climate change, uphold America's commitment to promoting human rights and democracy, and reassure traditional allies about US security commitments. They will pledge to combat foreign, and especially Russian, interference in American politics. Trump, of course, will claim that he has already restored American prestige and power. But whether or not Trump wins a second term, the challenges facing the American hegemonic system and the forces producing shifts in international order will continue. They predate Trump's election. They extend well beyond the overseas favorability ratings of any particular US president. They relate to basic shifts in the global economy and distribution of power.

We began this book by discussing anxieties about American decline in the 1980s. Recall that a series of political shocks and economic surprises erased those anxieties, leading to a period of "unipolar exuberance." The Soviet Union and its ordering infrastructure collapsed. Within a few years, the advanced industrialized economies, led by the United States, achieved a virtual "patronage monopoly" over the provision of international goods.

America experienced a technology-driven economic boom while Japan drifted into its "lost decade." The international ecosystem was dense with transnational networks promoting liberal order in the developing and post-Communist worlds. Now, these pathways head in the opposite direction—toward the exits.

New economic and political shocks may once again change the game. For example, China's seemingly unstoppable rise might derail in a wave of defaults triggered by maturing debt, a collapse in domestic credit markets, or the mismanagement of a financial crisis by Chinese authorities. After two decades of rule by President Putin, Russian domestic protests and elite defections might bring about a regime change that brings to power more, rather than less, Western-oriented leadership. But absent such developments, Washington cannot do much to reverse the global shifts in power that motor challenges from above, below, and within.

What the United States can do is to invest in those areas where it has lost momentum, including human capital, physical infrastructure, and research and development. It can increase its capacity to collect revenue in order to reverse record high deficits. It can take steps to shore up and defend its own liberal democracy. It can coordinate with those allies who remain committed to similar values. It can identify relationships where it still enjoys sufficient influence to push for liberalization. The European Union, if it gets its own house in order, will remain an important partner in any such efforts.

But Washington needs to recognize that its two decades as a global hegemon are likely over. Certainly, no amount of military spending will bring those back—because, in no small part, the most important sources of hegemonic unraveling are non-military in character, driven by alternative-order building and contention over liberal norms and governance. Regimes from around the world are unlikely, for better or for worse, to simply accept the kind of liberal ordering that the United States promoted in the 1990s and 2000s. The existence of alternative patrons brings with it new economic opportunities and sources of political leverage. Perhaps the prospect of turning to Beijing as a developmental model and source of foreign aid will become less appealing if China buckles under economic or political shocks, and if the United States and the European Union recover from their current crises of governance. But even then, we do not expect to see states abandon the pursuit of goods substitution and to cease their efforts to hedge against geopolitical change.

Washington can do little to comprehensively defeat counter-ordering activities. The policy environment that encourages contention over order and alternative-order building is unlikely to change in the near future. Russia and China will continue their ordering activities, regardless of who occupies the Oval Office. US-Russian relations will almost certainly further deteriorate. Sanctions against Russia appear likely to remain enshrined in US law. Russia's favorability ratings with the broader American public seem unlikely to improve very much from their current lows.[1] The last remnant of the nuclear arms control regime, the New Strategic Arms Reduction Treaty (New START), appears set to expire in February 2021. The 2020 presidential campaign will likely force candidates to position themselves as tough on Russia. When it comes to China, both sides of the aisle share concerns about Beijing's overseas economic activities, its trade practices, and its growing interest in asserting its strategic interests.

Finally, transnational counter-order movements are gaining traction, leading to a competitive ecology of liberal and illiberal networks. Populists, primarily but not exclusively on the right, threaten to erode liberal domestic democratic institutions and values. They will continue to challenge, or at least blunt, political-liberal elements of international architecture. Of course, attempts to push illiberal policies by exploiting the anxiety produced by immigration and shifts in traditional values will not always succeed; US public attitudes remain broadly supportive of immigration.[2] This is an arena where the outcome remains particularly uncertain. The fate of counter-order movements within democratic states will likely have a major impact on the sustainability of political-liberal ordering. In the past, though, these forces never gained power in the United States. Trump demonstrates that they can; as long as they remain a potent force in the Republican Party, then party polarization and politicization will make it difficult for the United States to combat the spread of right-wing populism, illiberal variants of cultural conservativism, and white nationalism. In fact, it is more likely that US foreign policy institutions like the United States Agency for International Development (USAID) or the Department of Justice's foreign outreach will be repurposed in the service of supporting faith-based organizations, promoting "religious freedom," and networking global evangelical communities.

ORDERS OF THE FUTURE?

What happens once we pass through the exit? We tend to be wary of predictions. They usually make the prognosticators look foolish. When such predictions prove correct, that's usually more of an accident than a sign of great wisdom. In fact, the degree to which we have already made judgments about the direction of current trends leaves us queasy. But it is necessary to consider possible futures; there is really no way to avoid it when making policy in the present.

We have no shortage of candidates for the next major phase of international ordering. Analysts often use terms like "multipolar" and "post-Western" to speculate about the contours of international order in the absence of American global leadership. But these often leave more questions on the table than they answer. In no small measure because they often fail to adequately disentangle unipolarity, the American hegemonic system, and broader international order.

What does seems pretty clear is that the "convergence" wager of the 1990s and 2000s proved wrong—that all of the pillars of liberalism did not, over the long term, reinforce one another. But we should be mindful that this does not mean the end of all liberal ordering. We think it quite likely that we will instead see further mutations in the mixtures of political, economic, and intergovernmental liberalism that characterize regional and international architectures. So, for the sake of focusing the mind, we consider three possible stylized futures of international order. Each strikes us as at least a *plausible* possibility. They are also not necessarily exclusive.

China's Rise: The G2 and a New Cold War

Over the next few decades, we could see a world increasingly dominated by strategic competition between the United States and China. At the extreme, that competition could morph into a new version of the Cold War. Note that even if China's economy stalls as a result of structural problems and the United States maintains healthy growth, China's current wealth, power, and technological capacity make it a formidable potential rival.

Some scholars and geopolitical analysts think that such a world already exists. As evidence, they point to growing rivalry in the Pacific, trade wars, military planning, and escalating competition in technology sectors. Others argue that as we saw in the Cold War, competition is becoming "multidimensional."[3] Some suggest that the trade wars of Trump's first term, combined with overall growing pressure for the United States to decouple from China economically, will reduce the possible role of trade interdependence in mitigating pressures for more intense competition.[4] Still others point to the potential structural effects of the Chinese leadership in the 5G wireless technology sector provided by the Chinese tech giant Huawei. They see competition over telecommunications infrastructure as seeding Cold War–style global divisions.[5] The argument goes that as American policymakers pressure third countries not to adopt Chinese technology standards—because of its accompanying security vulnerabilities, such as allowing embedded backdoors to intercept sensitive military and commercial data traveling on the network—governments will be forced to adopt either a Western or a Chinese platform. This will generate technological spheres of influence. Even intelligence-sharing networks among NATO countries or the Five Eyes (FVEY))—an intelligence cooperation agreement among Australia, Canada, New Zealand, the United Kingdom, and the United States— could break down as a result.[6]

As we saw in Chapter 7, there is even a line of thought that suggests Washington should abandon its hard-line policies toward Russia on issues like sanctions, democracy promotion, and NATO enlargement in an effort to pry Moscow from its current strategic partnership with Beijing. This basically echoes Cold War strategic calculations governing Sino-US rapprochement in the 1970s, which aimed to counter Soviet power in East Asia.[7]

Increasing competition between the United States and China does have the sound of inevitability. But we need to be careful about talk of a new Cold War. Many Americans, including policymakers and analysts, think that "Cold War" and "great-power competition" are basically synonyms. This makes it difficult to describe possible Sino-American rivalry other than through the lens of the Cold War. Moreover, the Cold War was nowhere near as uniform a strategic competition as it may seem in retrospect. The diplomatic historian Anders Stephanson convincingly argues that the Cold War, as such, only lasted from 1949 until around 1963. US-Soviet rivalry then went through a series of mutations until the Soviet invasion of Afghanistan helped kick off a "Second Cold War" that lasted from 1980 until 1987. We tend to overlook this heterogeneity because the collapse of the USSR in 1991—after the Cold War had ended, as evidenced by Gorbachev's abandonment of Moscow's Eastern and Central European satellites in 1989—creates a convenient bookend.[8]

The Cold War analogy runs into a number of problems. The US-Soviet rivalry involved a bipolar distribution of power and, at least by the later 1960s, a balance of nuclear forces. Moreover, the US-Soviet rivalry only became a Cold War during periods when at least one of the two sides rejected the fundamental legitimacy of the other and thus saw relations through the prism of an *existential struggle* between political systems (domestic and international) and their constitutive ideologies.[9] As Odd Arne Westad puts it, the Cold War "was a bipolar system of total victory or total defeat, in which neither of the main protagonists could envisage a lasting compromise with the other."[10] This meant the equivalent of "total war" but without direct (but plenty of very bloody and costly indirect) military confrontation.[11] You know a Cold War when you see it because nearly *every* possible field of competition—visual arts, music, sports, scientific achievements, chess, and so on—becomes, or is one step away from turning into, a zero-sum struggle to demonstrate the superiority of one of the two systems.[12]

It is possible that the future could come to resemble a new Cold War, but it will take active effort on the part of American and Chinese policymakers. However, we can be virtually certain that in a "two great powers above the rest" scenario, Washington and Beijing will compete to shape the emerging ecology of the international order. They will do so, among other things, by wooing states with the offer of economic and security assistance. But this is unlikely to produce two categorically distinct spheres of influence or rival orders. The Belt and Road Initiative represents a potentially powerful infrastructure of influence, but, at the same time, it is not creating clusters of client states in the way that the Cold War arranged Soviet and American clients. To do that, we need to have two distinct economic orders, with one of them relatively closed to outside trade and investment. Hence the attention to features of telecommunications competition.

However, the countries where China has increased both its economic and strategic presence—Cambodia, Djibouti, Pakistan, and Tajikistan—all appear to be aggressively courting multiple patrons to ensure that they get the best deals and the most goodies. They are all currently "post-Western," but none are exclusively "Chinese." As we have argued in this book, the order-disrupting activities of China stem not from its demands of exclusive partnership but rather from the way that Beijing empowers regimes to alter their position in Western and transatlantic ordering infrastructure.

For example, China's insistence in March 2019 that the Italian government sign a BRI memorandum stunned both EU and US officials, given that Italy has long been a pillar of the transatlantic architecture.[13] China's move westward into countries like Italy and Greece, and those of Eastern Europe seems less driven by the hope of producing subservient client states than by the desire to gain access to the European market and to get a more favorable hearing within established ordering institutions such as the European Union.

But, even if it committed to do so, could the United States effectively counter Chinese economic infrastructure and asset substitution in third areas like Africa, Eurasia, and Latin America? The Trump administration has issued far more critical assessments of the BRI and Chinese overseas investments than its predecessor.[14] In a speech about the new US strategy for Africa at the White House, former National Security Advisor John Bolton observed that China and Russia, as "great power competitors," are "deliberately and aggressively targeting their investments in the region to gain a competitive advantage over the United States."[15] Bolton added that "China uses bribes, opaque agreements, and the strategic use of debt to hold states in Africa captive to Beijing's wishes and demands," arguing that such "predatory actions" are a core part of the Belt and Road Initiative (BRI), which has the "ultimate goal of advancing Chinese global dominance."[16]

Washington's growing hostility to the BRI manifested in March 2019 when Washington and Beijing clashed over the inclusion of the mention of the BRI in a UN resolution to extend the body's political mandate in Afghanistan. In both 2016 and 2017, the BRI received mentioned as playing a part in Afghanistan's reconstruction efforts; US officials objected to including references to the Chinese initiative in 2019 given the initiative's "known problems with corruption, debt distress, environmental damage, and lack of transparency."[17] Despite growing concern in Europe over China's policy, the US has been unable to force a collective, transatlantic response to China's overseas development activities. Indeed, Washington's failure to halt traditional allies and partners from joining the Asian Infrastructure Investment Bank as founding members in 2015 seems more prelude than exception.

A similar type of dynamic may characterize China's role as a source of global political influence. On issues that Beijing considers central to its sovereignty and security, such as those related to its policies toward Tibet or the Uighurs in Xinjiang, Beijing will ignore international criticism. But it will also attempt to proactively reshape global architecture away from political-liberal principles and toward principles of sovereignty and non-interference associated with liberal intergovernmentalism. We have already seen how China secured a plurality of the members of the United Nations Human Rights Council in support of its Xinjiang mass "re-education camps." Its broader efforts are much more systematic.[18] In 2017, Human Rights Watch detailed how China has operated within the UN system to block expert and activist testimony on human rights committees, prevented NGOs that have criticized China from receiving UN accreditation, and intimidated and harassed UN staff on treaty bodies.[19] Beijing, along with Russia, has "led efforts to cut funding for key peacekeeping and human rights posts and missions, including 170 peace-related jobs."[20] In March 2018, China introduced a resolution titled "Promoting the International Human Rights Cause through Win-Win Cooperation" at the Human Rights Council in Geneva, which effectively called for replacing the system of universal periodic review that involves expert testimony, benchmarks, and public assessments with intergovernmental "dialogue" and "cooperation."[21]

More broadly, China will continue to erode liberal norms within global governance structures, including delegitimizing the standards and principles associated with international media openness, curtailing the power of nongovernmental watchdogs, and even clamping down on academic and scholarly research. It seems likely to continue exporting surveillance technologies across the world that will strengthen the hands of autocrats and make them dependent on Chinese standards. A 2018 report on digital freedoms from the watchdog Freedom House found that of 65 BRI partner countries, China had convened seminars or trainings on media or informational management with 36 of these; 38 countries have installed Chinese-manufactured internet and mobile equipment, including the new 5G networks.[22] Beijing is also likely to keep pressuring countries that host Uighur groups or communities to render them back to China, in contravention of international humanitarian norms and asylum procedures.

The United States may push back on some of these practices and, assuming a post-Trump administration, may even more aggressively advocate democratic values and human rights, but its credibility as a steward of norms and values will have been severely eroded.[23] More likely, Democrats and Republicans will converge on China's treatment of minorities as a common basis for criticizing Beijing, which will further fuel claims that Washington raises human rights issues selectively for geopolitical purposes. But it is hard to imagine something like a "Helsinki Act moment," where the

United States and China agree on a common set of values and principles and make commitments to respect them.

In sum, although the likelihood of US-China strategic competition is very real, the current trajectory suggests less a Cold War than a more typical great-power rivalry. Still, competition for influence will profoundly alter the ecology of international order, likely benefiting governments but also worsening global protection of civil, political, and human rights. Indeed, all of this assumes the political failure of Trumpism (or its successors) in the United States. If the United States moves decisively in the direction of right-wing populism and illiberalism, a Sino-US world will prove a very rough place for liberal democracy indeed.

Multipolarity without American Liberal Ordering

We might also see a world characterized by multipolar competition and, at best, an architecture with very little in the way of liberal elements.

In one version, associated with Trumpism, the United States would privilege its interactions with the most consequential powers around the world. Countries "that matter" would include militarily powerful states (like China and Russia), wealthy states (Saudi Arabia and Japan), and regional powers such as Brazil or Egypt. In this formulation, global commitments, such as providing foreign aid and humanitarian assistance, funding UN peacekeeping missions, supporting international institutions, and engaging in global regulatory efforts would be defunded or severely downgraded.

Moreover, trade deals might be taken out of the purview of global institutions like the World Trade Organization (WTO). Instead, they would be renegotiated as bilateral accords that are linked with non-trade issues such as payments for an American military presence or security guarantees. Indeed, according to one early exposé of the Trump administration, the emerging foreign policy of the White House or "Trump doctrine" was comprised of three sets of state interactions: "powers we can work with, powers we cannot work with, and those without enough power whom we can functionally disregard or sacrifice."[24] The withdrawal of the Trump administration from a number of international agreements, forums, and governance bodies is also driven by the desire to deprive these multilateral architectures of their purpose and power.

This future resembles a realist order, or perhaps a concert system divided into spheres of influence. In the Russian vision of a multipolar or polycentric world, for example, great powers that can claim a sphere of influence—based on military power, but also economic and cultural reach—get a seat at the table. In turn, great powers pragmatically cooperate and transact with other great powers while smaller powers lack agency and voice over broad rule-making. Critically, great powers would coordinate and link their respective infrastructures with those of other great powers, but without a hegemonic arbitrator or global rule-maker.

This could mean regional hegemonies with fairly extensive intergovernmental infrastructure, albeit hierarchical versions clearly dominated by leading powers. But note that it is *more* liberal—in terms of intergovernmentalism—than Trump's preferred order, which disdains multilateralism altogether. China, for its part, seems quite comfortable with alternative-order building that replicates liberal intergovernmentalism stripped of liberal norms.

Recall that Trump's case against international institutions is about more than the incompatibility of its liberal political values with his "nationalist" agenda. It is also a bet that weakening or even dismembering multilateral institutions will give the United States greater international leverage when negotiating international agreements. European states, for example, enjoy much greater market power when combined into the European Union than as individual countries negotiating on a bilateral basis. Such thinking also likely informs the continuing attempts to cut the budget of the State Department—including entire governance-related initiatives like combating AIDS or addressing climate change—while continuing to boost the Pentagon's budget. In this world of naked material competition, the use of selective incentives and reciprocity takes the place of universal principles and global compliance, thereby advantaging the most militarily powerful.

China and Russia do not support important aspects of American-led international order and certainly are not fans of US hegemony, but they are keenly aware of the power-political dividends that accrue from generating architectures and controlling infrastructures of order. China and Russia will continue to pursue liberal intergovernmentalism as the US retreats to bilateral transactionalism. If anything, by withdrawing from existing multilateral institutions the Trump administration makes it easier for Russia and China to get their way, thus making intergovernmentalism more, not less, attractive to illiberal states. Thus, rather than rendering international organizations and institutional arrangements irrelevant, Trump foreign policy only accelerates the process of transferring their control and leadership to geopolitical challengers. As we noted in the prior section, we are already seeing this dynamic play out.

Moreover, Trump-style foreign policy might actually stimulate the development of alternative ordering infrastructure that bypasses the United States altogether, thus further eroding American influence. Recall how the US withdrawal from the JCPOA (the Iran nuclear deal) and its use of its financial power to make other parties comply with the re-imposition of US sanctions, has prompted other states to propose creating new payment systems to settle trade accounts that will bypass US sanctions.[25]

The ultimate result might take a form that we could no longer really term "liberal intergovernmentalism" but would more accurately describe as "authoritarian intergovernmentalism," with the United States shifted to the periphery of ordering infrastructure. To make matters worse for Washington, the transition to bilateral transactionalism would likely prove quite painful—potentially collapsing relationships and ordering infrastructure the United States would prefer to maintain in a multipolar world.

Globalized Oligarchy and Kleptocracy

Our last possibility could emerge in either a bipolar or multipolar world, or one in which the United States was more or less engaged in ordering efforts. In this world, much of the existing global architecture as it pertains to economic liberalism and intergovernmentalism remains. But elements affirming political liberalism, especially in terms of democracy and good governance, significantly erode. Washington either does not use its economic power to tackle corruption and money laundering, or other states "routing around" its financial infrastructure robs it of effective tools to do so.

The current order supports and empowers the movement of money by powerful individuals with ties to their host governments. This future turns that up to eleven. Essentially, it entails the hijacking of specific elements of economic neoliberalism—such as capital mobility, financial deregulation, and the permeability of politics to moneyed interests—and the total cooptation of related infrastructure by oligarchs and kleptocrats.

A striking feature of the liberal international order is how relatively easy it is for authoritarian elites, kleptocrats, and oligarchs to use its institutions, rules, and organs for illiberal purposes, most notably the laundering of their money and their reputations on a global scale. In retrospect, the push for expansion of the global liberal economic architecture and the creation of a number of institutions and supporting services designed to facilitate financial liberalization proceeded without adequate safeguards. It gave birth to a transnational infrastructure built to facilitate grand corruption on an unprecedented global scale.[26]

At the heart of this apparatus lie the United States and Europe, the core of the liberal international order. For example, anonymous companies or shell companies are, contra popular perceptions, not the domain of exotic tax havens and Caribbean islands. They are mostly based in OECD jurisdictions within the UK and the United States (most notably the states of Delaware, Nevada, and Wyoming) that do not comply with Financial Action Task Force guidelines on transparency of ownership.[27] The Panama Papers offered a window into the industrial scale of production of shell companies and how individuals—many of them world leaders—and firms use them to minimize tax obligations and facilitate money laundering. For the extremely wealthy, an entire cohort of international asset managers uses legal mechanisms such as trusts, holding companies, and charitable foundations to dissociate assets from their owners, while Western service providers—including accountants, bankers, real estate brokers, and lawyers—also facilitate the laundering of questionable wealth.[28]

Once someone successfully moves money, he or she usually stores it in countries that guarantee property rights, such as by placing it in Western banks or buying luxury real estate in destinations such as London, New York, and the Côte d'Azur. The global market for citizenship and investor residency allows elites in one country to acquire the right of residency in exchange for investment.[29]

The connection between these aspects of contemporary international order and domestic political economy is becoming increasingly visible. In the United States, investments in infrastructure, education, healthcare, and research and development—all of which would benefit the "national interest" and which operated as pillars of American domestic political economy during the Cold War—have remained flat, failed to keep up with needs, or been reduced in favor of tax cuts that flow to the very top segment and exacerbate economic inequality.[30]

Such growing inequality is now a worldwide trend. The economist Gabriel Zucman showed that in the United States the top 1 percent owned an estimated 40 percent of wealth in 2016, as opposed to

25–30 percent in the 1980s. He estimated a similar rise of concentrated wealth in China and Russia in recent decades, and "a more moderate rise in France and the United Kingdom."[31] The offshore world is integral to global inequality, with another study estimating that the equivalent of 10 percent of the world's total GDP is now held in tax havens, with the percentages rising significantly to about 60 percent in the Gulf, Latin America, and Russia.[32] The same study also finds that the wealthiest .01 percent of households in the UK, Spain, and France store 30–40 percent of their assets offshore, with this number rising to over 60 percent in Russia. The global governance institutions and actors that in the 1990s appeared to promise transparency, democratization, and global liberal civil society now serve the interests of autocrats and kleptocrats in other ways as well—by providing opportunities for them to present themselves as respected cosmopolitan citizens and international philanthropists.[33]

Western public relations firms routinely take authoritarians as clients, helping to remake their images as "Westernizers" or "reformers" and assist them with campaigning, crisis management, and social-media strategy. The indictments of Paul Manafort, Donald Trump's campaign advisor—which led to his subsequent guilty plea in September 2018 for his activities as an unregistered foreign agent of Ukraine—reveal how this works. Manafort employed an international network of influencers—such as think tanks, journalists, former statesmen, and respected law firms—to soften the image of his kleptocratic client, Ukrainian President Viktor Yanukovych, to Western audiences. Manafort also helped Yanukovych's Party of Regions engineer its gerrymandered majority.[34] More broadly, elites and oligarchs increasingly use their own charities for philanthropic and cultural activities; they donate large sums to Western cultural institutions and universities. For example, in 2011 the London School of Economics came under fire for accepting a $1.5 million donation from Saif-al-Islam Qadafi, the then Libyan dictator's son; a subsequent report criticized the school for exercising "embryonic" diligence.[35]

Liberal international ordering sometimes privileges international oligarchy even at the expense of traditional state power. For example, after Oleg Deripaska—a Russian oligarch with ties to Manafort—was sanctioned along with his business holdings in April 2018 by the US Treasury, for "malign activity" around the world, he initiated a multipronged lobbying campaign that employed an extensive network of public relations firms and lawyers.[36] The campaign successfully appealed to the Trump administration to lift the sanctions on his business holdings, including the aluminum giant Rusal. In January 2019, the US Congress, after another lobbying campaign, failed to stop the Treasury Department from lifting the sanctions, falling short of the necessary two-thirds support in the Senate.[37] In response, in April 2019, Deripaska took the extraordinary step of suing the Treasury for sanctioning him in the first place, claiming that the sanctions had resulted in "the wholesale devastation of Deripaska's wealth, reputation, and economic livelihood."[38]

International oligarchy also requires a porous government or a foreign-policy apparatus that is susceptible to capture. The role of money in securing access and influence in American domestic policy has long been the subject of criticism. But the foreign-policy sphere has generally received less attention from champions of good governance. The Trump administration is helping to change that, especially because of concerns about how the private interests of the president and his family might shape US foreign policy.

The president's son-in-law Jared Kushner has been accused of using his position as senior advisor, and even access to highly classified information, to secure possible favors from foreign actors like the Saudi government.[39] At the very least, the White House's refusal to sanction, or even condemn, the Saudi leadership for the brutal abduction and murder of *Washington Post* columnist Jamal Khashoggi in the Saudi embassy in Ankara, raised the prospect that not only was the United States abandoning the sanctioning of human rights offenders, but that it had failed to even assign blame in the case because of potential private conflicts and personal ties. Similarly, China's favorable decision to grant trademarks to Ivanka Trump—the president's daughter and advisor—in the midst of an escalating trade war between the countries struck many as an attempt influence the administration. The same was true of China's decision to grant a cluster of patents to President Trump's business in 2017 after Trump met with Chinese president Xi Jinping.[40] Investigative reporting first uncovered in 2018 that then-candidate Trump had been secretly trying to secure a Trump Tower project in Moscow while he was campaigning for the Republican nomination.[41] In November 2018, Trump's former personal lawyer and fixer, Michael Cohen, pled guilty to a federal charge of lying to Congress about the duration and substantial involvement of Trump in these negotiations.[42]

As we discussed in Chapter 7, Trump stands at the nexus of right-wing populism and globalized oligarchy. What's most notable about this pattern of conflicts of interest is how typical it is in many parts of the world, where many leaders (and their supporters) extract rents from the state and then offshore their wealth. As the Panama Papers demonstrated, illegal, or technically legal but corrupt, extraction and expatriation of wealth through political connections and power is, in fact, a significant problem even within liberal democracies. Absent international efforts by democratic great powers to reverse these trends, they are likely to grow worse. Certainly, Russia and other illiberal great powers have little incentive to interfere with their own standard practices.

EXITING HEGEMONY

Whether we are entering a world of US-China competition, a multipolar system, an era characterized by international oligarchy, some combination of these possibilities, or a different international system altogether, it remains the case that the ecology of the order is undergoing major transformation. As we observed in our case studies, this transformation is accelerating and showing signs of positive feedback among its major proximate drivers: great-power challenges, bottom-up pressures, and counter-order transnational mobilization.

Some will welcome this shift and view it as giving rise to a more potentially peaceful and equitable distribution of power in the international system. Others will lament the passing of American influence and the liberal ideals that, however inconsistently and hypocritically, American leadership publicly championed. We readily admit that we can only guess at just what type of international system the United States will seek to promote in the future, let alone how its aims will interact with the preferences of other great powers.

What we can say with greater confidence is that the United States will no longer be able to exercise global hegemony, and that it will need to accommodate other powers to a much greater extent than it is used to. At the same time, the pathways that we identified will continue to transform the ecology of the institutions, rules, and norms that shape international political life. We can also confidently predict that regardless of the contours of this new order, the United States will continue to be the most consequential single actor for years, and possibly even decades to come. At the very least, it will be one of, at most, a small handful of first-tier great powers.

Devising a pragmatic, responsible, and publicly articulated strategy to cope with the different pathways comprising this international transition—as opposed to denial or maintaining a mystical American exceptionalism—remains the most important and urgent challenge confronting United States foreign policy.

Notes

CHAPTER 1

1. "Trump Blasts UK PM May's Brexit Plan, Says It Puts Trade Deal in Doubt," Reuters, July 11, 2018.

2. "Trump Calls EU a 'Foe' on Trade, *CBS News* Interview," Reuters, July 15, 2018.

3. In this chapter, we use terms such as "liberal international order" as a shorthand for how American and European powers have ordered significant dimensions of world politics. We discuss the concept, and its limitations, in more detail in subsequent chapters. For overviews of the relevant debates, see Graham Allison, "The Myth of the Liberal Order," *Foreign Affairs*, June 14, 2018, https://www.foreignaffairs.com/articles/2018-06-14/myth-liberal-order; Jeff D. Colgan and Robert O. Keohane, "The Liberal Order Is Rigged," *Foreign Affairs*, April 17, 2017, https://www.foreignaffairs.com/articles/world/2017-04-17/liberal-order-rigged; Alexander Cooley, "Ordering Eurasia: The Rise and Decline of Liberal Internationalism in the Post-Communist Space," *Security Studies* 28, no. 3 (June–July, 2019): 588–613, https://doi.org/10.1080/09636412.2019.1604988; Daniel Deudney and G. John Ikenberry, "The Nature and Sources of Liberal International Order," *Review of International Studies* 25, no. 2 (April 1999): 179–96; G. John Ikenberry, *Liberal Leviathan: The Origins, Crisis, and Transformation of the American World Order* (Princeton, NJ: Princeton University Press, 2011); G. John Ikenberry, "The Plot against American Foreign Policy: Can the Liberal Order Survive," *Foreign Affairs* 96, no. 1 (February 2017): 2–9; Rebecca Friedman Lissner and Mira Rapp-Hooper, "The Liberal Order Is More Than a Myth," *Foreign Affairs*, July 31, 2018, https://www.foreignaffairs.com/articles/world/2018-07-31/liberal-order-more-myth; Rebecca Friedman Lissner and Mira Rapp-Hooper, "The Day after Trump: American Strategy for a New International Order," *Washington*

Quarterly 41, no. 1 (January 2, 2018): 7–25, https://doi.org/10.1080/0163660X.2018.1445353; Paul Musgrave and Daniel Nexon, "American Liberalism and the Imperial Temptation," in *Empire and International Order*, ed. Noel Parker (London: Routledge, 2013), 131–48; Patrick Porter, *A World Imagined: Nostalgia and Liberal Order*, Cato Institute Policy Analysis No. 843 (Washington, DC: Cato Institute, June 5, 2018), https://www.cato.org/publications/policy-analysis/world-imagined-nostalgia-liberal-order.

4. "Nearly Half of Americans Link Defense of NATO to Allies' Spending: Reuters/Ipsos Poll," Reuters, July 18, 2018.

5. Paul Musgrave, "International Hegemony Meets Domestic Politics: Why Liberals Can Be Pessimists," *Security Studies* 28, no. 3 (June–July, 2019): 451–78, https://doi.org/10.1080/09636412.2019.1604983.

6. Daniel H. Nexon, "On American Hegemony, Part I," *Lawyers, Guns & Money* (blog), July 27, 2018, http://www.lawyersgunsmoneyblog.com/2018/07/american-hegemony-part.

7. See Kurt M. Campbell and Ely Ratner, "The China Reckoning," *Foreign Affairs*, August 2018; Thomas Wright, *All Measures Short of War: The Contest for the Twenty-First Century and the Future of American Power* (New Haven, CT: Yale University Press, 2017), chap. 1.

8. This assumes the rough accuracy of measurements of Chinese GDP.

9. See Chapter 2.

10. Robert Gilpin, *War and Change in World Politics* (Cambridge: Cambridge University Press, 1983). On Third World challenges to declining US power, see Stephen D. Krasner, *Structural Conflict: The Third World against Global Liberalism* (Berkeley: University of California Press, 1985).

11. Charles Poor Kindleberger, *The World in Depression, 1929–1939* (Berkeley: University of California Press, 1986).

12. Robert O. Keohane, *After Hegemony: Cooperation and Discord in the World Political Economy* (Princeton, NJ: Princeton University Press, 1984). Indeed, as Carla Norrlof and others have shown, American economic power may actually have increased in the wake of the collapse of Bretton Woods (see Chapter 2). Carla Norrlof, *America's Global Advantage: US Hegemony and International Cooperation* (Cambridge: Cambridge University Press, 2010).

13. Paul Kennedy, *The Rise and Fall of the Great Powers: Economic Change and Military Conflict from 1500 to 2000* (New York: Random House, 1987).

14. Ezra F. Voegel, *Japan as Number One: Lessons for America* (New York: Harper and Row, 1985).

15. George Friedman and Meredith Lebard, *The Coming War with Japan* (New York: St Martin's Press, 1991).

16. On the roles of Soviet republican nationalist movements and uncertain property rights, see, respectively, Mark Beissinger, *Nationalist Mobilization and the Collapse of the Soviet State* (Cambridge: Cambridge University Press, 2002); and Steven Lee Solnick, *Stealing the State: Control and Collapse in Soviet Institutions* (Cambridge, MA: Harvard University Press, 1998).

17. Initially, only a few commentators recognized this—among them, Charles Krauthammer, who coined the phrase "unipolar moment." See Charles Krauthammer, "The Unipolar Moment," *Foreign Affairs*, February 2, 1991, https://www.foreignaffairs.com/articles/1991-02-01/unipolar-moment. It would take the failure of European

powers to handle warfare and ethnic cleansing in the Balkans to make the new reality of American primacy absolutely clear.

18. Crude indicators, such as share of global military spending, suggest that it was, at least for the moment, the collapse of the Soviet Union, not an absolute rise in US military power, that drove this shift. See Nexon, "Hegemony, Part I." However, the 1990–1991 Gulf War demonstrated that American precision-strike and combined-arms capabilities easily exceeded those of other major powers—whose military planners took note. See Rebecca Rose Lissner, "Grand Strategic Crucibles: The Lasting Effects of Military Intervention on State Strategy" (thesis, Georgetown University, 2016), 236ff, https://repository.library.georgetown.edu/handle/10822/1042837; Jacqueline Newmyer, "The Revolution in Military Affairs with Chinese Characteristics," *Journal of Strategic Studies* 33, no. 4 (August 2010): 483–504, https://doi.org/10.1080/01402390.2010.489706; David S. Yost, "France and the Gulf War of 1990–1991: Political-military Lessons Learned," *Journal of Strategic Studies* 16, no. 3 (September 1993): 339–74, https://doi.org/10.1080/01402399308437522.

19. Francis Fukuyama, "The End of History?" *National Interest* 16 (1989): 3–18.

20. *Journal of Democracy* 1 (January 1990).

21. Alexander Cooley and Jack Snyder, eds., *Ranking the World* (Cambridge: Cambridge University Press, 2015).

22. On COMECON, see Randall W. Stone, *Satellites and Commissars: Strategy and Conflict in the Politics of Soviet-Bloc Trade* (Princeton, NJ: Princeton University Press, 1996).

23. The Russian federation maintained some institutional structures to cope with the Soviet dissolution and some governance and security issues in its former Soviet republics. For example, Russia concluded leasing arrangements to ensure continued access to a network of Soviet-era military and strategic installations, including the Black Sea fleet in Sevastopol (then part of Ukraine) and the Baikonur cosmodrome in Kazakhstan. And the very proclamation of December 25 that disbanded the Soviet Union established a looser Commonwealth of Independent States (CIS). All the post-Soviet states except the Baltic states and Turkmenistan eventually joined the CIS. However, it mostly served to manage the institutional legacies and coordination issues inherited from the Soviet system rather than to define a new basis for cooperation on regional matters; Russia organized and dispatched CIS peacekeepers to guard ceasefires between the government forces and breakaway territories in Georgia and Moldova, and decisively intervened on behalf of the government of Tajikistan during the Tajik Civil War (1992–1993).

24. Mary Elise Sarotte, *1989: The Struggle to Create Post-Cold War Europe*, updated ed. (Princeton, NJ: Princeton University Press, 2014).

25. The European Union came into being, as such, in 1993 as a result of the Maastricht Treaty.

26. Ronald D. Asmus, *Opening NATO's Door: How the Alliance Remade Itself for a New Era* (New York: Columbia University Press, 2004); Joshua R. Itzkowitz Shifrinson, *Rising Titans, Falling Giants: How Great Powers Exploit Power Shifts* (Ithaca, NY: Cornell University Press, 2018); James M. Goldgeier, *Not Whether but When: The U.S. Decision to Enlarge NATO* (Washington, DC: Brookings Institution Press, 2010).

27. Lissner, "Grand Strategic Crucibles."

28. Secretary of State Madeleine K. Albright, Interview on NBC-TV, *The Today Show* with Matt Lauer, Columbus, Ohio, February 19, 1998, As released by the Office of

the Spokesman, US Department of State. https://1997-2001.state.gov/statements/1998/980219a.html.

29. Robert Wade, "Japan, the World Bank, and the Art of Paradigm Maintenance: The East Asian Miracle in Political Perspective," *New Left Review* (1996): 3–37.

30. Valerie J. Bunce and Sharon L. Wolchik, "International Diffusion and Postcommunist Electoral Revolutions," *Communist and Post-Communist Studies* 39, no. 3 (2006): 283–304; Valerie Bunce and Sharon L. Wolchik, "Transnational Networks, Diffusion Dynamics, and Electoral Revolutions in the Postcommunist World," *Physica A: Statistical Mechanics and Its Applications* 378, no. 1 (May 2007): 92–99, https://doi.org/10.1016/j.physa.2006.11.049.

31. Janine R. Wedel, *Collision and Collusion: The Strange Case of Western Aid to Eastern Europe* (New York: St. Martin's Press, 1998).

32. Juliet Johnson, *Priests of Prosperity: How Central Bankers Transformed the Postcommunist World* (Ithaca, NY: Cornell University Press, 2016).

33. The seminal work in this area is Margaret E. Keck and Kathryn Sikkink, *Activists beyond Borders: Advocacy Networks in International Politics* (Ithaca, NY: Cornell University Press, 1998).

34. SIPRI Military expenditure database, https://www.sipri.org/databases/milex.

35. "Address by President of the Russian Federation." *President of Russia*, March 18, 2014, http://en.kremlin.ru/events/president/news/20603.

36. On the IMF's enhanced credibility in imposing its conditions in Africa in the 1990s, see Thad Dunning, "Conditioning the Effects of Aid: Cold War Politics, Donor Credibility, and Democracy in Africa," *International Organization* 58, no. 2 (2004): 409–23.

37. Joseph E. Stiglitz, *Globalization and Its Discontents*, (Norton: New York, 2002).

38. Steven Levitsky and Lucan Way, "The Rise of Competitive Authoritarianism," *Journal of Democracy* 13, no. 2 (2002): 51–65. On Central Asia's securitization and rising authoritarianism post-9/11, see Alexander Cooley, *Great Games, Local Rules: The New Power Contest in Central Asia* (New York: Oxford University Press, 2012). On similar dynamics in Africa, see Cédric Jourde, "The International Relations of Small Neoauthoritarian States: Islamism, Warlordism, and the Framing of Stability," *International Studies Quarterly* 51, no. 2 (June 2017): 481–503.

39. Larry Diamond, Marc F. Plattner, and Christopher Walker, eds., *Authoritarianism Goes Global: The Challenge to Democracy* (Baltimore, MD: Johns Hopkins University Press, 2016).

40. Judith Kelley, "The More the Merrier? The Effects of Having Multiple International Election Monitoring Organizations," *Perspectives on Politics* 7, no. 1 (2009): 59–64.

41. On the rise of the Russian-led CIS monitors, see Rick Fawn, "Battle over the Box: International Election Observation Missions, Political Competition and Retrenchment in the Post-Soviet Space," *International Affairs* 82, no. 6 (2006): 1133–53.

42. See Clifford Bob, *The Global Right Wing and the Clash of World Politics* (New York: Cambridge University Press, 2012).

43. Darin Christensen and Jeremy M. Weinstein, "Defunding Dissent: Restrictions on Aid to NGOs," *Journal of Democracy* 24, no. 2 (2013): 77–91. On the restrictions of foreign funding, see Kendra Dupoy, James Ron, and Aseem Prakash, "Hands Off My Regime! Governments' Restrictions on Foreign Aid to Non-Governmental Organizations in Poor and Middle-Income Countries," *World Development* 84 (2016): 299–311.

44. Stephen W. Kleinschmit and Vickie Edwards, "Examining the Ethics of Government-Organized Nongovernmental Organizations (GONGOs)," *Public Integrity* 19, no. 5 (2017): 529–46.

45. Ivan Krastev, *After Europe* (Philadelphia: University of Pennsylvania Press, 2017).

46. Anton Shekhovtsov, *Russia and the Western Far Right: Tango Noir* (London: Routledge, 2017).

47. See, for example, Stephen Brooks and William C. Wohlforth, "American Primacy in Perspective," *Foreign Affairs* 81, no. 4 (July 2002): 20–33; Ikenberry, *Leviathan*; Robert A. Pape, "Soft Balancing against the United States," *International Security* 30, no. 1 (Summer 2005): 7–45; T. V. Paul, "Soft Balancing in the Age of U.S. Primacy," *International Security* 30, no. 1 (Summer 2005): 46–71; William C. Wohlforth, "The Stability of a Unipolar World," *International Security* 24, no. 1 (Summer 1999): 5–41.

48. Paul Musgrave and Daniel Nexon, "American Liberalism and the Imperial Temptation," in *Empire and International Order*, ed. Noel Parker (London: Routledge, 2013), 131–48.

49. Thomas Wright, *All Measures Short of War: The Contest for the Twenty-First Century and the Future of American Power* (New Haven, CT: Yale University Press, 2017), 1.

CHAPTER 2

1. United States, *National Security Strategy of the United States* (Washington, DC: President of the US, December 1999), iii.

2. United States, *National Security Strategy of the United States* (Washington, DC: President of the US, December 2017), 2, https://www.whitehouse.gov/wp-content/uploads/2017/12/NSS-Final-12-18-2017-0905.pdf.

3. Stewart M. Patrick, "Can the Liberal World Order Survive Two More Years of Trump?," *World Politics Review*, January 15, 2019, https://www.worldpoliticsreview.com/insights/27192/the-liberal-world-order-is-dying-what-comes-next.

4. See G. John Ikenberry, *After Victory: Institutions, Strategic Restraint, and the Rebuilding of Order after Major War* (Princeton, NJ: Princeton University Press, 2001); G. John Ikenberry, *Liberal Leviathan: The Origins, Crisis, and Transformation of the American World Order* (Princeton, NJ: Princeton University Press, 2011).

5. Daniel Deudney and G. John Ikenberry, "The Nature and Sources of Liberal International Order," *Review of International Studies* 25, no. 2 (April 1999): 179–96; G. John Ikenberry, "Why the Liberal World Order Will Survive," *Ethics and International Affairs* 32, no. 1 (2018): 17–29, https://doi.org/10.1017/S0892679418000072; Paul Miller, *American Power and Liberal Order: A Conservative Internationalist Grand Strategy* (Washington, DC: Georgetown University Press, 2016), http://www.jstor.org/stable/j.ctt1ffjnqs. Crucially, liberal internationalists stress that *precisely* those features of liberal order that make American hegemony comparatively durable are the ones that Trump is challenging. As Schake argues: "Beginning in the wreckage of World War II, America established a set of global norms that solidified its position atop a rules-based international system. These included promoting democracy, making enduring commitments to countries that share its values, protecting allies, advancing free trade and building institutions and patterns of behavior that legitimize American power by giving less powerful countries a say." Trump, however, "seems bent on destroying the friendships and respect that bind America and its allies. If he succeeds, America will be seen as—and may even

become—no different from Russia and China, and countries will have no reason to assist America's efforts rather than theirs." Kori Schake, "The Trump Doctrine Is Winning and the World Is Losing," *New York Times*, June 15, 2018, https://www.nytimes.com/2018/06/15/opinion/sunday/trump-china-america-first.html.

6. Rohan Mukherjee, "Two Cheers for the Liberal World Order: The International Order and Rising Powers in a Trumpian World," H-Diplo | ISSF, February 22, 2019, https://issforum.org/roundtables/policy/1-5bo-two-cheers.

7. See, for example, Andrew Bacevich, *American Empire: The Realities and Consequences of U.S. Diplomacy* (Cambridge, MA: Harvard University Press, 2002); Tarak Barkawi and Mark Laffey, "The Imperial Peace: Democracy, Force and Globalization," *European Journal of International Relations* 5, no. 4 (December 1999): 403–34; James Fowler, "The United States and South Korean Democratization," *Political Science Quarterly* 114, no. 2 (1999): 265–88; Maria Höhn and Seungsook Moon, *Over There: Living with the U.S. Military Empire from World War Two to the Present* (Durham, NC: Duke University Press, 2010); Chalmers A. Johnson, *Blowback: The Costs and Consequences of American Empire* (New York: Metropolitan Books, 2000); Dov H. Levin, "When the Great Power Gets a Vote: The Effects of Great Power Electoral Interventions on Election Results," *International Studies Quarterly* 60, no. 2 (June 2016): 189–202, https://doi.org/10.1093/isq/sqv016; J. Patrice McSherry, "Death Squads as Parallel Forces: Uruguay, Operation Condor, and the United States," *Journal of Global South Studies* 24, no. 1 (Spring 2007): 13; Patrick Porter, *A World Imagined: Nostalgia and Liberal Order* (Washington, DC: Cato Institute, June 5, 2018), https://www.cato.org/publications/policy-analysis/world-imagined-nostalgia-liberal-order; Barbara Zanchetta, "Between Cold War Imperatives and State-Sponsored Terrorism: The United States and 'Operation Condor,'" *Studies in Conflict and Terrorism* 39, no. 12 (2016): 1084–102.

8. See, for example, Bacevich, *American Empire*; Barkawi and Laffey, "The Imperial Peace: Democracy, Force and Globalization"; Fowler, "The United States and South Korean Democratization"; Höhn and Moon, *Over There*; Johnson, *Blowback*; McSherry, "Death Squads as Parallel Forces"; Porter, "World Imagined"; Levin, "When the Great Power Gets a Vote"; Zanchetta, "Between Cold War Imperatives and State-Sponsored Terrorism."

9. Mukherjee, "Two Cheers."

10. This tripartite distinction resembles Anne L. Clunan's discussion of "charter liberalism" (intergovernmentalism), "liberal humanism" (political liberal governance), and "economic neoliberalism" (one variant of economic liberalism). Notably, she argues that Russia is fine with the first but not the other two. See Anne L. Clunan, "Russia and the Liberal World Order," *Ethics and International Affairs* 32, no. 1 (2018): 46.This discussion derives from Paul Musgrave and Daniel Nexon, "American Liberalism and the Imperial Temptation," in *Empire and International Order*, ed. Noel Parker (London: Routledge, 2013), 131–48. More broadly, see Deudney and Ikenberry, "Liberal International Order"; Michael W. Doyle, "Kant, Liberal Legacies, and Foreign Affairs," *Philosophy and Public Affairs* 12, no. 3 (Summer 1983): 205–35; Michael W. Doyle, "Kant, Liberal Legacies, and Foreign Affairs, Part 2," *Philosophy and Public Affairs* 12, no. 4 (Fall 1983): 323–53; Andrew Hurrell, "Kant and the Kantian Paradigm in International Relations," *Review of International Studies* 16, no. 3 (1990): 183–205; Ikenberry, *Leviathan*; Beate Jahn, *Liberal Internationalism: Theory, History, Practice* (New York: Palgrave Macmillan, 2013); Immanuel Kant, *Political Writings*, trans. H. B. Nisbet (Cambridge: Cambridge University Press, 1991).

11. The relevant literature is too voluminous to cite with any justice. But for examples that cover some of the debate about effectiveness and the scope of international rights law, see Emilie M. Hafner-Burton and Kiyoteru Tsutsui, "Justice Lost! The Failure of International Human Rights Law to Matter Where Needed Most," *Journal of Peace Research* 44, no. 4 (July 2007): 407–25, https://doi.org/10.1177/0022343307078942; Emilie M. Hafner-Burton, "Sticks and Stones: Naming and Shaming the Human Rights Enforcement Problem," *International Organization* 62, no. 4 (October 2008): 689–716, https://doi.org/10.1017/S0020818308080247; Emilie Hafner-Burton, *Making Human Rights a Reality* (Princeton, NJ: Princeton University Press, 2013); Linda Camp Keith, "The United Nations International Covenant on Civil and Political Rights: Does It Make a Difference in Human Rights Behavior?," *Journal of Peace Research* 36, no. 1 (January 1999): 95–118, https://doi.org/10.1177/0022343399036001006; Mona Lena Krook and Jacqui True, "Rethinking the Life Cycles of International Norms: The United Nations and the Global Promotion of Gender Equality," *European Journal of International Relations* 18, no. 1 (March 2012): 103–27, https://doi.org/10.1177/1354066110380963; Amanda M. Murdie and David R. Davis, "Shaming and Blaming: Using Events Data to Assess the Impact of Human Rights INGOs," *International Studies Quarterly* 56, no. 1 (March 2012): 1–16, https://doi.org/10.1111/j.1468-2478.2011.00694.x; Eric Neumayer, "Do International Human Rights Treaties Improve Respect for Human Rights?," *Journal of Conflict Resolution* 49, no. 6 (December 2005): 925–53, https://doi.org/10.1177/0022002705281667; Beth A. Simmons, *Mobilizing for Human Rights: International Law in Domestic Politics* (Cambridge: Cambridge University Press, 2009); Jana von Stein, "Making Promises, Keeping Promises: Democracy, Ratification and Compliance in International Human Rights Law," *British Journal of Political Science* 46, no. 3 (July 2016): 655–79, https://doi.org/10.1017/S0007123414000489; Susanne Zwingel, "How Do Norms Travel? Theorizing International Women's Rights in Transnational Perspective," *International Studies Quarterly* 56, no. 1 (March 2012): 115–29, https://doi.org/10.1111/j.1468-2478.2011.00701.x.

12. John Gerard Ruggie, "International Regimes, Transactions, and Change: Embedded Liberalism in the Postwar Economic Order," *International Organization* 36, no. 2 (1982): 379–415.

13. Mark M. Blyth, *Great Transformations: Economic Ideas and Institutional Change in the Twentieth Century* (Cambridge: Cambridge University Press, 2002).

14. Rawi Abdelal, *Capital Rules: The Construction of Global Finance* (Cambridge, MA: Harvard University Press, 2007).

15. Dani Rodrik, *The Globalization Paradox: Democracy and the Future of the World Economy* (New York: W. W. Norton, 2012).

16. Duncan S. A. Bell, "Empire and International Relations in Victorian Political Thought," *Historical Journal* 49, no. 1 (2006): 281–98; Jennifer Pitts, *A Turn to Empire: The Rise of Imperial Liberalism in Britain and France* (Princeton, NJ: Princeton University Press, 2006).

17. See Niall Ferguson, "A Victorian Idealist in the White House," *New Statesman*, February 17, 2003; Niall Ferguson, *Colossus: The Price of America's Empire* (New York: Penguin, 2004); Michael Ignatieff, "The Challenges of American Imperial Power," *Naval War College Review* 56, no. 2 (Spring 2003): 53–63; Michael Ignatieff, "The American Empire: The Burden," *New York Times Magazine*, January 5, 2003; Robert D. Kaplan, *Imperial Grunts: The American Military on the Ground* (New York: Random House, 2005); for discussions, see Paul K. MacDonald, "Those Who Forget

Historiography Are Doomed to Republish It: Empire, Imperialism and Contemporary Debates about American Power," *Review of International Studies* 35, no. 1 (2009): 45–67; Alexander J. Motyl, "Is Everything Empire? Is Empire Everything?," *Comparative Politics* 38, no. 2 (January 2006): 229–49; Daniel H. Nexon and Thomas Wright, "What's at Stake in the American Empire Debate," *American Political Science Review* 101, no. 2 (May 2007): 253–71.

18. See, for example, Neta Crawford, *Argument and Change in World Politics*, Cambridge Studies in International Relations (Cambridge: Cambridge University Press, 2002); Julian Go, "Global Fields and Imperial Forms: Field Theory and the British and American Empires," *Sociological Theory* 26, no. 3 (2008): 201–27; Julian Go, *Patterns of Empire: The British and American Empires, 1688 to the Present* (Cambridge: Cambridge University Press, 2012); Paul Musgrave and Daniel Nexon, "States of Empire: Liberal Ordering and Imperial Relations," in *Liberal World Orders*, ed. Tim Dunne and Trine Flockhart (Oxford: Oxford University Press, 2013), 211–30; Meghan McConaughey, Paul Musgrave, and Daniel H. Nexon, "Beyond Anarchy: Logics of Political Organization, Hierarchy, and International Structure," *International Theory* 10, no. 2 (2018): 181–218.

19. No spare account of the architecture of *any* real-world hegemonic or international order would meet the criteria of coherency and consistency demanded by those who see liberal order as a myth or reject the significance of liberal aspects of international order. The idea that they would is only plausible to the typical international-relations analysts because of their comparative familiarity with post-war and post-Cold War order. When one's knowledge of past international systems largely comes from extremely simplified, stylized accounts, one tends to think of them as simpler and more coherent than they actually were.

20. David A. Lake, *Entangling Relations: American Foreign Policy in Its Century* (Princeton, NJ: Princeton University Press, 1999), chap. 5.

21. Alexander Cooley and Daniel Nexon, "'The Empire Will Compensate You': The Structural Dynamics of the U.S. Overseas Basing Network," *Perspectives on Politics* 11, no. 4 (2013): 1036–37.

22. Victor D. Cha, "Powerplay: Origins of the U.S. Alliance System in Asia," *International Security* 34, no. 3 (2010): 158–96, https://doi.org/10.1162/isec.2010.34.3.158.

23. Glenn Dorn, "Perón's Gambit: The United States and the Argentine Challenge to the Inter-American Order, 1946–1948," *Diplomatic History* 16, no. 1 (Winter 2002): 1–20.

24. Ikenberry, *Leviathan*, 100–102; G. John Ikenberry, "Liberalism and Empire: Logics of Order in the American Unipolar Age," *Review of International Studies* 30, no. 4 (October 2004): 609–30.

25. See, for example, Gary J. Bass, *The Blood Telegram: Nixon, Kissinger, and a Forgotten Genocide* (New York: Knopf Doubleday, 2013); Kevin C. Dunn, *Imagining the Congo: The International Relations of Identity* (New York: Palgrave Macmillan, 2003), chap. 3; Jeane Kirkpatrick, "Dictatorships and Double Standards," *Commentary* 68, no. 5 (1979): 34; William M. Leogrande, "From Reagan to Bush: The Transition in US Policy towards Central America," *Journal of Latin American Studies* 22, no. 3 (October 1990): 595–621, https://doi.org/10.1017/S0022216X00020976; J. Patrice McSherry, "Tracking the Origins of a State Terror Network: Operation Condor," *Latin American Perspectives* 29, no. 1 (2002): 38–60; McSherry, "Death Squads as Parallel Forces: Uruguay, Operation Condor, and the United States"; Stephen Rabe, *Eisenhower and Latin America: The Foreign Policy of Anticommunism* (Chapel Hill: University of North Carolina Press, 1988).

26. Mukherjee, "Two Cheers"; indeed, the fact that United States exhibits hypocrisy or employs double-standards, perhaps paradoxically, may help to sustain the very principles that it violates. Otherwise, Washington would simply have to abandon even its situational and inconsistent commitments to liberal norms. As Martha Finnemore and Henry Farrell write, "This system needs the lubricating oil of hypocrisy to keep its gears turning." Henry Farrell and Martha Finnemore, "The End of Hypocrisy: American Foreign Policy in the Age of Leaks," *Foreign Affairs* 92, no. 6 (2013): 34; see also Martha Finnemore, "Legitimacy, Hypocrisy, and the Social Structure of Unipolarity: Why Being a Unipole Isn't All It's Cracked Up to Be," *World Politics* 61, no. 1 (January 2009): 58–85; for broader discussions of the role of hypocrisy in sustaining norms, see Nils Brunsson, *The Organization of Hypocrisy: Talk, Decisions and Actions in Organizations*, trans. Nancy Adler (New York: John Wiley, 1989); Stephen D. Krasner, *Sovereignty: Organized Hypocrisy* (Princeton, NJ: Princeton University Press, 1999).

27. Nexon and Wright, "American Empire Debate"; on electoral interference in particular, see Levin, "When the Great Power Gets a Vote"; Dov H. Levin, "Partisan Electoral Interventions by the Great Powers: Introducing the PEIG Dataset," *Conflict Management and Peace Science* 36, no. 1 (January 1, 2019): 88–106, https://doi.org/10.1177/0738894216661190.

28. Thomas Wright, *All Measures Short of War: The Contest for the Twenty-First Century and the Future of American Power* (New Haven, CT: Yale University Press, 2017), chap. 1.

29. See Larry Diamond, Marc F. Plattner, and Christopher Walker, eds., *Authoritarianism Goes Global* (Baltimore, MD: Johns Hopkins University Press, 2016); Anna Lührmann and Staffan I. Lindberg, "A Third Wave of Autocratization Is Here: What Is New about It?," *Democratization* 26, no. 7, published ahead of print (2019): 1–19, https://doi.org/10.1080/13510347.2019.1582029.

30. Scholars debate, sometimes rather vociferously, whether the story told by hegemonic-order theories actually makes sense. Some dispute the theoretical logic, others the interpretations of history. Many believe that both are fatally flawed. We think that the argument works better in some cases than in others. See, for example, Margit Bussmann and John R. Oneal, "Do Hegemons Distribute Private Goods? A Test of Power-Transition Theory," *Journal of Conflict Resolution* 51, no. 1 (February 1, 2007): 88–111, https://doi.org/10.1177/0022002706296178; Jonathan M. DiCicco and Jack S. Levy, "Power Shift and Problem Shifts: The Evolution of the Power Transition Research Program," *Journal of Conflict Resolution* 43, no. 6 (December 1999): 675–704; Andrew Q. Greve and Jack S. Levy, "Power Transitions, Status Dissatisfaction, and War: The Sino-Japanese War of 1894–1895," *Security Studies* 27, no. 1 (January 2, 2018): 148–78, https://doi.org/10.1080/09636412.2017.1360078; Isabelle Grunberg, "Exploring the 'Myth' of Hegemonic Stability," *International Organization* 44, no. 4 (Autumn 1990): 431–77; David A. Lake, "Leadership, Hegemony, and the International Economy: Naked Emperor or Tattered Monarch?," *International Studies Quarterly* 37, no. 4 (December 1993): 459–89; Douglas Lemke, *Regions of War and Peace* (Cambridge: Cambridge University Press, 2002); Douglas Lemke, "Great Powers in the Post-Cold War World: A Power Transition Perspective," in *Balance of Power: Theory and Practice in the 21st Century*, ed. T. V. Paul, James J. Wirtz, and Michel Fortmann (Stanford, CA: Stanford University Press, 2004), 52–75; Richard Ned Lebow and Benjamin Valentino, "Lost in Transition: A Critical Analysis of Power Transition Theory," *International Relations* 23, no. 3 (September 1, 2009): 389–410, https://doi.org/10.1177/0047117809340481; Duncan Snidal, "The

Limits of Hegemonic Stability Theory," *International Organization* 39, no. 4 (Autumn 1985): 579–614; A. F. K. Organski, *World Politics* (New York: Knopf, 1968); Steven Ward, *Status and the Challenge of Rising Powers* (New York: Cambridge University Press, 2017).

31. Perry Anderson, *The H-Word: The Peripeteia of Hegemony* (New York: Verso Books, 2017), 1.

32. Mark Edward Lewis, "The City-State in Spring-and-Autumn China," in *A Comparative Study of Thirty City-State Cultures*, ed. Mogens Herman Hansen (Copenhagen: C. A. Reitzals Forlag, 2000), 77n49.

33. Michael Doyle, *Empires* (Ithaca, NY: Cornell University Press, 1986), 11; David A. Lake, "Beyond Anarchy: The Importance of Security Institutions," *International Security* 26, no. 1 (Summer 2001): 56, 61; David A. Lake, "Anarchy, Hierarchy and the Variety of International Relations," *International Organization* 50, no. 1 (Winter 1996): 9; Nexon and Wright, "American Empire Debate."

34. See John Darwin, *The Empire Project: The Rise and Fall of the British World-System, 1830–1970* (Cambridge: Cambridge University Press, 2009); MacDonald, "Those Who Forget"; for theoretical elaborations, see McConaughey, Musgrave, and Nexon, "Beyond Anarchy"; G. John Ikenberry and Daniel H. Nexon, "Hegemony Studies 3.0: The Dynamics of Hegemonic Orders," *Security Studies* 3, no. 28 (2019): 395–421.

35. Wim Blockmans, *Emperor Charles V, 1500–1558* (London: Arnold, 2002); Geoffrey Parker, *The Grand Strategy of Phillip II* (New Haven, CT: Yale University Press, 1998); Daniel H. Nexon, *The Struggle for Power in Early Modern Europe: Religious Conflict, Dynastic Empires, and International Change* (Princeton, NJ: Princeton University Press, 2009); Richard Bonney, *The Thirty Years' War, 1618–1648*, Essential Histories (Oxford: Osprey, 2002); Peter H. Wilson, *The Holy Roman Empire, 1495–1806* (London: Macmillan, 1999); Peter H. Wilson, *The Thirty Years War: Europe's Tragedy* (Cambridge, MA: Belknap Press of Harvard University Press, 2009).

36. On the "British system," see Darwin, *The Empire Project*.

37. Ruggie, "Embedded Liberalism," 381; see also G. John Ikenberry and Charles Kupchan, "Socialization and Hegemonic Power," *International Organization* 44, no. 3 (Summer 1990): 283–315.

38. For a detailed account of this adjustment, see Kori N. Schake, *Safe Passage: The Transition from British to American Hegemony* (Cambridge, MA: Harvard University Press, 2017); see also Charles Kupchan, *How Enemies Become Friends* (Princeton: Princeton University Press, 2012), chap. 3.

39. Odd Arne Westad, *The Global Cold War: Third World Interventions and the Making of Our Times*, new ed. (New York: Cambridge University Press, 2007), 73–74, 79–86.

40. Among other things, Versailles also changed the landscape of Europe, largely by dissolving Austria-Hungary into constituent parts and creating new states—Austria, Czechoslovakia, Hungary, and Yugoslavia—out of them.

41. Adam Tooze, *The Deluge: The Great War, America and the Remaking of the Global Order, 1916–1931* (New York: Penguin Books, 2015), 6.

42. Bruce Russett, "The Mysterious Case of Vanishing Hegemony; or, Is Mark Twain Really Dead?," *International Organization* 39, no. 2 (1985): 213, https://doi.org/10.1017/S0020818300026953.

43. Stephen Wertheim, "Instrumental Internationalism: The American Origins of the United Nations, 1940–3," *Journal of Contemporary History* 54, no. 2 (April 2019): 265–83, https://doi.org/10.1177/0022009419826661. For a contemporaneous criticism of this kind of proposal, see Nicholas J. Spykman, *America's Strategy in World Politics: The*

United States and the Balance of Power (New Brunswick, NJ: Transaction Publishers, 2008), 459–60.

44. Mark Mazower, *No Enchanted Palace: The End of Empire and the Ideological Origins of the United Nations* (Princeton, NJ: Princeton University Press, 2009), 17.

45. Robert A. Pollard, "Economic Security and the Origins of the Cold War: Bretton Woods, the Marshall Plan, and American Rearmament, 1944–50," *Diplomatic History* 9, no. 3 (July 1985): 271–89, https://doi.org/10.1111/j.1467-7709.1985.tb00536.x.

46. Carla Norrlof, *America's Global Advantage: US Hegemony and International Cooperation* (Cambridge: Cambridge University Press, 2010), 161.

47. In fact, contemporary Chinese international-relations scholars draw an indigenous tradition to articulate a similar theory that posits two millennia from Chinese hegemonic management in East Asia. Some even turn the tables on European scholars, parsing the American system in terms of Chinese precedents. See, for example, Zhang Feng, "Rethinking the 'Tribute System': Broadening the Conceptual Horizon of Historical East Asian Politics," *Chinese Journal of International Politics* 2, no. 4 (2009): 545–74, https://doi.org/10.1093/cjip/pop010; David Kang, "Hierarchy, Balancing, and Empirical Puzzles in Asian International Relations," *International Security* 28, no. 3 (Winter 2003–2004): 165–85; Yuen Foong Khong, "The American Tributary System," *Chinese Journal of International Politics* 6, no. 1 (2013): 1–47, http://cjip.oxfordjournals.org/content/6/1/1.short; Ji-Young Lee, "Diplomatic Ritual as a Power Resource: The Politics of Asymmetry in Early Modern Chinese-Korean Relations," *Journal of East Asian Studies* 13, no. 2 (August 2013): 309–36, https://doi.org/10.5555/1598-2408-13.2.309; Ji-Young Lee, "Hegemonic Authority and Domestic Legitimation: Japan and Korea under Chinese Hegemonic Order in Early Modern East Asia," *Security Studies* 25, no. 2 (2016): 320–52, https://doi.org/10.1080/09636412.2016.1171970; Ji-Young Lee, *China's Hegemony: Four Hundred Years of East Asian Domination* (New York: Columbia University Press, 2016); Yuan-kang Wang, "Managing Regional Hegemony in Historical Asia: The Case of Early Ming China," *Chinese Journal of International Politics* 5, no. 2 (2012): 129–53, https://doi.org/10.1093/cjip/pos006; Feng Zhang, *Chinese Hegemony: Grand Strategy and International Institutions in East Asian History* (Stanford, CA: Stanford University Press, 2015); Yongjin Zhang and Barry Buzan, "The Tributary System as International Society in Theory and Practice," *Chinese Journal of International Politics* 5, no. 1 (2012): 3–36, https://doi.org/10.1093/cjip/pos001. Khong, "Tributary"; Feng, "Rethinking the 'Tribute System'"; Yaqing Qin, "A Relational Theory of World Politics," *International Studies Review* 18, no. 1 (March 2016): 33–47, https://doi.org/10.1093/isr/viv031; Zhang and Buzan, "The Tributary System as International Society in Theory and Practice."

48. Paul K. MacDonald, *Networks of Domination: The Social Foundations of Peripheral Conquest in International Politics* (Oxford: Oxford University Press, 2014); Andrew Phillips and J. C. Sharman, "Explaining Durable Diversity in International Systems: State, Company, and Empire in the Indian Ocean," *International Studies Quarterly* 59, no. 3 (September 2015): 436–48, https://doi.org/10.1111/isqu.12197; Andrew Phillips and J. C. Sharman, *International Order in Diversity: War, Trade and Rule in the Indian Ocean* (New York: Cambridge University Press, 2015).

49. See Jane Burbank and Frederick Cooper, *Empires in World History: Power and the Politics of Difference* (Princeton, NJ: Princeton University Press, 2010); Stacie E. Goddard, "Embedded Revisionism: Networks, Institutions, and Challenges to World Order," *International Organization* 72, no. 4 (2018): 763–97, https://doi.org/doi.org/10.1017/S0020818318000206; Go, *Patterns*; Charles A. Kupchan, "The Normative Foundations

of Hegemony and the Coming Challenge to Pax Americana," *Security Studies* 23, no. 2 (2014): 219–57; Andrew Phillips, "Contesting the Confucian Peace: Civilization, Barbarism and International Hierarchy in East Asia," *European Journal of International Relations*, no. 4 (2018), 740–64, https://doi.org/10.1177/1354066117716265.

50. Compare Bentley B. Allan, Srdjan Vucetic, and Ted Hopf, "The Distribution of Identity and the Future of International Order: China's Hegemonic Prospects," *International Organization* 72, no. 4 (2018): 5, https://doi.org/10.1017/S0020818318000267; Hedley Bull, *The Anarchical Society: A Study of Order in World Politics* (London: Macmillan, 1977), 8. For theoretically informed discussions of the nature of practices in world politics, see Emanuel Adler and Vincent Pouliot, "International Practices," *International Theory* 3, no. 1 (2011): 1–36, https://doi.org/10.1017/S175297191000031X; Rebecca Adler-Nissen and Vincent Pouliot, "Power in Practice: Negotiating the International Intervention in Libya," *European Journal of International Relations* 20, no. 4 (2014): 889–911, https://doi.org/10.1177/1354066113512702; Christian Bueger and Frank Gadinger, "The Play of International Practice," *International Studies Quarterly* 59, no. 3 (September 2015): 449–60, https://doi.org/10.1111/isqu.12202; Vincent Pouliot, "The Logic of Practicality: A Theory of the Practice of Security Communities," *International Organization* 62, no. 1 (2008): 257–88.

51. Academics will recognize this phrasing as virtually identical to that found in the "agent-structure problem": the notion that society and culture often appear as objective conditions that enable and constrain individuals, yet only exist by virtue of the beliefs and actions of those individuals. And, yes, this means that "international order" is just another way of talking about aspects of international structure. In international-relations theory, order is the new structure. And we'll probably eventually have the same debates about order that we had about structure. For theoretical discussions, see Margaret Archer, *Culture and Agency* (Cambridge: Cambridge University Press, 1988); Walter Carlsnaes, "The Agent-Structure Problem in Foreign Policy Analysis," *International Studies Quarterly* 36, no. 3 (1992): 245–70; David Dessler, "What's at Stake in the Agent-Structure Debate," *International Organization* 43, no. 3 (1989): 441–73; Martha Finnemore, *National Interests in International Society* (Ithaca, NY: Cornell University Press, 1996); Mlada Bukovansky, *Legitimacy and Power Politics: The American and French Revolutions in International Political Culture* (Princeton, NJ: Princeton University Press, 2002); Patrick Thaddeus Jackson and Daniel H. Nexon, "Relations before States: Substance, Process, and the Study of World Politics," *European Journal of International Relations* 5, no. 3 (1999): 291–332; Alexander Wendt, "The Agent-Structure Problem in International Relations Theory," *International Organization* 41, no. 3 (1987): 335–70; Colin Wight, *Agents, Structures and International Relations: Politics as Ontology* (Cambridge: Cambridge University Press, 2006).

52. In his discussion of the "lliberal international order," Charles Glaser complains that the concept is wooly (we agree!) because it is frequently treated as a means *and* an end. The same is true, of course, of the balance of power. He thus argues that "whether an order is a means or a constraint thus depends partly on the phase of its evolution. During its creation, an order is essentially a means to an end; once established, it can be at least partly a constraint. In the longer term, a sufficiently powerful state may be able to revise the order; therefore, in this time frame, the order is primarily a means." This is true to some degree, but we shouldn't let it obscure the fact that even those apparently well-institutionalized orders are sustained by dynamic patterns of practices and relations. See Charles L. Glaser, "A Flawed Framework: Why the Liberal International Order

Concept Is Misguided," *International Security* 43, no. 4 (April 1, 2019): 55–57, https://doi.org/10.1162/isec_a_00343.

53. On assemblages, see Michele Acuto and Simon Curtis, *Reassembling International Theory: Assemblage Thinking and International Relations* (New York: Palgrave Macmillan, 2013); McConaughey, Musgrave, and Nexon, "Beyond Anarchy"; Saskia Sassen, *Territory, Authority, Rights: From Medieval to Global Assemblages* (New York: Cambridge University Press, 2006).

54. One venerable school of thought, realism, sees *anarchy* as the fundamental ordering principle of international politics. That is, states lack a common authority, let alone a world government, to make and enforce rules. Organizations like the United Nations don't count as a common authority because they lack their own armies to enforce their decisions. They therefore need the support of the great powers and depend on the convergence of their member-states' interests. What about UN peacekeeping forces, you might ask? Realists point out that these forces are provided by nation-states, which can withdraw them whenever they choose. Realists recognize important differences between modern international politics and those of past international systems. They just don't think those differences affect the basic patterns of world politics, which they see as marked by a timeless struggle for power and security among states. See Kenneth N. Waltz, *Theory of International Politics* (New York: Addison-Wesley, 1979); Kenneth N. Waltz, "Reflections on Theory of International Politics: A Response to My Critics," in *Neorealism and Its Critics*, ed. Robert O. Keohane (New York: Columbia University Press, 1986), 322–46. Realists differ about the implications of anarchy. Some believe that it inclines states to adopt expansionist foreign policies. John Mearsheimer is the best-known contemporary advocate of this "offensive realist" position. See John Mearsheimer, *The Tragedy of Great Power Politics* (New York: W.W. Norton, 2001). Others think that anarchy favors prudent states that prioritize their security. In this view, some regimes may, for domestic or ideological reasons, pursue hegemonic domination. But a state that tries to maximize its power provokes other states to check its aggressive actions. Faced with an unfavorable shift in the balance of power, other states may respond by building up their own military capabilities or forming defensive security partnerships and alliances. Because domination-seekers trigger counterbalancing by other states, they wind up less secure than if they had never tried to expand in the first place. Realists in this camp point to the collapse of bids for hegemony by the Spanish Habsburgs, Bourbon France, Napoleon, and Nazi Germany as evidence that overly expansionist policies tend to backfire. Those outside of the realist camp also emphasize the short-lived character of most bids for system-wide hegemony. See Lebow and Valentino, "Lost in Transition," 405. For realist variations, see Christopher Layne, "The Unipolar Illusion: Why New Great Powers Will Arise," *International Security* 17, no. 4 (Winter 1993): 5–51; Jeffrey W. Taliaferro, "Security Seeking under Anarchy: Defensive Realism Revisited," *International Security* 25, no. 3 (Winter 2000): 128–61. Some bids for hegemony clearly fail, and fail disastrously. But Rome conquered the Mediterranean system and held it for centuries; East Asia saw multiple periods of hegemony under powerful Chinese dynasties; by the early twentieth century, the United States had established hegemony over much of the Western Hemisphere. The historical record suggests that both rough balances of power and hegemonic orders are common outcomes in world politics. Scholars of hegemony, some of whom belong to the realist school, disagree about the importance of anarchy as an ordering principle of world politics. They all agree that hegemons establish political orders of some kind, and that those orders influence the behavior and interests of

weaker states. But some think that hegemonic orders operate in the shadow of anarchy; for them, this "background anarchy" explains, among other things, why the decline of hegemons risks triggering great-power wars, and why particular international orders rarely outlast a transfer of hegemony. Others think that hegemonic orders, because they involve a preeminent power exercising governance over other political communities, are more hierarchical than anarchical. See Robert Gilpin, *War and Change in World Politics* (New York: Cambridge University Press, 1981), 230; Ikenberry, *Leviathan*, chaps. 1–2; Lemke, *Regions of War and Peace*, chap. 2; Stuart Kauffman, Richard Little, and William Wohlforth, "Introduction: Balance and Hierarchy in International Systems," in *The Balance of Power in World History*, ed. Stuart Kauffman, Richard Little, and William Wohlforth (New York: Palgrave, 2007), 1–21; William C. Wohlforth, "Gilpinian Realism and International Relations," *International Relations* 25, no. 4 (December 1, 2011): 499–511, https://doi.org/10.1177/0047117811411742. In our view, it really doesn't matter very much whether we think hegemonic systems operate within some broader condition of anarchy. The anarchical character of world politics may or may not account for basic features of international relations, but anarchy is not the alpha and omega of international order. To the extent that it does matter, we don't think that anarchy describes very much about world politics. Most contemporary international relations occur in a web of governance arrangements and asymmetric relations between states. We simply do not need to posit the shadow of anarchy to explain the persistence of power politics across time and space; we can also derive it from overlapping and inconsistent hierarchies—what Jack Donnelly refers to as "heterarchy." When it comes to hegemonic-order theories, it makes little sense to infer anarchy from what happens when hegemonic orders are contested or go into decline. That's like saying that Tsarist Russia was anarchical because prior to the Russian Revolution it experienced a civil war. See Jack Donnelly, "The Discourse of Anarchy in IR," *International Theory* 7, no. 3 (2015): 393–425; David A. Lake, *Hierarchy in International Relations* (Ithaca, NY: Cornell University Press, 2009); Janice Bially Mattern and Ayşe Zarakol, "Hierarchies in World Politics," *International Organization* 70, no. 3 (007 2016): 623–54, https://doi.org/10.1017/S0020818316000126; Nexon, *Religious Conflict*, chap. 2; McConaughey, Musgrave, and Nexon, "Beyond Anarchy"; Ayşe Zarakol, ed., *Hierarchies in World Politics*, Cambridge Studies in International Relations (Cambridge: Cambridge University Press, 2017), https://doi.org/10.1017/9781108241588.

55. See Goddard, "Embedded Revisionism"; Martha Finnemore, *The Purpose of Intervention: Changing Beliefs about the Use of Force* (Ithaca, NY: Cornell University Press, 2004); Stacie E. Goddard, *When Right Makes Might: Rising Powers and World Order* (Ithaca, NY: Cornell University Press, 2018); Rodney Bruce Hall, *National Collective Identity: Social Constructs and International Systems* (New York: Columbia University Press, 1999); John M. Owen, *The Clash of Ideas in World Politics: Transnational Networks, States, and Regime Change, 1510–2010* (Princeton, NJ: Princeton University Press, 2012); Christian Reus-Smit, "Constructing Anarchy: The Constitutional Structure of International Society and the Nature of Fundamental Institutions," *International Organization* 51, no. 4 (Autumn 1997): 555–89.

56. With a few possible exceptions, such as the Holy Roman Empire. The Catholic Church was a lot like an international organization, and even, in some respects, an intergovernmental one.

57. Tana Johnson, *Organizational Progeny: Why Governments Are Losing Control over the Proliferating Structures of Global Governance* (Oxford: Oxford University Press,

2014); see also Michael Barnett and Martha Finnemore, *Rules for the World: International Organizations in Global Politics* (Ithaca, NY: Cornell University Press, 2004); Reus-Smit, "Constructing Anarchy."

58. Stacie E. Goddard, Paul K. MacDonald, and Daniel H. Nexon, "Repertoires of Statecraft: Instruments and Logics of Power Politics," *International Relations* 33, no. 2 (2019): 308.

59. Sebastian Schmidt, "Foreign Military Presence and the Changing Practice of Sovereignty: A Pragmatist Explanation of Norm Change," *American Political Science Review* 108, no. 4 (November 2014): 817–29, https://doi.org/10.1017/S0003055414000434.

60. Alexander Cooley, *Base Politics* (Ithaca, NY: Cornell University Press, 2008); Cooley and Nexon, "Structural Dynamics"; Barry Posen, "Command of the Commons," *International Security* 28, no. 1 (2003): 16, 21; C. T. Sandars, *America's Overseas Garrisons: The Leasehold Empire* (Oxford: Oxford University Press, 2000).

61. Stephen Brooks, "The Globalization of Production and the Changing Benefits of Conquest," *Journal of Conflict Resolution* 43, no. 5 (October 1999): 646–70; Stephen G. Brooks, *Producing Security: Multinational Corporations, Globalization, and the Changing Calculus of Conflict*, Princeton Studies in International History and Politics (Princeton, NJ: Princeton University Press, 2005), http://library.georgetown.edu/search/i?=0691121516.

62. See Kalevi Holsti, *Peace and War: Armed Conflicts and International Order 1648–1989* (New York: Cambridge University Press, 1991), 22; Rebecca Friedman Lissner and Mira Rapp-Hooper, "The Liberal Order Is More Than a Myth," *Foreign Affairs*, July 31, 2018, https://www.foreignaffairs.com/articles/world/2018-07-31/liberal-order-more-myth; Andrew Phillips, *War, Religion, and Empire: The Transformation of International Orders* (Cambridge: Cambridge University Press, 2011), 331.

63. Ikenberry, *Leviathan*, 14–15.

64. Eric Grynaviski and Amy Hsieh, "Hierarchy and Judicial Institutions: Arbitration and Ideology in the Hellenistic World," *International Organization* 69, no. 3 (Summer 2015): 697–729, https://doi.org/10.1017/S0020818315000090; Reus-Smit, "Constructing Anarchy."

65. We need to stress that the existence of international order does not, in any way, imply either general peace or peace among the great powers. The settled rules and arrangements of many international orders treat war as a normal, and even desirable, means of achieving power, wealth, and glory. For example, as historian Michael Howard argues of late medieval Europe, the ruling aristocracy regarded "peace . . . as a brief interval between wars" that they filled with activities "to keep them fit for the next serious conflict." And "if European culture in the sixteenth century was becoming secularized, it nonetheless remained bellicose. Indeed, the entire apparatus of the state primarily came into being to enable princes to wage war. With few exceptions, these princes still saw themselves, and were seen by their subjects, essentially as warrior leaders, and they took every opportunity to extend their power." Michael Howard, *The Invention of Peace: Reflections on War and International Order* (New Haven, CT: Yale University Press, 2000), 12, 15.

66. Major variants of constructivist theory focus on the role of "intersubjective norms" in structuring international politics. We find it interesting that, despite the general decline of this flavor of norm constructivism, their understanding of how world politics is put together has come back in through the literature on hegemony and international order. See Finnemore, *Intervention*; R. Charli Carpenter, "Women and Children First: Gender

Norms and Humanitarian Interventions in the Balkans," *International Organization* 57, no. 4 (2003): 661–94; Jeffrey T. Checkel, "The Constructivist Turn in International Relations Theory," *World Politics* 50, no. 2 (1998): 324–48; Andrew P. Cortell and James W. Davis Jr., "When Norms Clash: International Norms, Domestic Practices, and Japan's Internalisation of the GATT/WTO," *Review of International Studies* 31, no. 1 (January 2005): 3–25; Audie Klotz, "Norms Reconstituting Interests: Global Racial Equality and the U.S. Sanctions against South Africa," *International Organization* 39, no. 3 (1995): 451–78; Jeffrey W. Legro, "Which Norms Matter? Revisiting the 'Failure' of Internationalism," *International Organization* 51, no. 1 (1997): 31–63; Katheryn Sikkink, *The Power of Human Rights: International Norms and Domestic Change* (Cambridge: Cambridge University Press, 1999).

67. Thus, international orders are just like many domestic political systems, which evolve and mutate as new institutions and practices get layered onto older ones. If one looks solely at its founding documents, the political order of the United States has undergone only a limited number of truly major shifts, such as from the Articles of Confederation to the Constitution, and in the Civil War amendments that ended slavery and expanded federal power. But through legal interpretation, political compromise, alterations in the role of political parties, the New Deal, wartime mobilization in the 1940s, and expansion of the national-security states during the Cold War, the American political order looks radically different from the way it did in the 1790s. See Daniel H. Deudney, "The Philadelphian System: Sovereignty, Arms Control, and Balance of Power in the American States-Union, circa 1787–1861," *International Organization* 49, no. 2 (1995): 191–228, https://doi.org/10.1017/S002081830002837X; Orfeo Fioretos, "Historical Institutionalism in International Relations," *International Organization* 65, no. 02 (2011): 367–99, https://doi.org/10.1017/S0020818311000002; Henry Farrell and Abraham Newman, "The New Politics of Interdependence: Cross-National Layering in Trans-Atlantic Regulatory Disputes," *Comparative Political Studies* 48, no. 4 (March 1, 2015): 497–526, https://doi.org/10.1177/0010414014542330; Ira Katznelson, *Fear Itself: The New Deal and the Origins of Our Time* (New York: W. W. Norton, 2013); Paul Musgrave, "Federation of Liberty: International Society and Hierarchy among the United States," Working Paper, University of Massachusetts, Amherst, January 28, 2019; McConaughey, Musgrave, and Nexon, "Beyond Anarchy," 198, 202; Kathleen Thielen, "Historical Institutionalism in Comparative Politics," *Annual Review of Political Science* 2, no. 1 (June 1999): 369–404.

68. When analysts characterize hegemonic orders in terms of their architectures, they sometimes look specifically at the intentional designs of dominant powers. Other times, they focus on foundational documents, such as the UN charter, or agreements, such as the Peace of Westphalia. See Daniel Philpott, *Revolutions in Sovereignty: How Ideas Shaped Modern International Relations* (Princeton, NJ: Princeton University Press, 2001). Still other times they look at the language used by states and international organizations, their practices, or other more dynamic evidence. Most often, they use a variety of different indicators. But generally, everyone is consciously simplifying the complexity of international orders by imputing to them some basic rules, norms, and procedures. There is nothing wrong with this. We do it ourselves. But those discussing international order need to keep in mind that international norms, rules, and procedures are often contradictory and contested. See Amitav Acharya, "How Ideas Spread: Whose Norms Matter? Norm Localization and Institutional Change in Asian Regionalism," *International Organization* 58, no. 2 (2004): 239–75; Nicola P. Contessi,

"Multilateralism, Intervention and Norm Contestation: China's Stance on Darfur in the UN Security Council," *Security Dialogue* 41, no. 3 (2010): 323–44, https://doi.org/10.1177/0967010610370228; Antje Wiener, "Contested Meanings of Norms: A Research Framework," *Comparative European Politics* 5, no. 1 (2007): 1–17; Lisbeth Zimmermann, "More for Less: The Interactive Translation of Global Norms in Postconflict Guatemala," *International Studies Quarterly* 61, no. 4 (2017): 774–85.

69. See Alex J. Bellamy, "International Law and the War with Iraq," *Melbourne Journal of International Law* 4, no. 2 (2003): 497–520; Adams Roberts, "The Law and the Use of Force after Iraq," *Survival* 45, no. 2 (June 1, 2003): 31–56, https://doi.org/10.1080/00396338.2003.100716061; Miriam Sapiro, "Iraq: The Shifting Sands of Preemptive Self-Defense," *American Journal of International Law* 97, no. 3 (July 2003): 599–607, https://doi.org/10.2307/3109845; John Yoo, "International Law and the War in Iraq," *American Journal of International Law* 97, no. 3 (July 2003): 563–76, https://doi.org/10.2307/3109841.

70. See Blockmans, *Emperor Charles V, 1500–1558*; J. H. Elliott, *Spain and Its World 1500–1700* (New Haven, CT: Yale University Press, 1989); J. H. Elliott, *Imperial Spain, 1469–1716* (London: Penguin, 1963); J. H. Elliott, "A Europe of Composite Monarchies," *Past and Present*, no. 137 (1992): 48–71; H. G. Koenigsberger, *The Practice of Empire*, emended ed. (Ithaca, NY: Cornell University Press, 1969); H. G. Koenigsberger, *The Habsburgs and Europe, 1516–1660* (Ithaca, NY: Cornell University Press, 1971); A. W. Lovett, *Early Habsburg Spain, 1517–1598* (Oxford: Oxford University Press, 1986); Nexon, *Religious Conflict*.

71. Darwin, *The Empire Project*; see also Peter Cain and Tony Hopkins, *British Imperialism, 1688–2000*, 2nd ed. (London: Longman, 2001); H. S. Ferns, "Britain's Informal Empire in Argentina, 1806–1914," *Past and Present*, no. 4 (1953): 60–75; Michael Fisher, "Indirect Rule in the British Empire: The Foundations of the Residency System in India (1764–1858)," *Modern Asian Studies* 18, no. 3 (1984): 393–428; McConaughey, Musgrave, and Nexon, "Beyond Anarchy."

72. See Hal Brands, "Fools Rush Out? The Flawed Logic of Offshore Balancing," *Washington Quarterly* 38, no. 2 (2015): 9, https://doi.org/10.1080/0163660X.2015.1064705; Miriam Kreiger, Shannon L. C. Souma, and Daniel Nexon, "US Military Diplomacy in Practice," in *Diplomacy and the Making of World Politics*, ed. Ole Jacob Sending, Vincent Pouliot, and Iver B. Neumann Cambridge University Press, 2015), 220–55; Frédéric Mérand, "Pierre Bourdieu and the Birth of European Defense," *Security Studies* 19, no. 2 (2010): 360, https://doi.org/10.1080/09636411003795780.

73. Cooley, *Base*; Cooley and Nexon, "Structural Dynamics"; Schmidt, "Foreign Military Presence and the Changing Practice of Sovereignty."

74. For discussions of the British Indian Army, see Tarak Barkawi, *Globalization and War* (Lanham, MD: Rowman and Littlefield, 2005); Tarak Barkawi, *Soldiers of Empire* (Cambridge: Cambridge University Press, 2017).

75. Ikenberry, "Why the Liberal World Order Will Survive," 24.

76. We owe many of the ideas in this section to Herman Schwartz, "Down the Wrong Path: Path Dependence, Increasing Returns, and Historical Institutionalism" (unpublished manuscript, 2014), http://www.people.virginia.edu/~hms2f/Path.pdf.

77. Benjamin Fordham and Paul Poast, "All Alliances Are Multilateral," *Journal of Conflict Resolution* 60, no. 5 (2016): 840–65, https://doi.org/10.1177/0022002714553108; Emilie M. Hafner-Burton and Alexander H. Montgomery, "Power Positions: International Organizations, Social Networks, and Conflict," *Journal of Conflict Resolution* 50, no. 1

(2006): 3–27; Brandon J. Kinne, "Dependent Diplomacy: Signaling, Strategy, and Prestige in the Diplomatic Network," *International Studies Quarterly* 58, no. 2 (June 2014): 247–59, https://doi.org/10.1111/isqu.12047; Zeev Maoz et al., "Structural Equivalence and International Conflict: A Social Networks Analysis," *Journal of Conflict Resolution* 50, no. 5 (2006): 664–89, https://doi.org/10.1177/0022002706291053.

78. On the last, see Rebecca Adler-Nissen, "Stigma Management in International Relations: Transgressive Identities, Norms, and Order in International Society," *International Organization* 68, no. 1 (2014): 143–76, https://doi.org/10.1017/S0020818313000337; Mattern and Zarakol, "Hierarchies in World Politics"; Daniel H. Nexon and Iver B. Neumann, "Hegemonic-Order Theory: A Field-Theoretic Account," *European Journal of International Relations* 24, no. 3 (2018): 662–86, https://doi.org/10.1177/1354066117716524; Shogo Suzuki, "Seeking 'Legitimate' Great Power Status in Post-Cold War International Society: China's and Japan's Participation in UNPKO," *International Relations* 22, no. 1 (2008): 45–63, https://doi.org/10.1177/0047117807087242; Ayşe Zarakol, *After Defeat: How the East Learned to Live with the West* (Cambridge: Cambridge University Press, 2011).

79. Adler-Nissen, "Stigma Management in International Relations: Transgressive Identities, Norms, and Order in International Society"; Ian Clark, *The Hierarchy of States: Reform and Resistance in the International Order*, rev. ed., Cambridge Studies in International Relations (Cambridge: Cambridge University Press, 1989); Edward Keene, "A Case Study of the Construction of International Hierarchy: British Treaty-Making against the Slave Trade in the Early Nineteenth Century," *International Organization* 61, no. 2 (2007): 311–39; Edward Keene, "The Standard of 'Civilisation,' the Expansion Thesis and the 19th-Century International Social Space," *Millennium—Journal of International Studies* 42, no. 3 (2014): 651–73, https://doi.org/10.1177/0305829814541319; Lee, "Diplomatic Ritual as a Power Resource: The Politics of Asymmetry in Early Modern Chinese-Korean Relations"; Phillips, "Contesting the Confucian Peace"; David Strang, "Anomaly and Commonplace in European Political Expansion: Realist and Institutional Accounts," *International Organization* 45, no. 2 (1991): 143–62; Steven Ward, "Race, Status, and Japanese Revisionism in the Early 1930s," *Security Studies* 22, no. 4 (2013): 607–39; Robert Vitalis, *White World Order, Black Power Politics: The Birth of American International Relations* (Ithaca, NY: Cornell University Press, 2015); Shogo Suzuki, "Japan's Socialization into Janus-Faced European International Society," *European Journal of International Relations* 11, no. 1 (2005): 137–64, https://doi.org/10.1177/1354066105050139; Suzuki, "Seeking 'Legitimate' Great Power Status in Post-Cold War International Society"; Shogo Suzuki, *Civilization and Empire: China and Japan's Encounter with European International Society* (London: Routledge, 2009), https://doi.org/10.4324/9780203880456; Ann Towns, "The Status of Women as a Standard of 'Civilization,'" *European Journal of International Relations* 15, no. 4 (2009): 681–706, https://doi.org/10.1177/1354066109345053; Zarakol, *After Defeat*.

80. Henry Farrell and Abraham Newman, "America's Misuse of Its Financial Infrastructure," *National Interest*, April 15, 2019, https://nationalinterest.org/print/feature/america%E2%80%99s-misuse-its-financial-infrastructure-52707; see also Barry E. Carter and Ryan M. Farha, "Overview and Operation of U.S. Financial Sanctions, including the Example of Iran," *Georgetown Journal of International Law* 44 (2013: 903–14; Viljar Veebel and Raul Markus, "At the Dawn of a New Era of Sanctions: Russian-Ukrainian Crisis and Sanctions," *Orbis* 60, no. 1 (January 1, 2016): 128–39, https://doi.org/10.1016/j.orbis.2015.12.001.

81. Compare Nexon, *Religious Conflict*, chap. 2.

82. Patrick Thaddeus Jackson, *The Conduct of Inquiry in International Relations: Philosophy of Science and Its Implications for the Study of World Politics* (London: Routledge, 2011), 145–55.

83. For an illustration of variation along this dimension from US-French ordering in Francophone Africa, see Peter J. Schraeder, "Cold War to Cold Peace: Explaining US-French Competition in Francophone Africa," *Political Science Quarterly* 115, no. 3 (2000): 395–419.

84. Compare Mustafa Emirbayer and Jeffrey Goodwin, "Network Analysis, Culture, and the Problem of Agency," *American Journal of Sociology* 99, no. 6 (1994): 1481; Barry Wellman, "Network Analysis: Some Basic Principles," *Sociological Theory* 1 (1983): 155–62; Harrison C. White, Scott A. Boorman, and Robert L. Breiger, "Social Structure from Multiple Networks. I. Blockmodels of Roles and Positions," *American Journal of Sociology* 81, no. 4 (1976): 733–34.

85. See Karen J. Alter and Sophie Meunier, "The Politics of International Regime Complexity," *Perspectives on Politics* 7, no. 1 (2009): 13–24, https://doi.org/10.1017/S1537592709090033; Marc L. Busch, "Overlapping Institutions, Forum Shopping, and Dispute Settlement in International Trade," *International Organization*, no. 4 (2007): 735–61; Daniel W. Drezner, "The Power and Peril of International Regime Complexity," *Perspectives on Politics* 7, no. 1 (2009): 65–70, https://doi.org/10.1017/S1537592709090100; Laura Gómez-Mera, "International Regime Complexity and Regional Governance: Evidence from the Americas," *Global Governance: A Review of Multilateralism and International Organizations* 21, no. 1 (2015): 19–42, https://doi.org/10.5555/1075-2846-21.1.19; Robert O. Keohane and David G. Victor, "The Regime Complex for Climate Change," *Perspectives on Politics* 9, no. 1 (2011): 7–23, https://doi.org/10.1017/S1537592710004068.

86. Alexander Cooley, "Ordering Eurasia: The Rise and Decline of Liberal Internationalism in the Post-Communist Space," *Security Studies*, 28, no. 3 (June–July 2019): 588–613.

87. Stacie E. Goddard and Daniel H. Nexon, "The Dynamics of Global Power Politics: A Framework for Analysis," *Journal of Global Security Studies* 1, no. 1 (2016): 4–18, https://doi.org/10.1093/jogss/ogv007; on wedging strategies more generally, see Timothy W. Crawford, "Wedge Strategy, Balancing, and the Deviant Case of Spain, 1940–1941," *Security Studies* 17, no. 1 (2008): 1–38; Timothy W. Crawford, "Preventing Enemy Coalitions: How Wedge Strategies Shape Power Politics," *International Security* 35, no. 4 (Spring 2011): 155–89, https://doi.org/10.1162/ISEC_a_00036; Victoria Tin-bor Hui, *War and State Formation in Ancient China and Early Modern Europe* (Cambridge: Cambridge University Press, 2005); Yasuhiro Izumikawa, "Binding Strategies in Alliance Politics: The Soviet-Japanese-US Diplomatic Tug of War in the Mid-1950s," *International Studies Quarterly* 62, no. 1 (March 2018): 108–20; Cooley and Nexon, "Structural Dynamics."

88. Goddard, "Embedded Revisionism"; see also Stacie E. Goddard, "When Right Makes Might."

89. Robert Jervis, "A Political Science Perspective on the Balance of Power and the Concert," *American Historical Review* 97, no. 3 (1992): 58; for different perspectives, see Korina Kagan, "The Myth of the European Concert: The Realist-institutionalist Debate and Great Power Behavior in the Eastern Question, 1821–41," *Security Studies* 7, no. 2 (1997): 1–57; Jennifer Mitzen, "Reading Habermas in Anarchy: Multilateral Diplomacy

and Global Public Spheres," *American Political Science Review* 99, no. 3 (2005): 401–17; Jennifer Mitzen, *Power in Concert: The Nineteenth-Century Origins of Global Governance* (Chicago: University of Chicago Press, 2013); Matthew Rendall, "Russia, the Concert of Europe, and Greece, 1821–29: A Test of Hypotheses about the Vienna System," *Security Studies* 9, no. 4 (2000): 55–96; Paul W. Schroeder, *The Transformation of European Politics, 1763–1848* (Oxford: Oxford University Press, 1994).

90. Keene, "A Case Study of the Construction of International Hierarchy."

91. For an example of how Washington used carrots and sticks to keep Japan firmly within its orbit during the Cold War, see Izumikawa, "Binding Strategies."

92. See Jeff D. Colgan and Nicholas L. Miller, "Rival Hierarchies and the Origins of Nuclear Technology Sharing," *International Studies Quarterly* 63, no. 2 (June 2019): 310–21; Eliza Gheorghe, "Proliferation and the Logic of the Nuclear Market," *International Security* 43, no. 4 (2019): 88–127, https://doi.org/10.1162/isec_a_00344; Rebecca Davis Gibbons, *American Hegemony and the Politics of the Nuclear Nonproliferation Regime* (PhD dissertation, Georgetown University, 2016); Rebecca K. C. Hersman and Robert Peters, "Nuclear U-Turns," *Nonproliferation Review* 13, no. 3 (2006): 539–53, https://doi.org/10.1080/10736700601071629; Nicholas L. Miller, "The Secret Success of Nonproliferation Sanctions," *International Organization* 68, no. 4 (2014): 913–44.

93. Charles Kindleberger, *The World in Depression 1929–1939* (Berkeley: University of California Press, 1973).

94. Goods vary in terms of whether they are, on the one hand, rivalrous or non-rivalrous or, on the other hand, excludible or non-excludible. These combine, in ideal-typical terms, to produce private goods (rival and excludable), such as "cars, clothes, food"; club goods (non-rival and excludable), such as "cable television"; public goods (non-rival and non-excludable), such as "air, public parks, national defense"; and common goods (rival and non-excludable), such as "water, fisheries." Hella Engerer, "Security as a Public, Private, or Club Good: Some Fundamental Considerations," *Defence and Peace Economics* 22, no. 2 (2011): 136–37, https://doi.org/10.1080/10242694.2011.542333; Elke Krahmann, "Security: Collective Good or Commodity?," *European Journal of International Relations* 14, no. 3 (2008): 379–404.

95. See Norrlof, *Global Advantage*; Carla Norrlof, "Dollar Hegemony: A Power Analysis," *Review of International Political Economy* 21, no. 5 (2014): 1042–70, https://doi.org/10.1080/09692290.2014.895773; Ruggie, "Embedded Liberalism."

96. Nexon and Neumann, "Hegemonic-Order Theory," 673; see also Dana P. Eyre and Mark C. Suchman, "Status, Norms, and the Proliferation of Conventional Weapons: An Institutional Theory Approach," in *The Culture of National Security: Norms and Identity in World Politics*, ed. Peter J. Katzenstein (New York: Columbia University Press, 1996), 79–113; Michelle Murray, *The Struggle for Recognition in International Relations: Status, Revisionism, and Rising Powers* (Oxford: Oxford University Press, 2018), chap. 8.

97. See Janice Bially Mattern, "Why Soft Power Isn't so Soft: Representational Force and the Sociolinguistic Construction of Attraction in World Politics," *Millennium* 33, no. 3 (2005): 583–612; Joseph S. Nye Jr., *Bound to Lead: The Changing Nature of American Power* (New York: Basic Books, 1990); Ikenberry and Kupchan, "Socialization"; Nexon and Neumann, "Hegemonic-Order Theory."

98. See, in general, Seva Gunitsky, *Aftershocks: Great Powers and Domestic Reforms in the Twentieth Century* (Princeton, NJ: Princeton University Press, 2017); see also Nexon and Neumann, "Hegemonic-Order Theory," 665ff.

99. Both Louis XIV (a member of the Bourbon dynasty) and Emperor Leopold (of the Habsburg dynasty) married, and had children by, sisters of Charles II of Spain, whose death without a direct heir triggered the conflict. John A. Lynn, *The Wars of Louis XIV, 1667–1714* (Essex, MA: Addison Wesley Longman, 1999), 105–6.

100. Nexon, *Religious Conflict*, 32, 94–95; see, generally, Richard Bonney, *The European Dynastic States: 1494–1660* (Oxford: Oxford University Press, 1991).

101. See Go, "Global Fields and Imperial Forms"; Go, *Patterns*; Robert P. Hager Jr. and David A. Lake, "Balancing Empires: Competitive Decolonization in International Politics," *Security Studies* 9, no. 3 (2000): 108–48.

102. Go, "Global Fields and Imperial Forms"; Go, *Patterns*; Nexon and Wright, "American Empire Debate."

103. At the height of the Cold War, Washington did covertly intervene in Italy to prevent a Communist electoral victory. This is only one example that complicates the more "benign" view of American leadership in Western Europe. See Levin, "When the Great Power Gets a Vote"; Michael Poznansky, "Stasis or Decay? Reconciling Covert War and the Democratic Peace," *International Studies Quarterly* 59, no. 4 (December 2015): 815–26, https://doi.org/10.1111/isqu.12193.

104. Valerie Bunce, "The Empire Strikes Back: The Evolution of the Eastern Bloc from a Soviet Asset to a Soviet Liability," *International Organization* 39, no. 1 (1985): 1–46; Lake, *Entangling Relations: American Foreign Policy in Its Century*, 10; Lake, "Beyond Anarchy: The Importance of Security Institutions," 139; Alexander Wendt and Daniel Friedheim, "Hierarchy under Anarchy: Informal Empire and the East German State," *International Organization* 49, no. 4 (1995): 689–721.

105. Note that some of the Republics in the Soviet Union, such as Ukraine, had seats at the United Nations. The International Postal Union, established in 1874, originally had seats designated for colonies, protectorates, and the like. So even the standard of "international personality" turns out to be rather complicated. See F. H. Williamson, "The International Postal Service and the Universal Postal Union," *Journal of the Royal Institute of International Affairs* 9, no. 1 (1930): 68–78.

106. The unofficial character of modern informal empires applies not only to *interstate* informal empires, such as the Soviet Union in Eastern Europe, but also to sovereign states that govern at least some of their territory through imperial logics and techniques. Both the Russian Federation and the People's Republic of China currently organize at least some of their domestic politics along imperial lines. Beijing has long engaged in settler colonialism—a conscious policy of shifting the ethnic composition of regions in favor of Han Chinese—in Tibet and Xinjiang. The Republic of Chechnya—a constituent political unit of the Russian Federation—is currently ruled by a local potentate, Ramzan Kadyrov, installed by Moscow and given wide latitude so long as he keeps it quiescent. Moreover, a number of sovereign states retain control of imperial dependencies. Consider the relationship between Guam and the United States or the British Overseas Territories, such as the Turks and Caicos Islands. See Charles King, "Crisis in the Caucasus: A New Look at Russia's Chechen Impasse," *Foreign Affairs* 82, no. 2 (March 2003): 134–39; Musgrave and Nexon, "States of Empire"; McConaughey, Musgrave, and Nexon, "Beyond Anarchy"; Ross Terrill, *The New Chinese Empire: And What It Means for the United States* (New York: Basic Books, 2004).

107. Paul Musgrave and Daniel Nexon, "Defending Hierarchy from the Moon to the Indian Ocean: Symbolic Capital and Political Dominance in Early Modern China and the Cold War," *International Organization* 72, no. 3 (2018): 662.

108. Patrick Thaddeus Jackson, "Defending the West: Occidentalism and the Formation of NATO," *Journal of Political Philosophy* 11, no. 3 (2003): 223–52; Patrick Thaddeus Jackson, *Civilizing the Enemy: German Reconstruction and the Invention of the West* (Ann Arbor: University of Michigan Press, 2006).

109. Alexander Cooley and Daniel Nexon, "Interpersonal Networks and International Security," in *The New Power Politics: Networks and Transnational Security Governance*, ed. Deborah D. Avant and Oliver Westerwinter (New York: Oxford University Press 2016), 74–102; Kreiger, Souma, and Nexon, "US Military Diplomacy"; Tom Long, *Latin America Confronts the United States: Asymmetry and Influence* (Cambridge: Cambridge University Press, 2015).

110. See Nikhil Kalyanpur, "Hegemony, Inequality, and the Quest for Primacy," *Journal of Global Security Studies* 3, no. 3 (2018): 371–84, https://doi.org/10.1093/jogss/ogy009; Carla Norrlof, "Hegemony and Inequality: Trump and the Liberal Playbook," *International Affairs* 94, no. 1 (2018): 63–88.

111. See Go, *Patterns*; Anders Stephanson, *Manifest Destiny: American Expansionism and the Empire of Right* (New York: Hill and Wang, 1995).

112. See Stephen Wertheim, "Tomorrow, the World: The Birth of US Global Supremacy in World War II" (PhD dissertation, Columbia University, 2015); Wertheim, "Instrumental Internationalism."

113. Michael Mastanduno, "Partner Politics: Russia, China, and the Challenge of Extending U.S. Hegemony after the Cold War," *Security Studies* 28, no. 3 (2019): 479–50.

114. Kreiger, Souma, and Nexon, "US Military Diplomacy," 229. Marina Henke shows that "diplomatic embeddedness"—"the sum of bilateral and multilateral institutional ties that link the United States to a third party"—gives Washington significant advantages when figuring out how to craft incentives for other states to join its military coalitions. Marina E. Henke, "The Politics of Diplomacy: How the United States Builds Multilateral Military Coalitions," *International Studies Quarterly* 61, no. 2 (June 2017): 410–11, https://doi.org/10.1093/isq/sqx017. On how American ordering activities build social capital, see Ikenberry, *Leviathan*, 353.

115. Lake, *Hierarchy*.

116. Abraham Newman and Daniel H. Nexon, "Trump Says American Allies Should Spend More on Defense. Here's Why He's Wrong," *Vox*, February 16, 2017, https://www.vox.com/the-big-idea/2017/2/16/14635204/burden-sharing-allies-nato-trump.

117. Brands, "Fools Rush Out?," 19; see also Norrlof, *Global Advantage*; Norrlof, "Dollar Hegemony."

118. Cooley and Nexon, "Interpersonal."

119. US foreign policy, the American system, and international order not only interact with and shape one another, but the boundaries among them shift over time. Moreover, international order is always a shorthand for a kind of amalgam of multiple regional and issue-specific orders; "liberal order" itself is often a blunt way of talking about liberal characteristics that can be found, to varying degrees, in each of the three.

120. See Daniel W. Drezner, "Counter-Hegemonic Strategies in the Global Economy," *Security Studies* 28, no. 3 (June–July 2019): 505–31, https://doi.org/10.1080/09636412.2019.1604985; Barry Eichengreen, *Exorbitant Privilege: The Rise and Fall of the Dollar and the Future of the International Monetary System* (Oxford: Oxford University Press, 2011); Norrlof, *Global Advantage*; Norrlof, "Dollar Hegemony"; Carla Norrlof and William C. Wohlforth, "Is US Grand Strategy Self-Defeating? Deep Engagement, Military Spending and Sovereign Debt," *Conflict Management and Peace*

Science 36, no. 3 (2019), 21, https://doi.org/10.1177/0738894216674953; Herman Mark Schwartz, "American Hegemony: Intellectual Property Rights, Dollar Centrality, and Infrastructural Power," *Review of International Political Economy* 26, no. 3 (2019): 490–519, https://doi.org/10.1080/09692290.2019.1597754; Susan Strange, "The Persistent Myth of Lost Hegemony," *International Organization* 41, no. 4 (1987): 551–74, https://doi.org/10.1017/S0020818300027600; Susan Strange, *States and Markets*, (London: Bloomsbury, 2015).

121. Thomas Oatley et al., "The Political Economy of Global Finance: A Network Model," *Perspectives on Politics* 11, no. 1 (2013): 140–41, https://doi.org/10.1017/S1537592712003593.

122. Compare John Mearsheimer, "Back to the Future: Instability in Europe after the Cold War," *International Security* 15, no. 1 (Summer 1990): 5–56; Mearsheimer, *The Tragedy of Great Power Politics*. In nominal terms, all of these countries had larger economies than Russia in 2014, the year that Moscow intervened in Ukraine.

123. Freedom House, "Freedom in the World 2007," https://freedomhouse.org/report/freedom-world/freedom-world-2007, accessed July 29, 2019.

124. Daniel W Drezner, *The System Worked: How the World Stopped Another Great Depression* (New York: Oxford University Press, 2014).

125. Ikenberry, *After Victory*; G. John Ikenberry, "America's Imperial Ambition," *Foreign Affairs* 81, no. 5 (September 2002): 44–60; Ikenberry, *Leviathan*.

126. See Daniel H. Nexon, "Toward a Neo-Progressive Foreign Policy," *Foreign Affairs*, September 4, 2018, https://www.foreignaffairs.com/articles/united-states/2018-09-04/toward-neo-progressive-foreign-policy.

127. The term has strongly anti-semitic overtones. See Rachel Barenblatt, "Yes, Ranting against 'Globalism' Is Anti-Semitic," *The Forward*, October 24, 2018, https://forward.com/scribe/412627/yes-ranting-against-globalism-is-anti-semitic/; Talia Lavin, "Conspiracy Theories about Soros Aren't Just False. They're Anti-Semitic," *Washington Post*, October 24, 2018, https://www.washingtonpost.com/outlook/2018/10/24/conspiracy-theories-about-soros-arent-just-false-theyre-anti-semitic/; Daniel H. Nexon, "Why the Right-Wing War on George Soros Matters," *Lawyers, Guns & Money* (blog), August 6, 2017, http://www.lawyersgunsmoneyblog.com/2017/08/right-wing-war-george-soros-matters.

128. Although US President Woodrow Wilson is often associated with liberal variants of national self-determination, his position on the matter was more complicated. For discussions, see Allen Lynch, "Woodrow Wilson and the Principle of 'National Self-Determination': A Reconsideration," *Review of International Studies* 28, no. 2 (2002), 419–36 https://doi.org/10.1017/S0260210502004199; Trygve Throntveit, "The Fable of the Fourteen Points: Woodrow Wilson and National Self-Determination," *Diplomatic History* 35, no. 3 (2011): 445–81, https://doi.org/10.1111/j.1467-7709.2011.00959.x.

129. Wright, *All Measures Short of War*, 16–29.

130. See Michael Desch, "America's Liberal Illiberalism: The Ideological Origins of Overreaction in U.S. Foreign Policy," *International Security* 32, no. 3 (Winter 2007/2008): 7–43; Jahn, *Liberal Internationalism*; Jonathan Monten, "The Roots of the Bush Doctrine: Power, Nationalism, and Democracy Promotion in U.S. Strategy," *International Security* 29, no. 4 (Spring 2005): 112–56; Musgrave and Nexon, "States of Empire"; Mukherjee, "Two Cheers"; Musgrave and Nexon, "American Liberalism and the Imperial Temptation"; Stephanson, *Manifest Destiny: American Expansionism and the Empire of Right*.

CHAPTER 3

1. Robert Gilpin, "The Theory of Hegemonic War," *Journal of Interdisciplinary History* 18, no. 4 (1988): 591–92.

2. Michael C. Horowitz, *The Diffusion of Military Power: Causes and Consequences for International Politics* (Princeton, NJ: Princeton University Press, 2010).

3. Historian Paul Kennedy makes much of overextension. See Paul Kennedy, *The Rise and Fall of the Great Powers: Economic Change and Military Conflict from 1500 to 2000* (New York: Random House, 1987).

4. On varieties of revisionism, see Alexander Cooley, Daniel H. Nexon, and Steven Ward, "Revising Order or Challenging the Balance of Military Power? An Alternative Typology of Revisionist and Status-Quo States," *Review of International Studies* 45, no. 4 (2019): 698–708; Steven Ward, "Race, Status, and Japanese Revisionism in the Early 1930s," *Security Studies* 22, no. 4 (2013): 607–39; Jason W. Davidson, *The Origins of Revisionist and Status-Quo States* (New York: Palgrave Macmillan, 2006); Randall L. Schweller, "Bandwagoning for Profit: Bringing the Revisionist State Back In," *International Security* 19, no. 1 (Summer 1994): 72–107; Steven Ward, *Status and the Challenge of Rising Powers* (New York: Cambridge University Press, 2017).

5. See Graham Allison, *Destined for War: Can America and China Escape Thucydides's Trap?* (Boston: Houghton Mifflin Harcourt, 2017); Stephen G. Brooks and William C. Wohlforth, "The Rise and Fall of the Great Powers in the Twenty-First Century: China's Rise and the Fate of America's Global Position," *International Security* 40, no. 3 (Winter 2015/ 2016): 7–53, https://doi.org/10.1162/ISEC_a_00225; Steve Chan, *China, the US and the Power-Transition Theory: A Critique* (London: Routledge, 2007); Alastair Iain Johnston, "Is China a Status Quo Power?," *International Security* 27, no. 4 (2003): 5–56; Jin Kai, *Rising China in a Changing World: Power Transitions and Global Leadership* (New York: Springer, 2016).

6. See Richard Ned Lebow and Benjamin Valentino, "Lost in Transition: A Critical Analysis of Power Transition Theory," *International Relations* 23, no. 3 (2009): 389–410, https://doi.org/10.1177/0047117809340481. One problem is that, until relatively recently, war was much more common than peace. Europe experienced pretty much constant warfare in the medieval and early modern periods. See H. G. Koenigsberger, *The Habsburgs and Europe, 1516–1660* (Ithaca, NY: Cornell University Press, 1971), 6; Michael Howard, *War in European History* (Oxford: Oxford University Press, 1976). The same is true of most recent international systems. See Peter C. Perdue, "Military Mobilization in Seventeenth- and Eighteenth-Century China, Russia, and Mongolia," *Modern Asian Studies* 30, no. 4 (1996): 757–93, https://doi.org/10.1017/S0026749X00016796. The East Asian system might be an exception, but this remains hotly contested. See David C. Kang, Meredith Shaw, and Ronan Tse-min Fu, "Measuring War in Early Modern East Asia, 1368–1841: Introducing Chinese and Korean Language Sources," *International Studies Quarterly* 60, no. 4 (December 2016): 766–77, https://doi.org/10.1093/isq/sqw032. Given constant warfare, it is difficult to pick out a particular "power-transition" conflict, especially because such wars can themselves produce rearrangements of the hierarchy of power. Keep in mind that data on economic growth and other indicators of power are fairly speculative until the last century or so. For a comprehensive discussion of these kinds of problems, see Lebow and Valentino, "Lost in Transition."

7. G. John Ikenberry, *After Victory: Institutions, Strategic Restraint, and the Rebuilding of Order after Major War* (Princeton, NJ: Princeton University Press, 2001),

chap. 7; see also Randall L. Schweller and William C. Wohlforth, "Power Test: Evaluating Realism in Response to the End of the Cold War," *Security Studies* 9, no. 3 (2000): 60–107.

8. See Odd Arne Westad, *The Global Cold War: Third World Interventions and the Making of Our Times*, new ed. (Cambridge: Cambridge University Press, 2007).

9. Robert S. Snyder, "Bridging the Realist/Constructivist Divide: The Case of the Counterrevolution in Soviet Foreign Policy at the End of the Cold War," *Foreign Policy Analysis* 1, no. 1 (2005): 60, https://doi.org/10.1111/j.1743-8594.2005.00003.x; for the potentially pivotal role of low oil prices in these developments, see Yuri Gaidar, *Collapse of an Empire: Lessons for Modern Russia* (Washington, DC: Brookings Institution Press, 2007), 105ff.

10. Schweller and Wohlforth, "Power Test: Evaluating Realism in Response to the End of the Cold War."

11. Mark R. Beissinger, *Nationalist Mobilization and the Collapse of the Soviet State*, Cambridge Studies in Comparative Politics (Cambridge: Cambridge University Press, 2002); Rey Koslowski and Friedrich V. Kratochwil, "Understanding Change in International Politics: The Soviet Empire's Demise and the International System," *International Organization* 48, no. 2 (1994): 215–47; Philip G. Roeder, *Where Nation-States Come From* (Princeton, NJ: Princeton University Press, 2007).

12. Beissinger, *Nationalist Mobilization*, 35.

13. There are many different sources of change in international orders. Some involve deep transformations that fundamentally alter politics. Here we might include drivers of some of the most important shifts in human societies, such as those associated with the development of agriculture, which made possible the foundation of cities and attendant increases in social complexity, and industrialization and electrification. We might also include the spread of various "global" religions, such as Christianity and Islam, or the emergence of modern scientific ways of knowing the world. The origins of fundamental change are a fascinating and weighty topic, but they aren't the subject of this book. Rather, we are interested in more proximate dynamics of transformations in international ordering and hegemonic systems. See Bentley B. Allan, *Scientific Cosmology and International Orders* (Cambridge: Cambridge University Press, 2018); Barry Buzan and George Lawson, "The Global Transformation: The Nineteenth Century and the Making of Modern International Relations," *International Studies Quarterly* 57, no. 3 (September 2013): 620–34, https://doi.org/10.1111/isqu.12011; Barry Buzan and George Lawson, *The Global Transformation: History, Modernity and the Making of International Relations* (Cambridge University Press, 2015); Paul Musgrave and Daniel Nexon, "The Global Transformation: More than Meets the Eye," *International Theory* 8, no. 3 (2016): 436–47, https://doi.org/10.1017/S1752971916000129; Andrew Phillips and J. C. Sharman, "Explaining Durable Diversity in International Systems: State, Company, and Empire in the Indian Ocean," *International Studies Quarterly* 59, no. 3 (September 2015): 436–48, https://doi.org/10.1111/isqu.12197; Phillips and Sharman, "Explaining Durable Diversity in International Systems."

14. See Cédric Jourde, "The International Relations of Small Neoauthoritarian States: Islamism, Warlordism, and the Framing of Stability," *International Studies Quarterly* 51, no. 2 (June 2007): 481–503; Parag Khanna, *The Second World: How Emerging Powers Are Redefining Global Competition in the Twenty-First Century* (New York: Random House, 2008).

15. Stacie E. Goddard, "Embedded Revisionism: Networks, Institutions, and Challenges to World Order," *International Organization* 72, no. 4 (2018): 763–97, https://doi.org/doi.org/10.1017/S0020818318000206.

16. See, for example, Rebecca Adler-Nissen and Vincent Pouliot, "Power in Practice: Negotiating the International Intervention in Libya," *European Journal of International Relations* 20, no. 4 (2014): 889–911, https://doi.org/10.1177/1354066113512702; Amy E. Eckert, "The Responsibility to Protect in the Anarchical Society: Power, Interest, and the Protection of Civilians in Libya and Syria," *Denver Journal of International Law and Policy* 41, no. 1 (2012): 87–100; Erna Burai, "Parody as Norm Contestation: Russian Normative Justifications in Georgia and Ukraine and Their Implications for Global Norms," *Global Society* 30, no. 1 (2016): 67–77; For a general overview, see Martha Finnemore, *The Purpose of Intervention: Changing Beliefs about the Use of Force* (Ithaca, NY: Cornell University Press, 2004).

17. See, for example, Amitav Acharya, "How Ideas Spread: Whose Norms Matter? Norm Localization and Institutional Change in Asian Regionalism," *International Organization* 58, no. 2 (2004): 239–75; Rebecca Adler-Nissen, "Stigma Management in International Relations: Transgressive Identities, Norms, and Order in International Society," *International Organization* 68, no. 01 (2014): 143–76, https://doi.org/10.1017/S0020818313000337; Nicola P. Contessi, "Multilateralism, Intervention and Norm Contestation: China's Stance on Darfur in the UN Security Council," *Security Dialogue* 41, no. 3 (2010): 323–44, https://doi.org/10.1177/0967010610370228; Alexander Cooley, "Countering Democratic Norms," *Journal of Democracy* 26, no. 3 (2015): 49–63; Jennifer M. Welsh, "Norm Contestation and the Responsibility to Protect," *Global Responsibility to Protect* 5, no. 4 (2013): 365–96; Antje Wiener, "Contested Meanings of Norms: A Research Framework," *Comparative European Politics* 5, no. 1 (2007): 1–17.

18. Charles E. Ziegler, "Russia as a Nationalizing State: Rejecting the Western Liberal Order," *International Politics* 53, no. 5 (2016): 565.

19. For a terrific synthesis of this line of argument, see Benjamin C. Denison and Emma M. Ashford, "Primacy, Regime Change and the Liberal International Order," Working Paper, Tufts University, Medford, MA, March 2019.

20. Cooley, Nexon, and Ward, "Revising Order"; see Ian Hurd, "Breaking and Making Norms: American Revisionism and Crises of Legitimacy," *International Politics* 44, no. 2–3 (2007): 194–213, https://doi.org/10.1057/palgrave.ip.8800184; Ward, "Race, Status, and Japanese Revisionism in the Early 1930s"; Ward, *Status*.

21. For background on these concepts, see Ronald S. Burt, *Structural Holes: The Social Structure of Competition* (Cambridge, MA: Harvard University Press, 1992); Timothy W. Crawford, "Wedge Strategy, Balancing, and the Deviant Case of Spain, 1940-1941," *Security Studies* 17, no. 1 (January 2008): 1–38; Timothy W. Crawford, "Preventing Enemy Coalitions: How Wedge Strategies Shape Power Politics," *International Security* 35, no. 4 (Spring 2011): 155–89, https://doi.org/10.1162/ISEC_a_00036; Mario Diani, "Brokerage," in *The Wiley-Blackwell Encyclopedia of Social and Political Movements* (Hoboken, NJ: Wiley-Blackwell, 2013), https://doi.org/10.1002/9780470674871.wbespm017; Mario Diani, "'Leaders' or Brokers? Positions and Influence," in *Social Movements and Networks: Relational Approaches to Collective Action*, ed. Mario Diani and Doug McAdam (Oxford: Oxford University Press, 2003), 105–22; Goddard, "Embedded Revisionism"; Stacie E. Goddard and Daniel H. Nexon, "The Dynamics of Global Power Politics: A Framework for Analysis," *Journal of Global Security Studies* 1, no. 1 (2016): 4–18, https://doi.org/10.1093/jogss/ogv007; Yasuhiro Izumikawa, "Binding Strategies in Alliance Politics: The Soviet-Japanese-US Diplomatic Tug of War in the Mid-1950s," *International Studies Quarterly* 62, no. 1 (March 2018): 108–20, https://doi.org/10.1093/isq/sqx070; Paul K. MacDonald, "Imperial Rule, Hierarchy, and Great Power Strategy" (PhD dissertation,

Columbia University, 2006); Daniel H. Nexon, *The Struggle for Power in Early Modern Europe: Religious Conflict, Dynastic Empires, and International Change* (Princeton, NJ: Princeton University Press, 2009), chaps. 2 and 4; Charles Tilly, *The Politics of Collective Violence* (Cambridge: Cambridge University Press, 2003).

22. Crawford, "Preventing Enemy Coalitions," 156; see also Stacie E. Goddard, "When Right Makes Might: How Prussia Overturned the European Balance of Power," *International Security* 33, no. 3 (Winter 2008–2009): 110–42; Stacie E. Goddard, *When Right Makes Might: Rising Powers and World Order* (Ithaca, NY: Cornell University Press, 2018); Victoria Tin-bor Hui, "Towards a Dynamic Theory of International Politics: Insights from Comparing Ancient China and Early Modern Europe," *International Organization* 58, no. 1 (2004): 175–205; Victoria Tin-bor Hui, *War and State Formation in Ancient China and Early Modern Europe* (Cambridge: Cambridge University Press, 2005).

23. See Alexander J. Motyl, *Imperial Ends: The Decay, Collapse, and Revival of Empires* (New York: Columbia University Press, 2001); Nexon, *Religious Conflict*, chap. 4.

24. Goddard and Nexon, "Global Power Politics," 13–14.

25. Doug McAdam, Sidney Tarrow, and Charles Tilly, *Dynamics of Contention* (Cambridge: Cambridge University Press, 2001), 142; see also Tilly, *Politics*.

26. Vincent Pouliot, *International Pecking Orders: The Politics and Practice of Multilateral Diplomacy* (Cambridge: Cambridge University Press, 2016).

27. See Marina E. Henke, "The Politics of Diplomacy: How the United States Builds Multilateral Military Coalitions," *International Studies Quarterly* 61, no. 2 (June 2017): 410–24, https://doi.org/10.1093/isq/sqx017; Marina E. Henke, "The Rotten Carrot: US-Turkish Bargaining Failure over Iraq in 2003 and the Pitfalls of Social Embeddedness," *Security Studies* 27, no. 1 (2018): 120–47, https://doi.org/10.1080/09636412.2017.1360077.

28. Kei Koga, "The Concept of 'Hedging' Revisited: The Case of Japan's Foreign Policy Strategy in East Asia's Power Shift," *International Studies Review* 20, no. 4 (2017), 7, https://doi.org/10.1093/isr/vix059; Deborah Welch Larson, "New Perspectives on Rising Powers and Global Governance: Status and Clubs," *International Studies Review* 20, no. 2 (2018): 2–3, https://doi.org/10.1093/isr/viy039.

29. Seva Gunitsky, *Aftershocks: Great Powers and Domestic Reforms in the Twentieth Century* (Princeton, NJ: Princeton University Press, 2017).

30. Parag Khanna refers to this process as a shift to the geopolitical "marketplace." See Khanna, *Second World*. But it can remain a market only if great powers don't shift to imperial modes of control in an effort to prevent exit. See Paul K. MacDonald, "Is Imperial Rule Obsolete? Assessing the Barriers to Overseas Adventurism," *Security Studies* 18, no. 1 (2009): 79–114.

31. Daniel W. Drezner, "Perspective: The 737 Max and the Changing World Politics of Regulation," *Washington Post*, March 13, 2019, https://www.washingtonpost.com/outlook/2019/03/13/max-changing-world-politics-regulation/; see also David Bach and Abraham L. Newman, "The European Regulatory State and Global Public Policy: Micro-Institutions, Macro-Influence," *Journal of European Public Policy* 14, no. 6 (2007): 827–46, https://doi.org/10.1080/13501760701497659.

32. Yu Zhou, "U.S. Trade Negotiators Want to End China's Forced Tech Transfers. That Could Backfire," *Washington Post*, January 28, 2019, https://www.washingtonpost.com/news/monkey-cage/wp/2019/01/28/u-s-trade-negotiators-want-to-end-chinas-forced-tech-transfers-that-could-backfire/.

33. Michael Allen, "Combatting Chinese Economic Coercion in the NSS," *Foreign Policy* (blog), December 15, 2017, https://foreignpolicy.com/2017/12/15/combatting-chinese-economic-coercion-in-the-nss/.

34. Deborah Welch Larson and Alexei Shevchenko, "Status Seekers: Chinese and Russian Responses to U.S. Primacy," *International Security* 34, no. 4 (Spring 2010): 63–95; Ward, *Status*; Wohlforth, William C. "Unipolarity, Status Competition, and Great Power War," *World Politics*, 61, no. 1 (2009): 28–57.

35. See Cooley, Nexon, and Ward, "Revising Order"; Judith Kelley, "Strategic Non-Cooperation as Soft Balancing: Why Iraq Was Not Just about Iraq," *International Politics* 42, no. 2 (2005): 15–173; Brock Tessman and Wojtek Wolfe, "Great Powers and Strategic Hedging: The Case of Chinese Energy Security Strategy," *International Studies Review* 13, no. 2 (2011): 214–40, https://doi.org/10.1111/j.1468-2486.2011.01022.x.

36. See Hal Brands, "South America Is a Battlefield in the New Cold War," *Bloomberg Opinion*, February 10, 2019, https://www.bloomberg.com/opinion/articles/2019-02-10/venezuela-crisis-south-america-is-a-battlefield-in-the-new-cold; Rocio Cara Labrador, "Maduro's Allies: Who Backs the Venezuelan Regime?," Council on Foreign Relations, February 5, 2019, https://www.cfr.org/article/maduros-allies-who-backs-venezuelan-regime.

37. Goddard, "Embedded Revisionism," 790; see also Larson and Shevchenko, "Status Seekers: Chinese and Russian Responses to U.S. Primacy,"; Ward, "Race, Status, and Japanese Revisionism in the Early 1930s"; Ward, *Status*; William C. Wohlforth, "Unipolarity, Status Competition, and Great Power War".

38. Goddard, "Embedded Revisionism," 789.

39. Karen J. Alter and Sophie Meunier, "The Politics of International Regime Complexity," *Perspectives on Politics* 7, no. 1 (2009): 13–24, https://doi.org/10.1017/S1537592709090033; Marc L. Busch, "Overlapping Institutions, Forum Shopping, and Dispute Settlement in International Trade," *International Organization* 61, no. 4 (2007): 735–61; Daniel W. Drezner, "The Global Governance of the Internet: Bringing the State Back In," *Political Science Quarterly* 119, no. 3 (2004): 477–98, https://doi.org/10.2307/20202392; Daniel W. Drezner, "The Power and Peril of International Regime Complexity," *Perspectives on Politics* 7, no. 1 (2009): 65–70, https://doi.org/10.1017/S1537592709090100; Laura Gómez-Mera, "International Regime Complexity and Regional Governance: Evidence from the Americas," *Global Governance: A Review of Multilateralism and International Organizations* 21, no. 1 (2015): 19–42, https://doi.org/10.5555/1075-2846-21.1.19; Edward Stoddard, "Authoritarian Regimes in Democratic Regional Organisations? Exploring Regional Dimensions of Authoritarianism in an Increasingly Democratic West Africa," *Journal of Contemporary African Studies* 35, no. 4 (2017): 469–86, https://doi.org/10.1080/02589001.2017.1347254.

40. See, in general, Nexon, *Religious Conflict*; John M. Owen, "When Do Ideologies Produce Alliances? The Holy Roman Empire, 1517–1555," *International Studies Quarterly* 49, no. 1 (March 2005): 73–99; John M. Owen, *The Clash of Ideas in World Politics: Transnational Networks, States, and Regime Change, 1510–2010* (Princeton, NJ: Princeton University Press, 2012).

41. John Brewer, *The Sinews of Power: War, Money and the English State, 1688–1783* (Cambridge, MA: Harvard University Press, 1990), 140.

42. Christian Leitz, *Nazi Foreign Policy, 1933–1941: The Road to Global War* (London: Routledge, 2004), 117–20.

43. Antony Best, *Britain, Japan and Pearl Harbor: Avoiding War in East Asia, 1936–41* (London: Routledge, 1995), 12.

44. William Roger Louis, *British Strategy in the Far East, 1919–1939* (Oxford: Clarendon Press, 1971), 218.

45. Peter Duus, Ramon H. Myers, and Mark R. Peattie, *The Japanese Informal Empire in China, 1895–1937* (Princeton, NJ: Princeton University Press, 2014), 3.

46. See Christopher Clark, *The Sleepwalkers: How Europe Went to War in 1914* (New York: Harper, 2012), 145, 337; Ross Hoffman, *Great Britain and the German Trade Rivalry 1875–1914* (Philadelphia: University of Pennsylvania Press, 1933), 173–74, 180–91; Charles Issawi, *The Fertile Crescent, 1800–1914: A Documentary Economic History* (New York: Oxford University Press, 1988), 211.

47. George F. W. Young, "German Banking and German Imperialism in Latin America in the Wilhelmine Era," *Ibero-Amerikanisches Archiv* 18, no. 1/2 (1992): 47–48; see also I. Briones and A. Villela, "European Bank Penetration during the First Wave of Globalisation: Lessons from Brazil and Chile, 1878–1913," *European Review of Economic History* 10, no. 3 (2006): 335, https://doi.org/10.1017/S136149160600178X.

48. George F. W. Young, "British Overseas Banking in Latin America and the Encroachment of German Competition, 1887–1914," *Albion: A Quarterly Journal Concerned with British Studies* 23, no. 1 (1991): 89, https://doi.org/10.2307/4050543.

49. Steven Liao and Daniel McDowell, "Redback Rising: China's Bilateral Swap Agreements and Renminbi Internationalization," *International Studies Quarterly* 59, no. 3 (September 2015): 401–22, https://doi.org/10.1111/isqu.12161.

50. Ji-Young Lee, "Hegemonic Authority and Domestic Legitimation: Japan and Korea under Chinese Hegemonic Order in Early Modern East Asia," *Security Studies* 25, no. 2 (2016): 337, https://doi.org/10.1080/09636412.2016.1171970; see also Ji-Young Lee, "Diplomatic Ritual as a Power Resource: The Politics of Asymmetry in Early Modern Chinese-Korean Relations," *Journal of East Asian Studies* 13, no. 2 (2013): 309–36, https://doi.org/10.5555/1598-2408-13.2.309; Ji-Young Lee, *China's Hegemony: Four Hundred Years of East Asian Domination* (New York: Columbia University Press, 2016).

51. On the ubiquity of contestation over norms and rules in world politics, see Burai, "Parody as Norm Contestation"; Contessi, "Multilateralism, Intervention and Norm Contestation"; Evelyn Goh, "Contesting Hegemonic Order: China in East Asia," *Security Studies* 28, no. 3 (2019): 614–44 ; Welsh, "Norm Contestation and the Responsibility to Protect"; Wiener, "Contested Meanings of Norms: A Research Framework"; Lisbeth Zimmermann, "More for Less: The Interactive Translation of Global Norms in Postconflict Guatemala," *International Studies Quarterly* 61, no. 4 (December 2017): 774–85.

52. Cooley, Nexon, and Ward, "Revising Order."

53. All hegemonic systems have cores and peripheries. It can be difficult to identify these until the system has unraveled, just as it can be difficult to know ahead of time which relationships are "lynchpins" and which are less essential to conserving the system. Still, it seems pretty obvious that NATO and the US-Japan alliance are both lynchpin partnerships and pretty central to the American system. Otherwise, your mileage may vary. For a discussion of lynchpin alliances and hegemonic orders, see Michael Mastanduno, "Partner Politics: Russia, China, and the Challenge of Extending U.S. Hegemony after the Cold War," *Security Studies* 28, no. 3 (2019): 479–504.

54. See Cooley, Nexon, and Ward, "Revising Order"; Alexander Cooley and Daniel Nexon, "'The Empire Will Compensate You': The Structural Dynamics of the U.S. Overseas Basing Network," *Perspectives on Politics* 11, no. 4 (2013): 1034–50; Koga, "Hedging"; Tessman and Wolfe, "Great Powers and Strategic Hedging."

55. James Raymond Vreeland, *The IMF and Economic Development* (Cambridge: Cambridge University Press, 2003).

56. Julia Bader, "China, Autocratic Patron? An Empirical Investigation of China as a Factor in Autocratic Survival," *International Studies Quarterly* 59, no. 1 (March 2015): 23–33, https://doi.org/10.1111/isqu.12148.

57. See, in general, Richard Bonney, *The European Dynastic States: 1494–1660* (Oxford: Oxford University Press, 1991); Olivier Christin, "From Repression to Toleration: French Royal Policy in the Face of Protestantism," in *Reformation, Revolt and Civil War in France and the Netherlands 1555–1585*, ed. Philip Benedict et al. (Amsterdam: Royal Netherlands Academy of Arts and Sciences, 1999), 201–14; Wim Blockmans, *Emperor Charles V, 1500–1558* (London: Arnold, 2002); Mack P. Holt, *The French Wars of Religion, 1562–1629* (Cambridge: Cambridge University Press, 1995); J. H. Elliott, *Richelieu and Olivares* (Cambridge: Cambridge University Press, 1984); De Lamar Jensen, "French Diplomacy and the Wars of Religion," *Sixteenth Century Journal* 5, no. 2 (October 1974): 23–46; R. J. Knecht, *The French Wars of Religion, 1559–1598* (New York: Longman, 1989); Nexon, *Religious Conflict*; D. L. Potter, "Foreign Policy in the Age of the Reformation: French Involvement in the Schmalkaldic War, 1544–1547," *Historical Journal* 20, no. 3 (September 1977): 525–44.

58. See, for example, Hans Heymann Jr., "Soviet Aid as a Problem for US Policy," *World Politics* 12, no. 4 (1960): 525–40.

59. Historian Elidor Mëhilli observes that "the Cold War created unexpected possibilities for small states to make big claims. Often mistreated in the international system and neglected in historical overviews of the twentieth century, small states should not be idealized either. They can be as cruel as any big power. Albania's unstructured regime, for example, used the Sino-Soviet split to step up its repression and fabricate more enemies. The point is not to show that small states matter but that Cold War confrontation endowed weak regimes with an outsized ideological significance." Elidor Mëhilli, *From Stalin to Mao: Albania and the Socialist World* (Ithaca, NY: Cornell University Press, 2017), 9.

60. Bruce Bueno de Mesquita and Alastair Smith, "Competition and Collaboration in Aid-for-Policy Deals," *International Studies Quarterly* 60, no. 3 (2016): 413–26, https://doi.org/10.1093/isq/sqw011.

61. David A. Lake, "Anarchy, Hierarchy and the Variety of International Relations," *International Organization* 50, no. 1 (1996): 1–33; David A. Lake, *Entangling Relations: American Foreign Policy in Its Century* (Princeton, NJ: Princeton University Press, 1999); MacDonald, "Obsolete?"

62. These exceptions include Gunitsky, *Aftershocks*; Nexon, *Religious Conflict*. Some work in the neo-Gramscian tradition, with which we do not engage, includes non-state actors, whether economic classes or intellectual elites. See Peter Burnham, "Neo-Gramscian Hegemony and the International Order," *Capital and Class* 15, no. 3 (1991): 73–92; Inderjeet Parmar, "'Mobilizing America for An Internationalist Foreign Policy': The Role of the Council on Foreign Relations," *Studies in American Political Development* 13, no. 2 (1999): 337–73; Inderjeet Parmar, *Foundations of the American Century: The Ford, Carnegie, and Rockefeller Foundations in the Rise of American Power* (New York: Columbia University Press, 2012).

63. Kennedy, *The Rise and Fall of the Great Powers*, 55.

64. Nexon, *Religious Conflict*. See also Blockmans, *Emperor Charles V, 1500–1558*; Philip Benedict, "The Dynamics of Protestant Militancy: France, 1555–1563," in *Reformation, Revolt and Civil War in France and the Netherlands 1555–1585*, ed. Philip Benedict et al. (Amsterdam: Royal Netherlands Academy of Arts and Sciences, 1999),

35–50; Carl C. Christensen, "John of Saxony's Diplomacy, 1529–1530: Reformation or Realpolitik," *Sixteenth Century Journal* 15, no. 4 (1984): 419–30; Martin van Gelderen, ed., *The Dutch Revolt* (Cambridge: Cambridge University Press, 1993); Abe J. Dueck, "Religion and Temporal Authority in the Reformation: The Controversy among the Protestants Prior to the Peace of Nuremberg, 1532," *Sixteenth Century Journal* 12, no. 2 (1982): 55–74; Mack P. Holt, "Review Article: Putting Religion Back in the Wars of Religion," *French Historical Studies* 18, no. 2 (1993): 524–51; Holt, *The French Wars of Religion, 1562–1629*; Jonathan Israel, *The Dutch Republic: Its Rise, Greatness, and Fall 1477–1806* (Oxford: Oxford University Press, 1995); Owen, "When Do Ideologies Produce Alliances?"; Owen, *Clash of Ideas*; Geoffrey Parker, *The Grand Strategy of Phillip II* (New Haven, CT: Yale University Press, 1998); Andrew Pettegree, "Religion and the Revolt," in *The Origins and Development of the Dutch Revolt*, ed. Graham Darby (London: Routledge, 2001), 67–83.

65. For perspectives on this claim, see Franz Ansprenger, *The Dissolution of the Colonial Empires* (London: Routledge, 2018); Tarak Barkawi, *Globalization and War* (Lanham, MD: Rowman and Littlefield, 2005); Adria Lawrence, *Imperial Rule and the Politics of Nationalism: Anti-Colonial Protest in the French Empire* (Cambridge: Cambridge University Press, 2013); Daniel Philpott, "Liberalism, Power, and Authority in International Relations: On the Origins of Colonial Independence and Internationally Sanctioned Intervention," *Security Studies* 11, no. 2 (2001): 117–63; Daniel Philpott, *Revolutions in Sovereignty: How Ideas Shaped Modern International Relations* (Princeton, NJ: Princeton University Press, 2001).

66. Owen, *Clash of Ideas*.

67. For a fantastic account of the relationship between power transitions and domestic political orders, one on which we lean heavily, see Gunitsky, *Aftershocks*.

68. Joseph Fronczak, "The Fascist Game: Transnational Political Transmission and the Genesis of the U.S. Modern Right," *Journal of American History* 105, no. 3 (2018): 564, https://doi.org/10.1093/jahist/jay279; "Butler Tale Unverified: Testimony before Congress Inquisitors Denies Plan for Revolution," *Los Angeles Times (1923–1995); Los Angeles, Calif.*, November 26, 1934, 20.

69. "Reputed Dictatorship Offer to Gen. Butler Will Be Fully Probed: Notables to Be Questioned, Committee Chairman Says Publicity Stunt, Declares Broker Reported Fascist Plan Called for Overthrow of Roosevelt," *The Sun* (1837–1993); Baltimore, MD, November 21, 1934, 1.

70. Fronczak, "The Fascist Game," 564–65. "Macguire Link with Alleged Plot Revealed: Congress Group Charges He Handled $75,000 for Unexplained Purposes. Money Came from Clark, Report Says. 'Somebody Is Trying to Shield Somebody,' Rep. Dickstein Concludes," *The Sun* (1837–1993); Baltimore, MD, November 26, 1934, 1.

71. Fronczak, "The Fascist Game," 567.

72. Jørgen Møller, Svend-Erik Skaaning, and Jakob Tolstrup, "International Influences and Democratic Regression in Interwar Europe: Disentangling the Impact of Power Politics and Demonstration Effects," *Government and Opposition* 52, no. 4 (2017): 579, https://doi.org/10.1017/gov.2015.37.

73. Arnd Bauerkämper, "Transnational Fascism: Cross-Border Relations between Regimes and Movements in Europe, 1922–1939," *East Central Europe* 37, no. 2–3 (2010): 236, https://doi.org/10.1163/187633010X534469; William C. Kirby, *Germany and Republican China* (Stanford, CA: Stanford University Press, 1984), 144–83.

74. Philip Morgan, *Fascism in Europe, 1919–1945* (London: Routledge, 2007), 172–76; Stanley G. Payne, *A History of Fascism, 1914–1945* (London: Routledge, 2016), 238–40; on the cycle of radicalization between left and right, see Fronczak, "The Fascist Game," 583.

75. "1,000 Irish Blue Shirts Offer to Fight for Italy," *Chicago Daily Tribune* (1923–1963), September 13, 1935, 10.

76. Payne, *A History of Fascism, 1914–1945*, 229.

77. See, inter alia, Gunitsky, *Aftershocks*; Kirby, *Germany and Republican China*; Payne, *A History of Fascism, 1914–1945*.

78. Møller, Skaaning, and Tolstrup, "International Influences and Democratic Regression in Interwar Europe," 561–62; see also Gunitsky, *Aftershocks*; Owen, *Clash of Ideas*; Kurt Weyland, "Diffusion Waves in European Democratization: The Impact of Organizational Development," *Comparative Politics* 45, no. 1 (2012): 25–45.

79. On the latter process, see Jack Snyder, *Myths of Empire: Domestic Politics and International Ambition* (Ithaca, NY: Cornell University Press, 1991).

80. And it should be no surprise that, as we see in Chapter 6, Moscow provided assistance to the pro-Brexit movement. England was one of its staunchest opponents in Europe, and throwing the country into chaos served its interests.

81. See, in general, Kevin McDermott and Jeremy Agnew, *The Comintern: A History of International Communism from Lenin to Stalin* (New York: Macmillan International Higher Education, 1996); Alexander Vatlin and Stephen A. Smith, "The Comintern," *The Oxford Handbook of the History of Communism*, January 1, 2014, https://doi.org/10.1093/oxfordhb/9780199602056.013.045.

82. Elliott, *Richelieu and Olivares*, 126–27.

CHAPTER 4

1. "Letter Dated 15 May 1997 from the Permanent Representatives of China and the Russian Federation to the United Nations Addressed to the Secretary-General," May 20, 1997, http://www.un.org/documents/ga/docs/52/plenary/a52-153.htm.

2. Henry Kissinger, "Moscow and Beijing: A Declaration of Independence," *Washington Post* May 14, 1996.

3. See Jeffrey Mankoff, *Russian Foreign Policy: The Return of Great Power Politics* (Lanham, MD: Rowman and Littlefield, 2009). On the importance of status and prestige for Moscow, see Andrei P. Tsygankov, *Russia and the West from Alexander to Putin: Honor in International Relations* (Cambridge: Cambridge University Press, 2012); and Deborah Welch Larson and Alexei Shevchenko, "Status Seekers: Chinese and Russian Responses to US Primacy," *International Security* 34, no. 4 (Spring 2010): 63–95.

4. At the Central Committee of the Communist Party of China's 2018 Central Conference on Work Relating to Foreign Affairs, Xi Jinping called for China to reform the global governance system, promoting the concepts of fairness and justice. See http://www.chinadaily.com.cn/a/201806/28/WS5b34179da3103349141df593.html.

5. See, for example, Ryan D. Griffiths, "States, Nations, and Territorial Stability: Why Chinese Hegemony Would Be Better for International Order," *Security Studies* 25, no. 3 (2016): 519–45, https://doi.org/10.1080/09636412.2016.1195628.

6. See, for example, Edward S. Steinfeld, *Playing Our Game: Why China's Rise Doesn't Threaten the West* (Oxford: Oxford University Press, 2010).

7. See especially Michael Beckley, "China's Century? Why America's Edge Will Endure," *International Security* 36, no. 3 (Winter 2011/2012): 41–78; Michael Beckley, "The Power of Nations: Measuring What Matters," *International Security* 43, no. 2 (2018): 7–44; Michael Beckley, *Unrivaled: Why America Will Remain the World's Sole Superpower* (Ithaca, NY: Cornell University Press, 2018).

8. Bobo Lo, *Axis of Convenience: Moscow, Beijing, and the New Geopolitics* (Washington, DC: Brookings Institution Press, 2009).

9. Data on UN voting convergence from the Votestar visualization tool at the Pardee Center for International Futures at the University of Denver, http://votester31.du.edu.

10. Milton Ezrati, "China Retreats Globally," *Forbes*, July 26, 2019, https://tinyurl.com/y2znxlxp; Derek Scissors, Derek Scissors, *China's Global Business Footprint Shrinks* (Washington, DC: American Enterprise Institute, July 2019), https://www.aei.org/wp-content/uploads/2019/07/Chinas-Global-Business-Footprint-Shrinks.pdf.

11. See Stephen Kotkin, "The Unbalanced Triangle—What Chinese-Russian Relations Mean for the United States," *Foreign Affairs*, 88 (2009): 130–38.

12. Jim O'Neill, "Building Better Global Economic BRICs," Goldman Sachs: Global Economics Paper no. 66 (2001).

13. O'Neill, "Building Better Global Economic BRICs," 10.

14. http://infobrics.org/page/history-of-brics/.

15. "Joint Statement of the BRIC Countries Leaders," Yekaterinburg, Russia, June 16, 2009, http://infobrics.org/document/3/.

16. See Hannes Ebert and Tim Maurer, "Contested Cyberspace and Rising Powers," *Third World Quarterly* 34, no. 6 (2013): 1054–74.

17. Vikram Nehru, "The BRICS Bank: Now Comes the Hard Part," Carnegie Endowment for International Peace, July 14, 2014, http://carnegieendowment.org/2014/07/17/brics-bank-now-comes-hard-part.

18. Natalia Khmelevskaya, "BRICS Financial and Payment Arrangements: A Locus of Intragroup Trade Development," in *BRICS and Global Governance*, ed. John Kirton and Marina Larionova (London: Routledge, 2018), 106–28.

19. Gabriel Stargardter, "Brazil's Courtship of U.S. Need Not Worry China: Foreign Minister," Reuters, July 26, 2019, https://www.reuters.com/article/us-brics-brazil-idUSKCN1UL2DO.

20. Andrew E. Kramer, "Russia Claims Its Sphere of Influence in the World," *New York Times*, August 31, 2008, https://www.nytimes.com/2008/09/01/world/europe/01russia.html.

21. Lai-Ha Chan, "Soft Balancing against the US 'Pivot to Asia': China's Geostrategic Rationale for Establishing the Asian Infrastructure Investment Bank," *Australian Journal of International Affairs* 71, no. 6 (2017): 568–90, https://doi.org/10.1080/10357718.2017.1357679; David Dollar, "China's Rise as a Regional and Global Power: The AIIB and the 'One Belt, One Road,'" *Brookings* (blog), July 15, 2015, https://www.brookings.edu/research/chinas-rise-as-a-regional-and-global-power-the-aiib-and-the-one-belt-one-road/; Sebastian Heilmann et al., "China's Shadow Foreign Policy: Parallel Structures Challenge the Established International Order," *China Monitor*, no. 18 (October 28, 2014): 9.

22. http://ceec-china-latvia.org/page/about.

23. Charles Clover, "Clinton Vows to Thwart New Soviet Union," *Financial Times*, December 6, 2012.

24. See, for example, Marcin Kaczmarski, "Non-Western Visions of Regionalism: China's New Silk Road and Russia's Eurasian Economic Union," *International Affairs* 93, no. 6 (2017): 1357–76; and Bobo Lo, *Russia and The New World Disorder*. Washington, DC: Brookings Institution Press, 2015.

25. See Alexei D. Voskresseni and Boglarka Koller, eds., *The Regional World Order: Transregionalism, Regional Integration, and Regional Projects across Europe and Asia* (Lanham, MD: Lexington Books, 2019); Alexander Lukin, "What the Kremlin Is Thinking: Putin's Vision for Eurasia," *Foreign Affairs* 93 (2014): 85–93. On Russian regionalism and emulation, see Yulia Nikitina, *The CSTO and the SCO: Models of Regionalism in the Area of Security* (Moscow, Russia: Navona: 2009). For an overview of Russian regionalism as a global orientation and critical responses, see the essays symposium "Power, Status and Entanglement," in *Russian Politics and Law* 54, no. 5–6 (2016): 415–526. Also see Angela Stent's analysis of Putin's "post-Western" strategies: Angela Stent, *Putin's World: Russia against the West and with the Rest* (London: Hachette, 2019).

26. See Bin Gu, "Chinese Multilateralism in the AIIB," *Journal of International Economic Law* 20, no. 1 (2017): 137–58; Xiao Re, "China as an Institution-Builder: The Case of the AIIB," *Pacific Review* 29, no. 3 (2016): 435–42; Shahar Hameiri and Lee Jones, "China Challenges Global Governance? Chinese International Development Finance and the AIIB," *International Affairs* 94, no. 3 (2018): 573–93. https://doi.org/10.1093/ia/iiy026; and Qin Yaqing, "International Society as a Process: Institutions, Identities, and China's Peaceful Rise," *Chinese Journal of International Politics*, 3, no. 2 (2010): 129–53.

27. "The Beleaguered BRICS Can Be Proud of Their Bank," *The Economist*, September 29, 2018, https://www.economist.com/finance-and-economics/2018/09/29/the-beleaguered-brics-can-be-proud-of-their-bank.

28. Naazneen Barma, Ely Ratner, and Steven Weber, "A World without the West," *National Interest*, no. 90 (2007): 23–30; Naazneen Barma et al., "A World without the West? Empirical Patterns and Theoretical Implications," *Chinese Journal of International Politics* 2, no. 4 (December 21, 2009): 525–44, https://doi.org/10.1093/cjip/pop013.

29. http://eng.sectsco.org/cooperation/.

30. For example, see David Kramer, "Why Europe Shouldn't Cooperate with Russia's Economic Bloc," *Politico.eu*, December 17, 2015, https://www.politico.eu/article/why-europe-shouldnt-cooperate-with-russias-economic-bloc/.

31. Evgeny Vinokurov, "Eurasian Economic Union: Current State and Preliminary Results," *Russian Journal of Economics* 3, no. 1 (2017): 54–70; Yuri Kofner, "Western Sanctions and Russian Counter Sanctions: Reasons and Effects," Russia International Affairs Council, December 31, 2018, https://russiancouncil.ru/en/blogs/GreaterEurasiaEnglish/western-sanctions-and-russian-counter-sanctions-reasons-and-effects/.

32. Jane Perlez, "U.S. Opposing China's Answer to World Bank," *New York Times*, October 9, 2014, https://www.nytimes.com/2014/10/10/world/asia/chinas-plan-for-regional-development-bank-runs-into-us-opposition.html; "Partnerships," Asian Infrastructure Investment Bank, n.d., https://www.aiib.org/en/about-aiib/who-we-are/partnership/index.html.

33. Peter J. Katzenstein, *A World of Regions: Asia and Europe in the American Imperium* (Ithaca, NY: Cornell University Press, 2005).

34. Martin Hutchinson and Agnes T. Crane, "Turning the Focus to Governance," *New York Times*, January 23, 2011, https://www.nytimes.com/2011/01/24/business/24views.html.

35. Michael Plummer and Peter A Petri. "The Case for RCEP as Asia's Next Trade Agreement," Brookings (blog), November 6, 2018, https://www.brookings.edu/blog/order-from-chaos/2018/11/06/the-case-for-rcep-as-asias-next-trade-agreement/.

36. Alexander Cooley, "What's Next for the Shanghai Cooperation Organization?" *The Diplomat* no. 43 (June 2018),

37. http://www.xinhuanet.com/english/2018-09/25/c_137490394.htm.

38. James Kynge and Michael Peel, "Brussels Rattled as China Reaches Out to Eastern Europe," *Financial Times*, November 27, 2017.

39. See Alexander Cooley, *Great Games, Local Rules: The New Great Power Contest in Central Asia* (New York: Oxford University Press 2012).

40. Peter Frankopan, *The New Silk Roads: The Present and Future of the World* (London: Bloomsbury, 2018).

41. See, in general, David F. Schmitz, *Thank God They're on Our Side: The United States and Right-Wing Dictatorships, 1921–1965* (Chapel Hill: University of North Carolina Press, 2009); Odd Arne Westad, *The Global Cold War: Third World Interventions and the Making of Our Times*, new ed. (Cambridge: Cambridge University Press, 2007).

42. See Lincoln Mitchell, *The Democracy Promotion Paradox* (Washington, DC: Brookings Institution Press, 2016), 94–104.

43. See, for example, Ellen Barry, "Putin Criticizes West for Libya Incursion," *New York Times*, April 26, 2011, https://www.nytimes.com/2011/04/27/world/europe/27putin.html; Angela Stent, *The Limits of Partnership: U.S.-Russian Relations in the Twenty-First Century* (Princeton, NJ: Princeton University Press, 2015), 247–49.

44. Saskia Brechenmacher, *Civil Society under Assault: Repression and Responses in Russia, Egypt, and Ethiopia* (Washington, DC: Carnegie Endowment for International Peace, 2017), 9–17, https://carnegieendowment.org/files/Civil_Society_Under_Assault_Final.pdf; Tyler Pager and Nick Gass, "Russia Brands McCain-Chaired NGO as 'Undesirable,'" *Politico*, August 18, 2016, https://www.politico.com/story/2016/08/international-republican-institute-russia-undesirable-227150.

45. "Clampdown in China Restrict 7,000 Foreign Organizations, *New York Times*, April 28, 2016, https://www.nytimes.com/2016/04/29/world/asia/china-foreign-ngo-law.html.

46. See Daniel Lynch's warning from 2007 that the CCP would not accept socialization into a global democratic norm and was likely to promote a counternorm: Daniel C. Lynch, "Envisioning China's Political Future: Elite Responses to Democracy as a Global Constitutive Norm," *International Studies Quarterly* 51, no. 3 (September 2007): 701–22.

47. Nate Schenkkan, "Nations in Transit 2018: Confronting Illiberalism," Nations in Transit, Washington, DC, Freedom House, 2018, https://freedomhouse.org/report/nations-transit/nations-transit-2018.

48. Christopher Walker, "What Is 'Sharp Power'?," *Journal of Democracy* 29, no. 3 (2018): 9–23, https://doi.org/10.1353/jod.2018.0041.

49. See Christopher Walker, "The Authoritarian Threat: The Hijacking of 'Soft Power,'" *Journal of Democracy* 27, no. 1 (2016): 49–63; Walker, "What Is 'Sharp Power'?"; Christopher Walker and Jessica Ludwig, "The Meaning of Sharp Power," *Foreign Affairs*, November 16, 2017, https://www.foreignaffairs.com/articles/china/2017-11-16/meaning-sharp-power.

50. Samuel Brazys and Alexander Dukalskis, "Grassroots Image Management: Confucius Institutes and Media Perceptions of China," AIDDATA, Working paper 69, January 2009, http://docs.aiddata.org/ad4/pdfs/WPS69_Grassroots_Image_Management.pdf.

51. This paragraph draws from Alexander Cooley, "Countering Democratic Norms," *Journal of Democracy* 26, no. 3 (2015): 49–63.

52. SCO, "Declaration on the Establishment of the Shanghai Cooperation Organization," 2001, www.eng.sectsco.org/load/193054. On how the "Shanghai Spirit" promotes regional authoritarianism, see Thomas Ambrosio, "Catching the 'Shanghai Spirit': How the Shanghai Cooperation Organization Promotes Authoritarian Norms in Central Asia," *Europe-Asia Studies* 60, no. 8 (2008): 1321–44.

53. Insightful accounts of the longer-term sources of the conflict appear in Samuel Charap and Timothy J. Colton, *Everyone Loses: The Ukraine Crisis and the Ruinous Contest for Post-Soviet Eurasia* (London: Routledge, 2018); and Rajan Menon and Eugene B. Rumer, *Conflict in Ukraine: The Unwinding of the Post–Cold War Order* (Cambridge, MA: MIT Press, 2015).

54. Charles Grant, "Is the EU to Blame for the Crisis in Ukraine?," Centre for European Reform, June 1, 2016, https://www.cer.eu/insights/eu-blame-crisis-ukraine; "Russia's Putin Took European States 'by Surprise' in Ukraine: Report," *NBC News*, https://www.nbcnews.com/storyline/ukraine-crisis/russias-putin-took-european-states-surprise-ukraine-report-n309406, accessed July 31, 2019.

55. http://en.kremlin.ru/events/president/news/20603.

56. Alexander Cooley and Lincoln A. Mitchell, "Engagement without Recognition: A New Strategy toward Abkhazia and Eurasia's Unrecognized States," *Washington Quarterly* 33, no. 4 (2010): 59–73.

57. United Nations General Assembly Resolution 68/262, "Territorial integrity of Ukraine" (adopted March 27, 2014),http://www.un.org/en/ga/search/view_doc.asp?symbol=A/RES/68/262.

58. In 2018, the NGO Airwars estimated civilian casualties as a result of Russian bombings as ranging from at least 3,445 to possibly as high as 18,000. See "Syria Conflict: 34% Rise in Civilian Deaths Caused by Russian Airstrikes, Report Finds," *Independent UK*, July 25, 2018. Russia continued to attack civilians in 2019.

59. Andrej Krickovic and Yuval Weber, "Commitment Issues: The Syrian and Ukraine Crises as Bargaining Failures of the Post–Cold War International Order," *Problems of Post-Communism* 65, no. 6 (2018): 373–84.

60. "President Xi Jinping Delivers Important Speech and Proposes to Build a Silk Road Economic Belt with Central Asian Countries," Ministry of Foreign Affairs of the People's Republic of China, September 7, 2013, https://www.fmprc.gov.cn/mfa_eng/topics_665678/xjpfwzysiesgjtfhshzzfh_665686/t1076334.shtml.

61. "Vision and Actions on Jointly Building Silk Road Economic Belt and 21st-Century Maritime Silk Road," March 28, 2015, http://en.ndrc.gov.cn/newsrelease/201503/t20150330_669367.html.

62. "One Belt, One Road Initiative Will Define China's Role as a World Leader," *South Morning China Post*, April 2, 2015.

63. The project may also be motivated by a desire to enhance Xi's legitimacy by positioning him as the leader who restored Chinese global prestige and influence; see Paul Musgrave and Daniel Nexon, "Zheng He's Voyages and the Symbolism behind Xi Jinping's Belt and Road Initiative," *The Diplomat*, December 22, 2017, https://thediplomat.com/2017/12/zheng-hes-voyages-and-the-symbolism-behind-xi-jinpings-belt-and-road-initiative/.

64. "A Thousand Miles Begin with a Single Step: Tax Challenges under the BRI," *International Tax Review*, November 28, 2017, http://www.internationaltaxreview.com/

Article/3772212/A-thousand-miles-begin-with-a-single-step-tax-challenges-under-the-BRI.html.

65. Matthew Erie, "The China International Commercial Court: Prospects for Dispute Resolution for the 'Belt and Road Initiative,'" *American Society of International Law, Insights* 22, no. 11 (2018), https://www.asil.org/insights/volume/22/issue/11/china-international-commercial-court-prospects-dispute-resolution-belt.

66. Jonathan Hillman and Matthew Goodman, "China's Belt and Road Mechanism to Challenge Current US-led order," *Financial Times*, July 24, 2018, https://www.ft.com/content/b64d7f2e-8f4d-11e8-b639-7680cedcc421.

67. Noah Barkin, "Chinese 'Highway to Nowhere' Haunts Montenegro," Reuters, July 16, 2018, https://www.reuters.com/article/us-china-silkroad-europe-montenegro-insi/chinese-highway-to-nowhere-haunts-montenegro-idUSKBN1K60QX.

68. Nick Cumming-Bruce and Somini Sengupta, "In Greece, China Finds an Ally against Human Rights Criticism," *New York Times*, June 19, 2017, https://www.nytimes.com/2017/06/19/world/europe/china-human-rights-greece-united-nations.html.

69. Nick Cumming-Bruce, "China's Retort over Its Mass Detentions: Praise from Russia and Saudi Arabia," *New York Times*, July 12, 2019, https://www.nytimes.com/2019/07/12/world/asia/china-human-rights-united-nations.html.

70. John Hurley, Scott Morris, and Gailyn Portelance, "Examining the Debt Implications of the Belt and Road Initiative from a Policy Perspective," Policy Paper 121 (March 2018), 11, Washington, DC, Center for Global Economic Development.

71. Maria Abi-Habib, "How China Got Sri Lanka to Cough Up a Port," *New York Times*, June 25, 2018, https://www.nytimes.com/2018/06/25/world/asia/china-sri-lanka-port.html.

72. Tom Hancock, "China Renegotiated $50bn in Loans to Developing Countries," *Financial Times*, April 29, 2019, https://www.ft.com/content/0b207552-6977-11e9-80c7-60ee53e6681d.

73. "US Vows to Tackle China's and Russia's 'Predatory' Practices in Africa," *Telegraph*, December 14, 2018, https://www.telegraph.co.uk/global-health/climate-and-people/trump-admin-vows-tackle-russia-chinas-predatory-practices-africa/.

74. Sergey Karaganov, "The New Cold War and the Emerging Greater Eurasia," *Journal of Eurasian Studies* 9, no. 2 (2018): 85–93.

75. Ben Westcott, Brad Lendon, and Yoonjung Seo, "Warplanes from Four Countries Face Off in Asian Confrontation," CNN, July 23, 2019, https://www.cnn.com/2019/07/23/asia/south-korea-russia-military-intl-hnk/index.html.

76. John Lee, "Russian Air Clash Is a Wake-up Call for South Korea," Nikkei Asian Review, https://asia.nikkei.com/Opinion/Russian-air-clash-is-a-wake-up-call-for-South-Korea, accessed July 31, 2019.

77. Clark Letterman, "Image of Putin, Russia Suffers Internationally," Pew Research Center, Global Attitudes and Trends, December 2018, https://www.pewresearch.org/global/2018/12/06/image-of-putin-russia-suffers-internationally/; Richard Wike, Bruce Stokes, Jacob Poushter, Laura Silver, Janell Fetterolf, and Kat Devlin, "Trump's International Ratings Remain Low, Especially among Key Allies," Pew Research Center, Global Attitudes and Trends, October 2018, https://www.pewresearch.org/global/2018/10/01/trumps-international-ratings-remain-low-especially-among-key-allies/

78. United States, "National Security Strategy of the United States," Washington, DC, President of the U.S., December 2017, 2–3ff, https://www.whitehouse.gov/wp-content/uploads/2017/12/NSS-Final-12-18-2017-0905.pdf.

CHAPTER 5

1. Cédric Jourde, "The International Relations of Small Neoauthoritarian States: Islamism, Warlordism, and the Framing of Stability," *International Studies Quarterly* 51, no. 2 (June 2007): 484.

2. On human rights verification, see Beth A. Simmons, *Mobilizing for Human Rights: International Law in Domestic Politics* (Cambridge: Cambridge University Press, 2009).

3. Joseph E. Stiglitz, *Globalization and Its Discontents* (New York: W.W. Norton, 2002).

4. Tijen Demirel-Pegg and James Moskowitz, "US Aid Allocation: The Nexus of Human Rights, Democracy, and Development," *Journal of Peace Research* 46, no. 2 (2009): 181–98, https://doi.org/10.1177/0022343308100714.

5. Thad Dunning, "Conditioning the Effects of Aid: Cold War Politics, Donor Credibility, and Democracy in Africa," *International Organization* 58, no. 2 (2004): 409–23; Xiaojun Li, "Does Conditionality Still Work? China's Development Assistance and Democracy in Africa," *Chinese Political Science Review* 2, no. 2 (2017): 201–20, https://doi.org/10.1007/s41111-017-0050-6; see also Bruce Bueno de Mesquita and Alastair Smith, "Competition and Collaboration in Aid-for-Policy Deals," *International Studies Quarterly* 60, no. 3 (2016): 413–26, https://doi.org/10.1093/isq/sqw011.

6. Emilie M. Hafner-Burton, "Sticks and Stones: Naming and Shaming the Human Rights Enforcement Problem," *International Organization* 62, no. 4 (October 2008): 689–716, https://doi.org/10.1017/S0020818308080247; Emilie Hafner-Burton, *Making Human Rights a Reality* (Princeton, NJ: Princeton University Press, 2013); Amanda M. Murdie and David R. Davis, "Shaming and Blaming: Using Events Data to Assess the Impact of Human Rights INGOs," *International Studies Quarterly* 56, no. 1 (March 2012): 1–16, https://doi.org/10.1111/j.1468-2478.2011.00694.x; Simmons, *Mobilizing*; on election monitoring becoming an international norm, see Susan D. Hyde, *The Pseudo-Democrat's Dilemma: Why Election Observation Became an International Norm* (Ithaca, NY: Cornell University Press, 2011).

7. Alexander Cooley and Jack Snyder, eds. *Ranking the World* (Cambridge: Cambridge University Press, 2015).

8. Randall W. Stone, *Lending Credibility: The International Monetary Fund and the Post-Communist Transition* (Princeton, NJ: Princeton University Press, 2002).

9. Stephen D. Krasner, *Sovereignty: Organized Hypocrisy* (Princeton, NJ: Princeton University Press, 1999).

10. See James Raymond Vreeland, *The IMF and Economic Development* (Cambridge: Cambridge University Press, 2003).

11. Alexander Cooley, Daniel H. Nexon, and Steven Ward, "Revising Order or Challenging the Balance of Military Power? An Alternative Typology of Revisionist and Status-Quo States," *Review of International Studies* 45, no. 4 (2019): 698–708.

12. This was a lesson many Asian governments learned after the 1998 Asian financial crisis. See Joshua Aizenman and Nancy Marion, "The High Demand for International Reserves in the Far East: What Is Going On?," *Journal of the Japanese and International Economies*, Financial Issues in the Pacific Basin Region, 17, no. 3 (2003): 370–400, https://doi.org/10.1016/S0889-1583(03)00008-X; Joshua Aizenman and Jaewoo Lee, "Financial versus Monetary Mercantilism: Long-Run View of Large International Reserves Hoarding," *World Economy* 31, no. 5 (2008): 593–611, https://doi.org/10.1111/j.1467-9701.2008.01095.x.

13. Douglas A. Johnson, Alberto Mora, and Averell Schmidt, "The Strategic Costs of Torture: How Enhanced Interrogation Hurt America," *Foreign Affairs* 95 (2016): 129.

14. Benjamin C. Denison and Emma M. Ashford, "Primacy, Regime Change and the Liberal International Order," Working Paper, Tufts University, Medford, MA, March 2019; see also Cooley, Nexon, and Ward, "Revising Order"; G. John Ikenberry, "America's Imperial Ambition," *Foreign Affairs* 81, no. 5 (September 2002): 44–60; Paul Musgrave and Daniel Nexon, "American Liberalism and the Imperial Temptation," in *Empire and International Order*, ed. Noel Parker (London: Routledge, 2013), 131–48.

15. See, for example, Associated Press, "China's Xi to Make 3-Nation Europe Visit Starting Thursday," *New York Times*, March 17, 2019, https://www.nytimes.com/aponline/2019/03/17/world/asia/ap-as-china-italy.html; Ferdinando Giguliano, "Italy Can't Keep Both China and Donald Trump Happy," *Bloomberg*, March 18, 2019, https://www.bloomberg.com/opinion/articles/2019-03-18/belt-and-road-italy-can-t-keep-both-china-and-donald-trump-happy.

16. See Richard Youngs, "Upholding Democracy in a Post-Western World," Working Paper, Rising Democracies Network, Washington, DC, Carnegie Endowment for International Peace, 2019, https://carnegieendowment.org/files/12_18_Youngs_Post-West_Democracy.pdf.

17. See Judith G. Kelley, *Ethnic Politics in Europe: The Power of Norms and Incentives* (Princeton, NJ: Princeton University Press, 2010). On EU conditionality, see Frank Schimmelfennig and Ulrich Sedelmeier, "Governance by Conditionality: EU Rule Transfer to the Candidate Countries of Central and Eastern Europe," *Journal of European Public Policy* 11, no. 4 (2004): 661–79. On NATO conditionality and socialization, see Alexandra Gheciu, *NATO in the New Europe: The Politics of International Socialization after the Cold War* (Stanford, CA: Stanford University Press, 2005).

18. Milada Anna Vachudova, *Europe Undivided: Democracy, Leverage, and Integration after Communism* (Oxford: Oxford University Press, 2005).

19. Jon C. Pevehouse, *Democracy from Above: Regional Organizations and Democratization* (New York: Cambridge University Press, 2005).

20. On the emerging link between authoritarianism and regionalism, see Anastassia V. Obydenkova and Alexander Libman, *Authoritarian Regionalism in the World of International Organizations: Global Perspective and the Eurasian Enigma* (New York: Oxford University Press, 2019).

21. Kim Lane Scheppele, "Other People's Patriot Acts: Europe's Response to September 11 Symposium on Immigration Law and Terrorism," *Loyola Law Review* 50 (2004): 89–148; Kim Lane Scheppele, "The Migration of Anti-Constitutional Ideas: The Post-9/11 Globalization of Public Law and the International State of Emergency," in *The Migration of Constitutional Ideas*, ed. Sujit Choudhry (Cambridge: Cambridge University Press, 2006), 347–73.

22. See Alexander Cooley and Matthew Schaaf, "Grounding the Backlash: Regional Security Treaties, Counternorms, and Human Rights in Eurasia," in *Human Rights Futures*, ed. Stephen Hopgood, Jack Snyder and Leslie Vinjamuri (Cambridge: Cambridge University Press, 2017), 159–88.

23. "GCC: Joint Security Agreements Imperils Rights," *Human Rights Watch*, April 26, 2014, https://www.hrw.org/news/2014/04/26/gcc-joint-security-agreement-imperils-rights, accessed July 31, 2019.

24. For an overview, see Marlies Glasius, "Extraterritorial Authoritarian Practices: A Framework," *Globalizations* 15, no. 2 (2018): 179–97, https://doi.org/10.1080/14747731.2017.1403781.

25. See Matteo Fumagalli, "Alignments and Realignments in Central Asia: The Rationale and Implications of Uzbekistan's Rapprochement with Russia," *International Political Science Review* 28, no. 3 (2007): 253–71.

26. Oz Hassan, "Undermining the Transatlantic Democracy Agenda? The Arab Spring and Saudi Arabia's Counteracting Democracy Strategy," *Democratization* 22, no. 3 (2015): 479–95, https://doi.org/10.1080/13510347.2014.981161; Mohammed Nuruzzaman, "Politics, Economics and Saudi Military Intervention in Bahrain," *Journal of Contemporary Asia* 43, no. 2 (2013): 363–78, https://doi.org/10.1080/00472336.2012.759406.

27. Hyde, *Pseudo-Democrat's Dilemma*.

28. On the role of election observers in the Color Revolutions, see Lincoln A. Mitchell, *The Color Revolutions* (Philadelphia: University of Pennsylvania Press, 2012). More broadly, see Daniela Donno, *Defending Democratic Norms: International Actors and the Politics of Electoral Misconduct* (New York: Oxford University Press, 2013); Daniela Donno, "Elections and Democratization in Authoritarian Regimes," *American Journal of Political Science* 57, no. 3 (2013): 703–16, https://doi.org/10.1111/ajps.12013.

29. On the origins of the CIS observers, see Rick Fawn, "Battle over the Box: International Election Observation Missions, Political Competition and Retrenchment in the Post-Soviet Space," *International Affairs* 82, no. 6 (2006): 1133–53.

30. Judith Kelley, "The More the Merrier? The Effects of Having Multiple International Election Monitoring Organizations," *Perspectives on Politics* 7, no. 1 (2009): 59–64.

31. The terms are used, respectively, by Christopher Walker and Alexander Cooley, "Vote of the Living Dead," *Foreign Policy.com*, October 31, 2013; and Maria J. Debre and Lee Morgenbesser, "Out of the Shadows: Autocratic Regimes, Election Observation and Legitimation," *Contemporary Politics* 23, no. 3 (2017): 328–47.

32. Lee Morgenbesser, "Casting a Shadow of a Doubt on International Election Monitoring Norms," *Power 3.0*, November 28, 2017, https://www.power3pointo.org/2017/11/29/authoritarian-corrosion-of-the-international-election-observation-norm/.

33. Lee Morgenbesser, "Fake Monitors Endorse Cambodia's Sham Elections," *ForeignPolicy.com*, July 30, 2018.

34. Walker and Cooley, "Vote of the Living Dead."

35. According to the organization, "EODE [Eurasian Observatory for Democracy and Election] denounces in particular the way the election monitoring is carried out by these Western NGOs and the monitoring missions of Western international organizations (US Congress, European Union, European Parliament, Parliamentary Assembly of the Council of Europe, OSCE, etc. . . .), to destabilize the countries non-aligned on the policy of the United States and NATO in Europe, Africa, Middle East, Asia, and Latin America and to support 'colour revolutions.' This concern is shared today by the CSTO, as this international organization has stated at its last summit," Eurasian Observatory for Democracy and Election, http://www.eode.org/contact/.

36. Charles Kindleberger, *The World in Depression 1929-1939* (Berkeley: University of California Press, 1973).

37. Moises Naim, "Rogue Aid," *Foreign Policy* 159 (2007): 96.

38. Julia Bader, "China, Autocratic Patron? An Empirical Investigation of China as a Factor in Autocratic Survival," *International Studies Quarterly* 59, no. 1 (March 2015): 23–33, https://doi.org/10.1111/isqu.12148.

39. Ngaire Woods, "Whose Aid? Whose Influence? China, Emerging Donors and the Silent Revolution in Development Assistance," *International Affairs* 84, no. 6 (2008): 1205–21, https://doi.org/10.1111/j.1468-2346.2008.00765.x.

40. Stefan Halper, *The Beijing Consensus: Legitimizing Authoritarianism in Our Time* (New York: Basic Books, 2012). For a response, see Deborah Brautigam, *The Dragon's Gift: The Real Story of China in Africa* (New York: Oxford University Press, 2011).

41. Stiglitz, *Globalization and Its Discontents.*

42. The first version of the dataset ranks Chinese aid projects around the world from 2000 to 2014 and includes 4,375 project records worth $354.4 billion. See https://www.aiddata.org/data/chinese-global-official-finance-dataset.

43. Axel Dreher, Andreas Fuchs, Roland Hodler, Bradley C. Parks, Paul A. Raschky, and Michael J. Tierney, "Aid on Demand: African Leaders and the Geography of China's Foreign Assistance," *Centro Studi Luca D'Agliano Development Studies Working Papers*, No 400, September 2016.

44. Dreher et al., "Aid on Demand," 32.

45. David Lewi, "The Failure of a Liberal Peace: Sri Lanka's Counter-Insurgency in Global Perspective," *Conflict, Security and Development* 10, no. 5 (2010): 647–71.

46. Richard A. Nielsen, Michael G. Findley, Zachary S. Davis, Tara Candland, and Daniel L. Nielson, "Foreign Aid Shocks as a Cause of Violent Armed Conflict." *American Journal of Political Science* 55, no. 2 (2011): 219–32.

47. Austin M. Strange, Axel Dreher, Andreas Fuchs, Bradley Parks, and Michael J. Tierney, "Tracking Underreported Financial Flows: China's Development Finance and the Aid–Conflict Nexus Revisited," *Journal of Conflict Resolution* 61, no. 5 (2017): 935–63.

48. Strange et al., "Tracking Underreported Financial Flows," 950, 955.

49. See David Lewis, John Heathershaw, and Nick Megoran, "Illiberal Peace? Authoritarian Modes of Conflict Management," *Cooperation and Conflict* 53, no. 4 (2018): 486–506.

50. See Crisis Group, "Central Asia: Decay and Decline," Asia Report no. 201, February 3, 2011, 17.

51. OCCRP, "Kyrgyzstan: PM Resigns amid Corruption Controversy," April 12, 2016, https://www.occrp.org/en/daily/5127-kyrgyzstan-pm-resigns-amid-corruption-controversy.

52. Ann-Sofie Isaksson and Andreas Kotsadam, "Chinese Aid and Local Corruption," *Journal of Public Economics* 159 (2018): 146–59.

53. Isaksson and Kotsadam, "Chinese Aid and Local Corruption," 157. Further, within Uganda, the authors also find that US- and Japanese-funded projects appear to lower corruption.

54. Samuel Brazys, Johan Elkink and Gina Kelly, "Bad Neighbors? How Co-Located Chinese and World Bank Development Projects Impact Local Corruption in Tanzania," *Review of International Organization* 12 (2017): 227–53, 250.

55. For critical assessments that emphasize the agency of Angolan elites in shaping the terms of the deal and negotiation dynamics, see Brautigham, *The Dragon's Gift*, 131–61; and Lucy Corkin, *Uncovering African Agency: Angola's Management of China's Credit Lines* (New York: Routledge, 2016).

56. Diego Hernandez, "Are 'New' Donors Challenging World Bank Conditionality?," *World Development* 96 (2017): 529–49.

57. Hernandez, "Are 'New' Donors Challenging World Bank Conditionality?," 522.

58. Erica Downs, *Inside China, Inc: China's Development Bank's Cross-border Energy Deals*, (Washington, DC: Brookings Institution Press, 2011), https://www.brookings.edu/wp-content/uploads/2016/06/1209_china_development_bank_downs.pdf.

59. "China to Import More Russian Coal, Lend $6 Billion," *Bloomberg*, September 7, 2020 https://www.bloomberg.com/news/articles/2010-09-07/china-will-take-more-russian-coal-imports-in-next-25-years-arrange-loan.

60. Bethany Allen-Ebrahimian, "Russia Is the Biggest Recipient of Chinese Foreign Aid," *Foreign Policy*, October 11, 2017, https://foreignpolicy.com/2017/10/11/russia-is-the-biggest-recipient-of-chinese-foreign-aid-north-korea/ .

61. Anthony Faiola, "Calling Foreign Debt 'Immoral,' Leader Allows Ecuador to Default," *Washington Post*, December 13, 2008, http://www.washingtonpost.com/wp-dyn/content/article/2008/12/12/AR2008121204105.html.

62. Chris Kraul, "Ecuador Faces a Huge Budget Deficit Because of Loans It Received from China," *Los Angeles Times*, December 10, 2018, https://www.latimes.com/world/la-fg-ecuador-loans-china-20181210-story.html.

63. Luke Harding, "China Signs Deal for 30 Years of Turkmen Gas," *The Guardian*, June 25, 2009, https://www.theguardian.com/business/2009/jun/25/china-turkmenistan-gas.

64. Sebastien Peyrouse, *Turkmenistan: Strategies of Power, Dilemmas of Development* (London: Routledge, 2015), 182–88.

65. Kevin Gallagher, Amos Irwin, and Katherine Koleski, "The New Banks in Town: Chinese Finance in Latin America," *Inter-American Dialogue* (February 2012), http://ase.tufts.edu/gdae/Pubs/rp/GallagherChineseFinanceLatinAmerica.pdf.

66. However, in both cases the regimes of Alexander Lukashenko and Kurmanbek Bakiyev accepted the funds but did not follow through on informal promises to accede to Moscow's wishes and rebuff the West. Belarus did not recognize the independence of the Georgian breakaway territories of Abkhazia and South Ossetia. The Kyrgyz and US governments announced a new agreement to extend access to the Manas Air Base in June 2009.

67. Ralph Clem and Anthony P. Maingot, *Venezuela's Petro-Diplomacy: Hugo Chávez's Foreign Policy* (Gainesville: University Press of Florida, 2011); and Tom Chodor and Anthea McCarthy-Jones, "Post-liberal Regionalism in Latin America and the Influence of Hugo Chávez," *Journal of Iberian and Latin American Research* 19, no. 2 (2013): 211–23.

68. See Bruce M. Bagley and Magdalena Defort, eds., *Decline of the US Hegemony? A Challenge of ALBA and a New Latin American Integration of the Twenty-First Century* (Lanham, MD: Lexington Books, 2015). For a critical account of ALBA as a counter-ordering institution, see Christopher Sabatini, "Meaningless Multilateralism," *Foreign Affairs*, August 8, 2014, www.foreignaffairs.com/articles/south-america/2014-08-08/meaningless-multilateralism.

69. Raymond Bonner, *Waltzing with a Dictator: The Marcoses and the Making of American Policy* (New York: Times Books, 1987).

70. Radoslav Yordanov, *The Soviet Union and the Horn of Africa during the Cold War: Between Ideology and Pragmatism* (Lanham, MD: Lexington Books, 2016).

71. Robert A. Pape, "Soft Balancing against the United States," *International Security* 30, no. 1 (Summer 2005): 7–45.

72. These two paragraphs draw on Alexander Cooley and Daniel H. Nexon, "The Empire Will Compensate You": The Structural Dynamics of the US Overseas Basing Network," *Perspectives on Politics* 11, no. 4 (2013): 1034–50.

73. Tyler Headley, "China's Djibouti Base: A One Year Update," *The Diplomat*, December 4, 2018, https://thediplomat.com/2018/12/chinas-djibouti-base-a-one-year-update/.

74. Costas Paris, "China Tightens Grip on East Africa Port," *Wall Street Journal*, February 21, 2019, https://www.wsj.com/articles/china-tightens-grip-on-east-african-port-11550746800.

75. Maria Abi-Habib, "China's 'Belt and Road' Plan in Pakistan Takes a Military Turn," *New York Times*, December 19, 2018, https://www.nytimes.com/2018/12/19/world/asia/pakistan-china-belt-road-military.html; and Gurmeet Kanwal, "Pakistan's Gwadar Port," *CSIS Brief*, April 2, 2018, https://www.csis.org/analysis/pakistans-gwadar-port-new-naval-base-chinas-string-pearls-indo-pacific.

76. Abi-Habib, "China's 'Belt and Road' Plan in Pakistan Takes a Military Turn."

77. Gary Shih, "In Central Asia's Forbidding Highlands, a Quiet Newcomer: Chinese Troops," *Washington Post*, February 19, 2019, https://www.washingtonpost.com/world/asia_pacific/in-central-asias-forbidding-highlands-a-quiet-newcomer-chinese-troops/2019/02/18/78d4a8d0-1e62-11e9-a759-2b8541bbbe20_story.html.

78. Craig Nelson and Thomas Grove, "Russia, China Vie for Influence in Central Asia as U.S. Plans Afghan Exit," *Wall Street Journal*, June 18, 2019, https://www.wsj.com/articles/russia-china-vie-for-influence-in-central-asia-as-u-s-plans-afghan-exit-11560850203.

79. Jeremy Page, Gordon Lubold, and Rob Taylor, "Deal for Naval Outpost in Cambodia Furthers China's Quest for Military Network," *Wall Street Journal*, July 22, 2019, https://www.wsj.com/articles/secret-deal-for-chinese-naval-outpost-in-cambodia-raises-u-s-fears-of-beijings-ambitions-11563732482; and John Reed, "China Construction Points to Military Foothold in Cambodia," *Financial Times*, July 24, 2019, https://www.ft.com/content/861d20ce-ad39-11e9-8030-530adfa879c2, https://www.ft.com/content/861d20ce-ad39-11e9-8030-530adfa879c2.

80. Page, Lubold, and Taylor, "Deal for Naval Outpost in Cambodia Furthers China's Quest for Military Network."

81. Data on Multilateral Debt as a % of Overall External Debt from World Bank Indicators, data.worldbank.org.

82. Jesse Johnson, "Maritime Rescue Center Opened on South China Sea Islet as Beijing Seeks to Reinforce Claims," *Japan Times*, January 29, 2019, https://www.japantimes.co.jp/news/2019/01/29/asia-pacific/maritime-rescue-center-opened-south-china-sea-islet-beijing-seeks-reinforce-claims/#.Xb5r0EVKiL4.

83. Jan-Werner Müller, *What Is Populism?* (London: Penguin, 2017).

84. https://budapestbeacon.com/full-text-of-viktor-Orbáns-speech-at-baile-tusnad-tusnadfurdo-of-26-july-2014/.

85. The report attributed the rating change to "sustained attacks on the country's democratic institutions by Prime Minister Viktor Orbán's Fidesz party, which has used its parliamentary super-majority to impose restrictions on or assert control over the opposition, the media, religious groups, academia, NGOs, the courts, asylum seekers, and the private sector since 2010." Freedom House, *Freedom in the World 2019: Democracy in Retreat*, p. 13, https://freedomhouse.org/sites/default/files/Feb2019_FH_FITW_2019_Report_ForWeb-compressed.pdf.

86. Patrick Kingsley, "Erdoğan Claims Vast Powers in Turkey after Narrow Victory in Referendum," *New York Times*, April 16, 2017, https://www.nytimes.com/2017/04/16/world/europe/turkey-referendum-polls-erdogan.html.

87. See Hanah Ellis-Petersen, "Duterte Confesses: 'My Only Sin Is Extra Judicial Killings," *The Guardian*, September 28, 2018, https://www.theguardian.com/world/2018/sep/28/duterte-confesses-my-only-sin-is-the-extrajudicial-killings. On the Mindanao death squads, see Human Rights Watch, "You Can Die at Any Time: Death Squad Killings in Mindanao," April 6, 2009, https://www.hrw.org/sites/default/files/reports/philippines0409web_0.pdf.

88. On the crackdown against human rights defenders, see International Federation for Human Rights (IFDH), "Philippines: Crackdown on Human Rights Defenders Likely to Intensify after President Rodrigo Duterte's Candidates Sweep Senate Elections," May 24, 2019, https://www.fidh.org/en/issues/human-rights-defenders/philippines-crackdown-on-human-rights-defenders-likely-to-intensify. On the targeting of the media, see Luke Hunt, "Duterte's Media War in the Philippines," *The Diplomat*, September 24, 2018, https://thediplomat.com/2018/09/dutertes-media-war-in-the-philippines/; and John Geddi and Martin Petty, "The Philippine Journalists Taking the Rap in Dutertes' Latest War," Reuters, March 29, 2019, https://www.reuters.com/article/us-philippines-media-insight/the-philippine-journalists-taking-the-rap-in-dutertes-latest-war-idUSKCN1R92VK.

89. Orban noted, "Today, the world tries to understand systems which are not Western, not liberal, maybe not even democracies yet they are successful." Honor Mahony, "Orban Wants to Build an 'Illiberal State,'" Euroobserver, July 28, 2014, https://euobserver.com/political/125128.

90. "Orbán: If the EU Doesn't Pay, Hungary Will Turn to China," *Budapest Business Journal*, January 11, 2018, https://bbj.hu/economy/Orbán-if-eu-doesnt-pay-hungary-will-turn-to-china_143836.

91. Aaron Mehta, "Turkey Officially Kicked Out of F-35 Program, Costing US Half a Billion Dollars," *Defense News*, July 17, 2019, https://www.defensenews.com/air/2019/07/17/turkey-officially-kicked-out-of-f-35-program/.

92. "Fed Up with the EU, Erdoğan says Turkey Could Join Shanghai Bloc," Reuters, November 20, 2016, https://www.reuters.com/article/us-turkey-europe-erdogan/fed-up-with-eu-erdogan-says-turkey-could-join-shanghai-bloc-idUSKBN13F0CY.

93. Renato Cruz De Castro, "The Duterte Administration's Foreign Policy: Unravelling the Aquino Administration's Balancing Agenda on an Emergent China," *Journal of Current Southeast Asian Affairs* 35, no. 3 (2016): 139–59.

94. "Presidential Remarks on China, Russia Send Investors Fleeing," *Business World Online*, September 27, 2016, http://www.bworldonline.com/content.php?section=Nation&title=presidential-remarks-on-china-russia-send-investors-fleeing&id=133993.

95. "China Hasn't Delivered on Its $24 Billion Philippines Promise," Bloomberg, July 25, 2018, https://www.bloomberg.com/news/articles/2018-07-25/china-s-24-billion-promise-to-duterte-still-hasn-t-materialized.

96. Maia de la Baume and Ryan Heath, "Parliament Denounces Hungary's Illiberalism, *Politico*, September 12, 2018, https://www.politico.eu/article/european-parliament-approves-hungary-censure-motion/.

97. Marc Santora, "George Soros-Founded University Is Forced Out of Hungary," *New York Times*, December 3, 2018, https://www.nytimes.com/2018/12/03/world/europe/soros-hungary-central-european-university.html.

98. According to the *New York Times*, Trump had praised Duterte in a phone call telling him he was doing an "unbelievable job on the drug problem." David E. Sanger and Maggie Haberman, "Trump Praises Duterte for Philippine Crackdown in Call

Transcript," May 23, 2017, https://www.nytimes.com/2017/05/23/us/politics/trump-duterte-phone-transcript-philippine-drug-crackdown.html.

CHAPTER 6

1. "Timeline of New Zealand Terror Attack," *Deutsche Welle*, March 15, 2919, https://www.dw.com/en/timeline-of-new-zealand-terror-attack/a-47940722.

2. Wajahat Ali, "The Roots of the Christchurch Massacre," *New York Times*, March 20, 2019, https://www.nytimes.com/2019/03/15/opinion/new-zealand-mosque-shooting.html.

3. Agence France-Presse, "New Zealand Mosque Gunman Claims Norway's Breivik Inspired Terror Attack," *The Local*, March 16, 2019, https://www.thelocal.no/20190316/how-norways-inspired-the-christchurch-mosque-attacker.

4. See Daniel Philpott, "Usurping the Sovereignty of Sovereignty?," *World Politics* 53 (2001): 297–324; Andrew Phillips, "The Protestant Ethic and the Spirit of Jihadism—Transnational Religious Insurgencies and the Transformation of International Orders," *Review of International Studies* 36, no. 2 (April 2010): 257–80, https://doi.org/10.1017/S0260210510000021.

5. See John Arquilla and David Ronfeldt, *Networks and Netwars: The Future of Terror, Crime, and Militancy* (Washington, DC: Rand, 2001).

6. John M. Owen, *The Clash of Ideas in World Politics: Transnational Networks, States, and Regime Change, 1510–2010* (Princeton, NJ: Princeton University Press, 2012); Kurt Weyland, "Crafting Counterrevolution: How Reactionaries Learned to Combat Change in 1848," *American Political Science Review* 110, no. 2 (2016): 215–31, https://doi.org/10.1017/S0003055416000174.

7. For major exceptions, see Seva Gunitsky, *Aftershocks: Great Powers and Domestic Reforms in the Twentieth Century* (Princeton, NJ: Princeton University Press, 2017); Owen, *Clash of Ideas*; Daniel H. Nexon, *The Struggle for Power in Early Modern Europe: Religious Conflict, Dynastic Empires, and International Change* (Princeton, NJ: Princeton University Press, 2009); Phillips, "The Protestant Ethic and the Spirit of Jihadism"; and Andrew Phillips, *War, Religion, and Empire: The Transformation of International Orders* (Cambridge: Cambridge University Press, 2011).

8. See Alexander Cooley, "Ordering Eurasia: The Rise and Decline of Liberal Internationalism in the Post-Communist Space," *Security Studies* 28, no. 3 (June–July, 2019): 588–613, https://doi.org/10.1080/09636412.2019.1604988; Stacie E. Goddard and Daniel H. Nexon, "The Dynamics of Global Power Politics: A Framework for Analysis," *Journal of Global Security Studies* 1, no. 1 (2016): 4–18, https://doi.org/10.1093/jogss/ogv007; Christopher Walker and Jessica Ludwig, "The Meaning of Sharp Power," *Foreign Affairs*, November 16, 2017, https://www.foreignaffairs.com/articles/china/2017-11-16/meaning-sharp-power; Christopher Walker, "What Is 'Sharp Power'?," *Journal of Democracy* 29, no. 3 (July 12, 2018): 9–23, https://doi.org/10.1353/jod.2018.0041.

9. Tamir Bar-On, "Transnationalism and the French Nouvelle Droite," *Patterns of Prejudice* 45, no. 3 (2011): 199–223.

10. Jacob Aasland Ravndal, "Explaining Right-Wing Terrorism and Violence in Western Europe: Grievances, Opportunities and Polarisation," *European Journal of Political Research* 57, no. 4 (2018): 845–66, https://doi.org/10.1111/1475-6765.12254.

11. Campbell Robertson, Christopher Mele, and Sabrina Tavernise, "11 Killed in Synagogue Massacre; Suspect Charged with 29 Counts," *New York Times*, October 29, 2018,https://www.nytimes.com/2018/10/27/us/active-shooter-pittsburgh-synagogue-shooting.html; Meghan Keneally, "Extremist-Related Killings in 2018 'Overwhelmingly Linked to Right-Wing' Movements: ADL," *ABC News*, March 12, 2019, https://abcnews.go.com/US/extremist-related-killings-2018-overwhelmingly-linked-wing-movements/story?id=60568464.

12. Hans-Georg Betz and Susi Meret, "Revisiting Lepanto: The Political Mobilization against Islam in Contemporary Western Europe," *Patterns of Prejudice*, 43, no. 3–4 (2009): 313–34; Hans-Georg Betz, "A Distant Mirror: Nineteenth-Century Populism, Nativism, and Contemporary Right-Wing Radical Politics," *Democracy and Security* 9, no. 3 (2013): 200–20; Clifford Bob, *The Global Right Wing and the Clash of World Politics* (New York: Cambridge University Press, 2012); Mary Fitzgerald and Calire Provost, "The American Dark Money behind Europe's Far Right," *New York Review of Books* (blog), July 10, 2019, https://www.nybooks.com/daily/2019/07/10/the-american-dark-money-behind-europes-far-right/; Ronald Inglehart and Pippa Norris, "Trump and the Populist Authoritarian Parties: The Silent Revolution in Reverse," *Perspectives on Politics* 15, no. 2 (2017): 443–54; Ishaan Tharoor, "Trump Turns to Europe's Far Right as He Detains Latin American Children," *Washington Post*, June 20, 2018, https://www.washingtonpost.com/news/worldviews/wp/2018/06/20/trump-turns-to-europes-far-right-as-he-detains-latin-american-children/?utm_term=.d7b8fd266e00; Cathrine Thorleifsson, "Disposable Strangers: Far-Right Securitisation of Forced Migration in Hungary," *Social Anthropology* 25, no. 3 (2017): 318–34; Ulrike M. Vieten and Scott Poynting, "Contemporary Far-Right Racist Populism in Europe," *Journal of Intercultural Studies* 37, no. 6 (2016): 533–40, https://doi.org/10.1080/07256868.2016.1235099; David Wollenberg, "Defending the West: Cultural Racism and Pan-Europeanism on the Far-Right," *Postmedieval* 5, no. 3 (2014): 308–19; Elisabeth Zerofsky, "Viktor Orbán's Far-Right Vision for Europe," The New Yorker, January 14, 2019, https://www.newyorker.com/magazine/2019/01/14/viktor-orbans-far-right-vision-for-europe.

13. Jackie Kerr, "Authoritarian Soft Power? Russia, International Cyber Conflict, and the Rise of 'Information Warfare'" (2018), https://tinyurl.com/y583fnv4; Jackie Kerr, "The Russian Model of Digital Control and Its Significance," in *AI, China, Russia, and the Global Order: Technological, Political, Global, and Creative Perspectives*, ed. Nicholas D. Wright, a Strategic Multilayer Assessment (SMA) Periodic Publication (US Department of Defense, 2018), 55–71.

14. Josh Rogin, "China's Interference in the 2018 Elections Succeeded—in Taiwan," *Washington Post*, December 18, 2018, sec. Global Opinions, https://www.washingtonpost.com/opinions/2018/12/18/chinas-interference-elections-succeeded-taiwan/.

15. Margaret E. Keck and Katheryn Sikkink, *Activists beyond Borders: Advocacy Networks in International Politics* (Ithaca, NY: Cornell University Press, 1998).

16. On the landmine ban as a classic transnational-activist campaign, see Richard Price, "Reversing the Gun Sights: Transnational Civil Society Targets Land Mines," *International Organization* 52, no. 3 (1998): 613–44. On the campaign against child soldiers, see R. Charli Carpenter, "Setting the Advocacy Agenda: Theorizing Issue Emergence and Nonemergence in Transnational Advocacy Networks," *International Organization* 51, no. 1 (March 2007): 99–120. For a more skeptical account that sees transnational advocacy networks as often instruments of states, see Iver B. Neumann

and Ole Jacob Sending, *Governing the Global Polity: Practice, Mentality, Rationality* (Ann Arbor: University of Michigan Press, 2010), chap. 4.

17. On NGO funding pressures and incentives, see Alexander Cooley and James Ron, "The NGO Scramble: Organizational Insecurity and the Political Economy of Transnational Action," *International Security* 27, no. 1 (Summer 2002): 5–39. On cross-organizational barriers to implementation, see Deborah Avant, "Conserving Nature in the State of Nature: The Politics of INGO Policy Implementation," *Review of International Studies* 30, no. 3 (July 2004), https://doi.org/10.1017/S0260210504006114. On marketing and framing, see Clifford Bob, *The Marketing of Rebellion: Insurgents, Media, and International Activism* (Cambridge: Cambridge University Press, 2005). On the critical role of gatekeepers at international organizations, see Carpenter, "Setting."

18. On the global trend in foreign funding restrictions, see Darin Christensen and Jeremy M. Weinstein, "Defunding Dissent: Restrictions on Aid to NGOs," *Journal of Democracy* 24, no. 2 (2013): 77–91; and Kendra Dupuy, James Ron, and Aseem Prakash, "Hands Off My Regime! Governments' Restrictions on Foreign Aid to Non-Governmental Organizations in Poor and Middle-Income Countries," *World Development* 84 (2016): 299–311.

19. Dupuy, Ron, and Prakash. "Hands Off My Regime!"

20. Kendra E. Dupuy, James Ron, and Aseem Prakash, "Who Survived? Ethiopia's Regulatory Crackdown on Foreign-Funded NGOs," *Review of International Political Economy* 22, no. 2 (2015): 419–56.

21. As Bethany Allen-Ebrahimian, a reporter specializing in Chinese government surveillance, notes, "On March 8, 2000, U.S. President Bill Clinton hailed the arrival of a new era, one in which the internet would mean the triumph of liberty around the world. He dismissed China's fledgling efforts to restrain online speech. 'Good luck,' quipped Clinton. 'That's sort of like trying to nail Jello to the wall.'" But "more than 16 years later, . . . it appears that China has largely succeeded in doing just that." China's "Great Firewall" is part of its famous government effort to simultaneously restrict the flow of information on social media and use telecommunications technologies to monitor and control its population. Authoritarian regimes everywhere have been developing, and even teaching one another, ways to turn cellular and internet communications into weapons of repression. Bethany Allen-Ebrahimian, "The Man Who Nailed Jello to the Wall," *Tea Leaf Nation—Foreign Policy* (blog), June 29, 2016, https://foreignpolicy.com/2016/06/29/the-man-who-nailed-jello-to-the-wall-lu-wei-china-internet-czar-learns-how-to-tame-the-web/; see also Ron Deibert, "Cyberspace under Siege," *Journal of Democracy* 26, no. 3 (2015): 64–78, https://doi.org/10.1353/jod.2015.0051; Justin Sherman, "How Authoritarian Regimes Use the Internet to Exert Control over Citizens," *Pacific Standard*, June 25, 2019, https://psmag.com/social-justice/how-digital-authoritarianism-is-spreading.

22. Bob, *The Global Right Wing and the Clash of World Politics*; see also Alan Bloomfield, "Norm Antipreneurs and Theorising Resistance to Normative Change," *Review of International Studies* 42, no. 2 (2016): 310–33, https://doi.org/10.1017/S026021051500025X; Louise Chappell, "Contesting Women's Rights: Charting the Emergence of a Transnational Conservative Counter-Network," *Global Society* 20, no. 4 (2006): 491–520, https://doi.org/10.1080/13600820600929853; Marcia Oliver, "Transnational Sex Politics, Conservative Christianity, and Antigay Activism in Uganda," *Studies in Social Justice* 7, no. 1 (2013): 83–105, https://doi.org/10.26522/ssj.v7i1.1056.

23. See Marlies Glasius, *The International Criminal Court: A Global Civil Society Achievement* (London: Routledge, 2006); M. Struett, *The Politics of Constructing the International Criminal Court: NGOs, Discourse, and Agency* (New York: Springer, 2008).

24. See Luke Glanville, *Sovereignty and the Responsibility to Protect: A New History* (Chicago: University of Chicago Press, 2013).

25. Bob, *The Global Right Wing and the Clash of World Politics*; on the effectiveness of counter-movements on blocking pro-LGBTQ advocacy networks, see Victor Asal, Amanda Murdie, and Udi Sommer, "Rainbows for Rights: The Role of LGBT Activism in Gay Rights Promotion," *Societies without Borders* 12 (2017): 20; Phillip M. Ayoub, "With Arms Wide Shut: Threat Perception, Norm Reception, and Mobilized Resistance to LGBT Rights," *Journal of Human Rights* 13, no. 3 (2014): 337–62, https://doi.org/10.1080/14754835.2014.919213; Fernando G. Nuñez-Mietz and Lucrecia García Iommi, "Can Transnational Norm Advocacy Undermine Internalization? Explaining Immunization against LGBT Rights in Uganda," *International Studies Quarterly* 61, no. 1 (2017): 196–209, https://doi.org/10.1093/isq/sqx011.

26. Seen from Moscow's perspective—and not without justification—its efforts to make the world safe for illiberal regimes are a reaction to American revolutionary revisionism privileging regime change over norms of sovereignty and seeking to expand its power in Eurasia. See Keith A. Darden, "Russian Revanche: External Threats and Regime Reactions," *Daedalus* 146, no. 2 (2017): 128–41; Benjamin C. Denison and Emma M. Ashford, "Primacy, Regime Change and the Liberal International Order," Working Paper, Tufts University, Medford, MA, March 2019; Gerard Toal, "Review of Sakwa, Richard, "Russia against the Rest: The Post-Cold War Crisis of World Order" (H-Diplo, H-Review, May 2018), https://www.h-net.org/reviews/showrev.php?id=51562.

27. See the legal overview in the International Center for Not-for-Profit Law, http://www.icnl.org/research/monitor/russia.html, accessed 20 July 2019.

28. Julie Hemment, "Nashi, Youth Voluntarism, and Potemkin NGOs: Making Sense of Civil Society in Post-Soviet Russia," *Slavic Review* 71, no. 2 (2012): 234–60.

29. Kristina Stoeckl and Kseniya Medvedeva, "Double Bind at the UN: Western Actors, Russia, and the Traditionalist Agenda." *Global Constitutionalism* 7, no. 3 (2018): 383–421.

30. Stoeckl and Medvedeva, "Double Bind at the UN," 396.

31. See H. G. Koenigsberger, "The Organization of Revolutionary Parties in France and the Netherlands during the Sixteenth Century," *Journal of Modern History* 27, no. 4 (1955): 333–51; Nexon, *Religious Conflict*; Wayne te Brake, *Shaping History: Ordinary People in European Politics, 1500–1700* (Berkeley: University of California Press, 1998).

32. See Samuel Huston Goodfellow, "Fascism as a Transnational Movement: The Case of Inter-War Alsace," *Contemporary European History* 22, no. 1 (2013): 87–106; Kurt Weyland, "Fascism's Missionary Ideology and the Autocratic Wave of the Interwar Years," *Democratization* 24, no. 7 (2017): 1253–70, https://doi.org/10.1080/13510347.2017.1322581.

33. Dov H. Levin, "When the Great Power Gets a Vote: The Effects of Great Power Electoral Interventions on Election Results," *International Studies Quarterly* 60, no. 2 (June 2016): 189–202, https://doi.org/10.1093/isq/sqv016; Dov H. Levin, "Partisan Electoral Interventions by the Great Powers: Introducing the PEIG Dataset," *Conflict Management and Peace Science* 36, no. 1 (2019): 88–106, https://doi.org/10.1177/0738894216661190; more generally, see Odd Arne Westad, "Has a New Cold War Really Begun? Why the Term Shouldn't Apply to Today's Great-Power Tensions," *Foreign*

Affairs, March 27, 2018, https://www.foreignaffairs.com/articles/china/2018-03-27/has-new-cold-war-really-begun.

34. See Kathleen R. McNamara, *The Politics of Everyday Europe: Constructing Authority in the European Union* (Oxford: Oxford University Press, 2015).

35. Tamir Bar-On, "The French New Right Neither Right, nor Left?," *Journal for the Study of Radicalism* 8, no. 1 (2014): 35; he traces many of these ideas to the French New Right and the 1970s. See also Bar-On, "Transnationalism and the French Nouvelle Droite."

36. Betz and Meret, "Revisiting Lepanto," 319. If this sounds familiar to Americans, that's because these concerns are also the bread-and-butter of Trumpism and right-wing populism in the United States.

37. Betz and Meret, "Revisiting Lepanto," 313.

38. See, for example, Shane Savitsky, "Populists Unite: Maréchal-Le Pen, Farage Join the Trump Show at CPAC," *Axios*, February 22, 2018, https://www.axios.com/cpac-marion-marechal-le-pen-nigel-farage-trump-c1559a17-2733-42a7-b33d-40a4b9d0e8bb.html; Adele M. Stan, "Le Pen, Salvini, and Europe's Far Right Increase Numbers in European Parliament, as Bannon Stays Close at Hand," *American Prospect*, May 29, 2019, https://prospect.org/article/le-pen-salvini-and-europes-far-right-increase-numbers-european-parliament-bannon-stays-close; Peter Walker and Paul Lewis, "Nigel Farage Discussed Fronting Far-Right Group Led by Steve Bannon," *The Guardian*, May 22, 2019, https://www.theguardian.com/politics/2019/may/22/nigel-farage-discussed-fronting-far-right-group-led-by-steve-bannon.

39. Ben Jacobs, "'France Is No Longer Free': Marine Le Pen's Niece Brings French Far Right to CPAC," *The Guardian*, February 22, 2018, https://www.theguardian.com/us-news/2018/feb/22/marion-le-pen-cpac-speech-2018-france-far-right.

40. Fitzgerald and Provost, "American Dark Money."

41. Anton Shekhovtsov, *Russia and the Western Far Right: Tango Noir* (London: Routledge, 2018).

42. Antonis Klapsis, *An Unholy Alliance: The European Far Right and Putin's Russia*, ed. Ingrid Habets (Brussels: Wilfried Martens Centre for European Studies, 2015), 13, https://www.martenscentre.eu/sites/default/files/publication-files/far-right-political-parties-in-europe-and-putins-russia.pdf.

43. Paul Sonne, "A Russian Bank Gave Marine Le Pen's Party a Loan. Then Weird Things Began Happening," *Washington Post*, December 27, 2018, https://www.washingtonpost.com/world/national-security/a-russian-bank-gave-marine-le-pens-party-a-loan-then-weird-things-began-happening/2018/12/27/960c7906-d320-11e8-a275-81c671a50422_story.html.

44. Klapsis, *An Unholy Alliance: The European Far Right and Putin's Russia*, 13–14.

45. John Shelton, "Austria: Secret Video Ensnares Far-Right Leader," *Deutsche Welle*, May 17, 2019, https://www.dw.com/en/austria-secret-video-ensnares-far-right-leader/a-48781845-0.

46. James Politi and Max Seddon, "Putin's Party Signs Deal with Italy's Far-Right Lega Nord," *Financial Times*, March 6, 2017, https://www.ft.com/content/0d33d22c-0280-11e7-ace0-1ce02ef0def9.

47. Franz-Stefan Gady, "Not All Russia-Friendly Policies Are Nefarious," *Foreign Policy*, March 30, 2018, https://foreignpolicy.com/2018/03/30/not-all-russia-friendly-policies-are-nefarious/; Amy Richards, "Italy-Russia Links Highlight Threat to EU

Democracy," *EU Observer*, February 25, 2019, https://euobserver.com/opinion/144255; *Russian Connections of the Austrian Far-Right* (Budapest: Political Capital, April 2017).

48. Alberto Nardelli, "Revealed: The Explosive Secret Recording That Shows How Russia Tried To Funnel Millions To The 'European Trump,'" *BuzzFeed News*, July 10, 2019, https://www.buzzfeednews.com/article/albertonardelli/salvini-russia-oil-deal-secret-recording.

49. Nardelli, "Revealed: The Explosive Secret Recording".

50. Note that, as of the end of July 2019, the revelations haven't damaged the Lega's position in the polls in the slightest. Nina dos Santos, "Investigation: Possible Scheme between Russia and Italian Political Party," *CNN*, July 11, 2019, https://www.cnn.com/2019/07/11/europe/investigation-league-salvini-russia-money-intl/index.html.

51. For possible explanations for why Russia's outreach to the right has been more successful, see Robert M. Entman and Nikki Usher, "Framing in a Fractured Democracy: Impacts of Digital Technology on Ideology, Power and Cascading Network Activation," *Journal of Communication* 68, no. 2 (2018): 298–308; Gayil Talshir, "Knowing Right from Left: The Politics of Identity Between the Radical Left and Far Right," *Journal of Political Ideologies* 10, no. 3 (2005): 311–35.

52. See, for example, Toby Archer, "Breivik's Mindset: The Counterjihad and the New Transatlantic Anti-Muslim Right"," in *Extreme Right Wing Political Violence and Terrorism*, ed. Max Taylor and Donald Holbrook (London: Bloomsbury Academic, 2013), 169–85; Richard Arnold and Ekaterina Romanova, "The 'White World's Future?': An Analysis of the Russian Far Right," *Journal for the Study of Radicalism* 7, no. 1 (2013): 79–107; Betz, "A Distant Mirror: Nineteenth-Century Populism, Nativism, and Contemporary Right-Wing Radical Politics"; Nigel Copsey, "'Fascism . . . but with an Open Mind.' Reflections on the Contemporary Far Right in (Western) Europe," *Fascism* 2, no. 1 (2013): 1–17; Johannes Due Enstad, "'Glory to Breivik!': The Russian Far Right and the 2011 Norway Attacks," *Terrorism and Political Violence* 29, no. 5 (2017): 773–92; Matt Golder, "Far Right Parties in Europe," *Annual Review of Political Science* 19 (2016): 477–97; David Neiwert, "Birth of the Alt Right," *The Public Eye*, Winter 2017, 4–11; Laurie Ouellette and Sarah Banet-Weiser, "Special Issue: Media and the Extreme Right: Editor's Introduction," *Communication, Culture and Critique* 11, no. 1 (March 23, 2018): 1–6, https://doi.org/10.1093/ccc/tcx021; Jens Rydgren, "The Sociology of the Radical Right," *Annual Review of Sociology* 33 (2007): 241–62; Jens Rydgren, "Radical Right-Wing Parties in Europe: What's Populism Got to Do with It?," *Journal of Language and Politics* 16, no. 4 (2017): 485–96; Wollenberg, "Defending the West: Cultural Racism and Pan-Europeanism on the Far-Right."

53. Doris Buss, *Globalizing Family Values: The Christian Right in International Politics* (Minneapolis: University of Minnesota Press, 2003), 83.

54. Buss, *Globalizing Family Values*, 85-87.

55. Kristina Stoeckl, "Transnational Norm Mobilization: The World Congress of Families in Georgia and Moldova," *Foreign Policy Centre* July 18. 2018, https://fpc.org.uk/transnational-norm-mobilization-the-world-congress-of-families-in-georgia-and-moldova/.

56. Adam Federman, "How US Evangelicals Fueled the Rise of Russia's 'Pro-Family' Right," *The Nation*, January 7, 2014.

57. See Melissa Hooper, "Russia's 'Traditional Values' Leadership," iForeign policy Centre. May 24, 2016. At: https://fpc.org.uk/russias-traditional-values-leadership/

58. Casey Michel, "How Russia Became the Leader of the Global Christian Right," *Politico* February 9, 2017, https://www.politico.com/magazine/story/2017/02/how-russia-became-a-leader-of-the-worldwide-christian-right-214755; Alina Polyakova, "Strange Bedfellows: Putin and Europe's Far Right," *World Affairs* 177, no. 3 (2014): 39; Klapsis, *An Unholy Alliance: The European Far Right and Putin's Russia*, 17–18.

59. Hannah Levintova, "Did Anti-Gay Evangelicals Skirt US Sanctions on Russia?," *Mother Jones*, September 8, 2014, https://www.motherjones.com/politics/2014/09/world-congress-families-russia-conference-sanctions/.

60. Laura Rosenberger and Thomas Morley, "Russia's Promotion of Illiberal Populism: Tools, Tactics, and Networks," Alliance for Securing Democracy, German Marshall Fund of the United States, March 11, 2019, https://securingdemocracy.gmfus.org/russias-promotion-of-illiberal-populism-tools-tactics-networks/.

61. As quoted in Southern Poverty Law Center, "World Congress of Families Holds Its Tenth Congress in Tbilisi, Georgia," May 13, 2016, https://www.splcenter.org/hatewatch/2016/05/13/anti-lgbt-hate-group-world-congress-families-gears-its-tenth-international-congress.

62. Robert Coalson, "'Family Values' Congress Brings Pro-Moscow Message to Georgia," *RFE/RL*, May 17, 2016, https://www.rferl.org/a/georgia-confress-families-antigay-moscow-oligarchs-bush/27741199.html.

63. "Hungary's Prime Minister Welcomes US 'Anti-LGBT Hate Group,'" *The Guardian*, May 26, 2017, https://www.theguardian.com/world/2017/may/26/hungary-lgbt-world-congress-families-viktor-orban.

64. Stoeckl, "Transnational Norm Mobilization."

65. See Timothy W. Crawford, "Wedge Strategy, Balancing, and the Deviant Case of Spain, 1940–1941," *Security Studies* 17, no. 1 (January 2008): 1–38; Timothy W. Crawford, "Preventing Enemy Coalitions: How Wedge Strategies Shape Power Politics," *International Security* 35, no. 4 (Spring 2011): 155–89, https://doi.org/10.1162/ISEC_a_00036; Stacie E. Goddard, "When Right Makes Might: How Prussia Overturned the European Balance of Power," *International Security* 33, no. 3 (Winter 2008/2009): 110–42; Stacie E. Goddard, "The Rhetoric of Appeasement: Hitler's Legitimation and British Foreign Policy, 1938–39," *Security Studies* 24, no. 1 (January 2, 2015): 95–130, https://doi.org/10.1080/09636412.2015.1001216; Stacie E. Goddard, Paul K. MacDonald, and Daniel H. Nexon, "Repertoires of Statecraft: Instruments and Logics of Power Politics," *International Relations* 33, no. 2 (2019): 304–21; Goddard and Nexon, "Global Power Politics"; Victoria Tin-bor Hui, "Towards a Dynamic Theory of International Politics: Insights from Comparing Ancient China and Early Modern Europe," *International Organization* 58, no. 1 (Winter 2004): 175–205; Nexon, *Religious Conflict*, chaps. 2–3.

66. Spencer S. Hsu and Tom Jackman, "Russian Maria Butina Pleads Guilty in Case to Forge Kremlin Bond with U.S. Conservatives," *Washington Post,* December 13, 2018, https://www.washingtonpost.com/local/legal-issues/russian-maria-butina-pleads-guilty-in-effort-to-forge-kremlin-bond-with-us-conservatives/2018/12/13/c27f2d26-fe4f-11e8-ad40-cdfd0e0dd65a_story.html.

67. Ruth May, "How Putin's Oligarchs Funneled Millions into GOP Campaigns," *Dallas Morning News*, December 15, 2017, https://www.dallasnews.com/opinion/commentary/2018/05/08/how-putin-s-oligarchs-funneled-millions-into-gop-campaigns/.

68. While Moscow had successfully cultivated relations with a number of Republicans, the GOP has, since at least George W. Bush's second term, been traditionally

more hard-line on Russia than Democrats. If Trump could reorient his party, that would count as an important gain. Still, Moscow has, and continues to, make overtures to the American left. Its main television propaganda arm, *RT*, employs a stable of left-wing Americans. Jill Stein, the 2016 Green Party candidate, sat at the same table as Putin at a now infamous *RT* anniversary dinner in Moscow.

69. Robert S. Mueller III, *Report on the Investigation into Russian Interference in the 2016 Presidential Election*, Volume I of II (Washington, DC: US Department of Justice, March 2019), 1.

70. Mueller, "Report," 4–8.

71. https://www.justice.gov/file/1035477/download.

72. https://www.justice.gov/file/1035477/download.

73. Craig Timberg and Tony Romm, "New Report on Russian disinformation, Prepared for the Senate, Shows the Operation's Scale and Sweep," *Washington Post*, November 1, 2017, https://www.washingtonpost.com/technology/2018/12/16/new-report-russian-disinformation-prepared-senate-shows-operations-scale-sweep/.

74. Kevin Collier, "Prominent 'GOP' Twitter Account, Allegedly a Russian Troll, Was Widely Quoted in US Media," *BuzzFeed News*, October 19, 2017, https://www.buzzfeednews.com/article/kevincollier/americans-helped-spread-an-alleged-russian-gop-accounts.

75. Permanent Select Committee on Intelligence (2018, June 18). Schiff statement on release of Twitter ads, accounts, and data. Retrieved from https://democrats-intelligence.house.gov/news/documentsingle.aspx?DocumentID=396;Darren L. Linvill and Patrick L. Warren, "Troll Factories: The Internet Research Agency and State-Sponsored Agenda Building," Clemson University, http://pwarren.people.clemson.edu/Linvill_Warren_TrollFactory.pdf.

76. Linvill and Warren, "Troll Factories," p. 7.

77. Linvill and Warren, "Troll Factories," p. 8.

78. Darren Linvill and Patrick Warren, "Russian Trolls Can Be Surprisingly Subtle, and Often Fun to Read," *Washington Post*, March 8, 2018, https://www.washingtonpost.com/outlook/russian-trolls-can-be-surprisingly-subtle-and-often-fun-to-read/2019/03/08/677f8ec2-413c-11e9-9361-301ffb5bd5e6_story.html.

79. Linvill and Warren, "Troll Factories," 12.

80. Ahmer Arif, Leo Stewart, and Kate Starbird, "Acting the Part: Examining Information Operations within #BlackLivesMatter Discourse," *Proceedings of the ACM on Human-Computer Interaction*, Vol. 2, No. CSCW, Article 20, November 2018.

81. Arif, Stewart, and Starbird, "Acting the Part," 12–13.

82. Leon Yin, Franziska Roscher, Richard Bonneau, Jonathan Nagler, and Joshua A. Tucker, "Your Friendly Neighborhood Troll: The Internet Research Agency's Use of Local and Fake News in the 2016 US Presidential Campaign," SMaPP Data Report, 2018:01, https://s18798.pcdn.co/smapp/wp-content/uploads/sites/1693/2018/11/SMaPP_Data_Report_2018_01_IRA_Links.pdf.

83. David A. Broniatowski et al., "Weaponized Health Communication: Twitter Bots and Russian Trolls Amplify the Vaccine Debate," *American Journal of Public Health*, 108, no. 10 (2018): 1378–84.

84. Broniatowski et al., "Weaponized Health Communication," 1378.

85. Goddard and Nexon, "Global Power Politics"; Goddard, MacDonald, and Nexon, "Statecraft."

86. See Laura A. Belmonte, *Selling the American Way: U.S. Propaganda and the Cold War* (Philadelphia: University of Pennsylvania Press, 2013); László Borhi, "Rollback,

Liberation, Containment, or Inaction? U.S. Policy and Eastern Europe in the 1950s," *Journal of Cold War Studies* 1, no. 3 (September 1, 1999): 67–110, https://doi.org/10.1162/152039799316976814; Charles Crabtree, David Darmofal, and Holger L Kern, "A Spatial Analysis of the Impact of West German Television on Protest Mobilization during the East German Revolution," *Journal of Peace Research* 52, no. 3 (May 1, 2015): 269–84, https://doi.org/10.1177/0022343314554245; Charles Crabtree, Holger L. Kern, and Steven Pfaff, "Mass Media and the Diffusion of Collective Action in Authoritarian Regimes: The June 1953 East German Uprising," *International Studies Quarterly* 62, no. 2 (June 1, 2018): 301–14, https://doi.org/10.1093/isq/sqy007; Holger Lutz Kern, "Foreign Media and Protest Diffusion in Authoritarian Regimes: The Case of the 1989 East German Revolution," *Comparative Political Studies* 44, no. 9 (September 1, 2011): 1179–205, https://doi.org/10.1177/0010414009357189.

87. Keir Giles, *Moscow Rules: What Drives Russia to Confront the West* (Washington, DC: Brookings Institution Press, 2019).

88. Elizabeth Dwoskin, Craig Timberg, and Adam Entous, "Russians Took a Page from Corporate America by Using Facebook Tool to ID and Influence Voters," *Washington Post*, October 2, 2017, https://www.washingtonpost.com/business/economy/russians-took-a-page-from-corporate-america-by-using-facebook-tool-to-id-and-influence-voters/2017/10/02/681e40d8-a7c5-11e7-850e-2bdd1236be5d_story.html; Daniel Nexon, "The Banality of Information Warfare," *Lawyers, Guns & Money* (blog), October 3, 2017, http://www.lawyersgunsmoneyblog.com/2017/10/banality-information-warfare.

CHAPTER 7

1. See, for example, William J. Burns, "How the U.S.-Russian Relationship Went Bad," *The Atlantic*, April 2019, https://www.theatlantic.com/magazine/archive/2019/04/william-j-burns-putin-russia/583255/?fbclid=IwAR2ZnKRY7Mumos8dIptUW6tAxer_xLo7hC1YZHsQVIb9sUU1CorZf2ICt24&utm_source=facebook&utm_medium=social&utm_campaign=share.

2. Shruti Godbole, "Changing Nature of International Order and the Role of U.S.," *Brookings Up Front* (blog), July 13, 2018,https://www.brookings.edu/blog/up-front/2018/07/13/changing-nature-of-international-order-and-the-role-of-u-s/.

3. See Paul K. MacDonald and Joseph M. Parent, "Graceful Decline? The Surprising Success of Great Power Retrenchment," *International Security* 35, no. 4 (2011): 7–44; Paul K. MacDonald and Joseph M. Parent, *Twilight of the Titans: Great Power Decline and Retrenchment* (Ithaca, NY: Cornell University Press, 2018); Aaron L. Friedberg, *The Weary Titan: Britain and the Experience of Relative Decline, 1895–1905* (Princeton, NJ: Princeton University Press, 2010).

4. See Chapter 2.

5. The general line of Republican attack against President Barack Obama was that he was insufficiently pro-NATO and too hesitant when it came to pushing back against great-power challengers.

6. Daniel W. Drezner, "Present at the Destruction: The Trump Administration and the Foreign Policy Bureaucracy," *Journal of Politics* 81, no. 2 (April 2019), published ahead of print, https://doi.org/10.1086/702230. In its 2020 budget, the Trump administration proposed draconian cuts of 23 percent to the State Department's budget. See Lindsay Wide and Brian Lowry, "Pompeo Defends Trump Budget; Says 23 Percent Cut

Won't Hurt State Department's 'Swagger,'" *Kansas City Star*, March 11, 2019, https://www.kansascity.com/news/politics-government/article227427189.html.

7. Matt Egan, "Jeb Bush on Trump: I Predicted a Chaos President—CNNPolitics," May 19, 2017, https://www.cnn.com/2017/05/19/politics/jeb-bush-trump/index.html.

8. Brian Blankenship and Benjamin Denison, Is America Prepared for Great Power Competition? *Survival* 61, no. 3 (2019): 43: 2.

9. Thomas Wright, "Trump's 19th Century Foreign Policy," *Politico* magazine, January 20, 2016, https://www.politico.com/magazine/story/2016/01/donald-trump-foreign-policy-213546.

10. Mark Landler, "Trump, the Insurgent, Breaks with 70 Years of American Foreign Policy," *New York Times*, December 28, 2017, sec. U.S., https://www.nytimes.com/2017/12/28/us/politics/trump-world-diplomacy.html.

11. Kori Schake, "The Trump Doctrine Is Winning and the World Is Losing," *New York Times*, June 15, 2018, https://www.nytimes.com/2018/06/15/opinion/sunday/trump-china-america-first.html.

12. Thomas Wright, "The Moment the Transatlantic Charade Ended," *The Atlantic*, February 19, 2019, https://www.theatlantic.com/ideas/archive/2019/02/mutual-distrust-2019-munich-security-conference/583015/.

13. Doug Stokes, "Trump, American Hegemony and the Future of the Liberal International Order," *International Affairs* 94, no. 1 (January 1, 2018): 135, https://doi.org/10.1093/ia/iix238; see also Geoffrey Gertz, "What Will Trump's Embrace of Bilateralism Mean for America's Trade Partners?," *Brookings* (blog), February 8, 2017, https://www.brookings.edu/blog/future-development/2017/02/08/what-will-trumps-embrace-of-bilateralism-mean-for-americas-trade-partners/; Dani K. Nedal and Daniel H. Nexon, "Trump Won't Get the Best Deals," *Foreign Affairs*, January 31, 2017, https://www.foreignaffairs.com/articles/2017-01-31/trump-wont-get-best-deals; Abraham Newman and Daniel H. Nexon, "Trump Says American Allies Should Spend More on Defense. Here's Why He's Wrong," *Vox*, February 16, 2017, https://www.vox.com/the-big-idea/2017/2/16/14635204/burden-sharing-allies-nato-trump; Stewart M. Patrick, "Trump and World Order," *Foreign Affairs*, February 13, 2017, https://www.foreignaffairs.com/articles/world/2017-02-13/trump-and-world-order; Schake, "Trump Doctrine Is Winning"; Martin Wolf, "Donald Trump's War on the Liberal World Order," *Financial Times*, July 3, 2018, https://www.ft.com/content/bec33c02-7de1-11e8-8e67-1e1a0846c475.

14. Jake Sullivan, "The World after Trump," *Foreign Affairs*, March 5, 2018, https://www.foreignaffairs.com/articles/2018-03-05/world-after-trump.

15. See Tarak Barkawi and Mark Laffey, "The Imperial Peace: Democracy, Force and Globalization," *European Journal of International Relations* 5, no. 4 (December 1999): 403–34.

16. Stephen Rabe, *Eisenhower and Latin America: The Foreign Policy of Anticommunism* (Chapel Hill: University of North Carolina Press, 1988).

17. Rachel Bronson, *Thicker than Oil: America's Uneasy Partnership with Saudi Arabia* (New York: Oxford University Press, 2008).

18. Susanne Jonas, "Guatemala: Acts of Genocide and Scorched-Earth Counterinsurgency War," in *Centuries of Genocide: Essays and Eyewitness Accounts*, ed. Samuel Totten and William S. Parsons (New York: Routledge, 2012), 355–94.

19. J. Patrice McSherry, "Tracking the Origins of a State Terror Network: Operation Condor," *Latin American Perspectives* 29, no. 1 (2002): 38–60; J. Patrice McSherry, "Death Squads as Parallel Forces: Uruguay, Operation Condor, and the United States,"

Journal of Global South Studies 24, no. 1 (2007): 13; Barbara Zanchetta, "Between Cold War Imperatives and State-Sponsored Terrorism: The United States and 'Operation Condor,'" *Studies in Conflict and Terrorism* 39, no. 12 (2016): 1084–1102.

20. See Tamar Jacoby, "The Reagan Turnaround on Human Rights," *Foreign Affairs* 64, no. 5 (1986): 1066–86; James Fowler, "The United States and South Korean Democratization," *Political Science Quarterly* 114, no. 2 (1999): 265–88; Andrew Yeo, "Signaling Democracy: Patron-Client Relations and Democratization in South Korea and Poland," *Journal of East Asian Studies* 6, no. 2 (2006): 259–87.

21. The most important articulation of the doctrine can be found in the 2002 *National Security Strategy of the United States*. For a discussion, see Robert Jervis, "Understanding the Bush Doctrine," *Political Science Quarterly* 118, no. 3 (2003): 365–88.

22. Paul Musgrave and Daniel Nexon, "American Liberalism and the Imperial Temptation," in *Empire and International Order*, ed. Noel Parker (London: Routledge, 2013), 131–48.

23. Brian C. Schmidt and Michael C. Williams, "The Bush Doctrine and the Iraq War: Neoconservatives versus Realists," *Security Studies* 17, no. 2 (2008): 200.

24. Graeme Wood, "Will John Bolton Bring on Armageddon—Or Stave It Off?," *The Atlantic*, April 2019, https://www.theatlantic.com/magazine/archive/2019/04/john-bolton-trump-national-security-adviser/583246/. A similar theme appears in the single most important public articulation of post–Cold War neoconservative thought: William Kristol and Robert Kagan, "Toward a Neo-Reaganite Foreign Policy," *Foreign Affairs*, July 1, 1996, https://www.foreignaffairs.com/articles/1996-07-01/toward-neo-reaganite-foreign-policy.

25. See G. John Ikenberry, *After Victory: Institutions, Strategic Restraint, and the Rebuilding of Order after Major War* (Princeton, NJ: Princeton University Press, 2001); G. John Ikenberry, *Liberal Order and Imperial Ambition* (Malden, MA: Polity Press, 2006).

26. Stokes, "Trump, American Hegemony and the Future of the Liberal International Order," 133.

27. Thomas Risse, "Beyond Iraq: The Crisis of the Transatlantic Security Community," *Die Friedens-Warte* 78, no. 2/3 (2003): 173–93.

28. Phillip Bump, "15 Years after the Iraq War Began, the Death Toll Is Still Murky," *Washington Post*, March 20, 2018, https://www.washingtonpost.com/news/politics/wp/2018/03/20/15-years-after-it-began-the-death-toll-from-the-iraq-war-is-still-murky/.

29. Steven Erlanger and Katrin Bennhold, "Rift between Trump and Europe Is Now Open and Angry," *New York Times*, February 19, 2019, sec. World, https://www.nytimes.com/2019/02/17/world/europe/trump-international-relations-munich.html; Stewart Patrick, "The World Order Is Starting to Crack," *Foreign Policy*, July 25, 2018, https://foreignpolicy.com/2018/07/25/the-world-order-is-starting-to-crack/.

30. Andrew Kohut et al., "Global Public Opinion in the Bush Years (2001–2008)," Pew Research Center, Global Attitudes and Trends, December 18, 2008, http://www.pewglobal.org/2008/12/18/global-public-opinion-in-the-bush-years-2001-2008/.

31. The most glaring exception is the Trump administration's approach to Venezuela, where it is perfectly willing to use traditional rhetoric associated with liberal ordering. It has also embraced a robust multilateral approach, which raises interesting questions about the workings of the Trump administration. See David A. Wemer, "Buy-In from Allies Critical for Effective Sanctions, Says Former US Treasury Secretary Lew," *New Atlanticist* (blog), February 19, 2019, https://www.atlanticcouncil.org/blogs/new-atlanticist/buy-in-from-allies-critical-for-effective-sanctions-says-former-us-treasury-secretary-lew.

32. As a number of specialists point out, trade deficits are about the balance of imports and exports, not one country taking money from the other.

33. Philip H. Gordon, "The Worst Deals Ever," *Foreign Affairs*, August 23, 2018, https://www.foreignaffairs.com/articles/2018-08-23/worst-deals-ever.

34. One also suspects that Trump does not enjoy how multilateral meetings dilute the spotlight.

35. Nedal and Nexon, "Trump Won't Get the Best Deals."

36. Charles Hankla, "What Is the TPP and Can the US Get Back In?," *The Conversation*, April 18, 2018, http://theconversation.com/what-is-the-tpp-and-can-the-us-get-back-in-95028; Emil Kirchner, "EU-Japan Trade Deal Comes into Force to Create World's Biggest Trade Zone," *The Conversation*, http://theconversation.com/eu-japan-trade-deal-comes-into-force-to-create-worlds-biggest-trade-zone-110729, accessed February 25, 2019. Phil Levy, "Trump to TPP: Don't Forget, America Last!," *Forbes*, April 12, 2018, https://www.forbes.com/sites/phillevy/2018/04/12/trump-to-tpp-dont-forget-america-last/#d3c79a711c65; Robert A. Manning, "Trump—Losing Asia?," *Nikkei Asian Review*, February 18, 2019, https://asia.nikkei.com/Opinion/Trump-losing-Asia.

37. Rebecca Friedman Lissner and Mira Rapp-Hooper, "The Day after Trump: American Strategy for a New International Order," *Washington Quarterly* 41, no. 1 (January 2, 2018): 7, https://doi.org/10.1080/0163660X.2018.1445353.

38. Glenn Thrush, "Trump Embraces Foreign Aid to Counter China's Global Influence," *New York Times*, October 14, 2018, sec. World, https://www.nytimes.com/2018/10/14/world/asia/donald-trump-foreign-aid-bill.html.

39. See Donald Trump, "Remarks by President Trump to the 73rd Session of the United Nations General Assembly, New York, NY," The White House, September 25, 2018, https://www.whitehouse.gov/briefings-statements/remarks-president-trump-73rd-session-united-nations-general-assembly-new-york-ny/. Even this is flatly hypocritical, as Trump policy toward Syria makes clear that "one does not need to hold a favorable view of Assad to admit that Iran's involvement in Syria comes with Damascus's express consent. Iran is not violating Syrian sovereignty, the United States is." Daniel H. Nexon, "Trumpism and the Sovereignty Paradox," *Lawyers, Guns & Money* (blog), October 10, 2018, http://www.lawyersgunsmoneyblog.com/2018/10/trumpism-sovereignty-paradox.

40. Gerard Toal, "Review of Sakwa, Richard, Russia against the Rest: The Post-Cold War Crisis of World Order" (H-Diplo, H-Review, May 2018), https://www.h-net.org/reviews/showrev.php?id=51562.

41. Robbie Gramer and Lynch Colum, "Trump Stealthily Seeks to Choke Off Funding to U.N. Programs," *Foreign Policy*, October 2, 2018, https://foreignpolicy.com/2018/10/02/trump-stealthily-seeks-to-choke-off-funding-to-un-programs/. Indeed, in 2019 Congress appropriated funding to peacekeeping operations, refugee aid, and other areas that the Trump administration has tried to cut. Emily Cochrane and Catie Edmondson, "Border Security, Foreign Aid and a Raise for Federal Workers: What You Need to Know about the Spending Package," *New York Times*, February 15, 2019, https://www.nytimes.com/2019/02/14/us/politics/congress-trump-border-deal-wall.html.

42. Thomas Adamson, "U.S. and Israel Officially Withdraw from UNESCO," *PBS NewsHour*, January 1, 2019, https://www.pbs.org/newshour/politics/u-s-and-israel-officially-withdraw-from-unesco; Maya Finoh, "Five Ways the Trump Administration Has Attacked the U.N. and International Human Rights Bodies," American Civil Liberties Union, September 24, 2018, https://www.aclu.org/blog/human-rights/five-ways-trump-administration-has-attacked-un-and-international-human-rights.

43. Eleanor Beardsley, "Critics Say U.S. Withdrawal from UNESCO Allows Different Agendas to Surface," *NPR.Org*, December 28, 2018, https://www.npr.org/2018/12/28/680616404/critics-say-u-s-withdrawal-from-unesco-allows-different-agendas-to-surface; Christal Hayes, "U.S. Pulls Out of UN Human Rights Council over Accusations of 'Bias,' Protecting Abusers," *USA TODAY*, June 19, 2018, https://www.usatoday.com/story/news/politics/2018/06/19/us-pulls-out-united-nations-human-rights-council/715993002/.

44. Finoh, "Five Ways"; Rick Gladstone, "U.S. Quits Migration Pact, Saying It Infringes on Sovereignty," *New York Times*, December 5, 2017, sec. World, https://www.nytimes.com/2017/12/03/world/americas/united-nations-migration-pact.html.

45. Claire Berlinski, "Europe's Dependence on the US Was All Part of the Plan," *Politico*, July 16, 2018, https://www.politico.eu/article/europe-dependence-on-the-us-was-all-part-of-the-plan-donald-trump-nato/.

46. Martin Dedman, *The Origins and Development of the European Union 1945–1995: A History of European Integration* (London: Routledge, 2006).

47. Patrick Kingsley, "Hungary's Leader Was Shunned by Obama, but Has a Friend in Trump," *New York Times*, October 15, 2018, sec. World, https://www.nytimes.com/2018/08/15/world/europe/hungary-us-orban-trump.html; see also Mark Landler, "Trump and Pompeo Embrace Autocrats and Disparage Opponents at Home," *New York Times*, January 11, 2019, sec. U.S., https://www.nytimes.com/2019/01/10/us/politics/trump-pompeo-china-cairo.html.

48. Alex Moraels, "Trump Hands a Gift to May in Predicting Post-Brexit Trade Bump," February 15, 2019, https://www.bloomberg.com/news/articles/2019-02-15/trump-sees-trade-with-u-k-rising-substantially-after-brexit; Jonathan Chait, "Brexit and Trumpism Have Failed Because Conservative Populism Is a Lie," *Intelligencer*, March 13, 2019, http://nymag.com/intelligencer/2019/03/brexit-trump-conservative-populism.html.

49. Natalie Nougayrède, "The Best Way to Scupper Putin and Trump? Scrap Brexit," *The Guardian*, December 27, 2018, sec. Opinion, https://www.theguardian.com/commentisfree/2018/dec/27/putin-trump-brexit-europe-britain-eu.

50. Donald Trump, "Remarks by President Trump to the People of Poland," The White House, July 6, 2017, https://www.whitehouse.gov/briefings-statements/remarks-president-trump-people-poland/.

51. Daniel H. Nexon, "Mr. Trump in Warsaw," *Lawyers, Guns & Money* (blog), July 6, 2017, http://www.lawyersgunsmoneyblog.com/2017/07/mr-trump-warsaw.

52. See Zack Beauchamp, "It Happened There: How Democracy Died in Hungary," *Vox*, September 13, 2018, https://www.vox.com/policy-and-politics/2018/9/13/17823488/hungary-democracy-authoritarianism-trump; Steven Erlanger, "'Fake News,' Trump's Obsession, Is Now a Cudgel for Strongmen," *New York Times*, August 7, 2018, sec. World, https://www.nytimes.com/2017/12/12/world/europe/trump-fake-news-dictators.html; Viola Gienger, "In 2019, Will the Global March of Authoritarianism Turn into a Stampede . . . or a Slog?," *Just Security*, January 14, 2019, https://www.justsecurity.org/62231/2019-global-march-authoritarianism-turn-stampede-slog/; Harold Meyerson, "Donald and Bibi's Tin-Pot International," The *American Prospect*, February 19, 2019, https://prospect.org/article/donald-and-bibis-tin-pot-international; John Shattuck, "How Democracy in America Can Survive Donald Trump," *American Prospect*, February 23, 2018, https://prospect.org/article/how-democracy-america-can-survive-donald-trump; Dan Slater, "After Democracy," *Foreign Affairs*, November 6, 2018, https://www.foreignaffairs.

com/articles/2018-11-06/after-democracy; Elisabeth Zerofsky, "Viktor Orbán's Far-Right Vision for Europe," January 14, 2019, https://www.newyorker.com/magazine/2019/01/14/viktor-orbans-far-right-vision-for-europe.

53. Scott Lemieux, "A Split Decision at the Supreme Court—Which Might Not Be Split for Long," *American Prospect*, June 27, 2019, https://prospect.org/article/split-decision-supreme-court-which-might-not-be-split-long.

54. Robert Mickey, *Paths Out of Dixie: The Democratization of Authoritarian Enclaves in America's Deep South, 1944–1972* (Princeton, NJ: Princeton University Press, 2015).

55. Anna Lührmann and Staffan I. Lindberg, "A Third Wave of Autocratization Is Here: What Is New about It?," *Democratization* 26, no. 7, published ahead of print (2019): 2, 10–12, https://doi.org/10.1080/13510347.2019.1582029.

56. Harriet Agerholm, "America Is Not a 'Full' Democracy, Report Finds," *The Independent*, February 5, 2018, http://www.independent.co.uk/news/world/americas/america-democracy-rated-donald-trump-not-fully-democratic-us-president-report-the-economist-a8195121.html; Dinorah Azpuru and Michael Hall, "Yes, Our 'Flawed' Democracy Just Got Downgraded. Here's Why," *Washington Post* (Monkey Cage), February 23, 2017, https://www.washingtonpost.com/news/monkey-cage/wp/2017/02/23/yes-our-flawed-democracy-just-got-downgraded-heres-why/.

57. Paul Musgrave, "International Hegemony Meets Domestic Politics: Why Liberals can be Pessimists," *Security Studies*, 28, no. 3 (June–July 2019): 451–78.

58. Richrd Wike et al., "America's International Image Continues to Suffer," Pew Research Center, Global Attitudes and Trends, October 1, 2018, http://www.pewglobal.org/2018/10/01/americas-international-image-continues-to-suffer/.

59. Richard Wike et al., "Trump's International Ratings Remain Low, Especially among Key Allies," Pew Research Center, Global Attitudes and Trends, n.d., 24, http://www.pewglobal.org/wp-content/uploads/sites/2/2018/10/Pew-Research-Center_U-S-Image-Report_UPDATED_2018-10-01.pdf.

60. Michael Hirsh, "How Russian Money Helped Save Trump's Business," *Foreign Policy*, December 21, 2018, https://foreignpolicy.com/2018/12/21/how-russian-money-helped-save-trumps-business/.

61. Casey Michael, "Hacked Emails List Right-Wing Fundraiser Partying with Russian Fascists and Oligarchs," *Think Progress*, January 30, 2019, https://thinkprogress.org/hacked-emails-list-right-wing-fundraiser-partying-with-russian-fascists-and-oligarchs-c964038dcbad/; Diana Pilipenko, "Cracking the Shell: Trump and the Corrupting Potential of Furtive Russian Money," Center for American Progress, February 13, 2018, https://www.americanprogress.org/issues/democracy/reports/2018/02/13/446576/cracking-the-shell/; Paul Waldman, "The Entire Republican Party Is Becoming a Russian Asset," *Washington Post*, July 20, 2018, https://www.washingtonpost.com/blogs/plum-line/wp/2018/07/20/the-entire-republican-party-is-becoming-a-russian-asset/.

62. Christopher Walker, "What Is 'Sharp Power'?," *Journal of Democracy* 29, no. 3 (July 12, 2018): 9–23, https://doi.org/10.1353/jod.2018.0041; Christopher Walker and Jessica Ludwig, "The Meaning of Sharp Power," *Foreign Affairs*, November 16, 2017, https://www.foreignaffairs.com/articles/china/2017-11-16/meaning-sharp-power.

63. Diana Pilipenko and Talia Dessel, "Following the Money: Trump and Russia-Linked Transactions from the Campaign to the Presidential Inauguration," Center for American Progress, December 17, 2018, https://www.americanprogress.org/issues/democracy/reports/2018/12/17/464235/following-the-money/.

64. Wike et al., "International Ratings."

65. Others see them as far too credulous concerning the notion of an American "liberal order." See our discussion in Chapter 2.

66. Daniel Larison, "Remembering Rumsfeld's Foolish 'Old Europe' Insult," *American Conservative*, December 29, 2011, https://www.theamericanconservative.com/larison/remembering-rumsfelds-foolish-old-europe-insult/.

67. Tara Copp, "US Committed to Europe Force Extension through 2020, Mattis Says," *Stars and Stripes*, June 28, 2017, https://www.stripes.com/news/us-committed-to-europe-force-extension-through-2020-mattis-says-1.475653; Jen Judson, "Funding to Deter Russia Reaches $6.5B in FY19 Defense Budget Request," *Defense News*, February 12, 2018, https://www.defensenews.com/land/2018/02/12/funding-to-deter-russia-reaches-65b-in-fy19-defense-budget-request/.

68. See Michael Crewell and Victor Gavin, "A History of Vexation: Trump's Bashing of NATO Is Nothing New," *War on the Rocks*, August 22, 2017, https://warontherocks.com/2017/08/a-history-of-vexation-trumps-bashing-of-nato-is-nothing-new/; Keith Hartley and Todd Sandler, "NATO Burden-Sharing: Past and Future," *Journal of Peace Research* 36, no. 6 (1999): 665–80; Newman and Nexon, "Trump Says American Allies Should Spend More on Defense. Here's Why He's Wrong."

69. Charles S. Sampson and James E. Miller, eds., in *Foreign Relations of the United States, 1961–1963*, vol. 13, Western Europe and Canada, Document 168, https://history.state.gov/historicaldocuments/frus1961-63v13/d168, accessed March 8, 2019.

70. Christina Wilkie, "Trump Pushes NATO Allies to Spend More, but so Did Obama and Bush," July 11, 2018, https://www.cnbc.com/2018/07/11/obama-and-bush-also-pressed-nato-allies-to-spend-more-on-defense.html.

71. James Kirchick, "Blaming Trump for Their Problems Is the One Thing Europeans Can Agree On," *Washington Post*, February 12, 2019, https://www.washingtonpost.com/opinions/2019/02/12/blaming-trump-their-problems-is-one-thing-europeans-can-agree/.

72. Charles Hawley, "The Legacy Battle: Bush-Schröder Enmity Continues in Memoirs," *Spiegel Online*, November 10, 2010, http://www.spiegel.de/international/world/the-legacy-battle-bush-schroeder-enmity-continues-in-memoirs-a-728336.html.

73. Francis J. Gavin, *Gold, Dollars, and Power: The Politics of International Monetary Relations, 1958–1971*, new ed. (Chapel Hill: University of North Carolina Press, 2007), 10. By the 1960s, American policymakers "began to worry about the balance of payments deficit because of its effects on *confidence*." One fear was that "as official liabilities held abroad mounted with success deficits, the likelihood increased that these dollars would be converted into gold" which the United States did not have enough of to cover total dollars in circulation. Michael Bordo, "The Operation and Demise of the Bretton Woods System: 1958 to 1971," *VoxEU.Org*, April 23, 2017, https://voxeu.org/article/operation-and-demise-bretton-woods-system.

74. Nick Wadhams and Jennifer Jacobs, "Trump Seeks Huge Premium from Allies Hosting U.S. Troops," March 2019, https://www.bloomberg.com/news/articles/2019-03-08/trump-said-to-seek-huge-premium-from-allies-hosting-u-s-troops.

75. Erlanger and Bennhold, "Rift between Trump and Europe Is Now Open and Angry"; Patrick, "America's Allies."

76. Yan Xuetong, "The Age of Uneasy Peace," *Foreign Affairs*, December 11, 2018, https://www.foreignaffairs.com/articles/china/2018-12-11/age-uneasy-peace. Some early predictions were much more "dire" about the costs to US influence; see Isaac Stone Fish, "China, Not Russia, Will Be the Big Winner of the Trump Administration," *Slate*

Magazine, January 30, 2017, https://slate.com/news-and-politics/2017/01/china-has-been-the-big-winner-from-trumps-policies-so-far.html.

77. Lara Seligman, "In Reversal, Trump Signals Further Boost in Defense Spending," *Foreign Policy*, December 2018, https://foreignpolicy.com/2018/12/27/in-reversal-trump-signals-further-boost-in-defense-spending-pentagon-iraq/; Leo Shane III, "This Trump Administration Effort to Increase Military Spending Is Likely to Spur Controversy. Here's Why," *Military Times*, February 25, 2019, https://www.militarytimes.com/news/pentagon-congress/2019/02/25/white-house-plans-to-use-temporary-war-funds-to-shift-billions-into-the-militarys-budget/; Connor O'Brien, "Trump's End Run on Defense Spending," *Politico*, February 24, 2019, https://politi.co/2TgZ7GU.

78. Ishan Tharoor, "The Trump Presidency Ushers in a New Age of Militarism," *Washington Post*, March 1, 2017, https://www.washingtonpost.com/news/worldviews/wp/2017/03/01/the-trump-presidency-ushers-in-a-new-age-of-militarism/.

79. Scott Cuomo, "It's Time to Make a New Deal: Solving the INF Treaty's Strategic Liabilities to Achieve U.S. Security Goals in Asia," *Texas National Security Review* 2, no. 1 (November 2018), https://tnsr.org/2018/11/its-time-to-make-a-new-deal-solving-the-inf-treatys-strategic-liabilities-to-achieve-u-s-security-goals-in-asia/; Dave Deptula, "Whether The U.S. Scraps the INF or Stays In, China Must Be Checked," *Forbes*, November 5, 2018, https://www.forbes.com/sites/davedeptula/2018/11/05/whether-inf-in-or-out-china-must-be-checked/; Michael Kofman, "Under the Missile's Shadow: What Does the Passing of the INF Treaty Mean?," *War on the Rocks*, October 26, 2018, https://warontherocks.com/2018/10/under-the-missiles-shadow-what-does-the-passing-of-the-inf-treaty-mean/.

80. Aarson Mehta, "Nuclear Posture Review Puts Russia Firmly in Crosshairs," *DefenseNews*, February 2, 2018, https://www.defensenews.com/space/2018/02/02/nuclear-posture-review-puts-russia-firmly-in-crosshairs/.

81. Strategically sound approaches to retrenchment usually entail pulling back from peripheral security commitments and regions. As of early 2019, it looks like the United States might withdraw from Afghanistan, which is a fairly major step. But it shows no indication of substantially reducing its security commitments in, say, the Middle East. Instead, Trump has focused his threats of abandonment on core allies in Europe.

82. Trump has floated major support for infrastructure projects but shown little commitment to making it happen. Critics raise significant doubts about whether the plans Trump has floated amount to much more than rents for the construction industry. Ronald A. Klain, "Trump's Big Infrastructure Plan? It's a Trap," *Washington Post*, November 18, 2016, https://www.washingtonpost.com/opinions/trumps-big-infrastructure-plan-its-a-trap/2016/11/18/5b1d109c-adae-11e6-8b45-f8e493f06fcd_story.html; Heather Long, "Trump Promised $1.5 Trillion in Infrastructure Spending. He's 1 Percent of the Way There," *Washington Post*, March 29, 2018, https://www.washingtonpost.com/news/wonk/wp/2018/03/29/trump-promised-1-5-trillion-in-infrastructure-spending-hes-1-percent-of-the-way-there/.

83. Hillary Clinton, "America's Pacific Century," *Foreign Policy*, October 11, 2011, https://foreignpolicy.com/2011/10/11/americas-pacific-century/.

84. John Ford, "The Pivot to Asia Was Obama's Biggest Mistake," *The Diplomat*, January 21, 2017, https://thediplomat.com/2017/01/the-pivot-to-asia-was-obamas-biggest-mistake/; Michael J. Green, "The Legacy of Obama's 'Pivot' to Asia," *Shadow Government—Foreign Policy* (blog), September 3, 2016, https://foreignpolicy.com/2016/09/03/the-legacy-of-obamas-pivot-to-asia/; David Hutt, "Has Obama's Pivot to Asia Been a Success or Failure?," *World Politics Review*, October 17, 2016, https://www.worldpoliticsreview.com/articles/20193/has-obama-s-pivot-to-asia-been-a-success-or-failure.

85. Michal Kolmaš and Šárka Kolmašová, "A 'Pivot' That Never Existed: America's Asian Strategy under Obama and Trump," *Cambridge Review of International Affairs* 32, no. 1, published ahead of print (2019): 1–19, https://doi.org/10.1080/09557571.2018.1553936.

86. This is not quite as strange as it sounds. In purely geopolitical terms, China presents a bigger long-term threat to Russia than the United States. There are also reasons to believe that for a variety of reasons, including racism, Russian policymakers have reason to worry about China's growing power and influence. But, as we discussed in Chapter 3, the current trajectory is the opposite.

87. https://harriman.columbia.edu/event/inaugural-columbia-nyu-new-york-russia-public-policy-seminar-%E2%80%9C-reset-trap%E2%80%9D.

88. Donald Kagan, Gary James Schmitt, and Thomas Donnelly, *Rebuilding America's Defenses: Strategy, Forces and Resources for a New Century* (Washington, DC: Project for the New American Century, 2000); see also Nana De Graaff and Bastiaan Van Apeldoorn, "Varieties of US Post-Cold War Imperialism: Anatomy of a Failed Hegemonic Project and the Future of US Geopolitics," *Critical Sociology*, November 15, 2010, 411–16, https://doi.org/10.1177/0896920510379446; Emre İşeri, "The US Grand Strategy and the Eurasian Heartland in the Twenty-First Century," *Geopolitics* 14, no. 1 (2009): 32, https://doi.org/10.1080/14650040802578658.

89. Zeeshan Aleem, "Trump Wants to Gut the State Department by 25 Percent. You Read That Right," *Vox*, February 12, 2018, https://www.vox.com/policy-and-politics/2018/2/12/17004372/trump-budget-state-department-defense-cuts.

90. Walter Pincus, "State Dept. Reeling from Budget Cuts," *Washington Post*, October 1, 2011, https://www.washingtonpost.com/world/national-security/state-dept-reeling-from-budget-cuts/2011/09/29/gIQAm87ODL_story.html.

91. See, for example, Greg Barnhisel, *Cold War Modernists: Art, Literature, and American Cultural Diplomacy* (New York: Columbia University Press, 2015); Laura A. Belmonte, *Selling the American Way: U.S. Propaganda and the Cold War* (Philadelphia: University of Pennsylvania Press, 2013); Paul Musgrave and Daniel Nexon, "Defending Hierarchy from the Moon to the Indian Ocean: Symbolic Capital and Political Dominance in Early Modern China and the Cold War," *International Organization* 72, no. 3 (2018): 561–90; Frances Stonor Saunders, *The Cultural Cold War: The CIA and the World of Arts and Letters*, (New York: New Press, 2013); Tony Shaw, "The Politics of Cold War Culture," *Journal of Cold War Studies* 3, no. 3 (2001): 59–76.

92. See Alexander Cooley and Daniel Nexon, "'The Empire Will Compensate You': The Structural Dynamics of the U.S. Overseas Basing Network," *Perspectives on Politics* 11, no. 4 (2013): 1034–50; Barry Posen, "Command of the Commons," *International Security* 28, no. 1 (2003): 45.

93. Associated Press, "Following Trump Tax Cut, Federal Budget Deficit up 77 Percent so Far This Budget Year," *USA TODAY*, March 5, 2019, https://www.usatoday.com/story/news/politics/2019/03/05/us-federal-deficit-up-budget-year/3074467002/; Tim Mahedy, "Trump's Big Tax Cuts Did Little to Boost Economic Growth," March 6, 2019, https://www.bloomberg.com/news/articles/2019-03-06/trump-s-big-tax-cuts-did-little-to-boost-economic-growth; Damian Paletta, "The Federal Deficit Ballooned at Start of New Fiscal Year, up 77 Percent from a Year Before," *Washington Post*, March 5, 2019, https://www.washingtonpost.com/business/economy/the-federal-deficit-ballooned-at-start-of-new-fiscal-year-up-77-percent-from-a-year-before/2019/03/05/ff8d31f6-3f75-11e9-9361-301ffb5bd5e6_story.html.

94. Receipts as a percentage of GDP dropped after the Reagan tax cuts, then went up as Reagan, H. W. Bush, and Clinton all responded to growing budget deficits by raising taxes. They then dropped significantly as a result of W. Bush's tax cuts, and are now dropping again as a result of Trump's tax cuts.

95. Concern about deficits drove both Ronald Reagan and George H. W. Bush to agree to tax increases during their terms. Combined with Clinton's 1993 tax hikes, these helped keep tax receipts as a percentage of GDP relatively constant. For an overview, albeit one less skeptical of tax cuts, see Justin Fox, "The Mostly Forgotten Tax Increases of 1982–1993," *Forbes*, December 15, 2017, https://www.bloomberg.com/opinion/articles/2017-12-15/the-mostly-forgotten-tax-increases-of-1982-1993. For speculation that political forces keep federal revenue below 20 percent of GDP, see David R. Henderson and Jeffrey Rogers Hummel, "The Inevitability of a U.S. Government Default," *Independent Review* 18, no. 4 (2014): 533–35.

96. Bruce Bartlett, "I Helped Create the GOP Tax Myth. Trump Is Wrong: Tax Cuts Don't Equal Growth," *Washington Post*, September 28, 2018, https://www.washingtonpost.com/news/posteverything/wp/2017/09/28/i-helped-create-the-gop-tax-myth-trump-is-wrong-tax-cuts-dont-equal-growth/.

97. For comprehensive discussions of the origins of these orthodoxies, see Mark M. Blyth, *Great Transformations: Economic Ideas and Institutional Change in the Twentieth Century* (Cambridge: Cambridge University Press, 2002); Mark Blyth, *Austerity: The History of a Dangerous Idea* (New York: Oxford University Press, 2013).

98. Thomas Oatley, *A Political Economy of American Hegemony* (Cambridge: Cambridge University Press, 2015); see also Nikhil Kalyanpur, "Hegemony, Inequality, and the Quest for Primacy," *Journal of Global Security Studies* 3, no. 3 (2018): 371–84, https://doi.org/10.1093/jogss/ogy009.

99. Moreover, a lot of this growth is driven by the medical sector.

100. Sean Kay, "America's Sputnik Moments," *Survival* 55, no. 2 (2013): 123–46, https://doi.org/10.1080/00396338.2013.784470; see also Ben Guarino, Emily Rauhala, and William Wan, "China Increasingly Challenges American Dominance of Science," *Washington Post*, June 3, 2018, https://www.washingtonpost.com/national/health-science/china-challenges-american-dominance-of-science/2018/06/03/c1e0cfe4-48d5-11e8-827e-190efaf1f1ee_story.html.

101. Carla Norrlof, "Hegemony and Inequality: Trump and the Liberal Playbook," *International Affairs* 94, no. 1 (2018): 63–88.

102. Daniel W. Drezner, "Perspective: The 737 Max and the Changing World Politics of Regulation," *Washington Post*, March 13, 2019, https://www.washingtonpost.com/outlook/2019/03/13/max-changing-world-politics-regulation/.

CHAPTER 8

1. From the 2019 Gallup survey, 24 percent of all respondents in the United States expressed a "favorable" view of Russia and 73 percent an "unfavorable"—a post–Cold War high. See https://news.gallup.com/poll/1642/russia.aspx.

2. In the 2019 Pew Survey, 62 percent agreed that "America's openness to people from all over the world is essential to who we are as a nation." This was down from 68 percent in 2018 and 2017. Claire Brockway and Carol Doherty, "Growing Share of Republicans Say U.S. Risks Losing Its Identity if It Is Too Open to Foreigners," Pew

Research Center, https://www.pewresearch.org/fact-tank/2019/07/17/growing-share-of-republicans-say-u-s-risks-losing-its-identity-if-it-is-too-open-to-foreigners/.

3. Hal Brands, "America's Cold Warriors Hold the Key to Handling China," *Bloomberg.com*, January 14, 2019, https://www.bloomberg.com/opinion/articles/2019-01-14/china-and-the-u-s-are-in-a-new-cold-war; see also Kurt M. Campbell and Ely Ratner, "The China Reckoning," *Foreign Affairs*, August 2018; Paul D. Gewirtz, "Can the US-China Crisis Be Stabilized?," *Brookings* (blog), June 26, 2019, https://www.brookings.edu/blog/order-from-chaos/2019/06/26/can-the-u-s-china-crisis-be-stabilized/; Robert D. Kaplan, "A New Cold War Has Begun," *Foreign Policy*, January 7, 2019, https://foreignpolicy.com/2019/01/07/a-new-cold-war-has-begun/.

4. Simon Lester, "Talking Ourselves into a Cold War with China," *National Interest*, January 6, 2019, https://nationalinterest.org/feature/talking-ourselves-cold-war-china-40612.

5. Zachary Karabell, "The Huawei Case Signals the New US-China Cold War over Tech," *Wired*, March 11, 2019, https://www.wired.com/story/huawei-case-signals-new-us-china-cold-war-tech/; and Adam Segal, "Year in Review: Huawei and the Technology Cold War," *Council on Foreign Relations*, December 26, 2018, https://www.cfr.org/blog/year-review-huawei-and-technology-cold-war.

6. See Emma Vickers, "The 70-year Spy Alliance the U.S. Says It May Cut Off," *Bloomberg Businessweek*, July 1, 2019; and Mike Gallagher and Tom Tugendhat, "Five Eyes Must Lead on 5G," *War on the Rocks*, April 25, 2019, https://warontherocks.com/2019/04/five-eyes-must-lead-on-5g/.

7. See Doug Bandalow, "A Nixonian Strategy to Break the China-Russia Axis," *National Interest*, January 4, 2017.

8. Anders Stephanson, "Fourteen Notes on the Very Concept of a Cold War," in *Rethinking Geopolitics*, ed. Gearóid Ó Tuathail and Simon Dalby (London: Routledge, 1999), 21.

9. For a similar line of argument, see Joshua Shifrinson, "The 'New Cold War' with China Is Way Overblown. Here's Why," *Washington Post*, February 8, 2019, https://www.washingtonpost.com/news/monkey-cage/wp/2019/02/08/there-isnt-a-new-cold-war-with-china-for-these-4-reasons/.

10. Odd Arne Westad, "Has a New Cold War Really Begun?," *Foreign Affairs*, March 27, 2018, https://www.foreignaffairs.com/articles/china/2018-03-27/has-new-cold-war-really-begun.

11. Odd Arne Westad, *The Global Cold War: Third World Interventions and the Making of Our Times*, new ed. (Cambridge: Cambridge University Press, 2007).

12. For this general line of reasoning, see Paul Musgrave and Daniel Nexon, "Defending Hierarchy from the Moon to the Indian Ocean: Symbolic Capital and Political Dominance in Early Modern China and the Cold War," *International Organization* 72, no. 3 (2018): 561–90; Paul Musgrave and Daniel Nexon, "Zheng He's Voyages and the Symbolism behind Xi Jinping's Belt and Road Initiative," *The Diplomat*, December 22, 2017, https://thediplomat.com/2017/12/zheng-hes-voyages-and-the-symbolism-behind-xi-jinpings-belt-and-road-initiative/.

13. Vernon Silver and Sheridan Prasso, "Italy's Embrace of China's 'Belt and Road' Is a Snub to Washington," *Bloomberg*, March 19, 2019.

14. For example, the Obama administration in Central Asia was generally favorably disposed to Chinese infrastructure investment as part of its policy of promoting regional

"connectivity." See the analysis in Andrew C. Kuchins, Jeffrey Mankoff, and Oliver Backes, *Central Asia in a Reconnecting Eurasia: U.S. Policy Interests and Recommendations* (Washington DC: Center for Strategic and International Studies, June 2015), https://csis-prod.s3.amazonaws.com/s3fs-public/legacy_files/files/publication/150507_Kuchins_CentralAsiaSummaryReport_Web.pdf.

15. "Remarks by National Security Advisor Ambassador John R. Bolton on the Trump Administration's New Africa Strategy," December 13, 2018, https://www.whitehouse.gov/briefings-statements/remarks-national-security-advisor-ambassador-john-r-bolton-trump-administrations-new-africa-strategy/.

16. "Remarks by National Security Advisor Ambassador John R. Bolton."

17. "U.S. and China Clash over 'Belt and Road' Resolution," Associated Press, March 19, 2019, https://www.apnews.com/8751180c77d14fa9855f3e1ef6f2ccaf.

18. See, for example, Ted Piccone, *China's Long Game on Human Rights at the United Nations* (Washington, DC: Brookings, September 2018), https://www.brookings.edu/wp-content/uploads/2018/09/FP_20181009_china_human_rights.pdf.

19. Human Rights Watch, "The Costs of Advocacy: China's Interference in United Nations Human Rights Mechanisms," 2017, https://www.hrw.org/sites/default/files/report_pdf/chinaun0917_web.pdf.

20. Piccone, "Long Game," 4.

21. Sophie Richardson, "As China's Grip Tightens, Global Institutions Gasp," *Human Rights Watch*, December 12, 2018, https://www.hrw.org/news/2018/12/12/chinas-grip-tightens-global-institutions-gasp.

22. Adrian Shahbaz, "Freedom on the Net 2018: The Rise of Digital Authoritarianism," FreedomHouse, https://freedomhouse.org/report/freedom-net/freedom-net-2018/rise-digital-authoritarianism.

23. On the role of state stewardship of human rights, see Emilie Hafner-Burton, *Making Human Rights a Reality* (Princeton, NJ: Princeton: Princeton University Press, 2013).

24. Michael Wolff, *Fire and Fury: Inside the Trump White House*. New York: Henry Holt, 227.

25. Henry Farrell and Abraham Newman, "Iran Unilateralism May Undermine America's Financial Hegemony," *Washington Post*, January 31, 2019, https://www.washingtonpost.com/news/monkey-cage/wp/2019/01/31/americas-financial-power-over-the-world-faces-a-big-big-challenge/; Henry Farrell and Abraham Newman, "America's Misuse of Its Financial Infrastructure," *National Interest*, April 15, 2019, https://nationalinterest.org/print/feature/america%E2%80%99s-misuse-its-financial-infrastructure-52707; and Henry Farrell and Abraham L. Newman, "Weaponized Interdependence: How Global Economic Networks Shape State Coercion," *International Security* 44, no. 1 (Summer 2019): 42–79, https://doi.org/10.1162/isec_a_00351.

26. Alexander Cooley and Jason Campbell Sharman. "Transnational Corruption and the Globalized Individual," *Perspectives on Politics* 15, no. 3 (2017): 732–53.

27. See Michael G. Findley, Daniel L. Nielson, and Jason Campbell Sharman, *Global Shell Games: Experiments in Transnational Relations, Crime, and Terrorism* (New York: Cambridge University Press, 2014).

28. See especially Brooke Harrington, *Capital without Borders* (Cambridge, MA: Harvard University Press, 2016).

29. See Atossa Araxia Abrahamian, *The Cosmopolites: The Coming of the Global Citizen* (New York: Columbia Global Reports, 2015); Luca Mavelli, "Citizenship for Sale

and the Neoliberal Political Economy of Belonging," *International Studies Quarterly* 62, no. 3 (September 1, 2018): 482–93, https://doi.org/10.1093/isq/sqy004.

30. Daniel Nexon, "Toward a Neo-Progressive Foreign Policy: The Case for an Internationalist Left," *Foreign Affairs*, September 4, 2018, https://www.foreignaffairs.com/articles/united-states/2018-09-04/toward-neo-progressive-foreign-policy.

31. Gabriel Zucman, "Global Wealth Inequality," *Annual Review of Economics* 11 (February 7, 2019): 19.

32. Annette Alstadsæter, Niels Johannesen, and Gabriel Zucman, "Who Owns the Wealth in Tax Havens? Macro Evidence and Implications for Global Inequality," *Journal of Public Economics* 162 (2018): 89–100.

33. Alexander Cooley, John Heathershaw, and J. C. Sharman, "Laundering Cash, Whitewashing Reputations," *Journal of Democracy* 29, no. 1 (2018): 39–53.

34. https://www.justice.gov/file/1007271/download; and https://int.nyt.com/data/documenthelper/300-paul-manafort-criminal-information/be0664938a2210067f25/optimized/full.pdf.

35. Jeevan Vasagr, "Gaddafi Donation to LSE May Have Come from Bribes, Inquiry Finds," *The Guardian*, November 30, 2011, https://www.theguardian.com/education/2011/nov/30/gaddafi-donation-lse-bribes-inquiry.

36. "Two Capitals, One Russian Oligarch: How Oleg Deripaska Is Trying to Escape U.S. Sanctions," *New York Times*, November 4, 2018, https://www.nytimes.com/2018/11/04/world/europe/oleg-deripaska-russia-oligarch-sanctions.html.

37. "Treasury Dept. Lifts Sanctions on Russian Oligarch's Companies," *New York Times*, January 27, 2019, https://www.nytimes.com/2019/01/27/us/politics/trump-russia-sanctions-deripaska.html.

38. "Oleg Deripaska Sues Treasury over Sanctions," *Financial Times*, March 15, 2019, https://www.ft.com/content/f6f5d2ee-473d-11e9-b168-96a37d002cd3.

39. Eduard Luce, "Jared Kushner and the Triumph of Saudi Arabia," *Financial Times*, February 21, 2019, https://www.ft.com/content/90d98374-3528-11e9-bb0c-42459962a812.

40. "China Grants Ivanka Trump Initial Approval for New Patents," *New York Times*, November 6, 2018, https://www.nytimes.com/2018/11/06/business/china-ivanka-trump-trademarks.html; and "In China, Trump Wins a Trove of New Patents," *New York Times*, March 8, 2017, https://www.nytimes.com/2017/03/08/business/china-trademark-donald-trump.html.

41. Anthony Cormier and Jason Leopold, "Trump Tower Moscow: The Definitive Story of How Trump's Team Worked the Russian Deal during the Campaign," *BuzzFeed News*, May 17, 2018, https://www.buzzfeednews.com/article/anthonycormier/trump-moscow-micheal-cohen-felix-sater-campaign.

42. https://int.nyt.com/data/documenthelper/501-michael-cohen-court-transcript/ddd84d2b0f5a3425ebc5/optimized/full.pdf#page=1.

Index

For the benefit of digital users, sindexed terms that span two pages (e.g., 52–53) may, on occasion, appear on only one of those pages.